T0322970

DIGITAL, CLASS, WORK

DIGITAL, CLASS, WORK

Before and During COVID-19

John Michael Roberts

EDINBURGH
University Press

Edinburgh University Press is one of the leading university presses
in the UK. We publish academic books and journals in our selected
subject areas across the humanities and social sciences, combining
cutting-edge scholarship with high editorial and production values
to produce academic works of lasting importance. For more
information visit our website: edinburghuniversitypress.com

© John Michael Roberts, 2022

Edinburgh University Press Ltd
The Tun – Holyrood Road
12(2f) Jackson's Entry
Edinburgh EH8 8PJ

Typeset in 11/13pt Sabon LT Pro
by Cheshire Typesetting Ltd, Cuddington, Cheshire, and
printed and bound in Great Britain

A CIP record for this book is available from the British Library

ISBN 978 1 3995 0293 1 (hardback)
ISBN 978 1 3995 0295 5 (webready PDF)
ISBN 978 1 3995 0296 2 (epub)

CONTENTS

ACKNOWLEDGEMENTS

═══════════

I would like to thank my mother, Jenny, sister, Tina, and Lucy and Isla for all their love and support while I've been writing this book. Lucy in particular has seen the start and finish of the writing process, and she has been a rock for me throughout, and I will always be grateful to her for this alone. Many thanks and much love to you. Isla has often wandered into the room where I write to give me excellent reasons why I should not be working but, instead, should be playing lots of games with her. She is always right, which is not bad for someone so young. This book is therefore dedicated to Isla with lots of love.

Chapter 1

INTRODUCTION: DIGITAL, CLASS AND WORK BEFORE AND DURING COVID-19

═══════════

INTRODUCTION

In late December 2019, reports started to circulate about a new virus in China that was spreading among people at an alarming rate. By the end of January, the World Health Organisation (WHO) confirmed that the virus, now called COVID-19, or coronavirus, was a global threat. Over the next few months, COVID-19 spread throughout the world, infecting more and more people, and causing countless deaths. COVID-19 was soon categorised as a global pandemic. Different to more recent viruses like SARS and MERS, suggests Mike Davis (2020: 13–14), coronavirus is a unique infection in three main ways. First, COVID-19 spreads in flu-like ways so that a person can have the virus without showing any clear signs or symptoms. Secondly, it has the potential to affect and damage heart tissue. Finally, early tests have shown that coronavirus has a hard and protective shell that allows it to survive longer in saliva, other body fluids and enjoy high resistance to outside conditions.

But it is also clear now that the pandemic has altered and fundamentally changed many social practices in society. Nowhere is this more apparent than with the relationship between digital technology, labour and work. In the United Kingdom, for example, one survey in April 2020 found that 46.6 per cent of people in employment did some work at home. And of those who did work at home, 86 per cent gave coronavirus as the reason for doing so (ONS 2020a). By June 2020, 49 per cent of the UK population said they had either exclusively worked at home or had worked from home while travelling to work (ONS 2020b). In America, a similar story of homeworking is evident. One study of a nationally representative sample of the US population found that, between 1–5 April 2020 to 2–8 May 2020, of those employed in the pre-COVID-19 times, nearly half were now working from home, with

35.2 per cent switching to working from home since the onset of the pandemic (Brynjolfsson et al. 2020).

For some, working at home has many positives. A UK consulting firm found in their survey that 57 per cent of 200 respondents said they have been 'significantly' or 'somewhat' more productive while working from home (Redfield & Wilton 2020). For others, though, working from home can elicit higher levels of work intensity and work-related stress. One survey in July 2020, and drawing on de-identified, aggregated meeting and email meta-data from 3,143,270 users, discovered that those now working from home in the United States, Europe and the Middle East had on average increased their daily working day by 48.5 minutes, or by an extra four hours per week. Meetings had also grown on average by 13 per cent, and there had been a rise in email activity (DeFilippis et al. 2020).

There are socio-economic factors at play here too. Research from YouGov shows that noticeable class effects are evident in and around homeworking. Among middle-class respondents, 53 per cent said they were now working from home, while only 23 per cent of working-class respondents said the same (Smith 2020). Another UK-based survey, this time of 2,000 office workers, suggests that working at home will become a permanent feature for many who would normally commute five days a week to their office workplace. Once the pandemic has subsided, about 62 per cent of senior office workers and 58 per cent of trainees still plan to split their working week between the office and home (BCO 2020). It is doubtful that this will be a choice afforded to those in working-class occupations. Felstead and Reuschke, for example, similarly discovered that in the first two months of lockdown in the United Kingdom, those who reported working at home tended to be from managerial, professional, administrative and secretarial occupations, while 'workers operating in lower skilled occupations continued to exclusively use the factory or office as their workplace both before and during the lockdown' (Felstead and Reuschke 2020: 9). Geographically, the authors also note that greater levels of homeworking were recorded in the more prosperous London regions and South East of the United Kingdom than in other regions. Looking at nationwide data for mid-April 2020, the UK Trades Union Congress (TUC) likewise revealed that 87 per cent of those in the information and communication sector could work at home during the first lockdown period, while of those in the accommodation and food sector, which have a large number of low paid working-class jobs, only 14 per cent could work from home (Collinson 2020).

This book is a critical exploration of digital labour and digital work both before and during the pandemic. It touches on some of the issues briefly explored above, particularly those that relate to social class dynamics. Social class and its socio-economic and socio-political effects, such as income and wealth inequalities, poverty levels, the clustering of certain groups based on race and ethnicity into different class occupations, and the appearance of different social classes in localities both within a nation and across the world, indicate that class analysis is a vital resource through which to understand crises. This is because social class acts as an important mediator for crises. As the examples above demonstrate, even working at home during the pandemic is mediated through class effects. More broadly, however, a crisis of the magnitude of COVID-19 brings to the fore the deeply embedded nature of social class and its effects across and within society as a whole. Indeed, one can plausibly argue that solutions to overcome a crisis like COVID-19 can only realistically materialise if they also include proposals on how to ameliorate, or better, eliminate, class relations and their negative effects. Writing in *The Lancet*, Richard Horton essentially makes this point when discussing the pandemic. He says that COVID-19 should not only be analysed by governments and experts as being a singular biological disease, but should also be investigated by the way in which it combines with and impacts on non-communicable diseases (NCDs), such as obesity, diabetes and heart disease. Research shows that there are strong links between NCDs and poverty, insofar as poverty will increase or harm a person's health outcomes. It is known that COVID-19 has different outcomes on people depending on which NCDs they have, or do not have, at the time of infection. Tackling NCDs, along with their association with socio-economic inequalities, must, Horton insists, therefore be part of a campaign to contain the spread of COVID-19. In fact, Horton more strongly argues that it is crucial to underline the social, and, we can add, class, origins of COVID-19 because, 'no matter how effective a treatment or protective a vaccine, the pursuit of a purely biomedical solution to COVID-19 will fail. Unless governments devise policies and programmes to reverse profound disparities, our societies will never be truly COVID-19 secure' (Horton 2020: 874).

This book also takes these issues seriously, and indeed traces the 'social origins' of the disparities Horton talks about to a number of structurally embedded, and contradictory, class relations. While the book therefore devotes some space and time to explaining and outlining these embedded class relations, it does so to provide a critical framework through which to explore the more concrete and specific relationship between social class, digital technology, and work both before and during the pandemic. Furthermore, the book places this relationship in a broader analysis of the changing nature of global capitalism and how global capitalism has shaped specific labour processes. Only then, in my view, can we begin to gain a comprehensive account of how the pandemic has impacted on digital technology, labour and work.

As far back as the 1970s, of course, many were heralding the rise of a 'knowledge economy' and, later on, a 'network economy'. During this time, a belief quickly established itself among many influential social theorists, economists, media pundits, managerial theorists, and politicians that a 'new economy', founded on creativity, information, knowledge and global digital networks, was now seen to be the pivotal force for economic success and wealth. In the words of Castells:

> It took the 1980s for micro-electronics-based machinery to fully penetrate manufacturing, and it was only in the 1990s that networked computers widely diffused throughout the information-processing activities at the core of the so-called services sector. By the mid-1990s the new informational paradigm, associated with the emergence of the network enterprise, was well in place and set for its unfolding. (Castells 2000: 255)

This basic idea, constantly spun in different narratives, which suggests we now live in 'new' digital times, also opens up a space to chastise, reprimand and ultimately reject claims made about society by critical theorists of the so-called industrial age (see also Boltanski and Chiapello 2003: 110). Nowhere is this clearer than in the case of Karl Marx, who is consistently cast aside by many contemporary thinkers as being a thinker for industrial capitalism, but no longer a thinker for our present-day digital and networked capitalism (see Böhm and Land 2012; Castells 2016, 2017; Hardt and Negri 2000). Given his supposed outdated theoretical framework, one might well therefore ask: how can Marx be used to make meaningful statements about contemporary digital networked capitalism, let alone a global pandemic that has materialised, indeed, has flourished, in a networked, mobile and globally connected world?

But is it really the case that Marx's insights on labour and work are no longer relevant or viable for our digital and pandemic times, or, at a minimum, only particular parts of Marx's ideas are applicable to our current age and beyond, while the vast majority of his insights can be jettisoned for newer ideas? While we can all agree that working conditions have changed substantially, does it necessarily follow that the core of Marx's 'labour theory of value' is also redundant? Naturally, it is plainly absurd to try to argue that Marx's analysis in his opus, *Capital*, can simply be grafted on to our current digital age, but it will be part of my argument that Marx's main ideas about class and exploitation can be both defended and then expanded and developed in order to provide a nuanced, rich and shrewd understanding of digital labour and work both before and during the pandemic. Indeed, one main point made throughout the book is to contend that without a Marxist understanding of class, exploitation and oppression, then approaches such as those put forward by some contemporary critical theorists are left wanting in terms of providing a full and rounded picture of labour and work both before and during the pandemic. Before we move to outline the book's main arguments and chapters, it is therefore worth considering, albeit briefly, this point in a little more detail.

CLASS, CRISES AND COVID-19 IN CONTEMPORARY CAPITALISM

For Marx, the historical uniqueness of capitalism resides in its ability to transform all social and natural life into a commodity, including that of labour itself. In slave societies, many people are forced at the point of death to work for others, whereas in capitalism, at least in 'developed' capitalist societies, nobody is forced to work for someone else. People are 'free' to sell their labour-power to whoever will purchase it. Productive capital will therefore purchase labour-power and the means of production in order to consume and exploit them as commodities and then generate more value, which Marx terms as surplus value (Marx 1988: 449; on surplus value, see also Chapter 3, below). But because workers have no ownership or control over how they produce, they are also alienated and dispossessed from their means of production. Alienated workers thus view capital as an objectified power that they must struggle in and against in order to gain control, rights and power over capital and the means of production. 'The basis for the whole of the capitalist system therefore resides in the separation of labour from the means of production' (Marx 1988: 270; see also Clarke 1991a).

Dispossession and separation also generate a number of crisis tendencies for capitalism. Separation of labour from the means of production creates a fragmented socio-economic system. Dispossession, for instance, reproduces a separation between sale and purchase, which provides the basis for more developed contradictions at specific points in time and in particular places. Dispossession, moreover, generates a system based not on catering for everybody's needs, but based in the needs of capital and profit. Even though the accumulation of surplus value and profit dominates capitalism, goods are nevertheless produced without knowing whether they will be sold for profit in the marketplace. Global competition places a pressure on individual capitals to accumulate surplus value and profit for the sake of accumulation without asking whether there

is a marketplace for the goods produced. External competition therefore establishes an unremitting restraint on capitals to be more productive than their rivals and, if necessary, to wipe out their rivals, devalue
capital, intensify the working conditions of labour, make some workers
redundant, but also, importantly, to reskill some workers and invest in
new technology to produce more profits than rivals (Clarke 1991b: 124).
Fragmented and uneven development of capitalism drives further the
separation between sales and purchase, which is itself grounded in the
separation of labour from its means of production. Crises are thereby
built on, generated by, and mediated through class relations that lie at
the heart of capital, which, as we will momentarily see, spill over into
class struggles in the capitalist labour process and in society more widely.

These basic 'core' elements of capitalism are still prevalent in our
digital times, they underline the response by policymakers to the pandemic, and they still provide the bedrock for the reproduction of capitalism. This is not to deny that capitalism changes its form and content
during particular moments in time, but it is to suggest that the underlying dynamism of these changes is the quest by capital to generate surplus
value, and, in the process, eventually, although unintentionally, unleash
contradictions and crises that arise from capitalist accumulation. Crises
are not therefore mere accidents, but are necessary events; they are part
of the very fabric and identity of capitalism. Crisis tendencies are structurally inscribed into the very nature of capitalism.

Catastrophic socio-economic crises have occurred regularly throughout the history of capitalism. Triggers at certain points in time push these
crisis tendencies to the fore, which then wreak havoc. COVID-19, as
Wolff argues, has been a trigger for yet another crisis of global capitalism.
For Wolff, US capitalism, which still represents the dominant form of
capitalism in the world, was already experiencing a number of problems
before the onset of the pandemic. Since the 2008 global financial crisis,
for instance, businesses and corporations have been able to borrow large
sums of money in the knowledge that interests rates were extremely low
(see also Roberts 2009). While this implied many businesses and corporations remained globally and, in many cases, ruthlessly competitive, it
also meant that when the pandemic started, these debts could no longer
be repaid, leading some businesses to go bust. Inequalities in the United
States and other capitalist countries had, moreover, been growing, while
private companies in healthcare and other public sector markets had
decided some time before COVID-19 that it was not profitable to stock-
pile protective goods, like healthcare masks, if a pandemic was to ever
break out (Wolff 2020). COVID-19 has subsequently acted as a crisis
trigger for a number of contradictions that had built-up from the 2008

financial collapse; contradictions that had not been resolved. Ironically, and as will become apparent as the book progresses, the crisis surrounding COVID-19 has in many ways given dominant governments in the world an opportunity to throw further funds at financial capital in order to try to once again assuage some of fallout from the 2008 financial collapse (see in particular Chapter 4, below). In my view, then, to really understand the impact that the pandemic is inflicting across the world, one simultaneously has to understand how capitalism works and operates globally *and* how the pandemic and capital fold into one another to create unique crises across the world.

Throughout the book, we will, of course, be exploring the nature and novelty of the crisis tendencies of contemporary global capitalism. One more point can be noted for now, however. Structural crises of capitalism are always mediated through specific conjunctures of class and group forces, practices, their institutions, organisations, ideologies, their alliances, their identities, and so on (Jessop 2008). Conjunctural mediation of crises therefore throw up strategic dilemmas for certain class and social forces about how to 'solve' these crises. Crises are thereby 'brought to life' through these strategic struggles and gain a 'reality' – they are named and narrated – through cultural, social, political, symbolic and economic forms in society (Lichten 1986: 47). Some social and political groups will therefore strategically employ a crisis to gain advantages for a socio-political agenda or project they are pursuing. Governments, for example, will treat a crisis as an occasion to construct and/or develop a particular agenda, or to win support from targeted populations in society for specific political programmes. Politicians, and their allies in places like the media or certain think tanks, will therefore 'narrate' the discursive contours of a crisis in a specific way, either through carefully used words, documents, phrases and images, and/or by demonising and scapegoating certain groups in society for being the 'cause' of a crisis, and/or by establishing the boundaries of 'acceptable' and 'reasonable' responses to and outcomes from a crisis (see Hay 1996; Walby 2015). A 'meaning system' will subsequently be created that helps to 'frame' ordinary people's subjective lived experiences of a crisis, and to 'guide' people in how they individually calculate the risks engendered by a crisis. A successful 're-imagining' of a crisis by a government entails, among other things, the institutional embedding in civil society of a particular meaning system in response to a crisis so that policies to 'manage' a crisis and outcomes are congruent with a government's political, societal and socio-economic agenda (Sum and Jessop 2015).

Neoliberal politicians and policymakers, as Philip Mirowski perceptively notes, have, to this extent, taken advantage of, and attempted to give meaning to, the COVID-19 pandemic in different ways to try to permanently embed a free-market and privatisation agenda into further areas of society. Indeed, COVID-19 has in many respects provided a strategic opportunity for neoliberal policymakers to divert attention away from the inherent contradictions of neoliberal financialisation as personified by the 2008 global financial crisis (see Chapter 4, below, for a discussion of this crisis). In the United States, neoliberal advocates have already exploited the crisis to extend the reach of private telemedicine, to embed and retain distance learning at all levels of education via assistance from private online providers, to reposition and rebrand in a positive light pharmaceutical companies, and to attack and allow the crisis to diminish what are perceived to be bureaucratic state-run agencies like the US Postal Service so that openings are created for private businesses to take over the running of these services (Mirowski and Doherty 2020). Some digital corporations, most notably Amazon, have similarly benefited from the crisis and have seen their profits soar, while other groups of capitalists, such as financial capitalists, have made yet more fortunes off the back of the virus. Such examples illustrate Marx and Engels' general point that crises not only destroy productive forces, but also open up prospects for some capitalists to conquer new markets and exploit existing ones more thoroughly to the detriment of their rivals (Marx and Engels 1964: 13).

Once again, we will provide more details of both points later in the book. Importantly, though, the current pandemic crisis, like all crises, creates the basis for new contradictions and crises, which give rise to fresh socio-economic absurdities and tragedies. Marx and Engels note, for instance, that during a capitalist crisis, food shortages often arise not because too little is produced to feed the world, but because too much is produced that cannot be sold for a profit and so the food is simply thrown away rather than given to those who need it most (Marx and Engels 1964). We see clearly how this particular absurdity has operated during COVID-19. Fresno County, California, is dominated by agriculture. In the course of the pandemic, however, some farmers in Fresno County have been throwing away their produce because certain markets have dried up and are no longer buying. One major farm producer of lettuce in the area was growing 204 acres of lettuce. This came to a grinding halt when restaurants shut up shop during lockdown and suddenly there was nowhere to sell the lettuce. Lettuce was left to rot in the fields as it was more cost-effective to do so rather than harvest it for the nearby Lanare food bank that was now serving unprecedented numbers of families hit hard by layoffs due to the pandemic (Tobias and Rodriguez 2020).

CLASS RELATIONS IN DIGITAL LABOUR AND DIGITAL WORK

Many critics of Marx, and also many defenders, claim that Marxism insists *all* workers are exploited labour, and so *all* workers create surplus value for the capitalist class. In this book, however, we will take a different theoretical route on Marx's theory of exploitation. Following, among others, the work of Simon Clarke, Guglielmo Carchedi, Nicos Poulantzas, Bob Jessop and Erik Olin Wright, we will employ a 'minimalist' definition of exploitation. Marx insists that alienated and dispossessed labour is the key to understanding capitalism. Through the ownership and control of the means of production, however, Marx also shows that *different forms* of dispossessed labour emerge in capitalism. Crucially, for Marx, it is only 'productive labour' that can be counted as exploited labour. Labour is productive in capitalism if materially or mentally (for example, through research and design) it transforms the use-value of an object into a new use-value to be exchanged, and does so under capitalist production relations in which labour works for capital. If these conditions are satisfied then *productive labour is labour that generates surplus value*. Examples of productive labour can be found in construction, manufacturing, agriculture, some occupations in the public and service sectors, as well as a number of other occupations and sectors such as transport (see also Chapter 3, below). Critically, Marx also notes that to count as being productive, labour must reproduce and increase the quantity, or mass, of surplus value, thereby expanding inter-capitalist competition (Marx 1988: 644; see also Mandel 1992: 42; Rotta 2018: 1369).

Other types of labour, such as those found in commercial sectors (retail, for example) or financial sectors, work for unproductive capitalists; unproductive in the sense that these capitalists do not seek to exploit labour in order to create surplus value. Any surplus generated by these unproductive workers represent surplus profits, but not surplus value (Carchedi 1991). This why unproductive labour is oppressed, but is not exploited, at least on this Marxist explanation. Unproductive capitalists are, however, vital to the circuit of capital, and, in particular, important for productive capitalists. For example, commercial capitalists, such as retailers, reduce the circulation time of capital and quicken up the realisation of surplus value for productive capitalists. Unproductive capitalists also circulate the gains of surplus value across different circuits of capital (see Marx 1992: 134–6). Unproductive capitals are essential for ideological reasons too because they help to mystify the origin of surplus value as being rooted in alienated productive labour (Marx 1991: 250; see also Mandel 1992: 17).

The capitalist labour process requires a group of people to organise and manage surplus value and profits, and to control the labour process in question. This group of 'non-labour' fall into a number of categories such as higher managers, middle managers and supervisors. Other class occupations can also be noted based on different degrees of ownership and control over their means of production. For example, somebody who is self-employed has some degree of autonomy over their means of production even if they do not employ other labourers, while freelancers often have some autonomy over their means of production even if they are hired for specified periods of time by other capitalist firms (see Chapter 3 for a more thorough discussion of these classes). So, while it might be the case that only a particular form of labour is exploited in capitalism, it does not follow that those other unproductive forms of labour or work should be discounted. As Shaikh and Tonak note, we should not think that productive activities are somehow better than unproductive activities. The distinction between productive labour and unproductive labour is not a moral one, but a distinction based in how capitalism actually operates (Shaikh and Tonak 1994: 20–1).

The theoretical approach sketched above is particularly advantageous when analysing the class dynamics of digital labour and digital work. Many accounts of these issues tend to conflate different forms of digital labour and work into one another (see, for example, Meil and Kirov's 2017 definition of 'virtual work'). In my view, what is actually required is a more careful theoretical distinction made between these different forms. On my understanding, therefore, the often-used term, 'digital labour', should instead be limited to exploring only relatively new types of platform work. So, for the purposes of this book, *digital labour* will refer to work that is processed and managed primarily through digital platforms so that, in theory at least, there is often no need for workers to be together in a permanent physical space to carry out certain work tasks. I have therefore deliberately restricted the use of digital labour to this category of platform labour – what is also sometimes referred to as 'gig work' – in order to make this term more precise and not to confuse it with other ways in which digital technology becomes associated with labour and work. This form of digital labour can be productive when it is directly brought within the remit of surplus value extraction; for example, if its labour is hired by capital to transform a use-value in order to realise more value. Digital labour can also be unproductive if it is employed to capture already produced surplus value. In Chapter 7, below, which focuses on platform-based gig work, we will see that, in the main, digital labour operates at present in the oppressive unproductive sphere of the economy rather than in the exploited productive sphere.

It is also true to say that while an increasing amount of work today is mediated and managed through digital platforms, not all work affected and impacted by digital technology can be labelled as digital labour. Instead, there has been a *digitisation of labour*. This simply refers to how 'technology turns physical goods and knowledge into data that can be easily replicated, shared and stored' (Dellot et al. 2019: 25). For the purposes of this book, then, we will use the term digitisation of labour to refer to the everyday use of digital technology in the workplace by management and supervisors in order to manage and supervise daily work tasks and create leaner workplaces and greater efficiencies when producing use-values from staff. Again, digitisation can be productive or unproductive.

We also know that the 'automation' of jobs has become an increasing point of debate and discussion for politicians, business leaders, policymakers and the general public. Automation normally refers to those situations in which artificial intelligence (AI), digital technology, robots, smart machines, and so forth 'complete tasks or changes who is responsible for undertaking them' (Dellot et al. 2019: 20). Leaving to one side for a moment the fact that the debate about automation has actually been raging at least since the 1950s (see, for example, Drucker 1993), it is true to say that AI, robots and smart machines work in tandem with digitisation and can, without doubt, enhance working conditions. Discussions about automation, though, also usefully alert us to concerns and questions about the extent to which some types of work will become fully digitised and replaced by machines (Dyer-Witheford 2015: 44; Frey and Osborne 2013: 38). For the purposes of this book, therefore, automation refers to a qualitative transformation in a workplace in which the *digitisation of labour* has overtime been transformed into *digitised labour*. Under these circumstances, the labour of 'real' people is replaced by the 'labour' of a machine, whether this is through AI or by a robot. Digitised labour can again be productive or unproductive.

It is also vital to remember that contemporary capitalism is run and managed through different groups of managerial and supervisory 'non-labour', or different types of managerial and supervisory 'work'. Again, these groups will be explored in greater detail throughout the book, but all I wish to emphasise for now is that this work will be categorised as *digital non-labour*; for example, those who manage platforms like Uber and monitor the performance of digital labour working for such platforms. Or, it can be categorised as the *digitisation of non-labour*; for example, when management has to adapt to, work with, and oversee new digital technology in their day-to-day working lives. Or, it can be categorised as *digitised non-labour*; for example, digitised labour also

	Digital labour	Digitisation of labour	Digitised labour
Productive labour			
Unproductive labour			
Non-labour (supervisors and managers)			
Other contradictory classes			

Diagram 1 Class Relations of Digital Labour and Work

needs to be managed and supervised by 'real' people, and so there is a distinct set of managers and supervisors who are also part of digitised labour whose main responsibility is to manage and monitor these 'automated' machines in a workplace (see Huws 2019: 100–4; Went et al. 2015). Finally, a number of other 'contradictory classes' can be found in all three spheres of digital work. For example, digital and IT consultants can be hired for a period of time to work for either a productive or unproductive business. Such consultants will enjoy a degree of autonomy over their means of production, but, at the same time, will sell their labour power to a capitalist and be subject to levels of managerial control and supervision during this time. Consultants can also be hired for a temporary period to take on managerial or supervisory roles in a productive or unproductive firm. Diagram 1 maps out these class relations of digital labour and work.

CONCLUSION

Throughout the book, the initial theoretical categories set out above will be developed and applied to a diverse array of workplaces and labour processes. Four main questions will guide this analysis. First, to what extent has the COVID-19 crisis been used strategically by certain socio-economic groups and socio-political groups to overcome the inherent contradictions and dilemmas of neoliberalism and financialisation, or to what extent has the crisis of COVID-19 been strategically used by certain socio-economic groups and socio-political groups to further develop and embed the ambitions of neoliberalism and financialisation across the globe? Secondly, how have these processes and dynamics operated in different circuits of capital and their class relations both before and during the pandemic? Thirdly, how have these processes and dynamics operated in specific concrete labour processes both before and during the pandemic? Fourthly, to what extent has the crisis surrounding the pandemic provided new opportunities, or developed existing opportunities, for particular classes in the capitalist workplace to campaign and struggle in and against neoliberal and financialised capital and/or struggle in and against capitalist power more broadly, or to what extent has the crisis surrounding COVID-19 constrained these class struggles? To provide some answers, the book is structured in the following way.

The issue of technology is discussed in the next chapter, which explores in more detail the idea that we have now arrived at a qualitatively new workplace from that prevalent in 'industrial capitalism'. There are two broad schools of thought on this issue. First, some argue that new digital technology has ushered in novel types of exploitation that blurs what were once thought to be taken-for-granted boundaries, such as the boundary between work and consumption. Secondly, other theorists are less concerned about new forms of exploitation and instead cast their analytical lens on how digital technology creates new types of cooperation and 'co-creation' between workers and users. Chapter 2 describes both schools, but concludes by suggesting that they each present one-sided accounts of more nuanced and complex labour and work processes. This paves the way in Chapter 3 to offer up an alternative framework, located in Marx's theory of alienated labour, through which to explore digital labour and work. A distinctive class theory is outlined, based in the categories of productive labour, unproductive labour and non-labour, which are then applied to forms of digital labour and work.

Chapter 4 explores the broader and global socio-economic and political background to class relations in contemporary capitalist societies and how COVID-19 has changed, as well as reinforced, certain patterns in these class relations. This chapter therefore sets out a number of observations and points that will prove crucial for the later chapters, which focus on specific labour processes, class relations and their relationship to digital technology. Chapter 4 begins by explaining the class forms of neoliberalism and financialisation. Neoliberalism, I argue, is best examined as a socio-political agenda in which different governments have developed a number of state strategies to pursue a marketisation policy programme based on the idea that deregulated markets, private property, flexible labour markets and entrepreneurial flair are some of the highest social goods in society (Harvey 2005; Jessop 2002). Financialisation is best examined as a socio-economic agenda in which interest-bearing capital trades debt through financial devices like securities. Financialisation also refers to the increasing use of finance, such as credit cards, in everyday life (Clarke 1992; Fine 2013). Both neoliberalism and financialisation have restructured class relations in a variety of ways. For example, neoliberalism has nurtured increasing inequalities in terms of income and wages between those in working-class occupations and those in top managerial occupations, while financialisation has, to a certain degree, remoulded class identities into consumer identities. The chapter then explains in detail, and through numerous pieces of evidence, how governments have the used the COVID-19 crisis to continue to underwrite neoliberalism and financialisation. For instance, the pandemic has granted governments another opportunity to bail out junk bonds. Furthermore, the pandemic has so far reinforced, and in some cases made worse, certain class inequalities associated with neoliberalism and financialisation.

Chapter 5 discusses how this unproductive financialised activity has been reproduced into the productive circuit of the global economy and labour processes; 'productive' in the sense that this is normally the circuit where surplus value is created. So-called lean management techniques, with the assistance of digital technology, have been at the forefront in pushing these financialised changes into the productive sphere, especially into the manufacturing sector. Emerging during the 1970s in the Japanese Toyota motor company, lean is built on the principle that organisations will use, 'highly flexible, increasingly automated machines to produce volumes of products in enormous variety' (Womack et al. 1990: 13). Through digitised automated labour, for instance, less human effort can produce more products than was the case under the older mass production system. Many firms in the productive sphere have also employed unproductive financialised business strategies to boost their profits. Moreover, digitised labour and finance have come together in many productive companies to attack the rights of workers. The chapter also explores the global uneven nature of manufacturing value chains, and how workers in the Southern hemisphere have more often than not experienced more intensified exploitation than workers in the Northern hemisphere. COVID-19 has exacerbated all these problems. But the chapter also details how productive workers have nevertheless sought to organise in and against deleterious working conditions.

Chapter 6 examines circuits of unproductive capital, such as the commercial and financial sectors. The chapter starts by elaborating and expanding on the distinction between productive and unproductive capital and labour. Following this, some analysis is presented of a number of specific properties of commercial capital; for instance, generally speaking, there are more investments made by commercial capitalists to brand their goods for consumers than is the case with industrial capitalists. From here, a discussion on how the pandemic has affected unproductive commercial capital, particularly retail, is presented. The chapter then moves on to consider labour processes in the unproductive circuit. In particular, there is a discussion of how digital technology and lean ideology has been used by management to control, monitor and 'standardise' different work patterns and the class relations within them to boost surplus labour and profit streams. Some examples taken from banking sector are used to illustrate these observations. The chapter also discusses examples of class struggle in unproductive circuits.

Chapter 7 focuses on the so-called creative industries. We will see that for all of the past hype surrounding the creative industries, for example, that they enjoy a high degree of 'flexibility' to adapt to changing circumstances, many creative sectors have been seriously damaged by the pandemic. Theoretically, the chapter also takes to task some insights made by Richard Florida, who argues that creative work signifies that we are in a qualitatively new phase of capitalism. Unlike Florida and like-minded scholars, the chapter argues that it makes more sense to analyse creative industries through the prism of value theory. These insights are developed through numerous illustrations, including many associated with the pandemic.

Chapter 8 focuses on platform, or 'gig', labour. This digital labour assumes a variety of guises but, generally speaking, it is argued that platform labour appears at present to be more prominent in unproductive circuits than productive circuits. The chapter also suggests that one innovative (if one can call it that) development of gig work is the way that owners and controllers employ platforms to manage workers in new ways. But the chapter also makes a number of other observations about digital platform labour. Most markedly, it argues that one overarching way to approach and analyse some important variants of digital labour is to understand it as the latest incarnation of casual labour, a form of labour that appears after a recession, rather than thinking digital platform labour is necessarily a brand new qualitatively distinct form of labour. Platform labour, however, also empowers workers by opening up spaces for them to campaign for greater worker rights and to form new worker organisations and unions at both the national and international level. As the chapter further shows, COVID-19, rather ironically, has undermined and negatively affected some well-known gig companies like Uber, while, at the same time, has presented gig workers with an opportunity to strengthen their activism around workers' rights in gig work, and, in particular, campaign for better health and safety in these workplaces.

Chapter 9 then considers state and public sector labour. In countries like the United Kingdom, digital technology and lean ideology has been applied to this type of labour in order to contract out the public sector to private firms. Hedge funds have a greater stake in the public sector, for example, and have taken over the running of some public sector services. Digital technology has helped to implement, guide and monitor these changes. In this case, then, such labour is transformed into unproductive labour and work because it is managed and controlled for the benefit of unproductive financial capital. However, in many of these state and public sector labour processes, workers manage to circumvent the worst excesses of lean ideology to reinstate their own preferred identity and status of public sector workers. Once more, we analyse many of these issues through the lens of the pandemic.

The concluding chapter, Chapter 10, argues that one factor that brings together diverse workplaces has been the intensification, through digital media, of productive and unproductive labour processes. This has involved implementing management strategies such as getting employees to work longer hours and complete more tasks during those hours, reducing wages, attacking yet more rights in the workplace, setting automated targets, monitoring the completion of these automated targets, tracking the movement of workers through digital media, and so on (Rigi 2014: 929). Importantly, though, subtle differences can also be noted in these different labour processes depending on factors as to whether a workplace is productive or unproductive, and the degree to which digital labour, the digitisation of labour and digitised labour operate, and the configuration of non-labour in each workplace. Generally, however, the belief that capital *is* crisis is a guiding thread throughout the book.

Chapter 2

DIGITAL PROSUMER LABOUR: TWO SCHOOLS OF THOUGHT

═══════════

INTRODUCTION

GitHub, a US company launched in April 2008, hosts a digital space where people can work on developing computer codes with others and share knowledge and skills about software. Today, GitHub is home to over 65 million developers, more than 3 million organisations, and in excess of 200 million code repositories (GitHub 2021). Individuals, groups, small start-up businesses and corporations can access on a mostly free basis these software codes, along with project spaces, code libraries and forums. Those utilising these resources and working with and on them must also ensure that they remain publicly available. According to its chief strategy officer, Julio Avalos, GitHub successfully demonstrates that the gap between 'enterprise versus consumer is going away' (cited in Peterson 2017). Avalos is alluding to one of the key ingredients of GitHub's steady growth. Software developers are encouraged to learn more about codes and increase their skills by working with others through GitHub. This, it is hoped, will lead companies and corporations to hire developers they have worked with on GitHub. To capitalise on this relationship between developers and corporations, GitHub introduced a fee service in the guise of GitHub Enterprise. For a price, corporations can get private accounts, host GitHub's platform on their own servers, get 24/7 support, and can also pay to keep their code private. Corporations can now also store work developed through GitHub onto cloud services. As Peterson reports:

> Its enterprise service has proven to be popular. In its recently released user report, the company said 52% of Fortune 50 corporations are GitHub Enterprise customers, as are 45% of those in the Fortune 100. Microsoft and Facebook run the two largest projects on GitHub's site. (Peterson 2017)

GitHub is an interesting example because it highlights some of the themes to be discussed in this chapter and throughout the book. First, GitHub alerts us to how people across the world can *share* their creative ideas and skills within a community in order to produce a good that, in most cases, is also publicly available to others and, subsequently, also open to common knowledge. Secondly, and related to the previous point, it focuses attention on practices of digital platform labour at work. In this instance, we see skilled digital labour working on software, but also working in many different spaces – at home, for corporations, in different networks and so on. Moreover, the digital labour operating at GitHub can be employed by a business or corporation. Someone might also use their IT skills for 'free' to work on a project in order to make contacts with others. Thirdly, then, we can also start to understand how a company like GitHub blurs different boundaries: public and private, commercial and non-commercial, organisations and non-organisations, vertical and horizontal networks and so on.

Fourthly, GitHub offers users, businesses and corporations, new ways of working and developing their technical expertise and software requirements. Through the platform, partnership networks are formed around distinctive projects that aim to benefit all the partners in question, which, further down the line, have advantages for others who might also learn from the finished project. In theory, this is a world of openness and collaboration that bypasses secrecy and closed doors that used to be commonplace certainly in the business environment. Fifthly, GitHub is noteworthy because it highlights a relationship between co-creativity on digital platforms and the corporate sector. In early June 2018, it was announced that Microsoft was to purchase GitHub for £7.5 billion. Acquiring GitHub strengthens Microsoft's repositioning of its image away from Windows operating system towards its developer-focused services (Hern 2018). The sharing nature of GitHub is thereby also captured by Microsoft and incorporated into its brand.

Finally, GitHub is interesting because it tells us something about the changing nature of digital work in an era of COVID-19. Through a study of the cadence data from January 2019 to March 2020 measuring the frequency, format and sequence of work patterns of 40,000 organisations that used GitHub developers, one GitHub report found that while developers' activity remained fairly regular with the onset of the pandemic, their actual work days grew on average by about an hour across the full seven-day week. Moreover, developers were increasing their workload as well as working longer hours. The report presents a number of reasons as to why developers initially felt this pressure to 'push more often'. 'Economic uncertainty' during the pandemic, along with 'the desire to do well and stay employed, using work as a distraction to combat boredom when stuck at home, pressure from management to get products to market, or team norms to push frequently to maintain fast and stable software delivery cadences' (Forsgren 2020), are some of the most prominent reasons given. At the same time, though, the report adds that collaboration increased during the start of the virus, especially on open source projects. For instance, the report found that there were 27.62 per cent more open source repositories created in late March 2020 compared with the previous year. One explanation that the report gives for this upsurge is that people have been online more during the pandemic and so have more time to focus and be more responsive to requests to view and comment on modifications and so on to a piece of software (Forsgren 2020). In relation to GitHub, therefore, COVID-19 has helped to produce a greater range of stressful work-related practices for developers through the likes of increased workloads and higher burnout rates, while, at the same time, collaboration and sharing has grown in stature during the pandemic.

The themes personified by GitHub have been the subject of discussion among many scholars, researchers and policymakers. For its part, this chapter will in particular flesh out in more detail two main schools of thought around the themes alluded to above. The first school of thought is a critical and post-Marxist take on these issues, and is encapsulated in the work of Hardt and Negri. For Hardt and Negri, Marx's labour theory of value has now been surpassed by a new type of 'immaterial' and 'free' labour, which represents the core of 'exploitation' in contemporary capitalism. The second school of thought that we will examine is arguably more 'positive' than Hardt and Negri to the extent that those within this second school argue that capitalism now has the potential to generate endless networks of creative labour across the globe. The emphasis with this school, then, is on collaboration, creativity and the ability of people to 'share' knowledge with one another for the benefit of all.

Still, both schools of thought come together by generally rejecting what they see as being an 'industrial' mode of thinking, and, more specifically, by rejecting Marx's core insights about the exploitation of labour in capitalism. At best, Marx is thought to offer up important insights about industrial capitalism, yet he is seen as being of limited use in understanding digital societies. That is to say, Marx is believed to be stuck in 'industrial' times. I suggest, however, that Marx is misinterpreted by the one-sided nature of each school of thought. While Marx argues that labour is alienated, exploited and oppressed under capitalism, he nevertheless celebrates the creativity of labour in its struggles to reclaim the means of production from capital and so overcome its alienated and objectified forms of existence in commodity production. Marx therefore produces a dialectical account of labour in capitalism, which is often missing or underdeveloped in the respective two schools. This starting point of critique is then developed in the chapter into more specific criticisms of each school. We start, though, by outlining the first school of thought.

LABOUR AS 'NEW' AND 'FREE' EXPLOITATION

According to Hardt and Negri, Fordist industrial factories of the sort that gained hegemony at the beginning of the twentieth century until the 1970s, based on factors like the mass production of standardised consumption, have qualitatively changed into what can today be described as post-Fordist working practices, based on factors like global network information flows, high-technology, computerisation, decentralised working practices, tertiary occupations and flexible (often cheap) labour (Hardt and Negri 2009: 132). This does not mean that industrial types of production – the production of cars, for example – are disappearing. But it is to argue that 'cognitive' abilities accumulated in and outside of work, 'interacting with automated and computerised . . . systems', so-called 'immaterial labour', is becoming 'directly productive of capital' (Hardt and Negri 2009: 132–3). Both in work and outside of work, people use digital media to communicate with one another about their ideas, emotions, passions, likes, dislikes and so on. Exploitation of labour today therefore resides in the exploitation, through the privatisation and centralisation of capital, of this common pool of knowledge; a common pool of knowledge initially created by different types of immaterial labour (Hardt and Negri 2004: 150). Unique to contemporary capitalism, much of the common pool of knowledge is created 'freely' by users during their leisure time – think, for example, of how many millions of people upload content onto YouTube every day – and this 'free' knowledge is subsequently captured by capital, commodified, and then packaged and sold for profit; for example, YouTube will package up the knowledge of their users and sell it as advertising revenue to other capitalists (Hardt and Negri 2004: 113–14; see also Hardt and Negri 2017: 172).

Fleming (2015) also makes a similar prognosis. Ideologies of work have now been dispersed throughout society into all sorts of nooks and crannies. We live in 'a gargantuan social factory that has colonised most facets of our lives' (Fleming 2015: 35). We check our work emails all the time irrespective of whether we are actually at work, for example, because this is the 'normal' thing to do. None of this is to suggest that class is no longer relevant either to people's everyday lives or as an explanatory category. Drawing on the post-Marxism of Negri and others, Mason (2015) argues that in present-day capitalism, manual labour and industrial production still obviously continue, but these are more apparent in countries like Brazil, Russia, India and China. In Western capitalist countries, by way of contrast, one finds a digital form of capitalism in which profits are generated through consumer behaviour in the creative, service and IT sectors. Consumers therefore have 'to be constantly fed coffee, smiled at, serviced by call centres . . .' (Mason 2015: 139). Contradictory dynamics spring from this global unholy global alliance between post-Fordist and Fordist work. 'We're living in an age of the network alongside the hierarchy, the slum alongside the web café . . .' (Mason 2015: 141). Yet the very contradictory dynamics of digital capitalism also elicit huge amounts of entertainment for users. One can use social media platforms to constantly post emotional comments and opinions on every issue under the sun, but do so without noticing that this very entertainment factor is gathered together by digital corporations to garner more profits (Jordan 2015: 135).

Such has been the potency of Hardt and Negri's 'post-Marxist' argument that some from other theoretical traditions assert similar arguments. From a Marxist perspective, Fisher (2012) argues that social media transcend some of the limitations of increasing surplus value through older types of mass media. Facebook and the like have led to an intensification of exploitation because they encourage users to spend more time on their sites throughout the whole day and in different places. Social media users therefore both produce and consume digital media content – they are social media 'prosumers'. This further implies that social media integrates more fully and in more precise detail than was the case in previous eras spheres of production, circulation and consumption (Fisher 2012: 181). Fisher therefore argues that social media sites represent new sources of surplus value in the capitalist economy and new outlets for accumulation, 'particularly the production of information through communication and sociability' (Fisher 2012: 179). Fuchs puts forward a similar argument. A digital media corporation like Facebook will take what is produced by its users, such as updated user profiles, and sell this information as commodities in the form of advertising revenue to third parties. Users are subsequently exploited unpaid labour (Fuchs 2016: 61; Fuchs and Sevignani 2013: 259–60).

'Free labour' has therefore become a 'strange attractor' that has propelled non-Marxist scholars to produce remarkably similar arguments to Marxists about the exploitation of prosumers. Ritzer and Jurgenson

(2010), for example, chide Marx for being overly concerned with production at the expense of consumption. Against Marx, then, Ritzer and Jurgenson (2010: 13) point out that 'in prosumer capitalism control and exploitation take on a different character than in the other forms of capitalism, there is a trend toward unpaid rather than paid labour and toward offering products at no cost, and the system is marked by a new abundance where scarcity once predominated'. Elsewhere, Ritzer insists that this trait of prosumption can be used to critique Marx's labour theory of value. After all, so Ritzer says, the Marxist theory of exploitation is based on capitalists *paying* workers less than the value of what they produce. Yet prosumers are paid nothing for their labours. This means that 'from a purely economic perspective, prosumers are exploited . . . to a greater extent than the proletariat' (Ritzer 2014: 20). Still, what Ritzer argues here concerning the exploitation of prosumers is very similar to the points made by a Marxist like Fuchs. The same can be said of Zwick et al. (2008) who make comparable observations to both Fuchs and Ritzer. They argue that many corporations encourage consumers to co-create goods, while consumers co-create and share knowledge with other consumers. This type of free 'playful production' is far from innocent. For Zwick et al., it constitutes a governing relationship through which production is collapsed into communication. Corporations gain value and profits through social communication with users, and so 'aim to secure the knowledge work of the collective consumer class as the repository for creative ideas and the driver of accelerated innovation so central to producing future profits under conditions of global competitive capitalism' (Zwick et al. 2008: 176).

COVID-19 has thrown up a number of cases that illustrate these perspectives. Let us just take one case as an illustration. When the pandemic started, Google and Apple said they would build smartphone apps to track COVID-19. The idea is that if a person tests positive for COVID-19, then they inform relevant health officials of the diagnosis through the app, which, in turn, informs anyone else, via tracking through Bluetooth, who has been in close proximity with the infected person in the last fourteen days. The apps would be used on Google Android Phones and Apple's iPhones. Both companies also insisted that any person infected would remain anonymous and that neither company would use personally identifiable information about any user (Bond 2020a). Initially, some policymakers and data-protection experts were critical about the involvement of two powerful digital media corporations being involved in accessing such personal user data. By April 2020, many governments in Europe, including Germany, Italy and Ireland, had decided to adopt a 'decentralised' approach to staring such data; an approach that Google and Apple champion through their technology (Scott et al. 2020).

This is just one illustration of how major tech corporations used the pandemic to embed their corporate brand more thoroughly into everyday life. But there are many other examples. As Naomi Klein documents, since the pandemic started, key tech figures, like Eric Schmidt, one-time CEO of Google, one-time executive chairman of Alphabet Inc., the parent company of Google, and who still has $5.3 billion shares in Alphabet Inc., campaigned for: 'massive public expenditures on high-tech research and infrastructure, for a slew of "public–private partnerships" in AI, and for the loosening of myriad privacy and safety protections – through an aggressive rebranding exercise. Now all of these measures (and more) are being sold to the public as our only possible hope of protecting ourselves from a novel virus that will be with us for years to come' (Klein 2020). In this instance, the crisis surrounding COVID-19 is being used as an opportunity for digital media corporations to gain access to yet more consumer markets and more user data.

Against this arguably pessimistic picture, there is, however, also a more optimistic outlook on the nature of digital labour. For Banet-Weiser and Castells (2017), changes in society towards all things digital also open up new possibilities and potential for people to communicate and share with one another in a way that is firmly rooted in the popular culture of ordinary lives and ordinary communities. More specifically, digital culture and digital platforms present ordinary people with opportunities and potential to expand sharing and community-building networks. We now turn our attention to this school of thought.

DIGITAL LABOUR: CO-CREATIVE AND PEER-TO-PEER NETWORKS

One way to understand more positive accounts of digital labour is to look at how popular management texts have both developed and appropriated the 'prosumer' term. Back in 1996, the well-known management guru, Don Tapscott, noted that as mass production whittles away to be replaced by 'mass customisation', then organisations and companies will be forced to create goods that respond to the specific tastes of individuals customers. Gone are the days of the 'old economy' when people simply gazed at their TV sets. Prosumers can be more active in how they interact with TV shows, from inputting their views directly to TV channels and networks via specific webpages of shows, to selecting their top shows and preferred TV stations, and watching TV during their chosen time and space (Tapscott 1996: 62–3). Consumers are also increasingly empowering themselves in bypassing IT experts and instead creating software and databases through collaboration unleashed by the Internet (Tapscott 1996: 70).

Tapscott was, of course, drawing, in part, on Alvin Toffler's use of the prosumer term. Back in 1980, in *The Third Wave*, Toffler argued that businesses are successful to the extent that they 'find ingenious ways of applying the latest technology to the individualization of products and services' (Toffler 1980: 265). One 'ingenious way' to build success was that of 'prosumption'. At the heart of prosumption is a DIY ethic; the idea that consumers take on a more active role in the production of consumer goods (Toffler 1980: 280–1). Shoe stores, supermarkets, banking and so on, by the end of 1970s, relied less on the skills of support workers, salespeople or advisers, and more on the customer performing tasks that were once the remit of professional employees. As a result, there has been a progressive blurring of the boundaries between production and consumption (Toffler 1980: 278). In a later and more well-known book, *Wikinomics*, Tapscott and his co-author, Anthony Williams, develop the insights on prosumption in relation to the ubiquitous presence of digital media. Online digital games, for example, are for Tapscott and Williams ideal illustrations of digital prosumption at work. Individual consumers can co-create a virtual games world by designing online game characters and by co-creating virtual businesses in which virtual money can be used to buy and sell game characters and which can be exchanged for real money.

Importantly, for Tapscott and Williams, prosumption highlights the possibilities and potential of prosumers to engage in self-organisation and mass collaboration with one another in co-creating an object of consumption and adding value to it. DIY prosumer culture in technological innovation has therefore blossomed. Individuals form groups and clusters around co-creating and co-designing products, 'ranging from the Toyota Prius to the Apple iPod' (Tapscott and Williams 2007: 129). Lego is another company willing to let creative control be given back to its consumers. Mindstorms.lego.com is the company website specifically devised to encourage Lego enthusiasts to develop Lego software. Indeed, Tapscott and Williams recommend unleashing peer-to-peer creativity to an even greater extent. For example, the media industry needs to harness the collective intelligence of readers and enable them to co-create new stories through a type of citizen journalism, especially through self-publishing tools and by submitting user-generating content to media outlets (Tapscott and Williams 2007: 146).

During the first COVID-19 lockdown, there have been numerous examples of ordinary people coming together with both public and private organisations in order to share their experiences about living through the pandemic and to connect virtually with others for amusement, education, fun and so on. One survey of a 1,000 people between 29 April and 1 May 2020 reported that 41 per cent of people said they were reading more books since the lockdown (Nielsen Book 2020). Such figures are reflected in terms of library use. In the United Kingdom online membership for public libraries soared, up by nearly 770 per cent in some places. For instance, in Wolverhampton, England, more than 700 people had joined or restarted their library membership by mid-May 2020, while 1,200 people had used the virtual library service (Public Library News 2020). In the first three weeks of the UK's lockdown, 120,000 new members of libraries were registered, accompanied by a 205 per cent surge in ebook library loans (Chandler 2020). Libraries used these changed practices to encourage online collaborative activities between themselves and their members and users. In Greenwich, London, librarians turned their gardens, living rooms, and kitchens into creative spaces for producing new content for members, with activities that included unique children's storytelling sessions and space for members to post comments and join in these sessions. Norfolk libraries, in East Anglia, held virtual 'just a cuppa' groups for people to meet and socialise, while Kingston libraries in London's suburbs put on interactive virtual book and rhyme-times for children (Public Library News 2020). It was a similar story in other countries. Libraries in America employed social media – Facebook Live and Stories, Instagram, Discord, Zoom, GoToMeeting, and YouTube – in order to design and deliver numerous interactive programmes to the public, such as online book clubs (Freudenberger 2020). Smart technology is integral generally for people to get involved in their local communities. Mobile technologies made it easier for people to crowdfund charity events and raise money in communities to help local people impacted by the virus. And smart technologies can enhance the collaborative economy to connect business and volunteers together to help build community resilience in the face of the pandemic (Baeck and Reynolds 2020).

In many respects, the innovative and collaborative use of digital media by libraries taps into what some see as a relatively new sense of 'creativity' in society. Doyen of the idea that a 'creative class' is at the forefront of progressive ways of living and working in society, Richard Florida recommends, among other things, that children need to be given an active and creative form of learning at an early age, and so 'become emotionally attached to learning' (Florida 2012: 391). This goal can be achieved by encouraging the 'sparkling imaginations' of children to grow and prosper by taking risks in what and how they think. In some ways, the innovative and collaborative response of libraries to COVID-19 is closely aligned to devising new and creative activities for its users, including children (see also Galvagno and Dalli 2014; Potts et al. 2008a, 2008b; and see Chapter 7, below, for a critical analysis of Florida's main ideas about the creative class).

A guiding principle of this more optimistic picture of prosumer digital labour is that it is mediated through 'sharing'. As Bruns observes, digital culture today is premised on the fact that ordinary digital users, along with other partners like businesses, the third sector and policy officials, collaborate with one another by sharing content (Bruns 2008: 20; see also Gauntlett 2011: 95). In the eyes of Clay Shirky, we therefore produce and share media through 'social production' – 'the creation of value by a group for its members, using neither price signals nor managerial oversight to coordinate participants' efforts' (Shirky 2010: 118). Cultures of sharing are springing up everywhere. Free software projects, in which a community shares a computer code so that others can develop and improve it for everyone, not only creates a new object, in this instance a new piece of software, but also generates a *culture* of community sharing. Sharing thus becomes a norm (Shirky 2010: 143; see also Banet-Weiser and Castells 2017: 30).

What might be termed as a COVID-19 collaborative and sharing culture has certainly appeared during the pandemic. In January 2021, we were told that major enterprises had increased their use of open source software so that they could function more efficiently and resourcefully to cater for new market demands in these new pandemic times. Around 72 per cent of Fortune 50 companies went to GitHub Enterprise to help develop open source solutions for some of their tools and products, while, generally, open source collaborations proliferated by the start of the March 2020 lockdown. GitHub estimated that there was 25 per cent more contribution to open source projects on its site during 2020, while 35 per cent more repositories were created. 'This is exciting', opined Git Hub, 'especially as so many of us are at home right now. Open source gives us an opportunity to make and create, to learn and collaborate, and to share with our community' (GitHub 2020: 17). TikTok, which lets users upload 15-second clips of themselves, has also grown in popularity during successive lockdowns. Not only have people posted humorous clips of their experiences about living in lockdown, but many others have posted clips of how the pandemic has unsettled their lives, 'from school closures to hospital births to canceled sports seasons. Others have posted videos of getting tested for the virus. Ultimately, being able to vent and share experiences online helps to create a sense of digital community in the midst of the crisis' (Haasch 2020). Another illustration comes in the guise of Lego. For instance, the Lego corporation announced in late March 2020 that it was donating $50 million to support children most in need during COVID-19 (Lego Foundation 2020).

The pandemic has also had a knock-on effect of inspiring more people to become involved in voluntary work in their communities. Another study published in May 2020 estimated that in the United Kingdom one in every five adults, or 19 per cent of the adult population, gave their time freely to help out in their communities from the start of the first lockdown in March 2020. Of these people, 67 per cent of volunteers helped out in collecting groceries for others, 26 per cent delivered or collected medicines for others, and 16 per cent volunteered to call people to combat loneliness. Digital media has helped to develop and deepen these voluntary networks. For example, digital media alleviated to some extent socialising time lost during the lockdown. People were on average spending an extra 2 hours per week socialising through platforms like WhatsApp and Skype. Many who took part in the survey felt that the lockdown had brought local communities together to help one another – a fifth (19 per cent) strongly agreed with this statement, while a 45 per cent tended to agree. According to the study, this voluntary sharing economy represents the equivalent economic value of £357 per week (Legal and General 2020).

These examples illustrate a broader trajectory of a novel 'DIY citizenship' that has been with us now for a number of years. With the arrival of digital media and new networks of communication and sharing, opportunities open up for ordinary people to be 'critical makers' by creating, producing and using technology, objects, emotions, and so on, in often new and inventive ways in order to engage in 'politically transformative activities' (Ratto and Boler 2014: 1), and, in the process, generate their own sense of community and grassroots activism. Indeed, other positive effects have appeared from this emerging, pandemic collaborative culture. There been an upsurge in ordinary people believing that after the pandemic, society will be more united, equal and fairer. One survey from the Office for National Statistics (ONS) found that 61.1 per cent of its sample believe Britain will be a more united place in a post-COVID-19 world (this figure was only 21.4 per cent before the pandemic), while 42 per cent believed that Britain was somewhat or very kind before the coronavirus pandemic, and a larger proportion of 61 per cent said that Britain would be kinder once we have recovered from the coronavirus pandemic (ONS 2020c).

BEYOND THE TWO SCHOOLS

Two contemporary schools of thought on digital labour have now been mapped out. Yet, in my opinion, there is also something amiss with them. In their respective approaches, they tend to present a one-sided narrative on technology and labour. The first school of thought suggests that digital technology represents the latest mode of labour exploitation, while the second school of thought suggests that digital technology represents the latest mode of labour cooperation and collaboration. Both schools thereby sever the dialectical relationship and interplay between work, technology, and the material and objective world, and, in the process, sever the dialectical relationship between cooperation and exploitation.

To understand the ramifications of these problems in each respective school, let us momentarily go back to Marx, and, in particular, how Marx attempts to think through these dialectical relationships. The first point to note is that even at a general and trans-historical level of analysis, Marx believes that it is only through labouring on the objective world, and developing the tools and technology to do so, that we come understand both ourselves as being part of a community, our needs and our individual freedom, while, at the same time, we gain a greater understanding of nature and the natural world. Through labouring on the objective world, we also satisfy current needs and develop new needs and wants. Labouring activity therefore also alters its form and content historically; our natural and social capacities, powers and consciousness develop through time as we labour upon the changing external and objective world (Sayers 2011: 17).

This dialectical and historical moment to Marx's thinking is crucial in how he conceptualises exploitation and cooperation in the more complex, developed and unique system of capitalism. As we mentioned in Chapter 1, and will explore in more detail in Chapter 3, a capitalist market, for Marx, is historically unique to the extent that labour is involved directly by itself in the buying and selling of its labour to a capitalist because labour is free from ownership of the means of production (Fine 1998: 255). Furthermore, a worker's labour power increases in value during the production process and generates surplus value for the capitalist. Surplus value thus provides lubricant for the engine of capitalism. Crucially, the separation of labour from the means of production implies that the objective conditions of living labour appear as alienated, dispersed and detached from everyday life. Living labour produces the wealth of society, but under capitalism this wealth expresses itself externally in the guise of commodities created by past dead labour, 'so that living labour appears as a mere means to realise objectified, dead labour' and the products of living labour appear as 'alien, independent existences' (Marx 1973: 461). Alienation is thus a *constant condition* for workers who labour for a capitalist. Human labour now appears in the form of 'the properties of things', such as commodities and money, so that products of labour confront workers as an objective power; products which then appear to control workers rather than the other way round (Clarke 1991a: 325).

At the same time, workers are pushed together as commodities, and so they start to recognise common experiences of exploitation and oppression amongst themselves, and forge links of solidarity in the capitalist chain. Or, in the words of Marx: 'As the number of the cooperating workers increases, so too does their resistance to the domination of capital. And, necessarily, the pressure put on by capital to overcome this resistance' (Marx 1988: 449). Even so, constant competitive pressure placed on each capital to capture ever larger amounts of surplus value generates, in its wake, more complex relationships between different circuits of capital, their class relations and social divisions of labour in the capitalist workplace. Subsequently, varying degrees of socio-economic exploitation, socio-economic economic oppression *and*, by default, degrees and increasing forms of cooperation are all found in advanced capitalist class relations. That is to say, capitalism simultaneously expands alienated class relations across the globe, while it also complexifies those class relations, including their cooperative relations among class forms of labour. For example, some members of the 'working class' are employed mainly by industrial capital and so create surplus value and are exploited. Other members of the 'working class' are employed by commercial capital and so do not generate surplus value. They are, instead, oppressed workers because they create profits for a commercial capitalist through their surplus labour (see Chapter 3, below). Yet all these different classes of workers will likewise create their own representative bodies and trade unions that then advocate and push forward their class interests in and against capital.

In my view, both schools of thought fail to fully understand the contradictory basis to the very essence and identity of capitalism. This is particularly noticeable in how they both compare contemporary capitalist societies with past capitalist societies. According to each school, the Internet, social media and other developments in the expansion of digital technology mean we longer have to erect sharp divides between production, distribution and consumption. In its industrial place, then, we have arrived at a new digital period of capitalist history. These respective accounts, though, more often than not employ linear and descriptive historical narratives in which 'industrial capitalism' is said to have been surpassed by 'digital/informational/network capitalism'. By constructing this linear historical narrative, however, a whole host of other binary oppositions, dualisms and linear histories are let loose. Industrial capitalism, for instance, is said to be predicated on vertical networks, whereas digital capitalism is predicated on flatter horizontal networks. So-called industrial thinkers, like Marx, are also brushed off as writers for a bygone age industrial age.

Gere (2008) is typical in following this linear narrative. In his otherwise highly readable account on the history digital culture, Gere argues that Marx tended to emphasise that the abstract and standardisation of goods in society – how goods are produced, packaged and exchanged for the abstract measurement of money – occurs primarily in nineteenth- and early twentieth-century industrial factories (Gere 2008: 24). As history moves forward, however, so Marx drops out of view. Abstraction and standardisation, according to Gere, is replaced during the mid-twentieth century by 'complexity' in which digital systems start to become self-regulating, while in the twenty-first century we witness the hegemony of a participatory and prosumer culture immersed in social media and an internet of things – 'assemblages' of digital devices, digital machines and humans – that communicate with one another in predictable and unpredictable ways. Theorist of liquid life, Zygmunt Bauman (2000: 141), similarly notes that Marx mainly talks on behalf of 'industrial societies, not our present complex, fluid and unstable conditions. Social media shows us that people's energies can be exploited by corporations in the safety of one's bedroom.' Stiegler (2010: 33) makes essentially the same point. Trapped in an industrial logic, Marx could not possibly predict that an empowered digital capitalism would thrive by exploiting people's cognitive abilities as well as their physical labour. Even for a Marxist like Fuchs, digital and informational capitalism can be compared with an earlier industrial capitalism (see Fuchs 2020: 180–1). This leads Fuchs to offer a somewhat non-dialectical reading of capitalism. He claims that capitalist 'exploitation' has moved beyond the 'industrial factory' and reaches into every area of society. As such, the exploited 'proletariat' is now found everywhere in society, including in the sphere of the 'commons' (Fuchs 2020: 214).

Problematically, however, we begin to see here how this linear narrative, in which 'industrial society' is pitted against 'digital society', starts to unravel. This is particularly noticeable when these theorists sketch out how ordinary people might 'resist' power relations at play in digital societies. This is trickier than at first might be appreciated. After all, for these theorists, exploitation is now firmly embedded in digital technology across society. Everyone is therefore subsumed in exploitative power relations both inside the workplace, but also outside of it too, as when they use social media in their 'private' spaces. More optimistically, though, this expansion of social exploitation also unintentionally throws up 'new' types of 'resistance' to capitalism. Mediated through an array of 'workers' that Marx would never have the opportunity to get to know – 'computer programmers, advertising copywriters, graphic designers, workers in roboticised factories, art workers, and so on' (Gere 2008: 166) – digital capitalism unleashes novel capacities and potentialities of resistant subjectivities beyond the industrial factory gates. Similarly, Fuchs wants to suggest that while 'digital capitalism deepens exploitation', it also builds 'new foundations for autonomous realms that transcend the logic of capitalism' (Fuchs 2019: 62). Global social movements like the Occupy movement are an obvious illustration of the radical potential unleashed by new horizontal networks of communications.

Fuchs, however, paints a strangely ahistorical picture of these radical potentials. After all, for Fuchs, the proletariat is simply defined as 'all those who produce goods and commons that are appropriated by capital' (Fuchs 2020: 214). Thus, the definition presented by Fuchs of the 'proletariat' is so all-encompassing that it misses the dialectical complexities and subtleties of Marx's original analysis of class relations; for instance, Fuchs fails to distinguish different labour processes at play in digital workplaces, which are themselves refracted through different circuits of capital. Fuchs' definition of the proletariat is also so generic that it can feasibly be said to share remarkable similarities with the definition of collaboration presented by the more positive school of thought. A theorist like Bruns sees 'produsage' as being 'the collaborative and continuous building and extending of existing content in pursuit of further improvement' (Bruns 2008: 21). This is essentially the same as the definition bequeathed to us by Fuchs, with the difference being that Fuchs arguably gives more space to explaining the 'exploitative' aspects of these practices by capital.

Interestingly, these problems are reproduced in new ways in some accounts that aim to overcome certain dualisms in thinking about these issues. Jordan (2020: 125–6), for example, argues that networks of collaboration are always mediated and organised through pre-programmed and hierarchical protocols, the latter of which are strictly controlled by dominant powers. Most obviously, social media companies encourage users to co-create and collaborate with one another mainly to the extent that these user practices benefit the commercial strategies of large-scale digital media corporations. Jordan's observations, though, throw up more questions than answers. We are still none the wiser, for example, whether, from Jordan's account, some types of prosumer activity create surplus value, while other types help to generate profits. Like Fuchs, this is because Jordan does not explore in enough detail or depth the different circuits of capital and their contradictions or different class relations in the digital labour process. Finally, Jordan tends to operate, theoretically, with a fragmented view of capitalist social relations. To give one illustration, he argues that alienation is one 'factor' of user activity on social media. 'Liking' somebody on Facebook is an 'inalienable' factor of a friendship network (Jordan 2020: 122). Effectively, Jordan therefore conceptualises 'alienation' at a subjective level as being one moment of a person's everyday interaction on social media. As we will see in the next chapter, it is more fruitful to think about alienation in the first instance as a historically specific essential property of capitalism; arguably, the most essential condition of the class relation of capitalism insofar as it constitutes a daily and total experience for all those who work in capitalism.

Politically, the two schools of thought respective description of contemporary capitalism also advances, in their own ways, a rather thin understanding of how we might 'resist' capitalist power in the world today. Fleming, for example, holds a parallel view of capitalism to that of Fuchs to the extent that both believe that capital extends its exploitative grip beyond the industrial factory walls and now seeks to exploit the common pool of knowledge created by users in digital networks based in individual's everyday emotions, intelligence and personalities. For Fleming, one way to 'resist' this newer type of exploitation is for political movements to refuse to enter into dialogue with new types of capitalist power. Radicalised silence therefore recognises that capitalism today, especially in its digital and social media guise, wants to insert itself into our everyday subjectivity. Political movements subsequently need to simply engage in 'turning away from power' (Fleming 2015: 143), to refuse to recognise or to be recognised by capitalist work and power, by not participating in dialogue with representatives of this power at the moment that one struggles against it.

In Chapter 10, we look at these sorts of political argument in more empirical detail. But for now, we can say that it represents a rather thin political practice to the extent that it advocates, once more, a rather generic set of political practices. For example, what exactly does it mean to say that progressive political groups should engage in 'radical silence' against forms of new capitalist power? Does this mean that the anti-neoliberal political movement started by Jeremy Corbyn in the United Kingdom or Bernie Sanders in the United States were doomed to fail from the start because they both tried to win state power for radical and progressive causes and movements? Should anti-neoliberal social and political movement always refuse to enter into dialogue with the state or other more conventional institutions such as large-scale trade unions? Fleming's perspective provides little guidance on such issues.

Similar observations can be made about the more positive school of thought. Advocates of the school suggest that digital technology has thrown up new collaborative and sharing opportunities for society. Theoretically, though, without the adequate conceptual means to understand the historical specificity of capitalism, other problematic issues arise when trying to grasp more empirical questions about 'resistance' to capital. Again, COVID-19 provides us with an illustration of this critical point. As we know, the pandemic has motivated people to become involved in voluntary activity. However, voluntary activity by itself does not necessarily lead to clear-cut benefits for society as a whole, nor does it imply that people are somehow building a 'commons' of resistance. As Dhillon notes, the term 'mutual aid' was associated many years ago with anarchist groups and workers' cooperatives, and mutual aid was part of their broader respective activism to build and foster cooperative movements beyond the centralising forces of capitalist state bureaucracies. Under the pandemic, COVID-19 Mutual Aid in London was set up to coordinate care efforts for people self-isolating because of the virus, and it soon grew to become a national organisation. Yet this contemporary pandemic mutual aid organisation is obviously not the same as past anarchist or socialist forms of mutual aid. In fact, contemporary mutual aid charities and voluntary networks can often get pulled into doing the sort of work, and plugging the policy gaps, that the welfare state once provided (Dhillon 2020). Through the 'hollowing out of the welfare state', voluntarism can therefore often soon become part and parcel of a neoliberal workfare state project in which ordinary people are encouraged by governments to take up the welfare slack, but to do so for free (Roberts 2004; see also Chapter 4 on neoliberal and austerity-imposed cutbacks to welfare services).

This latter point hints at some further problems for the more positive school of thought on prosumer digital labour. Often, this school omits questions from its respective analysis about the impact that wider social factors such as changing state and governance agendas have on collaborative networks in society. Keeping momentarily with volunteering, the pandemic has exposed the precarious and underfunded nature within which many charities and voluntary organisations have to operate in our current austere times. One UK research report published in June 2020 found, for example, that on average charities received 29 per cent less income during lockdown than they had originally budgeted for, while

91 per cent of the charities that responded said they are forecasting that their budged income will fall for the year ahead, with 35 per cent expected a 'significant decrease'. Redundancies in the UK charity sector will follow this loss of income, alongside a significant decrease in the services the sector can offer (NCVO 2020). Reduced support for voluntary sectors has a direct impact on trying to support an online collaborative and sharing culture in society. Wallace et al. (2020), for instance, found that during 2019/20, more people in the United Kingdom felt that their wellbeing, based on a range of factors such as a sense of personal wellbeing, one's relationships, health, what a person does on a daily basis, where they live, finances, one's job, and one's surrounding environment, was 6.79 out of 10, whereas the figure was 6.89 in 2018/19. The report presents a number of possible solutions to raise the UK's wellbeing score. One useful recommendation is to increase investment and support in equality of participation for ordinary people in a range of community endeavours and spheres, which will directly affect them, and to invest in IT literacy and digital inclusion (Wallace et al. 2020: 31). Cutbacks to the voluntary sector, however, already place a substantial barrier to successfully implementing this policy.

Our pandemic times have, however, also thrown up mutual aid groups more attuned to anarchist and socialist principles. Cooperation Kentish Town, London, established in December 2019, is based in a community centre on a housing estate. It took its inspiration from similar groups in the United States, which had formed 'to build community autonomy and resilience through establishing a network of workers' cooperatives' and to assemble working-class education collectives (Anderson 2020). Originally tasked with distributing food parcels to households on the estate, the Kentish Town cooperative soon started to deliver food parcels across the London borough of Camden once the pandemic emerged. Soon, Cooperation Kentish Town launched the Cooperation Towns network across Britain (Anderson 2020). In my view, these forms of voluntarism, mutual aid and workers' cooperatives represent a more organised, and often localised, assault on capital. They are class conscious and recognise that their local activism is a small but significant contribution towards building a genuine anti-capitalist 'commons' than is the case with other types of volunteering and mutual aid. However, by developing a rather ahistorical account of the 'commons', as is evident, in my opinion, with some ideas in the two schools of thought, it is soon theoretically difficult to gain a qualitative dimension to activities like 'helping out' in a local community in the sense of having the adequate theoretical tools make qualitative judgements as to the socio-political and ideological effects of types of voluntary work, or, more broadly, one's contribution to the commons. Do some types of voluntary work and online collaboration, for example, actually serve to support neoliberalism more so than other types?

CONCLUSION

Naturally, ideas should never be sacrosanct, and must always be developed, updated and improved to take account of social changes and the passing of time. Still, in a seemingly frantic need to generate 'new' theoretical frameworks, many misread and misapprehend the thinkers they wish to surpass. In the case of Marx, he is misleadingly said to be a thinker of 'industrial' capitalism, even though Marx is more interested in setting out some of the core contradictions and problems of capitalism as a system, rather than explain the workings of any distinct phase of capitalism, whether this is imperialist capitalism, industrial capitalism, Keynesian welfare capitalism and so on. As my book is, in part, a defence and extension of Marx's labour theory of value and social class, we need therefore to spend some time in presenting an adequate account of these key areas in Marx's thought. The next chapter starts to undertake this task by setting out Marx's value theory and its relationship to social class. This discussion is vital if we wish to gain a critical understanding of the state of digital work both before and during COVID-19.

Chapter 3

ALIENATED LABOUR AND CLASS RELATIONS

INTRODUCTION

We know that many contemporary critical theorists believe that the core ideas of Marx are somewhat archaic. In particular, Marx's labour theory of exploitation is thought to be rather obsolete in explaining the nature of present-day capitalism. Marx's main ideas cannot be used to understand how exploitation is now prevalent across society and not just in the industrial factory, and they cannot explain how digital technology unleashes co-creative energies in communities. If truth be told, however, criticisms of Marx's value theory are not particularly new. Variations of them have been made throughout the years; indeed, they were made way before the emergence of digital media. The first major critique of Marx's labour theory of value was in fact articulated a mere twelve years after his death. In 1896, Eugen von Böhm-Bawerk published, *Karl Marx and the Close of His System*. Böhm-Bawerk argues that Marx arbitrarily favours abstract labour as the common substance that allows commodities to exchange with one another, whereas, in reality, there is no historical reason why this should be the case (Böhm-Bawerk 1949: 75). In making his case, Böhm-Bawerk set the template for a critique of Marx that others have subsequently followed, even if they if rarely acknowledge the debt to him. Today, of course, it is countless digital theorists who reject, or at least distance themselves from, Marx's theory of value in favour of terms like 'information', 'networks', 'free labour', 'co-creation' and so forth.

The aim of this chapter is to defend a version of Marx's value theory and Marxist class theory. According to Marx, capitalism is first and foremost a *class* society with an antagonistic relation at its core; a relation 'in which unpaid surplus-labour is pumped out of the direct producers' (Marx [1966] 1991: 927). But more than this, Marx wishes to discern *why* labour takes a *historically specific* class form under capitalism, and he endeavours to understand the political results of this class relation (Marx: 1988: 173–5; see also Elson 1979: 123). Marx tells us, for example, that labour in capitalism is not 'a general category', but assumes 'a *definite historical* form' (Marx 1969: 285). For Marx, this 'definite historical form' is labour's *alienated* nature under capitalism; 'alienated' because every-day acts of work in capitalism are founded on the historic dispossession of labour from the means of production. Dispossession further implies that labour is alienated from the capitalist means of production and the commodities flowing from them; commodities that labour produces in the first place. Capitalists instead own and control these commodities.

I want to suggest that this particular Marxist viewpoint provides a basis to overcome the dualism between conceiving digital labour and work as representing concrete and generic exploited free labour, or conceiving labour as representing co-creative networks of cooperation. Exploited labour is, instead, dialectically entwined with creativity; with the desire and need for labour to struggle against and overcome alienation and exploitation. But this is the case only if one places labour in its class context and recognises that the circuits of capital are constituted through class relations and class struggle. In this chapter, therefore, I show how the contradiction between labour and capital imposes an external competitive constraint on capital to expand and develop itself across the globe through both productive and unproductive labour processes and class forces. I subsequently provide a brief theoretical sketch of class relations in the contemporary labour process and outline how a number of social classes develop in 'late capitalism'. I then apply these classes to different digital labour processes. But first things first. We need to say more about what is meant by alienated labour and how this term is also associated with Marx's theory of abstract labour.

ABSTRACT AND ALIENATED LABOUR

For Marx, the basic appearance of capitalism is the commodity. Capitalism is, after all, a system dominated and determined by commodity production. Marx wants to understand how commodities actually exchange with one another given that, at a very basic level, each commodity is created and produced by people who, at least initially, are isolated and separated from one another. Commodities are also different to one another. So, what enables at least two different objects to exchange with one another? Marx believes this 'something' is human labour power, which appears in a homogeneous form as *abstract human labour* mediated through the *socially necessary labour time* taken on average to produce a commodity. In other words, the concrete labour time that produces a commodity is judged as having a *value* in the marketplace, and, in particular, it has an *exchange-value*, not only to the extent that someone wants to purchase the commodity, but also to the extent that the commodity embodies the socially necessary labour time that went into producing it. If the commodity takes longer to produce than on average, it will tend to have a lower exchange-value at the point of exchange in a marketplace than those commodities that possess the average socially necessary labour time.

Concrete and private labour embodied in one commodity is, according to Marx, expressed as abstract homogeneous and undifferentiated labour when exchanged for another commodity. In other words, a commodity only gains *value*, namely, it assumes a *value-form*, in the moment of exchange (Marx 1988: 125 ff.). Commodities must therefore be 'socially validated' in the marketplace by being exchanged for something else; for example, exchanged for another commodity or, more normally, exchanged for money. This simple point is true even today. People take products to the marketplace in the hope that the products – the commodities – have universal exchangeability. 'In other words, do not those involved in production and distribution expect to be able to purchase the commodities they want or need from the proceeds from selling their products?' (Smith 2019: 81–2). At this most simple and basic level of analysis, the historical peculiarity of capitalism lies in the fact that concrete labour is transformed into its opposite, into abstract labour, during exchange. The measurement of abstract labour is the socially necessary labour time it takes to produce specific commodities, and whose appearance is money (Bonefeld 2010: 263–5).

Marx further suggests that production and circulation are moments in the circulation and reproduction of alienated labour. Certainly, 'the material dimension of this reproduction is the production and circulation of use-values, and the quantity of use-values available to circulation is determined within production' (Clarke 1994: 141; see also Murray 2011; Saad-Filho 2002). Production and circulation are, however, an interconnected totality. Production is a social process that cannot be conceived in isolation from other social relations, such as distribution and circulation. In the *Grundrisse*, Marx writes: 'Production creates the material, as external object, for consumption; consumption creates the need, as internal object, as aim, for production' (Marx 1973: 93). Even at the most basic level of analysis, use-values in capitalism gain value only if they can be exchanged for another commodity; that is, if they can be consumed by others as exchange-value. Use-values must therefore enter into circulation (Elson 1979: 127–31). So, the use-value of a commodity is not achieved directly, but is achieved indirectly through a complex division of labour and social production.

At a more developed level of analysis, one can say that capitalists enter into an exchange relation with dispossessed labour – labour that does not own its means of production and is forced to sell itself to capital for a wage – in order to produce goods to sell in the marketplace. Workers are thereby transformed into a commodity in the capitalist labour markets and bought for money, for a wage, by a capitalist. Alienated labour is subsequently at the core of this relation. Production and exchange are only moments in this class relation; a relation founded on dispossessed labour. Use-values are not consumed directly by the labour that produces them, but are exchanged in the marketplace in order to realise their value (Clarke 1991a: 102). Alienated labour is thus concrete labour, which is socially validated only to the extent that it produces value for others and is only generally recognised in a complex division of socially necessary labour time, 'i.e., labour which proves that it is universal social labour only by the suppression of its original character in the exchange process' (Marx 1972: 45). An alienated and objective compulsion is thereby readily apparent in which 'the possessor of labour-power . . . must rather be compelled to offer for sale as a commodity that very labour-power which exists only in his living body' (Marx 1988: 272; see also Kicillof and Starosta 2007: 33; Moseley 2000: 307). 'Things', such as commodities, whose substance ultimately dwells in abstract labour, or value, are assessed through money, and it is money that enables one to play an active every-day role in capitalism. Money thus acts as the universal equivalent, a social relation of capitalist commodity production, which expresses a relationship between the labour of the individual and the labour of society (Clarke 1991a).

While Marx argues that capitalism transforms us into commodity 'things' to be bought and sold in labour markets, he also recognises that workers come together as a collective and cooperative unit to produce commodities for a capitalist (see Holloway 1992: 151). Indeed, dispossessed labour also creates the material conditions for the appropriation of surplus value, which is the main source of wealth in capitalism. In order to gain the means to subsistence, a dispossessed labourer sells not her/his labour, but her/his capacity to work, or labour power, to a capitalist for a certain length of time during a day. Surplus value arises from the difference between the sum of value accrued by the capitalist on the sale of the product and the sum paid out for the purchase of labour power and means of production. The 'fictitious' nature of labour power reveals itself when we are therefore made aware that the capitalist does not purchase labour power to enjoy it directly, but purchases it only as a means of gaining surplus value. Similarly, commodities are not generated to appease consumption wants, but only to expand capital (Marx 1988: 1061; see also Banaji 2011).

Marx's theory of alienated labour might sound interesting to many, and can provide an understanding into how radical nineteenth-century thinkers portrayed capitalism, but can it really help us to understand contemporary forms of labour and work, and, in particular, forms of digital labour and work? I think it can, and so I now outline a number of advantages to Marx's theory of alienated labour for improving our interpretation of contemporary forms of digital labour and work.

ADVANTAGES OF MARX'S THEORY OF ALIENATED LABOUR

One advantage to Marx's approach is that a focus on alienated labour alerts us to how workers will often develop a feeling of disempowerment in their workplace. Of course, workers can also express solidarity and loyalty with their employers, particularly against rival firms. Class experiences in the workplace are therefore contradictory and subject to strategic dilemmas depending on changing circumstances (Gough 2003). Resistance and dissent by workers in and against their conditions of work therefore assumes a diverse array of guises. In today's world, this might take the appearance of workers writing critical comments in online forums and blogs about their managers, or employees creating spaces so that they can skive and avoid work, employees feeling degrees of resentment at a new managerial rule, or annoyed that no pay rises are imminent, or the emergence of new worker collectives and unions that bring dispersed workers together to campaign for better pay and working conditions, and so on (Thompson 2016).

I would wish to go further, though, and argue that the class relations analysed and described by Marx provide the bedrock for these everyday class experiences. The capital–labour relation, and the contradictory processes associated with these relations, impart a total social experience for workers. Before the circuit of capital can proceed, it requires the capital–labour relation to be in place. Dispossession and alienation therefore provide the parameters through which the vast majority experience the world of work and social life, and both mediate our economic, political and cultural relations (Clarke 1994). None of this is to deny the significance of other socio-cultural experiences of people in their daily lives. We are all defined by a whole array of identities. Class relations are therefore also expressed through a variety of social identities – age, disability, race and ethnicity, gender, sexuality and so forth – and this implies that class relations encompass a set of complex dynamics in actual contexts and different labour processes (Moore 2011: ch. 1). Even so, capitalism will, for its own ends, make use of different types of socio-cultural identity and experiences to further the expansion of capitalist accumulation, and, by default, ensure that dispossessed and alienated labour remains the bedrock for accumulation. Racism, for example, has been used to further capitalist expansion across the world. Late seventeenth- and eighteenth-century colonialism depicted black slaves as less than human just as the increasingly proletarianised working class in the dominant capitalist nations like Britain were being represented as formally free and equal participants in the wage contract with their capitalist masters. Black slaves were therefore ideologically positioned as being 'non-persons standing outside the normal universe of freedom and equality' (Wood 1995: 269). Importantly, capitalism will also ameliorate specific types of oppression, whether these are related to racism, sexism, disability, sexuality and so forth, if it suits the purposes of accumulation. Capitalism, though, can never rid itself of the class relations of exploitation because this exploitation is essential to the very survival of capitalism.

Class struggles are, accordingly, complexly structured and, as such, experienced in real-time by people through a number of strategic dilemmas and strategic opportunities. These strategic dilemmas and opportunities include the ability of some classes to articulate their interests in the economic and political arenas, the ideological formation of state projects at a particular point in time (for example, whether a state pursues a Keynesian project or a neoliberal project), the role of media discourses in supporting or criticising specific state projects and programmes, the ability of certain institutions to attach themselves to a dominant state project and provide support for that state project, the role that particular social movements, collective identities and cultural organisations might play in policy formation, and so forth (Jessop 2008: ch. 1). Strategic dilemmas and strategic opportunities are particularly prominent during crises. This is because a crisis will create new prospects to give meaning to society. Politicians, for instance, will represent a crisis through specific media discourses and use a crisis to push forward a specific policy agenda onto society. But crises also provide occasions for workers to struggle in and against their sense of alienation. As we will see throughout the book, COVID-19 illustrates this point in relation to relatively new types of union organisations representing workers employed by digital media companies.

Another advantage to Marx's ideas on alienated labour is a theoretical one. Marx's insights provide a way to combat and overcome more problematical technologically determinist approaches to digital media and labour. Marx's primary focus of attention is on contradictory social relations between classes that mediate and give form to technological innovation, rather than a focus on individuals *and* technological innovation (see Clarke 1979: 141–2). The difference between these two approaches is discernible if we briefly turn our attention to the highly influential thinker, Manuel Castells. According to Castells, products made by some informational corporations and social media companies are increasingly targeted at financial markets in order to gain positive valuations by these markets, which then increase interest from other investors, and so forth. 'But to reach the financial market, and to vie for higher value in it', continues Castells, 'firms, institutions, and individuals have to go through the hard labour of innovating, producing, managing, and image-making in goods and services' (Castells 2000: 160). Technological innovation is therefore at the heart of this profit-making machine alongside financial markets. In fact, Castells suggests technological innovation constitutes a 'mode of development', which he defines as 'the technological arrangements through which labour works on matter to generate the product, ultimately determining the level and quality of surplus' (Castells 2000: 16). Yet Castells' idea that progress is achieved primarily through a continuous technological innovation economy implies, problematically, that technology has become (relatively) detached from the contradictory dynamics associated with value relations and alienated labour (cf. Fitzgerald 2012: 70–1).

In contrast to Castells, then, it is vital to understand that technological innovations, including digital breakthroughs, are not autonomous of capitalist class relations. Technological breakthroughs are mediated by the tendency of capital to accumulate surplus value and profits without regard to the limits of the marketplace by driving out competitors from markets, by developing new technology, and by intensifying the working conditions of labour (Clarke 1992: 135). Valorisation of capital, and the accumulation of surplus value, therefore drives the tendency to overproduce (Marx 1988: 769).

External competitive pressure placed on individual capitals gives rise to a 'struggle between firms for technological advantage . . . (and) a pattern of leap-frogging innovations in technological and organisational forms' (Harvey 2017: 9). Technological breakthroughs in some workplaces, for instance, produce use-values, but they also create new ways to reduce the turnover time of production; design sophisticated new software in order to monitor fluctuations in prices on stock markets; build new databases to process information on the health, welfare and well-being of labour; and manufacture new transport and communication systems to increase the mobility of capital. That is to say, each 'technological' accumulation regime requires the construction of social norms and habits across varying branches of production that will support this newly emerging accumulation regime. Over a time period, it will be hoped by capitalists and policymakers that a convergence will also emerge between transformations in production and transformations in consumption (Lipietz 1988: 29–31). Under these circumstances, a 'mode of development' is theorised as being less about technological innovations, but more as a way to *regulate* distinctive, although contradictory, accumulation regimes at points in time (Boyer 1988: 8–9). These are contradictory regimes because they refract the class antagonism of labour and capital. Technological innovations, for example, often replace labour by machines, but this in turn reduces the source of surplus value for capital, and detaches profit from its source in productive social labour (Harvey 2014: 98–104).

A further advantage to Marx's ideas on alienated labour relates to social class. For Marx, only productive labour creates and transforms a use-value into a new use-value for exchange and in so doing, generates surplus value for a productive capitalist. In exchanging its labour-power against capital, productive labour thereby increases the value of capital. At the same time, the value generated then confronts productive labour as capital and reproduces the class relation between capital and labour (Marx 1988: 1039–43; see also Poulantzas 1978: 219). Unproductive labour, however, is labour that does not create or transform a use-value into surplus value, but circulates and transfers already created surplus value and transforms it into profit (see also Tregenna 2011: 288). While surplus value lies at the heart of capitalist accumulation and is generated by alienated labour, Marx therefore argues that actual profits are derived through the distribution of surplus value among various capitals. Unproductive capitals, such as commerce, finance and rent, gain profits from already produced and circulating surplus value, but they do not necessarily add any surplus value themselves. Instead, they help to 'equalise profit' through competition, but they are not 'productive' as they do not create surplus value. Prices thereby allocate a share of surplus value to individual capitals through capitalist competition. Indeed, capitalist competition ensures that commodities do not exchange at prices that correspond to their values, but instead exchange 'at prices corresponding to the equalisation of the rate of profit' (Clarke 1991a: 138–9).

Capital must subsequently expand itself through these circuits, but as it does so it builds complex arrangements, labour processes and systems to realise more profits. In particular, surplus value is distributed through *different* labour processes – productive and unproductive labour processes – to develop other markets and lines of profit. Each labour process will have distinct configurations of social classes that include different types of non-labour in the guise of managerial and supervisory workers as well. It is for this reason that we need to understand the different class forms and class configurations assumed by alienated labour in contemporary digital capitalism. Some workers represent productive labour, some are unproductive, while others will be managerial and supervisory non-labour. It is true that on one level all labour represents dispossessed labour, which is subject to 'precarious labour markets and pressure to secure the profitability of her employer as the basis of sustained employment' (Bonefeld 2014: 107; see also Moraitis and Copley 2017: 106). It is also the case, however, that qualitative class differences can be recognised between different forms of dispossessed labour (Poulantzas 1978: 222). Not all labour creates surplus value and not every capitalist is interested in producing surplus value. A segment of people in the workplace will, moreover, manage and supervise discrete labour processes and subject workers to control and surveillance (see also Carchedi 1991: 40).

One final advantage in employing Marx's theory of alienated labour is that it provides a coherent and critical way to analyse how capitalist class relations are reproduced not just economically, but also politically, socially and culturally. This is so in two related senses. In the first instance, class relations, as we will see in the next section, are reproduced in the labour process through exploitative and oppressive social relations that are also founded on the ability of capitalists and managers to retain political and legal relations of control on workers. Moreover, workers develop distinctive social and cultural identities and work patterns, which sometimes spill over into overt modes of resistance to the control exerted by capitalists and managers; for instance, when workers go on strike or when resistance appears in 'small acts', such as skiving off from work. There might also be a cultural pattern of employees working cooperatively with management, and so on.

In the second instance, class relations need to be managed and regulated by political forms. Most obviously, class relations are governed by the capitalist state and the latter's ability to impose the abstract rule of law and order in civil society and impose the abstract rule of money in civil society. Law and order and money are both forms of appearance of alienated class relations in capitalism that the state seeks to govern and regulate (on the class nature of the capitalist state, see also Chapters 4 and 9, below). At a basic level of analysis, the state manages and regulates both labour power as a commodity and the circulation and flow of money. Labour power is managed through welfare provision, law and order, industrial relations, market labour and so on. Money is managed and regulated through a monetary system that includes national monetary policies and standards that operate alongside global monetary systems and standards. Monetary policy is devised nationally and internationally and is managed through different channels. Notably, banks and central banks become crucial to making policies and regulating money and capital. For example, states can set policies for banks and establish lines of credit for various class interests in civil society (Bonefeld et al. 1995: 12). Globally, national states act as conduits in global accumulation regimes. National states certainly set their own aims and goals in relation to labour and money within their borders, but they are also locked into different global price mechanisms. '(W) orld money transcends national currency' (Bonefeld et al. 1995: 28), and so governments must respond to international financial markets and will often cooperate with other governments to gain advantages in this global marketplace.

Correspondingly, class struggles in different countries will affect how governments impose monetary policies and regulate labour and civil society within their borders, all of which will in their own way impact on global monetary flows. Through local policies, national states facilitate investment opportunities for global money and, in turn, aim to attract investments into national economies. States must also discipline different groups of workers through coercion and consent to ensure workers operate within the limits of capital. Governments therefore pass policies to regulate labour power in all of its concrete guises. For instance, states will pass legislation about different types of welfare that then impact on the daily social and cultural experiences of black workers, disabled workers, gay and lesbian workers, female workers and so on. National states will likewise enter into global pacts with other states to ensure global money and finance can flow around the world and provide new outlets for capitalist accumulation, while, simultaneously, all states enter into conflict with one another about socio-economic competition and political disagreements about how best to alleviate different crises and problems in global capitalism (Bonefeld et al. 1995: 26–8).

The next section now outlines in more detail some of the characteristics of these different class forms in relation to the labour process, while the next chapter starts to explore class relations in relation to the nation state and global capital.

THE CAPITALIST CLASS

Separation of labour from the means of production is 'the given starting point' for understanding specific class relations in the workplace (Marx

1991: 120). In a capitalist labour process, this separation appears as a relationship between the owner of the means of production and those workers who own nothing but their labour power. This class relation compels workers to sell their 'commodity' of labour power to an owner – a capitalist – in order to obtain a wage and then use this to purchase necessities to live. In the *capitalist* labour process these basic prerequisites therefore assume a peculiar form in which labour is *free* from *ownership of the means of production*, while capitalists enjoy, first, *ownership* of the means of production, as well as, secondly, *control* or *possession* of the means of production (Poulantzas 1978: 18). There is also a third relation at play in the ownership of the means of production, which is associated with 'title'. Capitalists naturally require legal rights to the means of production, but title can also refer to 'the sort of calculations which govern the circulation of legal titles' (Jones 1982: 77). The transfer of liquid assets between corporations, for instance, not only depends on legal rights, but also involves making calculations about other important elements, such as stock market expectations, government policies, predicted rates of return and so on. If surplus value is to be generated, the capitalist class consequently requires possession over the means of production, control over the labour process, and a legal right over its possession to control the labour process and make binding calculations about it (Woodiwiss 1990: 177; see also Wright 1978: 73). Workers, in contrast, are dispossessed of the means of production, and so are also dispossessed of control and legal rights over the means of production (Wright 1978: 73). These class relations are the foundation of the capitalist workplace because labour power only appears as a wage commodity in a society that dispossesses labour of its means of production (Clarke 1979).

For Marx, the rise of manufacture builds the conditions for the transformation of the capitalist mode of production and paves the way for the establishment of modern class relations. Manufacturing is important to Marx because it advances and develops the capitalist division of labour and enables capital to take root in society. This, then, provides the ground to create a greater amount of surplus value (Marx 1988: 293). These conditions also provide stronger foundations for productive capital; the latter of which is defined primarily as capital that, through money capital, purchases the commodities of labour power and the means of production in order to consume these and convert them into commodities to generate more value (Marx 1992: 131). Productive capital is so vital for Marx's analysis because without it there can be no industrial capital. It is the latter – industrial capital – that completes the circuit of capital and generates a greater mass of surplus value than the previous cycle of production (Marx 1992: 131–3). The following circuit can thus represent industrial capital:

$$M - C \ (LP + MP) \dots P \dots C^1 - M^1$$

(Marx 1992: 137)

Here, M represents money capital exchanged for the commodities of labour power (LP) and means of production (MP). Both LP and MP are put to use in the process of production (P) to create commodities (C^1) of more value than was initially laid out in the production process. Transforming an object into commodity capital (C^1) enables a capitalist to sell the commodity for more money than was spent in production. Profit (M^1) is then realised.

While contemporary forms of productive capital and industrial capital are explored in Chapters 4 and 5, below, it is also worth noting that in numerous cases today owners of the means of production delegate control and possession to corporate directors, CEOs and top executives. In previous years, an 'old' capitalist class often had both legal and real ownership and possession of the means of production, and employed a few people in the workplace. Corporate, multinational capitalism and, more recently, the financialisation of society (see Chapter 4), in which financial capital becomes a dominant mode of accumulation, have nevertheless ushered in a relatively new capitalist and executive management class group. Managers and CEOs of large corporations, for example, enjoy high wages and other remuneration packages that invariably include financial assets as well. Between 2000 and 2005, for instance, CEOs in America's top fifty firms received only 40 per cent of their compensation from income and salaries, while stocks represented 23 per cent and options 37 per cent (Weil 2014: 48). Capitalists similarly gain income flows from the likes of financial assets alongside capital income. As a result, the division between high managers and capitalists has in many cases become blurred (Duménil and Levy 2011: 85).

Capitalist managers are involved in strategic control and decisions about how to employ and allocate resources in a firm in and around certain interests (Wright 1978). Under corporate capitalism, strategic control is always intimately related to ownership of a corporate entity despite the formal separation that obtains today between ownership and control. As Jones (1982) observes, corporate control is concerned with making, breaking and re-organising corporate social relations. Control of a workforce in global value chains, for example, is connected to matters about whether a particular plant might be relocated to another region or country, and with issues like subcontracting, severance and so on.

Corporate control, therefore, is first and foremost about how a corporation makes calculations on a range of diverse factors and then how they bring them together into a range of factors; for example, 'the choice of locations and products for investment, the division of the overall profit and the general objectives concerning the labour force, finance, and so on' (Jones 1982: 96).

Corporate and multinational capitalism consequently signifies the integration in new ways of industrial capital and financial capital, which has spread across the globe through the likes of global value chains, global outsourcing chains and global financial networks. One study conducted in 2011 found that 1,318 multinational corporations collectively own, through shares, the majority of blue-chip companies (those multinational companies that are seen as being relatively stable and have good reputable brands like Disney, McDonalds or Coca-Cola) and collectively own, again through shares, manufacturing companies, which together represent 60 per cent of global revenues. These multinational companies also operate 20 per cent of global operating revenue so that, in total, they actually comprise 80 per cent of the world's revenue (Robinson 2017: 177). Robinson further observes: 'In effect, less than 1 per cent of the companies were able to control 40% of the entire network. Revealingly, the top 50 were mostly major global financial institutions, among them, the Goldman Sachs Group, JP Morgan Chase and Co, and Barclays Bank, and global financial institutions and insurance companies dominated the top 50' (Robinson 2017: 177). CEO pay of the top corporations has, moreover, soared since the 1980s. A report by the Chartered Institute of Personnel and Development (CIPD) calculates that in the FTSE 100 – the largest publicly listed companies in the United Kingdom – CEO median pay packages were about £3.6 million for the year ending in 2019. These individuals therefore earn 119 times more than the median UK earnings of the average full-time worker, which stands at £30,353 (CIPD 2020).

Given all of this, it should come as no surprise that corporate capitalism has also promoted the interests of a distinct group of rentier capitalists (Livingstone 1983). For Schutz, rentiers are located in a small group of people who have inherited financial portfolio wealth after selling stakes in the ownership of major corporations or large-scale businesses. These are 'people wealthy enough to live comfortably on the returns on their portfolios without having significant business management positions' (Schutz 2011: 93). Some, of course, keep their ownership of businesses, but most rentiers lack immediate employer power. For this reason, the rentier class can be described as a 'functionless investor' who gains profits from financial market activity through their ownership of financial firms and financial assets (Epstein and Jayadev

2005: 48–9). Many rentier capitalists are part of the broader category of unproductive financial capitalists who gain revenue by lending money to others. Unproductive capitalists are also those who own land, buildings or intellectual property rights and gain revenue by renting those assets to others. Commercial capitalists, such as retailers, who buy, sell and trade in already produced commodities, are also unproductive (see Foley 1986: 106). Unproductive capitalists employ workers who create surplus labour and profits, but not surplus value. Only productive capitalists and productive workers generate surplus value (on commercial capitalists, see Chapter 6, below). We now move on to discussing labour and the working class.

THE WORKING CLASS:
PRODUCTIVE AND UNPRODUCTIVE LABOUR

One way to think about the identity of the working class is through the terms 'productive labour' and 'unproductive labour'. Taking his cue from Marx, Poulantzas (1978) says that the productive or unproductive nature of labour can be discerned only through its social form, namely, its position in the social relations of production. 'In the capitalist mode of production, productive labour is that which directly produces surplus value, which valorises capital and is exchanged against capital' (Poulantzas 1978: 211; see also Marx 1988: 644). Surplus value can only emerge in a society based in the separation of labour from the means of production in which labour has no possession over the means of production, no control over the labour process, and no legal right to control the labour process and make binding calculations about it. Under these circumstances, capitalists do not purchase the work of labour as such, but the *ability* of labour to work. And bound up with the purchase of the ability to work is at the same time the capitalist's 'right' to control the labour process and working day (Atzeni 2010: 4). Unlike previous socio-economic systems, a product does not emerge when the exchange between a worker and capitalist has been finalised. This ensues through the 'free' subjective will of the labourer and after a capitalist has paid a wage to the labourer (Clarke 1991). By the 'superordinate control over labour and production policies' (Livingstone 1983: 55), the capitalist class therefore aims to bend the will of labour to producing surplus value for capital. This is achieved both through coercion – for example, through rules and regulations – and through consent – for example, through a workplace rewards system. Capitalist relations of production are subsequently forged through economic, political and ideological mechanisms of class power (Poulantzas 1978).

The need for capital to develop sophisticated modes of control and surveillance in the labour process is part and parcel of how capitalism operates. Control and surveillance of the workplace are mainly the function of managerial non-labour; of which more in a moment. But it is also the case that some types of labour coordinate the labour process, and help to bring degrees of unity to how a labour process operates in specific workplaces. Coordinators, unlike managers or supervisors, are therefore still classed as labour, and can be productive or unproductive (Carchedi 1991: 35). For their part, productive capitalists must ensure that the productive capitalist labour process is mediated through the ability of labour power to affect and/or transform a use-value into a new use-value. While this is found in all types of societies, only in capitalism does labour power have the potential, during production, to affect and/or transform a use-value into a new use-value that can be exchanged in the marketplace and therefore be converted into surplus value over and above the exchange-value of labour power (Carchedi 1991: 11–12).

Productive labour includes occupations found in construction, certain public sector and service industry occupations directly implicated in surplus value generation, agriculture, manufacturing, mining, types of technical and scientific labour that directly help to create commodities with surplus value, transportation that moves productive commodities to places to be circulated and eventually sold, those working in warehouses that store productive commodities, and planning and coordinating production activities within sectors employing productive labour (Moseley 1992; Rotta 2018). Official government and policy data do not, of course, analyse the labour force through Marxist categories, but, nevertheless, some figures are available about what can be termed as productive labour. Globally, for example, the Organisation for Economic Cooperation and Development (OECD) estimates that in 2019 about 665.9 million people across OECD countries were part of the global labour force. Of this figure, nearly 30 million were employed in agriculture, which represents a slight decline across the decade, while over 137.7 million people were employed in industry (OECD 2020).

Intriguingly, Marx (1988: 574) notes that as capitalist industry begins to exploit labour power, so it is the case that capitalism starts to employ a greater number of workers as unproductive labour. In its search for profits, capitalism assumes complex forms as it grows, and it moves away from productive branches and the generation of surplus value towards unproductive areas of employment. For Marx, a typical illustration is the growth of a luxury consumer marketplace, much of which is not generated through productive avenues. The growth of some areas in the service sector and service employment is another illustration of some occupations in unproductive areas of the economy (cf. Marx 1988: 573–4; see also Chapter 6, below). Unproductive labour is also found in occupations which circulate and distribute already generated surplus value, such as accountancy, finance, advertising, legal services, certain government sectors, research, retail and rental sectors. As noted, services house many unproductive occupations, and for 2019 the OECD estimated that 462.4 million people gained employment in services (OECD 2020). Broadly speaking, unproductive labour generates unpaid surplus labour that provides the basis of profits for unproductive capitalists. Unproductive labourers are subsequently oppressed rather than exploited (Carchedi 1977, 1991). They, too, perform unpaid labour for unproductive capitalists – but 'from the standpoint of the social capital as a whole and its reproduction, their remuneration is an unproductive expense and forms part of the *faux frais* of capitalist production' (Poulantzas 1978: 212).

In order to be clear about the nature of the distinction between productive and unproductive labour, two further observations need to be made at this juncture. First, productive labour is labour that *reproduces* the value of commodities; 'where value takes on in turn the form of money and commodities, culminating in . . . exceeding initial investment' (Smith 2019: 109). In other words, productive labour is not labour that merely produces commodities and re-establishes an original production time in the past, but is labour that can reproduce commodities with new quantities of value and thus further the system of inter-capitalist competition as a whole (Rotta 2018: 1369; see also Mandel 1992: 42). Productive labour, in this sense, increases the total mass of surplus value (Marx 1988: 644) and completes the circuit of industrial capital and prepares the way for a new cycle. Secondly, unproductive labour can be extremely useful for a productive capitalist to realise surplus value. For instance, a commercial capitalist, say, a retailer, can help a productive capitalist reduce the time it takes to sell a commodity. It does not follow, however, that the retailer is productive. Retailers do not *directly* create surplus value. Certainly, a retailer helps in its own way to circulate already produced commodities, but the retailer does not add value as such. The retailer is unproductive, even though it forms part of productive activities (Marx 1992: 210; see also Chapter 6, below). Unproductive activities can generally help to *indirectly* increase demand and profits for productive activities, but they do not directly create new surplus value (Rotta 2018: 1368; see also Olsen 2015: 39). Coordinators of the labour process are equally important not only because they help to organise the production of surplus value and surplus labour, but they do so by directly participating in this production as labourers and so also help to bring unity to the labour process. As such, they perform the function of labour (Carchedi 1991: 34; see also Chapter 6, below).

In terms of the capitalist labour process, it is also important to observe another vital characteristic of the class relation between capital and labour. As previously observed, there is a tendency for capitalists to introduce new technology in order to cut costs and accumulate more surplus value and profits than rivals. Capitalism undertakes this task by de-skilling some workers, standardising their work-related tasks and replacing labour with technology. To remain competitive, capital must also invest in the latest technological innovations and technical instruments of production, which propels it to re-skill some workers and to invest in their technical and learning capacities. Some workers are thereby de-skilled and others laid off, while some workers are re-skilled, trained in new forms of knowledge, and given some autonomy in how they operate new technology. This contradiction is related with another one. In laying off workers in favour of new technology, capital loses its capacity to generate surplus value and realise increased profits. This is another reason why capitalists turn to unproductive means to generate profits (Livingstone 1983: 52–5). We now move to consider non-labour and other middle-class occupations.

MANAGERIAL AND SUPERVISORY 'NON-LABOUR'

We have already mentioned high-level management which blurs into the capitalist class, but of course there are different management layers in capitalist societies. As capitalism matures, capitalists no longer have to directly oversee the production process, but can hand the task of 'direct and constant supervision' of labour to a special subset of workers.

> An industrial army of workers under the command of a capitalist requires, like a real army, officers (managers) and NCOs (foremen, over-seers), who command during the labour process in the name of capital. The work of supervision becomes their established and exclusive function. (Marx 1988: 450)

In capitalism, there is a predisposition for this intermediate stratum to emerge. In particular, observes Marx, as capitalist firms grow in size, there is 'the tendency to separate this function of managerial work more and more from the possession of capital, whether one's own or borrowed . . . (A)nd since . . . the mere manager . . . takes care of all real functions that fall to the functioning capitalist as such . . . the capitalist vanishes from the production process as someone superfluous' (Marx 1991: 512). We need to be clear, however, that, as noted earlier, while there is a separation between ownership and control, it is nevertheless the case that control is still integrally related to ownership relations. Management of a corporate enterprise is therefore required to help to make strategic calculations, control the labour process and give it operational direction.

For Carchedi, this social class of managers and supervisors represents neither productive nor unproductive labour, but can instead be labelled as 'non-labour' (Carchedi 1991: 35). Those in non-labour management positions *expropriate* surplus value, but because they are not owners, they cannot *appropriate* it as well (Carchedi 1991: 35). So, while many top managers assume the role of possessors, and are dependent owners of the means of production, they also delegate some of their power to middle managers. Middle managers have no legal ownership claims over the means of production and therefore sell their labour power to capitalists. Their main function is to apply a distinct set of control and surveillance techniques in order to ensure that surplus value or surplus labour is produced. Frequently, managers have a degree of delegated ownership powers over labour, which include a 'right' to enact disciplinary measures and hire and fire workers. Managers will also control the daily work-related tasks associated with social and technological relations of production, such as the technical design and planning of specific units of production (Livingstone 1983: 55). Supervisors are another layer of management with disciplinary powers, but often with little or no influence on the technical design of the labour process or role in investment decisions about the workplace. There are also 'non-supervisory professional employees' who work primarily in problem-solving with technical design and operating systems of relations of production. Generally, this class group has no supervisory powers over other workers. Managers, supervisors and non-supervisory professional employees all have the potential to be productive workers if they are employed by a productive capitalist as well as all enjoying the potential to contribute to the control and surveillance of labour (Livingstone 1983: 55–6). Middle managers and supervisors therefore do not have ownership powers, but they nevertheless perform the function of capital in the workplace, particularly over the control and supervision of labour in the workplace (Carchedi 1991: 37–8).

In terms of class, the contradictions inherent in technological relations of production create an artificial division between mental and manual labour. Some employees will conceive, design and/or plan technological productive relations, while others will execute and run the technology. Technological tasks must also be managed along with the speed, intensity and duration of technological work tasks (Gough 2003: 31). But the division between mental and manual labour is an artificial and socially imposed management division because, in reality, *all* types of labour are manual and mental at one and the same time. Capitalist and management thereby create an artificial division in order to control labour in new ways. These technological relations again can be productive or unproductive (Livingstone 1983: 52–5).

Many who occupy management and supervisory positions might also occupy a similar social position to workers even if they have some degree of power over other workers (Schutz 2011: 95). Lower-level managers, for example, can work long hours, are given a large number of tasks to complete on a daily basis, and have limited incomes. Above all else, those managerial middle-class employees who do not have either legal or real ownership of the means of production will combine 'in a varying balance . . . the global function of capital and the collective worker' (Carchedi 1977: 88). They are part of what Marxists will term as occupying, 'contradictory class locations' (Wright 1978: 63; 1997: 54–5).

OTHER 'CONTRADICTORY' CLASSES

Managerial and supervisory non-labour are also known as the petite bourgeoisie. But there are also a number of other petite bourgeois groups in society. Classically, the 'petite bourgeoisie' are thought to be small-scale producers and traders. Typically, they own their own property – they are self-employed – and realise their own labour power rather than employing more than two other workers. Self-employed workers therefore appear as their own wage-labour with their own means of production, and 'as his own capitalist he puts himself to work as wage-labourer' (Marx 1988: 1042). These petite bourgeois members subsequently exist outside the direct class relation of capital and labour even if those relations subsume and mediate how they operate and work (Clement and Myles 1994: 14–15). Under corporate and financialised capitalism, even newer petite bourgeois groups are readily apparent. Think for a moment of the array of middle-class occupations created by financial capital. Hedge funds, financial trading, financial management consultancy, pension funds, private equity, global governance bodies dealing with finance and so on, all generate various middle-class occupations (as well as some working-class occupations). There are, moreover, a range of occupations that deal with financial issues, such as audit partners, consultants, corporate lawyers, stock market analysts, traders and dealers, those who devise financial mathematical models, new financial language and so on (Hall 2009; Folkman et al. 2007: 557). Then, there are 'creative' and service sectors (see Chapters 6 and 7, below), each of which will have numerous middle-class occupations.

To ascertain whether these occupations form part of the petite bour-geoisie will depend on the class criteria already sketched out, namely, the extent to which they enjoy elements of ownership, control and legal title over their means of production. For example, some of the occupations in the financial sector noted above will no doubt be inhabited by self-employed people who run their own businesses, such as financial con-sultants, and who are hired on temporary contracts by financial firms. Those who are self-employed under these circumstances are, perhaps ironically, part of the 'old' middle-class and are therefore also members of the petite bourgeoisie. Novel types of digital labour, sometimes known as platform labour, are also often thought to constitute new categories of freelancing and self-employed work. While Chapter 8, below, investi-gates the class characteristics of digital and platform labour, it is worth noting that much of the work that falls into this group is in fact a pro-letarianised variety of work. Many people who work for digital and platform labour, for example, working as a taxi driver for Uber, are not self-employed, but instead sell their labour to a service-sector platform company. People who work for these platform companies often do so under relatively poor conditions, enjoy few or no union rights, and are subject to excessive digital control and surveillance by managers. Many platform companies can therefore simply be seen as the latest incarna-tion of offering 'new forms of marginal, semi-proletarian, and poorly paid' employment (Clement and Myles 1994: 53). Arguably, the differ-ence today is that some platform companies also want to claim that their workers are self-employed so that the employer can then escape some legal requirements to respect certain worker rights, such as paid holiday entitlements.

'Non-supervisory professional employees' are often involved in detailed problem-solving activities, especially in relation to technical design and operation systems, but they are subordinated to higher man-agers or supervisors (Livingstone 1983: 56). These are sometimes 'semi-autonomous' employees who have to sell their labour power, but who also enjoy a degree of autonomy in how they work due to their special-ist skills (Wright 1997). For example, university lecturers and medical doctors enjoy a degree of semi-autonomy in how they work (Callinicos 1987).

Usefully, Choonara (2017) highlights another class concept developed by Marx called 'complex labour', which can help us understand the class location of some workers. According to Marx, 'complex labour' is labour that has yet to be rendered 'simple', 'abstract' and subject to commodity exchange. Labour is complex to the extent that it is the monopoly of a few workers. For example, a relatively small number of workers might have expert knowledge to undertake certain job tasks. These workers therefore have a 'monopoly' over this knowledge. Those with the latest knowledge about digital breakthroughs can command a monopoly over their technical expertise, at least initially. By investments into education, or by the 'mechanisation' of this expert knowledge, capital will, though, attempt to make this labour abstract and exchangeable by 'generalising' this knowledge across workers in different sectors, ensuring that it is no longer a monopoly of a small number of workers (see also Marx 1988: 135).

Now that we have outlined social classes in capitalist society, it is time to explore how the digital labour and work maps onto these class relations. The digital labour process harbours all class forms, both productive and unproductive, which we have elaborated above. Chapter 1 set out three types of digital labour and work in the capitalist labour process – *digital labour*, *digitisation of labour* and *digitalised labour* – which are, in turn, managed by a number of non-labour managerial classes. Based in and developed from numerous studies on the digital and labour, these three types ensure that an analysis of the digital labour process is relatively clear and simple, empirically applicable to a wide range of contexts, and allow for further divisions between productive labour, unproductive labour and non-labour. Value relations and social class therefore remain at the heart of an analysis of digital labour and work. We therefore turn our attention to exploring in more detail these issues.

THE DIGITAL LABOUR PROCESS

As Chapter 1 noted, *digital labour* is often correlated with a diverse array of digital work. Problematically, this mixes together types of digital work that are qualitatively different from one another. To avoid this analytical difficulty, it is preferable, in my view, to restrict the way we define 'digital labour' to work that is processed and managed primarily through digital platforms. Uber is a well-known and controversial illustration of digital labour on this understanding, but other platform work includes skilled and professional freelance workers who gain employment through a platform like Upwork. Digital labour is also found in types of 'participatory labour', or 'prosumer labour', in which people might not be paid a regular wage as such for uploading or working on material on platforms for online audiences, but who nevertheless can gain monetary payment through other avenues like advertising streams. Through their personalised channels, YouTube users can constantly upload their own material, gain subscribers to their channel and interest from other parties and traffic, and then attract advertisers to place adverts on their personalised YouTube channel, which can gain real streams of revenue for the user (Postigo 2014). While money is accumulated through these digital mechanisms, the people running personalised channels on YouTube are not being paid a wage as such. But their 'digital labour' can potentially give the user some financial rewards to varying degrees through advertising streams. The digital activity of a user will also, of course, generate profits for YouTube. But one important point to note is that YouTube 'prosumers' still have their work mediated through the YouTube platform, and this particular platform is owned and controlled by Google. YouTube users are still therefore, first, dispossessed from the YouTube means of production, and, secondly, subject to the control and surveillance of a corporate capitalist entity, namely, Google. At the same time, the 'digital labour' of a YouTube user is arguably less regulated and formalised than somebody working for, say, Uber. For example, there's often more 'play' associated with digital labour on YouTube in the sense that somebody might create and then upload a video in their leisure time, and also work on content that is immediately connected to their own sense of identity, culture and enjoyment. Some term this as 'playlabour' (Scholz 2017: ch. 2).

I believe the *digitisation of labour* can be contrasted to digital labour because digitisation points towards the processes by which objects, practices and life in general are progressively captured, reshaped, repackaged, transported, and then reordered through digital codes, databases and other digital formats. Digitisation is therefore reliant on computer technology, digital networks, and the digitisation of media and information content, rather than being reliant only on digital platforms (Flew 2008; Will-Zocholl 2017). For Will-Zocholl (2017), the digitisation of labour subsequently refers to those developments that transform analogue information in the workplace into digital information. Data and information can then be transmitted across work spaces more easily than in the days of analogue. This includes the transmission of digital models and representations about specific work processes. Correspondingly, this digital expansion has been accompanied by a separation 'between humans and the phenomena that are represented. Digitisation thus means the separation of material and non-material objects of labour' (Will-Zocholl 2017: 65). We must be cautious, however, about the degree to which one argues that 'material and non-material' objects of labour now remain separated from one another. Digitisation of productive or unproductive labour works in tandem with 'normal' work routines in ordinary and regular workplaces. For instance, and it is an example we will look at in more detail in Chapter 5, there has been a 'computerisation' of productive labour across many factories in range of different countries. In numerous cases, however, computerisation has made the labour process more 'material' in the sense that it has reinforced and extended materially embedded surveillance of individual worker outputs. Digitisation of labour is therefore best thought of, in the first instance, as simply being the development and extension of digital technology in a workplace, which occurs in productive and unproductive labour processes.

Digitised labour taps into debates about the rise of automation, AI and robots in the workplace, and the degree to which tasks in certain occupations become fully automated and replaced by smart machines. In their well-known article on this subject, Frey and Osborne (2013) argue that the twenty-first century has ushered in a new technological revolution based on the likes of smart machines that can learn to undertake tasks and adapt them to changing circumstances, mobile robotics whereby robots can uproot themselves from one place to work next to people, computational statistics and data mining. Other examples of digital automation include machines and their parts – a whole array of material devices, home appliances and so on – which have the power to communicate with one another through the so-called Internet of Things and engage in self-regulation with one another (Krzywdzinski 2017: 249). These advanced intelligent machines now have the capability and potential to undertake not only routine types of manual and cognitive work based on rule-following, but also non-routine work that requires a degree of discretion, such as deciphering handwriting. When 'real' labour and teams of people in a workplace have been replaced by robots it is therefore plausible to say that we have witnessed the emergence of digitised labour in that workplace. Here, the digitisation of labour makes a qualitative transformation into digitised labour. Of course, robots need to be regulated, managed and supervised by 'real' people, who monitor, re-programme and repair the machines as required. This group of 'overseers' of automation might also be classed as digitised labour to the extent that their jobs and livelihoods are defined through automation. It goes without saying, digitised labour can be productive or unproductive.

Naturally, and it will be a point explored throughout this book, much of what is said about AI, automation and smart machines is part of hegemonic discourses that aim to reconstruct labour relations in firms and workplaces with the intention normalise new micro-systems of control over workers (Pfeiffer 2017; Spencer 2017). Even so, there can be no doubt that automation, smart machines and robots have replaced, and will replace, some types of labour. For example, the relatively cheap cost of making digital sensors could lead to an increase in the automation of public transport and its logistics, while the sophistication of databases makes it likely that more routine administrative and office work will be subject to automation (Frey and Osborne 2013: 38). Nevertheless, it is also important to be vigilant in making any generalisations here, and, anyhow, the replacement of labour by machines in one place often then leads to the creation of new paid labour in another place.

Finally, it is vital to remember that contemporary capitalism is run and managed through different groups of 'non-labour', or different types of management and supervision. As mentioned already in reference to the work of Carchedi, non-labour can be seen in the rise of numerous management groups in contemporary capitalism. Again, these groups will be explored in greater detail throughout the book, but all I wish to emphasise for now is that work can be categorised as *digital non-labour*, for example, those who manage platforms like Uber and monitor the performance of digital labour working for such platforms; or it can be categorised as the *digitisation of non-labour*, for example, when management have to adapt to and work with new digital technology in their day-to-day working lives; or it can be categorised as *digitised non-labour*, for example, those whose main responsibility is to manage and monitor automation in a workplace. Again, similar to the labour categories, those who work in non-labour occupations might lose their jobs to automation. There is, therefore, a level of precariousness associated with non-labour, which we discuss in subsequent chapters.

CONCLUSION

Some critical theorists suggest that key defining characteristics of the capitalist labour process include relations of control, oppression and power between managers and workers (see Smith and Thompson 1998; Thompson 1990; Thompson and Smith 2017). While this is correct, we have also argued it is equally true to say that issues around workplace factors like control and power are moments in capitalist *class relations* (cf. Carchedi 1991: 17). 'Control' of workers in the labour process, at a basic and essential level of analysis, is dialectically fused with issues concerning the incessant requirement of capital to create and/or mediate surplus value and reproduce the class relation of capital, namely, the constant dispossession of labour from the means of production (Marx 1973: 458; see also Albritton 2007: 69; Braverman 1974: 413; Clarke 1994: 140; Spencer 2000: 232). At a more concrete level of analysis, different labour processes are subsumed and mediated through two fundamental forms of capital and their accompanying circuits: productive capital and the circuit of industrial capital; and unproductive capital and the circuits of commercial capital, financial capital, rent capital and so forth. The reason why it is important to include value relations and the dialectical interplay of productive and unproductive circuits of capital is because they enable us to present a more nuanced analysis of the contradictory dynamics of class relations at work in different labour processes. This can be appreciated further if we momentarily reflect on non-Marxist and Marxist accounts that do not share the same theoretical concerns as those outlined.

In respect to non-Marxist accounts, Kivinen (1989) claims that a more realistic account of the new middle class should take note of resources that this class has to hand to pursue strategies of autonomy and professionalisation through the 'mental work' of designing and planning their work. Strategies of professional autonomy can help to organise the politics and ideologies of organising production in a workplace. To this extent, Kivinen maps out seven new middle-class categories. To generate these middle-class categories, Kivinen explicitly rejects a Marxist approach and instead draws on other sociological approaches that pay attention to the power resources each different middle-class position employs to gain professional autonomy. So, for instance, some managerial and supervisory positions work almost in harmony in generating autonomy alongside the needs of capital, while those in the caring and reproduction middle classes face many obstacles in pursuing professional autonomy because they are employed in hierarchical and bureaucratic state structures.

Problematically, however, Kivinen's theoretical framework veers towards a type of Weberian sociology in which *individuals* gain their class position in a *marketplace* based on how these individuals use power resources as *calculated means and ends* to achieve professional autonomy (Bonefeld et al. 1995: 10–11). Yet this approach does not adequately address how these middle-class groups are themselves part, or a moment, in the various circuits and class relations of capital as a whole. By analysing the middle class through this framework, we are immediately alerted to the different capitalist circuits – industrial, commercial, financial and so forth – which mediate productive and unproductive middle-class occupations alongside the political and cultural mediations of class. This point is crucial in how we explore the middle classes because it places them in the changing contradictions of class relations. Kivinen, however, has a rather static understanding of the middle class. We see this in relation to his understanding of 'caring' middle-class occupations, such as those middle-class members who work in health occupations. Kivinen claims that these professionals find it difficult to translate their power resources into full professional autonomy because they more often than not work in bureaucratic public sectors that stifle professional autonomy. An alternative more Marxist-inspired approach, though, investigates this question from the perspective of class relations as a whole. As we will see in Chapter 9, professional occupations in the UK state and public sector have been subject to an aggressive contracting out to financial capital and some commercial capital, which has then also entailed new management regimes being rolled out in this sector. State legislation has been passed to support this contracting-out process. Yet there have been pockets of resistance and struggle by public sector staff in and against these new unproductive regimes, which has then reinforced the professionalisation, knowledge and autonomy of these middle-class public sector staff members. Unfortunately, Kivinen's typology does not enable us to gain a full insight into these class dynamics and class struggles.

In respect to a Marxist account, Vidal (2020) argues that the capitalist labour process is beset by two basic contradictions. The first contradiction is related to management and revolves around conflicting pressures this class has about whether to coordinate and unify workers and thereby empower workers, or whether managers should use their power to discipline workers. The second contradiction concerns the capitalist tendency to socialise workers and bring them together as a cooperative force in a workplace that can potentially then act against the interests of capital, versus the tendency of capitalism to alienate workers. Without placing these contradictions within value processes, however, a number of weaknesses emerge in Vidal's analysis.

Vidal's use of the term 'productive', is instructive here. For Vidal, 'productive' refers to how workers come together through multiple skills to form a socialised and empowered unit in order to work and increase production. Management is thereby seen to be 'productive' when it increases organisational efficiency by coordinating the division of labour through competent and effective design, planning, training and so on. Management is unproductive when it enacts discipline in a labour process; for example, by directly observing workers. Vidal notes that management can also be both coordinative and disciplinary at one and the same time (Vidal 2019: 254; Vidal 2020: 187). Vidal thereby renders the concepts 'productive' and 'unproductive' as being empirically bounded in the sense they are used to explore how workers literally 'produce' more outputs in everyday concrete workplaces.

At the heart of Vidal's analysis is therefore a general theory of exploitation. As Vidal himself notes, 'exploitation . . . refers to *all* forms of wage labour that produce surplus labour for employers . . .' (Vidal 2019: 244; added emphasis). In other words, exploitation is a generic mode of power that is used by a generic category of capitalist 'employers' to control and coordinate the labour of a generic category of 'workers'. What is thereby missing is an explanation of how these labour processes are mediated through specific forms of class relations and different circuits of capital. The last point also raises the important issue of differentiation and functions in distinct circuits of capital. Those who work in the public sector, for example, will often work against, or ignore, certain ideological themes found in other circuits. Indeed, as we will note in Chapter 9, public sector workers are often less concerned with the accumulation and profit motive, but more aware of the need to gain legitimacy for their professions, to promote a caring ethic, to be responsible to the communities they serve, and to maintain cost-effectiveness for their tax-paying local users of public services. Of course, other capitals may try to penetrate the public sector and change these ideological themes – and, again, in Chapter 9 we explore how financial capital has attempted to do just this – but, interestingly, evidence demonstrates that public sector workers often 'resist' these attempts to do so in order to retain, as far as possible, what they perceive to be their 'unproductive' public sector identity. Similarly, unproductive financial capital might try to gain access to a productive workplace and transform a collective endeavour by labour to generate surplus value into fragmented and discrete units to sell to financial markets and thereby generate, at least in part, surplus profits but not surplus value (see also Crompton and Gubbay 1980: 173).

Further dilemmas in Vidal's account arise from these observations. For example, 'productive' managers in Vidal's explanation are those individuals who increase organisational efficiency. Yet this does not grant us an insight into how these managerial actions might impact on value relations and the creation, or not, of surplus value. To take one illustration, management at Facebook might very well develop extraordinarily efficient organisational structures for its employees, which then lead to higher profits for Facebook. From a value perspective, however, these larger profits occur in the unproductive circuits of capital and so arguably have a negative impact on the production of surplus value in other productive areas of the economy. In this respect, managers at Facebook are unproductive, not productive, from a Marxist point of view. The main point to make is that Vidal conflates Marx's use of 'productive' with the more empirically bounded term of 'producing', and, in so doing, he deprives himself of the necessary theoretical tools with which to analyse the impact of different circuits of capital in different labour processes.

In place of these class relations, Vidal tends to put workers into groups based on occupational factors like skills, autonomy, labour intensity and rationalisation. He then uses these categories to compare the work experience of different groups of workers. But by doing so, Vidal strays, like Kivinen, close to a Weberian theory of class based on factors like the ownership of skills a worker has in labour markets; factors which then grant that worker a certain amount of autonomy in the workplace. This means that rather than distinguish workers through the prism of value relations, Vidal opts to mix productive and unproductive workers together through his more resource-based approach. So, for example, Vidal tells us that assemblers and machine operators, who, under a Marxist framework, would normally constitute part of the productive working class, are in fact part of the 'tightly constrained working class, which includes phone operators and bank tellers' (Vidal 2020: 193–4). In my view, Vidal creates 'chaotic abstractions' with these class occupational categories, which fail to fully place class relations within the deeper capitalist relations of production. Capital certainly exploits, but it is productive capital that does this in the contours of a productive labour process, while unproductive capital oppresses workers in an unproductive labour process.

None of this is to deny that autonomy and skills are unimportant to the capitalist labour process. In fact, they are crucial elements in various ways. Again, though, skills and autonomy are mediated through the contradictions embedded in value relations. Workers who enjoy a relatively high level of autonomy and skills in the workplace often tend to enjoy higher levels of satisfaction in their job because they have more discretion and variety in what they do in the workplace. They are therefore also sometimes in a position to engage in offensives against management to preserve this autonomy. On the flipside, high levels of autonomy and skills in a workplace can also breed a more conservative culture in which workers collaborate with management to uphold their skilled status rather than engage in class struggles against management (Gough 2003: 276–7). Nevertheless, all workers are subordinated to wage relations and therefore to value relations too. Workers also compete for jobs, and all firms need to remain profitable and subject themselves to different capitalist circuits (Gough 2003: 34). Each labour process therefore gives rise to unique collective experiences for workers depending on their specific value relations, alongside unique contradictions and dilemmas that arise from capitalist class relations (see also Lucio and Stewart 1997: 71–3).

Elsewhere Vidal (2013; 2014) examines different labour processes in respect to the global political economy. He argues that from the 1950s up until the 1970s, the main mode of accumulation was a Fordist one predicated on mass production, oligopolistic competition, producer-led national supply chains and a financially autonomous Keynesian state that operated under an international system of capital and trade controls (Vidal 2014: 86). Vidal further claims that Fordism went into crisis during the 1960s when stagflation became a problem. Governments and policymakers initially tried to ignore declining profit rates, but by the 1970s they started to restructure their economies and industries so that by the early 1980s a new post-Fordist mode of accumulation was the dominant force in advanced capitalist nations. While Vidal draws on Marxism to put forward his main arguments here, there are once again certain limitations in what he argues.

As noted previously, class relations in capitalism are mediated economically, politically and culturally. While Vidal makes some pertinent points about the crisis tendencies and 'dysfunctional' characteristics in different regimes of accumulation at an 'economic level', he does not fully embed these in a political analysis too. As noted earlier in the chapter, class relations are managed and regulated by the state. The capitalist state also aims to capture a slice of surplus value in terms of the supply of global money. This relationship between the 'political' sphere and the 'economic' sphere is the appearance of class relations at this level of analysis. Vidal therefore certainly investigates many of the problems associated with accumulation regimes, but he also misses some core elements of them. For example, while he notes that Fordism experienced rapid dips in its profit rates from the 1960s onwards, he does not tell us why or how this occurred. It is therefore difficult to understand the underlying processes of how and why one accumulation regime merged into another accumulation regime. Neither does Vidal present a comprehensive account of the role of the state in passing policy after policy to stem the class struggle of labour in and against accumulation regimes. While Vidal does mention how employers under post-Fordism have reduced labour's share of national income, he effectively centres his analysis around whether this reduced labour share has led to a crisis of under-consumption for capitalism (Vidal 2013: 465). In effect, then, Vidal focuses on whether the structure of a regime of accumulation corresponds to a necessary labour process and mode of consumption. Class struggle, under this analysis, therefore appears to be 'only a factor facilitating rather than contradicting the immanent development of the structure' (Gartman 1983: 661). Class contradictions and strategic dilemmas between different forms of labour and capital – industrial, commercial, financial and rent, for example – are thereby noticeable by their absence.

An alternative class-based account to that proposed by Vidal is presented in the next chapter. We explore how class relations have been maintained and regulated by states and global governance institutions, and how these have prepared the way for neoliberal and financialised unproductive circuits to gain hegemony across the world, and the imperialist form these circuits assume today. Digital media is also related in different ways to the rise of financialisation, and so we map out key aspects of the relationship between both. Moreover, the analysis will also be illustrated by reference to the pandemic and, in particular, how the neoliberal and financialised relations analysed have impacted on the class-based experiences of COVID-19.

Chapter 4

NEOLIBERALISM, FINANCIALISATION AND CLASS RELATIONS BEFORE AND DURING COVID-19

INTRODUCTION

Free markets, the power of finance and the general deregulation of the economy across the globe has led to the growing power of monopolies. Digital corporations provide a good illustration of this tendency in action. Take Snapchat. Like many big tech companies, Snapchat expends a considerable amount of money on acquisitions. In 2017, it spent an estimated $352.4 million on acquiring other companies, which was five times more than in 2016, and over six years up until 2017 it had purchased around twenty-four companies (Heath 2017). Snapchat's rationale in extending its reach through these acquisitions is its desire to bridge the gap between software and hardware by entering a variety of marketplaces. In 2017, Snapchat was also floated on the stock market with a market valuation of $28.3 billion. Evan Spiegel, one of the founders, made $5 billion from this floatation. Spiegel and his other co-founder of Snapchat, Bobby Murphy, own all of the 'C' shares of Snapchat, which carry most voting rights. The *New York Post* dubs this practice, 'Silicon Valley CEO authoritarianism' (Trugman 2017), while for the *Financial Times* it shows a glaring lack of corporate governance and accountability in major digital media companies (Plender 2017). So, Snapchat not only demonstrates the monopolistic tendencies of tech companies, and how they guard their power closely even when floating their companies on financial markets, but also the broader point that finance is a vital channel in furthering the expansionist ambitions of capital (Lapavitsas 2013: 201).

This chapter maps out in more detail some of the broader changes and impacts that neoliberalism, financialisation and digital media have made in society and on class relations. The discussion will not only extend, at a more concrete level of analysis, the account of social class provided in

66

Chapter 3, it will also provide a necessary backdrop to the consideration of productive and unproductive digital work and digital labour in the chapters that follow. In particular, we will see in this chapter that the incessant thirst for profits across the globe has driven some corporations, particularly digital corporations, to take on a financialised form. Over time since the 1980s, financialisation become increasingly autonomous of productive capital and labour. According to Marx, financial capital tends to gain a more independent existence as capitalism develops into more complex forms. Interest linked with credit-money is a case in point. As capitalism expands, interest-bearing capital increasingly detaches itself from the production of surplus value (Marx 1991: 968). A more subtle, intangible and, arguably, insidious financial form thereby grows in importance and stature. Trading in financial assets, such as bonds and derivatives, gains momentum and increasingly becomes its own trading world. This 'fictitious' capital is a claim, or speculation, on *future* quantities of surplus value being produced. Unproductive financial assets are now traded at some distance from the actual process of industrial production and thereby gain their own prices (Marx 1991: 598; see also Rotta and Teixeira 2016: 1197). As a consequence, labour power's productivity is soon believed to be derived from interest-bearing capital rather than from productive capital, thus furthering the fetishism of capital (Marx 1991: 596).

Financialisation has also been supported by a neoliberal state. A liberal financial system emerged most forcefully during the 1980s under the state projects of Thatcherism in the United Kingdom and Reaganism in the United States. Both governments freed capital from certain market boundaries and entered the realm of competitive regulation of 'free markets'. Under these conditions, labour power is sold in strict accordance with the free market, thus ensuring there is no necessity to remain committed to policies like national wage rates in certain sectors or committed to 'universal' welfare state benefits like national social housing (Jessop 2002). In this chapter, we examine how neoliberalism and financialisation operate in the wider context of the crisis tendencies of capital, and how these tendencies are associated with the contemporary neoliberal state and financialised accumulation strategies. In many respects, financialised capitalisation does represent more destructive crisis tendencies than previous eras. In particular, it has seeped into the productive sphere of major economies, and has done so through digital technology. This chapter discusses these points in detail, and also explains how COVID-19 has, in a short space of time, exacerbated many of the problems that were already apparent in the global economy and in contemporary class relations.

NEOLIBERAL CLASS FORMS

Capitalist class relations are generally sustained through political forms as well as economic forms. Unique to capitalism, while economic and political forms of power appear on the surface to represent different types of dominance, in reality they are part of the same basic capitalist relations of production. 'It is a relation that depends on the reproduction of the worker as "free", a reproduction that is determined outside the immediate process of production by the subordination of the working class to capital within the circuit of capital and to capitalist state power' (Clarke 1979: 142). Under neoliberalism, these class relations have been reproduced through market relations, which are said by their advocates to provide 'efficiency, income distribution, economic growth, and technological progress' (Kotz 2015: 12). Significantly, neoliberals exploit the crisis tendencies of capitalism to try to capture state power so that they can then develop and pursue neoliberal class and political strategies in civil society. It is not entirely a coincidence that neoliberalism came to prominence during the crisis of the post-war welfare settlement in the 1970s, and neoliberals took advantage of this crisis to push forward new policies and politics that aimed to supplant the social agenda of Keynesian welfarism with policies attuned to the interests of money-capital and finance (Jessop 2019: 975).

Underpinning neoliberalism is therefore a class-based project of seeking to constrain and curb the power and rights of labour. Among other things, this has meant that public services have been steadily privatised through an audit culture based on targets, internal markets, and internal competition within and between public services, so that these services then become attractive to the private sector to invest in and/or to administer and run them (Mirowski 2013: 57). Neoliberal state policies can also be used to bolster deregulation, protect the intellectual property of large corporations and thereby privatise knowledge, push society towards entrepreneurial activity, and ensure leaders from the private sector sit on boards and committees associated with the public sector (Harvey 2005: 64–7). A class of managers have been also empowered with ensuring companies maintain high rates of return and value to their shareholders (Duménil and Levy 2011: 84).

Welfare-to-work policies have, moreover, grown in importance as a means to make those in receipt of welfare assistance employable, while labour markets and wage policies become more 'flexible', meaning that they change according to the demands of markets. Supply-side policies place the responsibility of being employable onto the shoulders of workers. 'Individuals', not classes with specific needs, are therefore forced to make themselves employable. Trade unions have likewise seen their influence considerably diminished through successive neoliberal state legislation. Throughout the 1970s and early 1980s, labour militancy pushed forward demands for better working conditions, greater workplace democracy and higher wages in and against capital. In major European capitalist countries – the United Kingdom, France and Sweden, for example – the early 1970s saw left-wing parliamentary parties promising to extend worker ownership of major industries through nationalisation policies (Cahill 2014: 94). Neoliberalism sought to drastically reduce the power wielded by unions, and has been successful in this task particularly in the United Kingdom and the United States.

A key moment in establishing the class power of neoliberalism came in 1979 when the Federal Reserve Bank, under the leadership of Paul Volcker, increased interest rates from 10 per cent to 15 per cent and then to 20 per cent. Why did the Federal Bank carry out this policy? The official reason was to tackle high inflation and stagnation, the so-called disease of 'stagflation'. But this only provides a very partial answer. As Brenner (1998) notes, finance capital and neoliberalism did not cause the crisis in the 1970s, even if they exacerbated it. Before the 1970s, productive capital, especially in the area of manufacturing, had been on a downward slide. The post-war Keynesianism state, according to Clarke, had for a number of years integrated the working class into the circuit of productive capital and it had worked alongside the construction of international credit so that governments could pursue productive growth. Domestic and international credit rocketed during the 1950s and 1960s, which had the negative effect of leading to an over-accumulation of capital that soon came up against the barriers of profitable outlets in the marketplace. Productivity slowed and the wages of workers were attacked by capital and states (Clarke 1991b).

Stagflation, then, was the result of the tendency to develop productive forces without limit; a tendency which is imposed on all capitalists through competition, resulting in the over-accumulation of capital. Among other things, the Volcker shock further liberated financial capital by introducing low interest rates and thereby flamed the demand for US bonds because of the low interest paid on them. At the same time, the neoliberal state attacked the rights of labour in the United States and the United Kingdom, and ensured that wages stagnated (Panitch and Gindin 2009: 10–11). Credit was thus harder to come by for ordinary consumers, and this was coupled with higher interest rates and cuts in investments in manufacturing. Unemployment rose, wage rates declined and management gained power in the workplace. By the end of the 1980s, productive labour had been subject to disciplinary mechanisms and had lost its capacity and potential to create 'a hegemonic-societal project against capital' (Antunes 2013: 29). The effects of the 'Volcker shock' had achieved what it intended. 'Wages and inflation were tracking down; profits were tracking up' (McNally 2011: 36), while global investors rushed to put money into US finance and implement financial constraints on their operations through forms such as shareholder value.

Since this time, neoliberals have used the state and different crises, including that of the 2008 global crisis, to embed neoliberalism ever more into society. Austerity politics, imposed in the United Kingdom, the United States and elsewhere in the aftermath of the 2008 crisis, has cut even further into the welfare state and transformed neoliberalism and marketisation into a new and harsher ideology at some distance from the touchy-feely neoliberalism of the mid-1990s and early 2000s 'Third Way' under leaders like Tony Blair. Ideologically, austerity is driven by a desire to reduce public spending and public deficits. The financial crisis was employed as an opportunity by some politicians to manufacture a specific fear in society that suggested 'we' might fall off a 'fiscal cliff' unless public and welfare spending was 'brought under control'. Public spending has therefore been dramatically cut back, even while, at the same time, austerity policies also include extending corporate tax breaks, underwriting the financialised economy and protecting defence spending (Jessop 2015: 29). Yet austerity politics have been a dismal failure. In the United Kingdom, and because of austerity, GDP growth has not surpassed 2 per cent and is also forecast for the next few years not to move beyond this figure (O'Leary 2020a/b). Austerity has also increased government debt, lessened outputs, and has created less demand in the economy as wage levels decline and households struggle to pay off debts (Whitfield 2014).

Practically, neoliberal state policies have over time shifted income and wages away from labour and towards capital. In the United Kingdom, the Institute for Public Policy Research (IPPR) 'Commission on Economic Justice' argues that over the last forty years, only 10 per cent of national income growth has gone to the bottom half of the income distribution, while nearly two-fifths has gone to the richest 10 per cent (IPPR 2018: 6); many of whom are to be found in the capitalist class identified in the previous chapter. In 2020, the Joseph Rowntree Foundation claimed that around 14 million people in the United Kingdom, which equates to one in five or 22 per cent of the population, lived in income poverty – people living on 60 per cent or less income of the national average. In 1998, this figure was one in four of the population, which then fell to one in five of the population in 2004/5, or 20 per cent. Since 2004/5, then, income poverty has risen by 2 per cent. Significantly, child poverty has been climbing since 2011/12. In 2020, Joseph Rowntree calculated that 4 million UK children lived in income poverty, a rise of 500,000 in five years. The vast majority of this increase has taken place in working families. Around 56 per cent of people in poverty are now in a working family. In 1998, 10 per cent of individual workers were in poverty, whereas now, at the time of writing, this figure stands at 13 per cent. Overall, in-work poverty has been rising higher than UK employment levels. Experiences of poverty and social class vary of course depending on one's social background. The risk of poverty is greater for Black, Asian and Minority Ethnic (BAME) and disabled people than it is for non-disabled and White workers. Moreover, some occupations contain larger numbers of people experiencing in-work poverty than other sectors. Unproductive sectors of accommodation and catering have the highest levels of in-work poverty, while retail and residential care also contain high levels (JRF 2020). The United States has also shown marked rises in income inequality under neoliberalism. During the post-war Keynesian era, the richest 1 per cent of the US population received about 10 per cent of the total US income. Between 1981 and 2007, a period when neoliberalism was firmly embedded in American society, this figure reached 23.5 per cent of the total income. In 1978, a CEO in charge of a large corporation could be expected to receive twenty-nine times more in pay than the average worker. In 2007, this had rocketed to 351.7 times more pay (Kotz 2015: 95–6).

In Chapter 10 we explore further the relationship between wages and social class, but for now we can note that neoliberalism has been accompanied by inequalities in terms of income and wealth, with those in working-class occupations having seen a decline in both, while those at the top have seen them increase (Cahill 2014: 101). Below, we will see how COVID-19 strengthens these class relations, but for now we move on to consider financialised class forms.

FINANCIALISED CLASS FORMS

Financialisation is certainly associated with neoliberalism, but it is also different. Whereas neoliberalism, in my view, involves a socio-political project in which the state actively restructures society in favour of marketisation policies, financialisation is a socio-economic project that has spread throughout the global economy and has helped to further the interests of unproductive financial accumulation in the economy. But before we explore in more concrete detail some of the class relations associated with financialisation, we need, first of all, to develop two theoretical points about credit and finance. First, then, credit and finance not only lay the foundation for capitalist expansion across the world, but also contribute towards the crisis tendencies of capitalism. It is therefore vital to theoretically comprehend why credit and finance enjoy this potential for crisis.

Competition between capitals places an enormous pressure on each capitalist to overproduce goods, which eventually leads to a crisis. Marx suggests there are at least two ways for capitalists to 'succeed' in this global competitive race. 'On the one hand by enforced destruction of a mass of productive forces; on the other, by the conquest of new markets, and by the more thorough exploitation of old ones' (Marx and Engels 1964: 13). Finance, especially in the form of credit, is particularly useful for capital in this competitive quest to dominate national and global markets. By financing new projects and keeping unprofitable enterprises afloat, credit and finance can *suspend* the barriers and crisis-tendencies inherent in capitalist accumulation (Clarke 1990–91: 463). Credit and other financial mechanisms therefore support some capitalists during times of crisis by facilitating fresh cycles of accumulation, increasing the basis and capacity for some capitals to assert their global dominance in certain markets, and furthering the tendency towards centralisation of capital to the detriment of rivals (Marx 1988: 778–9). In civil society, the expansion of credit also provides the means for people to keep consuming goods.

But credit also reproduces and expands the power of unproductive capital and labour, as well as propping up unprofitable capitals (Clarke 1988). Sooner or later, then, the contradictory limits of the market can no longer be so readily overcome by credit, or by other financial mechanisms. Capital is then devalued, productive capacity destroyed and labour made redundant. In other words, a crisis erupts. 'The productive forces at the disposal of society no longer tend to further the development of the conditions of bourgeois property' (Marx and Engels 1964: 12). Crises result in the ruthless and vicious destruction of some capitals in favour of others, and crises are used politically to restructure and re-order the social fabric of society; 'a process that brutally restores the contradictory unity' of accumulation (Boyer 1990: 35; see also Lipietz 1988: 13). Over time, however, stability soon turns into its opposite. Embedded contradictions will always eventually reassert themselves. What once provided stability now turn into the fetters of capital by paving the way 'for more extensive and more destructive crises', which, in turn, diminishes 'the means whereby crises are prevented' (Marx and Engels 1964: 13).

Secondly, credit and finance obtain at least two distinct forms in mature capitalist societies. The first form has already been alluded to above. Money is lent to a capitalist, which allows the capitalist to create a commodity or a service, that then makes money, and part of this money is given back in the form of interest to the lender. That is to say, the money lent is valorised and increases its value. If the money lent is part of the circuit of industrial capital, then the lender gains a slice of surplus value. Credit-money in its guise as capital is therefore different to money, as such. In everyday life, money is used to purchase goods, but not necessarily to become capital, whereas credit-money is employed as capital. Types of credit are lent to other capitals and consumers within the margins of the general rate of profit, which is itself based in the distribution of surplus value among productive and some unproductive circuits like commercial capital (see Chapter 3, above). For example, many companies will give credit to a customer so that the customer can then afford to purchase a product from the company.

But there is another type of credit-money that can be termed 'interest-bearing capital', which constructs its own marketplace, especially a marketplace dealing with debt. Consumer credit – mortgages, credit cards, student loans and the like – represent this type of credit-money. One major development in this respect has been the pooling together by banks of various debt cash flows from assets (for example, mortgages or car loans) into securities. These debt assets, officially known as 'collateralised debt obligations' (CDOs), thus have a foreseeable income stream emanating from the continuous debt that is being repaid with interest from a bank's customers (for example, the continuous debt generated from individual customers who have taken out mortgages or car loans) and are attractive enough for banks to trade them with other investors on secondary markets (Foster and Magdoff 2009). Unlike the previous form of credit-money, which, as we saw, is used to generate surplus value and surplus profits for different capitals, interest-bearing capital gains its value through interest payments and fees. Interest-bearing capital is therefore money that generates money, or $M - M^l$.

Marx shows how the debt embodied as $M - M^l$ lays the foundation for the emergence of a novel type of financial capital that takes on a market life of its own. Debt itself can now be traded and gain monetary value 'that may or may not correspond to the potential to realize that value in the application of the money advanced as capital by whoever took the loan' (Fine 2013: 50). In this respect, interest-bearing capital acts relatively autonomously of industrial and commercial capital and gains a surplus in the form of interest *before* surplus value is circulated across different capitals (Fine 2013: 54). This *fictitious* capital is a claim, or speculation, on *future* quantities of surplus value being produced elsewhere. 'All these securities actually represent nothing but accumulated claims, legal titles, to future production' (Marx 1991: 599). Profits for those trading in interest-bearing capital are made by dealing in financial assets irrespective of whether surplus value is being produced in the here and now. For Fine, this type of interest-bearing capital, in which portfolios of debt streams are bundled up with other debt streams and sold as assets to financial investors, is what is today known as financialisation. While different definitions of financialisation are readily apparent, for the purpose of this chapter and book, financialisation will be explored through this Marxist lens. This has the added benefited of ensuring that class relations, contradictions and crisis tendencies of capitalism are at the forefront of how we will approach financialisation.

As we know, it was during the 1970s that capital started to produce surplus profits through financial means, and this included generating massive debt in society alongside 'the diversion of surplus capital into unproductive and increasingly speculative channels' (Clarke 2001: 86). Interest-bearing capital is constantly on the lookout for new assets to buy and sell, and money generated from financialised assets is also used for capitalisation and investment purposes in other areas of the economy (Marx 1991: 597). The neoliberal state has likewise prepared the way for interest-bearing capital to trade in a whole number of assets in society, including non-financial corporations and institutions like car manufacturing (see Chapter 5, below), as well as commercial sectors like retail (see Chapter 6, below), and the state and public sector (see Chapter 9, below). In so doing, financialised capitalist class interests have encroached ever further into different workplaces and have endeavoured to transform workers in these sectors into unproductive financialised labour.

Today, then, interest-bearing capital has become a powerful means of making money in different marketplaces because it can attach itself to a whole host of activities from which it was previously absent. Financial markets and debt streams have, moreover, enabled lenders to generate money, which they can then pass on to increasing numbers of households, with the latter getting into more debt and so on. Among other things, lenders target those households in debt to persuade them to get into more debt. Lifestyles, for example, are sold to consumers on the premise that these can be 'bought' through credit. Such is the 'normalisation' of personal debt that in June 2019 it was reported that the total consumer debt in the United States, accumulated from the likes of credit cards, mortgages, auto loans, student loans and so on, had reached $14 trillion. This is actually an increase on the $13 trillion consumer debt in 2008 just before the great financial crash. Unlike 2008, however, economists believed that the US economy was more stable than in 2008, with GDP having expanded 3.1 per cent in the first quarter of 2019 (DeCambre 2019). In the United Kingdom, the increase in consumer debt has been equally impressive. In June 2017, it was reported that it had reached £201.5 billion and credit card debt stood at £68.7 billion, an all-time high (Montgomerie 2018: 149).

Class relations are noticeable in the debt industry in another related way. In their study of the United States from the 1980s to the mid-2000s, Mian et al. (2020: 37) show that American households in the top 10 per cent income distribution – which includes members of the capitalist class identified in Chapter 3 – increased their holdings of US household debt by 26 per cent of national income. This amounts to gaining almost half of the overall increase in household debt during this period. By buying debt assets, this richest 10 per cent of US households has in effect been taking money and saving it from the bottom 90 per cent of US households, many of whom are of course in working-class households. This explains, in part, why the bottom 90 per cent have experienced a fall in their savings during this same time period. That is to say, the bottom 90 per cent tended to save less but borrow more, while the top 10 per cent saved more because they gained much of their extra income through the debt accumulated by the bottom 90 per cent. In the words of Mian et al.: 'The results show that the rise in household debt owed as a liability was driven by the bottom 90 percent of the income distribution, whereas the rise in household debt held as a financial asset was driven by the top 10 percent of the income distribution' (Mian et al.: 2).

Later in the chapter, we will see how COVID-19 has shaped debt relations and the relative surplus population. For now, however, it is important to note there is a strong relationship between digital media and finance (see also Mandel 1995: 66–7). As stated in Chapter 1, capital will invest in technology to remain competitive and seek to overcome the barriers of the global capitalist marketplace. This remains true today in relation to investments in digital technology. Venture capital and other financial forms of capital have also invested heavily in digital technology. By the late 1990s, the US stock market had grown by more than 60 per cent. This can be accounted for by the huge increase in technology stocks that soared upwards by 300 per cent from 1997 to 2000. 'At the peak of the bubble, total market capitalization approached US$15 trillion, while the technology stocks soared above US45 trillion, or 35% of the total, up from 12% in 1997' (Perez 2009: 784). In the United Kingdom, for example, emerging internet service providers (ISPs) were seen by many in the City of London as a new and continuous stream for making lots of money very quickly. The first phase in establishing the

UK ISP market from 1995 to 1999 was accompanied by major investors keen on getting a slice of this opportunity. Financial backers also had stakes in other global ISP markets. A US-based company, FMR Corporation, for example, made investments in America Online (AOL), Verio and WorldCom, 'all of which were active in the ISP market in the United Kingdom' (Mansell and Javary 2004: 232).

Today, there is still a scramble to invest in high-tech companies. In January 2018, the video streaming service, Netflix, gained a financial valuation of $100 billion. This valuation was based to a large degree on Netflix's announcement it had added another 8.33 million subscribers globally in the three-months leading up to December 2017, taking it up to 109 million members across 190 countries (Rushe 2018). In mid-August 2020, during the pandemic, Apple became the first listed company in the United States with a $2 trillion market valuation, helped, in a large part, by the popularity of Apple's wearable devices along with dominance in the iPhone ecosystem. Financial analysts and speculators, confident that Apple will not only retain its reputation among consumers, but will also continue to diversify its product range and grow, believe that the corporation is a safe bet for investment (Eadicicco 2020).[1]

Digital media is also an attractive option for financial investors because digital media corporations have now monopolised online consumption and ecommerce markets. Amazon is the main beneficiary of this online consumer trend. In February 2020, it was reported that, in the fourth quarter of 2019, Amazon made $79.8 billion in US online gross merchandise volume, which is a 19 per cent increase from the year previously. At the time, it was stated that this was set to increase in the foreseeable future, with online gross merchandise volume for Amazon rising by another 15.7 per cent throughout 2020 (Duggan 2020). In fact, Amazon has seen its sales and profits rise even further since the onset of the pandemic (see below). Digital technology has, moreover, been integral in tracking financial consumer tastes by gaining detailed informa-

---

[1] But not all these financial investments go as planned. Tech start-up WeWork, for example, founded in 2010 to rent out real and virtual co-working spaces, particularly to other tech start-ups. It soon grew as a company, helped along the way by investments from a whole host of major financial backers like JP Morgan and Goldman Sachs. In April 2019, WeWork filed for an IPO, and in August the same year they filed the necessary paperwork to make the company public. WeWork initially had a massive valuation of $47 billion, yet in preparing its paperwork to go public, WeWork also had to report that they were losing money. Indeed, the company did not even indicate how it would go into profit once it became an IPO. In fact, it lost two dollars for every dollar it made (Campbell 2019). Soon, the negative publicity moved WeWork's managers to halt their IPO.

tion about ordinary people's digital history (Langley 2014), while digital innovations, such as high-frequency trading (HFT), a finance-trading platform that is programmed to make huge numbers of automated financial transactions across the world (see Lange et al. 2016: 153), has empowered financial trading across the globe.

While investments in technology have often countered falling profits, the contradictions of capitalism, and, in particular in recent times, excessive investments and speculations in unproductive circuits, has meant that even the low costs for capital brought about by technological innovations has not helped to reverse the decline in the profits rate for capitalism over the last two decades. The section moves on to considering why this has been the case.

THE NEOLIBERAL AND IMPERIALIST STATE OF FINANCE

Unproductive accumulation and employment have increased significantly since the 1970s. As Rotta observes in relation to the United States:

> After 1980 . . . the economy shifted to faster unproductive accumulation and faster growth in the stock of unproductive assets . . . The total income of unproductive activities quadrupled relative to the total value generated in productive activities during the 1947–2011 period. (Rotta 2018: 1368–9; see also Lapavitsas 2013: 201–4)

Certainly, investments in unproductive financial capital, particularly interest-bearing capital, have acted as a counter-tendency to the overall profit rate to fall. Indeed, during the 1980s and 1990s profitability steadily rose. Between 1982 and 1997, for example, the average rate of profit in the United States grew by 19 per cent. Excessive unproductive investments in the financial sector during this period eventually meant that by 1997 the average rate of profit, based in real GDP growth comprising productivity growth and employment growth, began to shrink. Between 1997 and 2008 it declined by 6 per cent (Carchedi and Roberts 2018: 15). Since the global recession of 2008, the average profit rate has waned still further to under 1 per cent per year (Roberts 2016: 240). For Naisbitt et al., world trade growth had fallen to 1.2 per cent per year just before the pandemic took hold; a figure not seen since 2009 (Naisbitt et al. 2020: 37). According to Michael Roberts, this steep decline is due to a large extent to capitalists trying to find profitable sources in financial and property speculations.

At the heart of this global system has been the imperialist power of the US state. Successive US governments have passed legislation to deregulate banking practices. In 1982, for example, the Garn–St. Germain

Act opened up opportunities for different savings banks to trade in junk bonds and engage in risky financial ventures in order to increase their own money supply and then compete with other banks for a share of household deposits (Lazonick and O'Sullivan 2000: 17). The Gramm–Leach–Bliley Act of 1999 simplified and relaxed banking regulations still further, making bank acquisitions easier and strengthening links between commercial and investment banking (Panitch and Gindin 2012: 267). These changes were part of a larger qualitative transformation in financial markets, leading to the eventual hegemony of financialised capitalisation across the globe and the move away from productive sectors in the economy.

US imperialism is also embedded globally through by the dollar being the number one currency in the world and its power to discipline and regulate other currencies. Even in our post-2008 crisis era, there is little willingness by major and emerging countries to try to challenge the regulatory global nature of the US dollar (Drezner 2010: 399). It is still the case that the United States uses its own currency to determine the flows and liquidity of financial markets. One paper suggests that the US dollar's supremacy as the main foreign currency for international borrowing has risen. Dollar credit to the non-bank sector outside the United States rose from 9.5 per cent of global GDP at the end of 2007 to 14 per cent in the first quarter of 2018 (Aldasoro and Ehlers 2018). However, there are some signs that the global power of the dollar has weakened in the last couple of years. The main threat to its hegemonic position is from China. Since 2015, the People's Bank of China has allowed its own currency, the renminbi, to gain some freedom in how it trades in global markets. China also now has the biggest trade surplus with the United States. The renminbi therefore acts as a guide to whether the United States is drawing in enough investment to fund its trade deficit with China. Since 2017, and more so since China has emerged out of their worse stages of COVID-19, the renminbi has appreciated in its value, which signals a weakening of the dollar (Mohi-uddin 2020). At the time of writing, though, it is too early to tell whether these developments will topple US dollar hegemony. Moreover, other major countries, including China, might still prefer for the foreseeable future to maintain strong export growth rather than act as 'a strong currency and the associated large current-account deficits that come with meeting the global demand for safe assets (government bonds)' (Roubini 2020). Countries across the world therefore remain committed to investing in US dollars, and this ensures that the US state has a strong voice in establishing the rules of the 'international financial architecture'. To gain entry to these financial networks, other countries have to abide by neoliberal conditions and rules set out by US policy officials and global institutions like the World Bank (Kiely 2010: 145; Norfield 2013: 164; Panitch and Gindin 2009: 10–11).

Since the 2008 financial crash, little has thus been done by governments, policymakers and global institutions to stem the tide of the worst excesses of financialisation. Sure enough, some regulatory mechanisms have been put in place, but as Martin Wolf notes, policymakers have largely failed to act against rising company and consumer debt or to properly regulate highly risky financial trading practices (Wolf 2018). Far from prompting governments to abandon financialisation for more rational means of regulating financial markets, politicians bailed them out. Most graphically, after 2008, the US state pumped trillions of dollars into the financial markets to 'calm' and 'steady' investors. An audit in July 2011 of the Federal Reserve's emergency lending programmes showed that the US state had given over $16 trillion to corporations and banks for the purposes of 'financial assistance' during and after the 2008 financial collapse (Greenstein 2011). In the space of just over one year alone, between 2008 and 2009, the US government established a $700 billion Troubled Asset Relief Program to help the failing markets, and then, in 2009, Obama passed a bill to provide another $787 billion for fiscal stimulation over ten years (*Forbes* 2018).

With such support from the state, a global financial elite has become more prosperous. Those who are already wealthy have reproduced and increased their wealth through the likes of inheritance, marriage, social networks, housing, low tax, private pensions and education. But, as indicated in the previous chapter, the main types of wealth today are financial forms, which include private pension wealth, net property wealth and net financial wealth. According to *Capgemini World Wealth Report 2019*, the global wealth of high net-worth individuals (HNWIs), which are those individuals who have a minimum of $1 million in investable assets, has slightly decreased from a figure of $70.2 trillion in 2017 to $68.1 trillion in 2018. Nevertheless, the global wealth of HNWIs had from 2011 to 2017 been increasing year on year. In 2011, their overall wealth stood at $42 trillion, rising to $56.4 trillion by 2014, to the figure of $70.2 trillion by 2017. The United States has the largest number of HNWIs, standing at just over 5.3 million individuals, followed by Japan at over 3.1 million (*Capgemini* 2019). Similarly, the *World Ultra Wealth Report 2019*, which defines the ultra-wealthy as those with $30 million or more in net worth, estimates that those in this group have expanded so that by 2018 it numbered 265,490 individuals. This is an increase of nearly 13 per cent across two years. In 2018, the ultra-wealthy saw their net worth decline, but by only 1.7 per cent to stand at $32.3 trillion.

Prior to 2018, the ultra-wealthy had increased their net wealth by 16.3 per cent (*World Ultra Wealth Report 2019*). During 2012–2014, the average net wealth held by UK adults in the top 10 per cent topped £1 million. This group accounted for nearly half (49 per cent) of all Britain's wealth in 2012–2014, with the top 1 per cent alone owning 14 per cent of the wealth (D'Arcy and Gardiner 2017: 17).

The growth and hegemony of this financial aristocracy has underpinned the wealth gap between the mega-rich and other sections of society. Before COVID-19, one report discovered that this widening gap was especially noticeable in London. To give just one illustration:

> (In London) the value of household assets such as property, pensions, financial assets and possessions swelled to 12.8 trillion pounds ($17 trillion) in 2014–2016 from pre-crisis levels of 10.1 trillion pounds, after adjusting inflation ... The wealth of the richest grew 22 per cent compared with 13 per cent for the poorest. (Liimatainen 2018)

Somewhat predictably, financial markets have been reaping the rewards from the support they have received from governments in the decade or more since 2008. Wall Street's pre-tax profits reached $13.7 billion in the first half of 2018, which was an increase of 11 per cent on the previous year. Moreover, the average salary in the securities industry shot up by 12 per cent in 2017 to $403,100, which is the third highest salary figure for these occupations ever recorded after adjusting for inflation (Hennelly 2018). Federal Reserve analysts reported in March 2019 that the richest 10 per cent in the United States represented 70 per cent of all US wealth, which was an increase from 60 per cent in 1989. Assets provide a key route to wealth concentration. 'The share of assets held by the top 10% of the wealth distribution rose from 55 percent to 64 percent since 1989, with asset shares increasing the most for the top 1 percent of households' (Batty et al. 2019: 26). The neoliberal state has also passed flagrant class laws to support the interests of this massively wealthy class. Most graphically, President Trump passed the Tax Cuts and Job Act 2017, which served to benefit those who already have extraordinary wealth. To give just one illustration, Sheldon Adelson, the nineteenth richest man in the world according to *Forbes*, and CEO of the Sands Corporation that operates casinos, gained a $670 million tax break (Ryan 2018).

CLASS RELATIONS, INTERNATIONAL STATES AND THE PANDEMIC

In their June 2020 *World Economic Outlook*, the OECD stated that the world was and is facing its deepest recession since the Great Depression in the 1930s. The OECD predicted two possible scenarios. In the first scenario, the world is 'hit' by one COVID-19 wave. World GDP will then decline by 6 per cent by the end of 2020, but will regain its pre-crisis level by the end of 2021. In the next scenario, a second COVID-19 wave will 'hit' global economies towards the end of 2020. World GDP will then decline by 7.6 per cent and remain short of its pre-crisis levels at the end of 2021 (OECD 2020). In its *Economic Outlook: Interim Report*, published in September 2021, the OECD was now predicting global GDP to increase by 5.7 per cent in 2021 and 4.5 per cent in 2022. While global GDP levels now surpassed pre-pandemic levels, the OECD nevertheless noted that output and employment gaps remained in many countries. High debt and rising inflation remained a problem for emerging economies, while the global economic recovery would be uneven. Vaccination rollouts and macroeconomic support for certain economic sectors have diverged across nations, for example (OECD 2021).

The next chapter discusses how COVID-19 has affected digital work in the productive areas of the global economy, such as in the manufacturing sector. For now, however, it is worth asking the following question: has there been a policy shift away from neoliberalism and financialisation since the onset of COVID-19? In their *Global Financial Stability Report: Markets in the Time of COVID-19*, the IMF argues that the pandemic has exposed weak spots in global credit segments, emerging markets and banks. For example, risky credit market segments – high-yield bonds, leveraged loans and private debt – all expanded rapidly following the 2008 financial crisis, eventually reaching around $9 trillion globally (IMF 2020a: 3). Private debt markets alone reached $1 trillion (IMF 2020a: 30). Since the pandemic, prices of risk assets have plummeted, the volatility of markets increased, and borrowing costs have escalated in anticipation of defaults (IMF 2020a). At the same time, since the 2008 crisis banks had lessened their exposure to financial leverage – financing business assets through borrowing. Yet, continues the IMF, the interconnections between banks and other financial institutions appear to be increasing. Since 2013, bank lending to non-financial institutions has nearly doubled in the United States to stand at $1.4 trillion (IMF 2020a: 35). Interconnections between banks and non-bank financial institutions are formed through complex ecosystems which are obscure and opaque. COVID-19, therefore, 'may entail risks to the banking system, whereby adverse shocks may be transmitted broadly across financial institutions and possibly amplified by the layering of visible and invisible leverage' (IMF 2020a: 40).

In an update to their report published two months later in June 2020, the IMF predicted that global growth in 2020 would be worse than initially predicted and will end up at −4.9 per cent, but by 2021 global GDP was expected to just about exceed its level for 2019. For the advanced economies, growth was projected to be −8 per cent in 2020, recovering to 4.8 per cent during 2021, which is still 4 per cent below its 2019 level. For emerging market and developing economies, the forecast was at −3 per cent growth in 2020, rising to 5.9 per cent in 2021; a rise which, to a large extent, was due to China's predicted growth in this year at 82 per cent. If China is excluded from the picture, then the growth rate for these countries was predicted to be 4.7 per cent in 2021, which is slightly below the rate in 2019 (IMF 2020b: 5–8). In terms of the global financial system, the IMF (2020c) noted that since their earlier April report, financial markets had rebounded somewhat from their initial dip. Several reasons account for this bounce back, including a noticeable fall in interest rates and a strengthening of risk asset market valuations, equity markets also bounced back, intervention by central banks, such as the US Federal Reserve announcing in March it would provide $2.3 trillion in crisis-era credit facilities. Central banks in emerging economies also announced new policies, such as buying a range of assets, in the hope of attracting external investment. Governments in these regions also provided emergency measures to support financial markets, and there was growing investor confidence towards emerging economies.

At the time of writing, the IMF *World Economic Outlook* report suggests that global growth will be 6 per cent for 2021, moving to 4.4 per cent for 2022. These more positive projections are due to progress made with vaccines along with large-scale fiscal support for major economies, most notably, for example, in the United States. The IMF cautions, however, that only a mild recovery is predicted in Latin America and the Caribbean because, among other things, most countries in these regions do not have enough supplies of vaccine for their populations, and major business opportunities linked to the likes of tourism have been revised down. Sub-Saharan Africa – countries such as Ghana, Kenya, Nigeria and South Africa – will continue to experience heavy losses both in human terms and in economic terms. In 2020, the region saw an economic contraction of −1.9 per cent. In 2021, this was set to grow to 3.4 per cent, which would still be below pre-COVID-19 predicted trends (IMF 2021).

So, markets seem to have made a bounce back of sorts at the time of writing. A note of caution is, though, also thrown into the mix by the IMF. Financial markets exhibit a 'bullish mood' about investment opportunities, detects the IMF in one of their earlier COVID-19 reports, but this is largely because financial investors expect the state to keep supporting financial markets. As such, these very same investors thought, at least initially, that there would be a quick 'V-shaped' recovery, but in making this assumption, they did not appreciate the deep-seated nature of the global downturn. Investors were betting too strongly on central banks giving them unprecedented support in the long term. 'This tension can be illustrated, for example, by the recent rally in the US equity market, on the one hand, and the steep decline in consumer confidence, on the other hand' (IMF 2020c: 4). Moreover, continues the IMF, one reason to sound alarm bells is that the pandemic might aggravate financial vulnerabilities built up over the last decade. For example, aggregate corporate debt and household debt is at historically high levels, which will suffer in economies that experience severe downturns. Insolvencies will test the banking sector, and might also impact heavily on non-bank financial companies; the latter of which now have a greater role in the global financial system than in previous years, which is due to the financialisation of the global economy (IMF 2020c). Given the scale of the problems unleashed by the pandemic onto financial markets, it should come as no great surprise that the IMF recommends, among other things, that the relevant authorities should further extend support to risky credit markets, and that in a post-COVID-19 world, policy-makers need to promote greater transparency in credit markets (IMF 2020a: 44–5). Possibly, these might provide workable solutions in supporting complex global financial markets during and after the pandemic. Vigilance, though, is required when assessing the potential of such proposals for a number of reasons, which we now map out.

State Protection of the Financial System

First, and as the IMF suggests, highly risky financial trading in what we have termed as interest-bearing capital, along with other financialised business practices, has not ended despite the pandemic. In fact, the signs so far suggest that it will continue at least for the foreseeable future. During the 2008 global crisis, governments pumped in trillions to save the global financial system from going under. In effect, they bolstered and strengthened financialisation. The same has happened again, which is clear if we focus momentarily on the US state actions to tackle the virus. In March 2020, the Federal Reserve injected $1.5 trillion into the short-term credit market for financial investors. The Federal Reserve also engaged in quantitative easing by announcing that it would purchase $500 billion in Treasury securities and $200 billion in mortgage-backed securities. The Federal Reserve then decided to buy $1 trillion in unsecured corporate debt from issuers who had been experiencing problems selling corporate paper. By buying up corporate debt, the Fed effectively gave the issuers selling the debt some much-needed funds so that they could ensure their workers were paid, and so on. Cheaper lines of credit therefore magically appeared for many corporations, including major corporate players like Boeing, airline Delta, Exxon Mobil and T-Mobile (Dayen 2020).

The Coronavirus Aid, Relief, and Economic Security Act, or CARES Act, was signed into law by President Trump on 27 March 2020. CARES was at the time the largest stimulus package in US history with $2.2 trillion available in funds to be spread across the economy and society, ranging from funds available to individuals, to corporations, small businesses, public health and state and local officials. Some of the funds could be leveraged up so that the government then had the potential to make far higher loans if it deemed it necessary to do so. In fact, the Fed is also empowered to leverage $425 billion of the bailout so that it can generate a further $4.5 billion bailout fund for corporations (Jackson 2020). Still, only a fraction of these funds – $250 billion – went to households. The rest were employed to subsidise banks and other businesses. Certainly, workers earning less than $75,000 per year were able to claim $1,200, but they could only do so for three months. Precarious workers – the unemployed, those without unemployment insurance and so on – could not even claim these benefits. For Burke, then, 'the actual beneficiaries of the Trump bailout are big businesses and the banks' (Burke 2020).

Of course, Trump lost the next race for the White House in 2020, and Joe Biden assumed office. Almost immediately, Biden passed the American Rescue Plan Act (ARP), which is a $1.9-trillion stimulus package to help the US recovery from the economic and health impacts of COVID-19. Among the other measures, ARP will invest $160 billion to provide health supplies, protective equipment, testing and vaccines to stop the spread of COVID-19 across the United States, provide another $130 billion to ensure that all schools still serve students, give all working families $1,400 along with extending unemployment insurance benefits and eligibility. Emergency aid will also be given to those struggling to pay rent, and assistance will be given to those struggling with mortgages due to the pandemic. Child tax credit will be increased from $2,000 per child to $3,000 per child, while more child care assistance will be introduced through schemes such as additional tax credit to help cover the costs of childcare for some struggling families. Health insurance premiums will be lowered or even eliminated for millions of lower- and middle-income families, which will mean many uninsured Americans will be able to access health coverage. Emergency grants, lending and investment will also be made available to struggling businesses, while $360 billion will be distributed to state, local and territorial governments to help in their fight against the spread of COVID-19 (The White House 2021).

Biden's rescue plans have been applauded by many, and there is much to welcome in the package. For some progressives, the recovery programme is good news for a number of reasons, not least because it promotes the idea of 'government spending as a potential good in itself, the broadening of the concept of investment to include care expenditures, and raising taxes on the wealthy and corporations' (Meadway 2021: 29). A more critical analysis, however, should recognise many of its limitations. Three observations in particular can be made. First, and as the critical US commentator, Chris Hedges, observes, the Biden plan will not alter structural inequalities in the United States. For example, the ownership and control of healthcare, insurance and pharmaceutical corporations will still remain mostly privatised. Indeed, these corporations will prosper still further from the ARP because the US state will, in effect, be subsidising more people to take out private medical insurance. Hedges goes on to argue: 'This act will, at best, provide a momentary respite from the country's death spiral ... Much of (the extra) money will be instantly gobbled up by landlords, lenders, medical providers and credit card companies' (Hedges 2021). It is also unclear how ordinary people hit hard by the pandemic will make ends meet once the extra temporary government support stops.

Secondly, the stimulus plan is based on injecting huge amounts of money into the economy, both to get consumers to spend more and to give funds to businesses. Yet, and as we noted in previous chapters, capital develops its technological methods of production when it is forced to by global competition. Increasing its profits is the main motivation for capital, not demand for goods. If profits can be made by raising prices, or by cutting innovation, then capitalists will take these routes. So, if large amounts of government money is fed into the economy, this will not necessarily convince capitalists to invest in innovation and technology in order to increase labour productivity and raise real growth. It might be the case that, as O'Leary (2021) notes, the Biden recovery package will artificially stimulate growth in the very short term, but fail to tackle the underlying weak economic growth that has been with the United States for a number of years now.

Thirdly, the package introduced by Biden does not challenge neoliberalism and financialisation, but works within these contradictory constraints. A strong state that intervenes in society is not incompatible with neoliberalism or financialisation. If anything, a strong interventionist state has been a bedrock for both since Thatcher and Reagan came to power in the early 1980s. One way to look at Biden's plan, then, is to see it as enacting a set of measures that places marketisation and financialisation, at least temporarily and in certain areas, within a more European-form of neoliberalism. Biden's intervention is much higher than we have seen in Europe, but this is because social support mechanisms for its population have for years been lower than in Europe. When the pandemic subsequently hit the United States, therefore, its lower public spending on areas like unemployment benefits and families, when compared with dominant European nations, were shown up to be inadequate. US unemployment, for example, reached much higher peaks during the pandemic than in Europe (Watkins 2021: 16). In one important sense, therefore, APR introduces a number of temporary welfare measures into American society, but without creating a real welfare state. So, for example, APR gives \$32 billion to 'underserved communities', but this represents only 6 per cent of the total money being spent by the stimulus package (Watkins 2021: 17). In the meantime, neoliberal and financialised class relations remain intact, and indeed have got worse during the pandemic (see below).

It is a similar story in the United Kingdom. State subsidies for those who have been furloughed certainly guaranteed some people's wages, but not their full wages, while others have simply been made jobless. Yet different types of private financial capital have been protected by the UK state. At the start of the pandemic, for example, the British government introduced the Coronavirus Business Interruption Loan Scheme, which empowered the state to underwrite lending to commercial banks, who then issued credit in the form of loans to businesses. Banks, however, were condemned for being slow in handing out loans to struggling businesses, and when they have done so, many banks have introduced high interest rates for loans after their first year of lending. While the government therefore had to intervene to ensure banks act more fairly with the loans, Berry et al. (2020) observe that this scheme was one illustration of the UK state initially empowering and supporting a small number of commercial banking interests over and above other groups in society. Furthermore, continue Berry et al., if the average working household spent £147 per month on debt repayments, £135 on rent and £177 on mortgage costs, then about 45 per cent of the Job Retention Scheme went to landlords or to banks in the form of rent, debt repayments or mortgages. For Berry et al., the Job Retention Scheme was therefore 'in part an indirect means of protecting income streams for asset owners' (Berry et al. 2020: 20). For those in low income working-class households, who normally spend most of their income on 'essential' items, having a reduced income meant less money for essentials and the need to take on more debt to compensate for this loss of income (see also below).

But, as we have already indicated, the US economy and its financial system was already teetering on the edge of crisis *before* the pandemic started. The average rate of profit in the United States had declined over the years and unproductive capital was a shackle on productive investments. What can be added to this picture is that while banks after the 2008 crisis might not have been as exposed to financial leverage to the extent they were before the crisis, they were still acting as conduits for global financial risks. Willing to transform loans into assets for a secondary loan market, banks were instruments for encouraging the rise of opaque finance currently floating around the United States and in other major economies; a type of finance that precipitated the subprime crash in 2008. Central banks had been regularly 'buying up financial assets of diverse kinds, handing out new cash produced out of thin air, to private financial firms. In return they receive titles to future income streams from debtors of all sorts, turning private debt into public assets, or better: into assets of public institutions with the privilege unilaterally to determine an economy's money supply' (Streeck 2017: 19). In December 2017, it was reported that major central banks continued to hold astoundingly high assets – \$21 trillion to be exact – and many of these were not in good health. The European Central Bank (ECB) started to buy corporate bonds in June 2016, and by December 2017 it was estimated to hold \$152 billion in these bonds. Some of the companies issuing the bonds, such as Steinhoff International Holdings, were, however, declining in value (Grant 2017).

Given these circumstances, it is perhaps to be expected that the financial system should have started to experience high levels of instability before the onset of COVID-19. In August 2019, stock markets had already plummeted as markets were growing fearful of trade wars between America and China. Subsequently, short-term US bonds surpassed those of long-term US bonds, giving rise to the so-called inverted V-curve, which is often seen by some as the prelude to a global crisis (Marte 2019). In response, the Fed, in September 2019, entered the emergency repurchase (repo) loan market; the first time it had done so since the 2008 financial crash. 'The Fed's emergency repo loans outstanding last year hit a peak of \$236.6 billion on December 18, 2019 – \$100 billion more than during the worst financial crisis since the Great Depression' (Martens and Martens 2020).[2] Importantly, financial markets had reached this point because of their toxicity, which, overall, had not been successfully governed or regulated since 2008.

Ironically, COVID-19 *might* give this toxic system a new lease of life through government bailouts. The reason for remaining cautious with the word *might*, is that there are also signs of the financial sector

---

[2] For a succinct summary of repo loans, see Cheng and Wessel (2020).

struggling to come to terms with the pandemic. For example, the Lloyds Banking Group in late July 2020 posted a pre-tax loss of £676 million in the second quarter of that financial year compared with a pre-tax profit of £1.3 billion a year previously. One of the main reasons for its loss is that Lloyds had set aside £2.4 billion to cover future possible default loans from its customers, taking its total to £3.8 billion put to one side to cover bad loans (Megaw 2020). Even so, there are still plenty of opportunities for financial investors during the crisis, as we will now see.

Crisis Opportunities for Financial Investors

As noted above, some venture capitalists, financial investors and speculators see the crisis surrounding COVID-19 as an opportunity to make even more money. As Mathur and Thorne (2020) note, during the 2008 global financial crash, venture capitalists took the opportunity to buy into fledging digital companies like Uber. Today, there is a similar sense of optimism among many investors. At the same time, continue Mathur and Thorne, aggressive growth models could make way in a post-COVID-19 world for more reflective investment strategies in which 'sustainability and profitability' in start-ups surpass 'growth at all costs' (Mathur and Thorne 2020).

But while some venture capitalists might be troubled by engaging in old practices, it is not true of all large financial investors. The pandemic has provided a chance for governments to gift new opportunities to investors in the financial system. Two examples serve to illustrate this point. First, the IMF has given funds to poorer nations to help them tackle the pandemic within their own borders. Jubilee Debt Campaign claims, however, that $11.3 billion of IMF loans to twenty-eight out of thirty-three highly indebted countries, which include Ghana, Jordan, Kenya, Pakistan and Tunisia, are in fact being used to pay off private lenders. Problematically, the IMF itself argues that debts are maintainable despite evidence to the contrary. In 2019, before the onset of COVID-19, countries in the Southern hemisphere were already paying on average 14.1 per cent of government revenue on external debt repayments, which amounted to a 100 per cent increase since 2010. With the arrival of COVID-19, the thirty-three countries have seen their GDP decline, but 'the IMF continues to bail out previous lenders rather than say that debt restructurings are needed and help governments to implement them' (Jubilee Debt Campaign 2020: 11).

The second example is taken from early June 2020 when the Trump administration allowed private equity firms to be included in workers' retirement accounts. According to Appelbaum (2020), this policy was carried out by stealth under the cover of the pandemic and Black Lives Matter protests. Private equity firms had been lobbying for access to these pension pots for some time. About $6.2 trillion is locked away one pension account – the 401(k) account – while another $2.5 trillion can be found in the IRA pension accounts. Appelbaum estimates that if only 5 per cent of these retirement funds are available to private equity funds, then up to $435 billion could fall into the laps of private equity investors and managers. These pensions funds will then, however, be exposed to high risk, with many recently launched private equity funds underperforming on stock markets (Appelbaum 2020). By sanctioning this practice, according to Sirota (2020), the Trump administration was handing to private equity firms what is known as, 'dumb money'. This is money held by bodies like pension funds and controlled and managed by paid officials, the latter of whom are often willing to pay high fess to private equity firms for these firms to make investments with their pension funds. Fees paid to private equity firms are, though, often astronomical, and pension funds potentially stand to lose millions of dollars, much of which could have gone to their members. There is no reason why the pandemic might not be used in other bellicose ways to generate large profits.

Austerity, the Pandemic and Government

The evidence so far is that the neoliberal politics of attacking welfare and implementing austerity are still very much with us. Before the pandemic, and as we alluded to at the start of this chapter, a certain ideological agenda on the right of the political spectrum in the United States, United Kingdom and elsewhere started to come of age in the 1980s. In the United States, Ronald Reagan used his presidency to realign welfare entitlements towards a workfare agenda by shifting the administration of welfare delivery from the federal government to the private sector. Subsequent presidents have all proceeded along the same structural route under the belief that a system of 'empowerment' and the creation 'responsible' individuals who work with the private and voluntary sector in looking after their own welfare provisions is a vital ingredient for a prosperous society (Boyle and Silver 2005). This was also a key mantra of the UK's Conservative governments in the 1980s and early 1990s. New Labour under Tony Blair likewise pushed, albeit in new directions, this neoliberal workfare agenda in the late 1990s and early 2000s. Certainly, New Labour moved beyond the strict neoliberal approach of the Conservatives in the area of social policy and gave more resources over to active welfare programmes of assistance to those who need it.

Nonetheless, New Labour also redefined welfare provisions in a way that adopted elements of Conservative thinking on these issues. Blair, his ministers and advisers spoke about the 'rights' and 'responsibilities' of 'conditioned' welfare provisions based upon the duty of individuals to take care of their own welfare. What this meant in practice was that New Labour endeavoured to promote, 'a particular type of moral community in which citizens earn access to their social rights through a combination of hard work, responsible behaviour and personal contribution' (Dwyer 2002: 274).

After 2010, austerity further entrenched workfare ideology into British society, which included estimates that £37 billion less would be spent on UK welfare by 2021. By 2019, UK public service spending was around 8 per cent of GDP, whereas in 2007/8 it stood at just over 11 per cent (Shaheen and Jesse 2020: 45–6). Cuts to the public sector also meant cuts to jobs in the public sector. In the North of England, public sector employment fell by 19 per cent, while London underwent a 10 per cent reduction. And while council spending on services fell by 13 per cent across England between 2009/10 and 2018/19, local government spending in the North has seen dramatic reductions in council spending, falling by 20 per cent, which is the equivalent of £364.94 per person (Johns 2020).

Since the pandemic, the signals sent by government is that authoritarianism neoliberalism, austerity and workfare will not end any time soon. In his COVID-19 budget in March 2020, Rishi Sunak, the UK Chancellor of the Exchequer, made the headline-grabbing announcement of an extra £30 billion to help to support the economy during the pandemic. Beneath the headlines, though, masked another reality. Austerity was very much at the forefront of the budget. Forecasts suggested at the time that UK total government spending would actually decrease from 2019/20 to 2024/25 to stand at 40.5 per cent of GDP. Yet in the six years before 2019 this figure stood at 40.8 per cent of GDP. Furthermore, public sector spending in areas such as health and welfare was also set to drop in the forthcoming years from 36.5 per cent of GDP to 35.5 per cent of GDP (O'Leary 2020a).

For sure, initial welfare assistance by the Conservative government, particularly the £9 billion increase to welfare expenditure, helped to cushion the impact of the pandemic for the lowest earners. But, during this earlier period in the pandemic, the Conservatives also made it clear that by April 2021, benefit cuts would be made. This would mean that basic unemployment support would be reduced back to its lowest level since 1990/1 and that support for renters would be diminished, particularly through a reduction in housing allowance for two-bedroom properties. At the time, it was predicted that Council Tax Support enhancement would likely be removed as well. At the time, it was estimated that '6 million households (22 per cent) – containing 18 million people (27 per cent) – will lose over £1,000 in 2021/22; reducing the average income of the bottom half of the income distribution by around £800 (4 per cent)' (Brewer et al. 2020: 51).

In early July 2020, Sunak made a 'summer statement', a sort of mini-budget, setting out further policy and spending commitments to help to tackle the socio-economic effects of the pandemic in the United Kingdom. Up to £25 billion of extra public spending was made available, but this really only added up to 1 per cent of GDP. Sunak also announced that he had set the jobs furlough scheme to end in October 2020, which meant employers would then pay 100 per cent of the wages of their retained workers. As O'Leary (2020b) observed, many employers already struggling would simply cut their workforces. Indeed, the evidence at the time did show job losses and unemployment steadily rising. One survey in July 2020 from the employer's organisation, the British Chamber of Commerce, found that 29 per cent of the 7,400 UK businesses who responded expected to decrease the size of their workforce in the three months before the Job Retention Scheme ended, while only 12 per cent would increase their workforce (BCC 2020). Government data showed that by June 2020, the number of UK employees on payrolls was down by 650,000 compared with March 2020. Even so, the rate of unemployment had started to slow in June. Moreover, in the year March to May 2019–March to May 2020 the actual weekly hours worked in the United Kingdom fell by 16.7 per cent, which was the largest annual decrease since records began in 1971 (ONS 2020d).

Due to mounting public pressure from some quarters, Sunak partially relented in his March 2021 budget on some cutbacks he had earlier planned. One of his most attention-grabbing proposals was to extend the £20 uplift to Universal Credit and Working Tax Credit for another six months – it was due to be phased out in April 2021. In the end, it was phased out by early October 2021. Some believed its ending would place 500,000 people, including 200,000 children, into poverty. Furthermore, there was little in the March 2021 budget to help families already in rent arrears (Innes and Schmuecker 2021).

In his budget at the end of October 2021, Sunak announced that the government would reduce the taper rate of the withdrawal of Universal Credit – the amount of money a claimant loses when they work and earn over a certain threshold – from 63 per cent to 53 per cent. This will soften the blow of the end to the £20 uplift to Universal Credit. The October budget also pledged to make large increases to government department spending, totalling £150 billion over the next few years. Nevertheless, the years of austerity will still linger in British society. Despite extra funding being available, only one-third of 'unprotected' government departments that suffered austerity cuts from 2010 onwards will see real-term reversals in spending by 2024/25 (Resolution Foundation 2021: 2). Moreover, wages are forecast to grow by just 2.4 per cent over the coming years, with households looking overall at a 'flat recovery'. 'The country is still in the weakest decade for pay growth since the 1930s' (Resolution Foundation 2021: 2). Higher inflation, estimated to rise by 4.4 per cent in 2022, means, for example, that at least for the next two or so years disposable household income will also fall (Resolution Foundation 2021: 12). Still, Sunak found space to give tax concessions to some business and financial sectors, which will cost the government about £3 billion over the next few years (Resolution Foundation 2021: 36).

Chapter 9 explores in more detail how coronavirus has impacted on the state and public sector, and as we will see then, and as the present section indicates, government social and welfare policies so far on COVID-19 indicate a continuation of Thatcherism and neoliberalism, not a restructuring away from these ideologies. In practical terms, this means that despite the pandemic, the government is still pursuing welfare policies that effectively individualise social problems by placing the responsibility on welfare claimants and those on low incomes to make themselves 'employable' (see Bonefeld et al. 1995: 149).

Occupations and COVID-19

Evidence from the United Kingdom suggests that COVID-19 has distinct effects on a person due to their social class and occupation. For example, men in low-skilled manual jobs are four times more likely to die from the virus than what might be termed as 'middle-class' occupations. The study looked at the 2,494 COVID-19 deaths in England and Wales up to and including 20 April 2020. For men, the highest rate of death was found in 'elementary workers' – those people who work in construction or cleaning. The group with the next highest rate was caring, leisure and other service occupations (17.9 deaths per 100,000 males, or 72 deaths), which include occupations such as nursing assistants, care workers and ambulance drivers. Process, plant and machine operatives also had 15.5 deaths per 100,000 males, or 242 deaths.

For women in the United Kingdom, caring, leisure and other service occupations had a rate of 7.5 deaths per 100,000 females, equivalent to 130 deaths, followed by women working in low skilled elementary occupations. What these figures suggest is that men working in productive spheres, such as construction, have a higher death rate than many other occupations, but so do some unproductive working-class occupations. Overall, and when the study reported its findings, men in low-skilled jobs are four times more like to die from COVID-19 than those doing professional jobs. So, for example, among men, a number of occupations were found to have higher COVID-19 death levels, including taxi drivers and chauffeurs (36.4 deaths per 100,000); bus and coach drivers (26.4 deaths per 100,000); chefs (35.9 deaths per 100,000); and sales and retail assistants (19.8 deaths per 100,000) (ONS 2020e).

Evidence further suggests that people working in higher paid jobs have better opportunities to work from home. One survey found that about four-in-five workers in the top earnings quintile were working from home at the start of the pandemic some or all of the time, compared with less than half those in the bottom quintile. In other words, it is workers in jobs with lower earnings who are more likely to expose themselves to the risk of the virus by travelling to a workplace and interacting with fellow employees (Gardiner and Slaughter 2020).

Geography and Social Class

There is also a spatial element to the relationship between social class and COVID-19. We know that capitalism fosters uneven development between countries, but it equally true to say that uneven development occurs also both between and within regions and localities. Older industrial areas in the United Kingdom – cities and towns found in Northeast England and the South Wales Valleys, for example, along with some seaside towns and a number of London boroughs – have tended to struggle in recent years to attract investment. They therefore on average have higher levels of deprivation and poverty than other areas. As Beatty and Fothergill (2016) note, the more deprived the local authority, then the more welfare entitlements they would lose because of the reforms. Towns like Blackburn and Blackpool in Lancashire with high clusters of working-class neighbourhoods would each lose £560 per working age adult because of the post-2015 reforms, for example, compared with the wealthier town of Guilford in Surrey, which would lose £150, or the loss of £130 in the Hart district of Hampshire (Beatty and Fothergill 2016: 3).

COVID has strengthened many of these spaces of austerity. Other analysis on the United Kingdom demonstrates that deaths involving the virus are twice the rate in the most deprived neighbourhoods in England (55.1 deaths per 100,000 people) compared with the least deprived (25.3 deaths per 100,000) (ONS 2020f). Places of deprivation, like Newham in London, have local authorities that lack resources to fully help their residents cope with the effects of the pandemic. As a result, working-class, lower income families have to rely on their own resources to cope on a day-today basis. But this then entrenches even further certain inequalities. Children from poorer families, for example, have been disadvantaged during lockdown, while working-class parents often find it harder to get access to computers for their children. Overall, the Institute for Fiscal Studies (IFS) claim that children from middle-class families are spending more time on almost every single educational activity than children in the worse-off fifth of families. Children from middle-class families also received higher-quality support from their respective schools during the crisis than worse-off families (Blundell et al. 2020: 17–18). Another study published in September 2020, shortly before UK children were set to return to school after six months away from formal education, and based in a weighted sample of 3,000 school leaders and teachers, found that teachers in the most deprived schools were three times more likely to report that their children were four months or more behind their curriculum learning compared with teachers in the least deprived schools (Sharp et al. 2020).

Class, Wealth and the Pandemic

COVID-19 has contributed to widening the huge gap between the capitalist class and the world's poor. One the one hand, the massively wealthy seem to have got wealthier. In 2020, America had 614 billionaires. At the start of 2020, their combined wealth stood at $2.947 trillion; by the second week in April 2020, however, US billionaire wealth had risen to $3.229 trillion. Overall, US billionaire wealth grew by 10 per cent from March to April 2020, which meant an extra $282 billion (Collins et al. 2020). In the United Kingdom, though, the combined wealth of the richest 1,000 people has fallen by £54 billion during the pandemic (Smithers 2020). A slightly later study by the Institute for Policy Studies in the United States calculated that the global 2,365 billionaires have watched, with some delight I'm sure, their wealth grow in the pandemic by $4 trillion, or a whopping 54 per cent. In one year, from March 2020 to March 2021, their combined wealth increased from $8.04 trillion to $12.34 (Collins and Ocampo 2021).

Obviously, the world's ultra-wealthy employ private wealth management advisory firms to manage their financial and investment portfolios. These advisory firms, or so-called 'family offices', have been using the crisis as an opportunity to gain higher returns for their clients. One report suggests that more than three-quarters (77 per cent) of family offices claimed that their managed portfolios had performed in line with, or above, respective target benchmarks from the beginning of 2020 to May 2020. Almost half of those surveyed (45 per cent) were looking to raise allocations in real estate, while the same number were looking to increase allocations in market equities (UBS 2020).

During the pandemic, CEO pay tended initially to remain the same as before the crisis. In the United Kingdom, for instance, only thirty-six FTSE 100 firms cut CEO pay because of COVID-19. Generally, these firms reduced by 20 per cent the fees and salaries of executive directors or non-executive directors. But salaries only normally account as a minority of total CEO earnings. Typically, CEOs are paid through remuneration packages that include bonuses paid in the form of shares. Some of these companies have also used the government's Job Retention Scheme, which, in effect, means that the state has been paying for furloughed workers even though the CEOs of these very same companies were still holding onto to their huge remuneration schemes (CIPD 2020).

A more recent UK report argues that on average households have increased their nominal savings by around £125 billion more than expected due to the pandemic. Among other things, this is because more households are paying off consumer card debts and managing to save. Indirect changes in asset prices have risen even more steeply, with an estimation that the value of total wealth in the United Kingdom has grown by over £750 billion. And it has been changes in asset prices, according to the report, that has had a wider impact on the level and distribution of wealth. The report notes:

> We . . . find that the pandemic's effects on asset prices raised wealth levels by as much as 7 per cent in the middle of the wealth distribution. Those in the middle of the distribution had the largest proportional rises because they tend to hold more housing wealth as a share of total wealth than richer or poorer families – and house price increases outpaced returns on other assets. But the largest absolute increases in wealth were for those at the top of the distribution: the richest 10 per cent of families gained, on average, £44,000 in net wealth per adult from higher asset prices. (Leslie and Shah 2021: 7)

When savings on consumer spending and debts are also factored into the picture, then the authors of the report found that the richest 10 per cent of households gained just over £50,000 extra per adult in wealth during the pandemic, whereas the poorest 30 per cent gained just over £86 per adult.

Class, Wealth, and Race and Ethnicity

Class-based effects of the pandemic are also experienced differently depending on one's cultural and social identity. For instance, UK per capita COVID-19 hospital deaths, *'are highest among the black Caribbean population and three times those of the white British majority.* Some minority groups – including Pakistanis and black Africans – have seen similar numbers of hospital deaths per capita to the population average, while Bangladeshi fatalities are lower' (Platt and Warwick 2020, added emphasis). Bangladeshi COVID-19 hospital deaths are, however, twice as high as white British. Platt and Warwick claim that one reason for the disparity in hospital deaths is because many in ethnic minority groups find employment in key worker occupations, such as health and care work, and so are therefore at greater risk of being exposed to the virus. Furthermore, some ethnic minority groups have a high percentage of older people with underlying health conditions. Those in black and ethnic minority groups can also often be found in more economically vulnerable jobs or work in economically vulnerable circumstances. Bangladeshis, Black Caribbeans and Black Africans likewise have the most limited savings to provide a financial buffer if laid off, for instance, while some ethnic minority groups are employed in industries that have been shut down during the pandemic (Platt and Warwick 2020).

Another report finds a link between the types of employment undertaken by BAME members and the barriers they face in their respective workplaces in shielding from coronavirus. It is estimated that a third of BAME members were more likely to working outside their home during the pandemic compared with just over a quarter of White people. More BAME groups are likewise represented in key worker jobs than White people. For example, Black African and Black Caribbean people are especially over-represented in front-line health and social care employment. As a consequence, the report finds that increased numbers of BAME key workers (32 per cent) said they had not been issued with adequate PPE equipment at work compared with their White colleagues (20 per cent). And given that a higher percentage of BAME people have to work outside their home, then this also means that a higher proportion of BAME members have been using public transport to travel to their workplaces, which again leads to greater exposure to COVID-19 (Haque et al. 2020).

The pandemic has likewise exposed, and indeed reinforced, disparities between wealth and race. In the United States, one study argued that the crisis has had a disproportionate effect on the wealth divide between White and Black, Brown and Native populations in America.

Black people, for example, were 3.57 times more likely to be at risk from dying of coronavirus than White Americans, while for Latino Americans the death risk was 1.88 times higher than for Whites. Similar to the United Kingdom, one reason for such differences lies in the occupations of each group. Roughly, nearly 38 per cent of Black people are employed in 'essential industries' compared with around 27 per cent of Whites, while 40 per cent of Black workers are more likely to be found in the hospital sector. During the pandemic, Black and Latino workers in the United States have carried the burden of job and income losses. 'Sixty-one percent of Latino households and 44 percent of Black households have had a job or wage loss due to the pandemic, compared to 38 percent of White households' (Hamilton et al. 2020: 8).

Wealth in the United States is, as one might expect, structured through lines of race and ethnicity. Of Black and Latino families, 37 per cent and 33 per cent, respectively, have zero or negative wealth compared with 15.5 percent of White families. Yet, between March and June 2020, as the virus took hold of American society, the combined wealth of all billionaires in America increased by more than $637 billion, which equates to more than 13 per cent of *all* pre-virus Black wealth. As the report notes: 'People of color, with less savings on average than whites, will have a harder time covering the cost of basic needs if they experience loss of income' (Hamilton et al. 2020: 10).

Gender and the Pandemic

There are gender inequalities and gender imbalances in how COVID-19 has affected society. An early study of these issues, just after the first UK lockdown, found that women were about one third more likely to work in a sector that had been shut down because of the pandemic. These sectors were in retail and hospitality, where many occupations are defined as being unproductive working-class jobs insofar as employees within these sectors neither own, control nor have legal title over their means of production. One in six female employees surveyed worked in these sectors compared with one in seven male employees (Joyce and Xu 2020). Government data from the beginning of July 2020 through to the end of December 2020 similarly found that the highest proportion of workers furloughed was found in the accommodation and food services sectors followed by the wholesale and retail sectors. Government data also shows that more jobs with women employees were furloughed than with male employees. By the end of November 2020, 1.92 million female employees were furloughed, with this figure decreasing slightly to 1.88 million by the end of December 2020. The figures for male employees were 1.79 million and 1.85 million, respectively (Coronavirus Job Retention Scheme statistics: January 2021). Later figures from 1 July to 31 May 2021, however, show that for the first time since the outbreak of the pandemic more male job holders had been furloughed than female job holders. By the end of May 2021, 1.20 million male employees were furloughed, whereas the figure for female employees stood at 1.13 million. Part the reason for this decrease in female furloughed employees was because of the gradual opening up of the UK retail and hospitality sectors (Coronavirus Job Retention Scheme statistics: 1 July 2021).

Work, gender and the pandemic are related in other ways too. Insecure work is employment that does not have guaranteed regular hours or income (for example, casual and temporary work), or it is work that is low-paid self-employment. According to the TUC, this type of work accounts for around one in nine workers in the United Kingdom. Many key workers – carers, delivery drivers and so on – can also be counted as engaging in insecure work. Around 7.1 per cent of women are in insecure work compared with 6 per cent of men, while BAME women are about twice as likely as white workers to have insecure employment. Insecure workers have found it more difficult during the pandemic to get government support, such as statutory sick pay (SSP). There are a number of reasons for this. To claim SSP, for instance, 'an employee must, on average, earn £120 per week. This excludes 1.8 million employees, 70 per cent of whom are women' (TUC 2021a: 6).

Gender inequality is noticeable in other areas as well. Before COVID, women tended to do more unpaid housework than men. During the first UK lockdown when schools closed, one study found that on average parents undertook childcare duties for nine hours during the day, whereas before the pandemic this figure was about five and a half hours. And because more women were furloughed, they spent more time doing household duties and responsibilities. In May 2020, it was estimated that on average women were spending two more hours per day on childcare and housework because of the pandemic. But while fathers still did less childcare than mothers, they had nevertheless nearly doubled the time they spent on childcare duties (Andrew et al. 2020). Other data suggest that women on average have experienced higher levels of anxiety, loneliness, worry and depressive symptoms due to the pandemic than is the case with men. Loneliness in the United Kingdom was found to be the main driver of anxiety at the start of the first lockdown in 2020, with women 1.3 times more likely to report loneliness than men at this time (ONS 2021). Another report of parents with children aged 4–12 found that between April 2020 and November 2020 both mothers and fathers in this group reported worse mental health than a comparable sample of parents interviewed before the pandemic. The study discovered that mothers suffered worse mental effects than fathers, with, once again, loneliness being the main factor in causing mental health issues (Blanden et al. 2021).

Poverty and the Pandemic

Data suggests that the pandemic will eradicate any progress made to improve the lives of the world's poor. The World Bank has estimated that the pandemic could push 71 million people into extreme poverty, which represents the first increase in global extreme poverty since 1998. And a large percentage of the those who will find themselves in extreme poverty live in countries that already have large numbers of people in poverty, such as South Asia and Sub-Saharan Africa (World Bank 2020a). Another report suggests that the pandemic will actually push 176 million people into poverty at the $3.20 poverty line. 'Far from being the "great leveller"', argues Philip Alston in his final report as Special Rapporteur on extreme poverty and human rights for the Human Rights Council, 'COVID-19 is a pandemic of poverty, exposing the parlous state of social safety nets for those on lower incomes or in poverty around the world' (Alston 2020: 9).

Research from Oxfam states that new centres of hunger are spreading across the globe due to the virus. Owing to the economic and social consequences of COVID-19, a predicted 122 million people could be thrusted into near starvation conditions. The irrationalities of global capitalism and the pandemic are acutely on show here because, at the same time, eight of the biggest food and beverage companies give £18 billion to shareholders, which is more than ten times the funding required to get enough food and agricultural assistance to those who will be hardest hit globally by the virus. The ten most severe 'hunger spots' include Afghanistan, Syria and South Sudan, and emerging epicentres of hunger in countries like India, South Africa and Brazil. For example, border closures around Afghanistan have caused a drop in food supplies, while travel restrictions in India have meant that farmers can no longer hire migrant labour. One knock-on effect of these changing circumstances is that a rise in unemployment amongst migrant workers has caused a downturn in remittance flows – the money migrant workers send to their families. As the Oxfam report notes: 'Global remittances totalled $554bn in 2019 and are a lifeline for millions of families that are living in poverty. The World Bank estimates that the pandemic will result in a 20 percent decline in remittances to low- and middle-income countries – which amounts to more than $100bn' (Oxfam 2020: 3).

Another report from Christian Aid claims that if COVID-19 leads global consumption to fall by a fifth, then between 420 million and 580 million people will fall into poverty. Unemployment has, furthermore, soared in many developing countries because of the pandemic (on unemployment, see also the next sub-section). In India, for example, 80 million migrant workers have lost their jobs in major cities. Refugees have similarly suffered to greater extent since the pandemic, especially since refugees in developing countries are often placed in cramped makeshift camps with limited facilities (Christian Aid 2020).

Since 2020, poverty has also increased in different and more affluent Northern countries, and this has partly been caused by the pandemic. For an illustration, let us look at Britain. The Social Metrics Commission (SMC) in the United Kingdom develops a poverty indicator by considering core and recurring living costs like housing, childcare and the extra costs of disability. It also considers people's wider resources, such as post-tax earnings and income, liquid assets. The SMC measure sets a poverty threshold of 55 percent of median total available resources – the total weekly resources required for families to meet their needs. The SMC's 2020 report claimed that 14.4 million people in the United Kingdom were in poverty (which is a similar figure to that given by the Joseph Rowntree Foundation). About 8.5 million in poverty are working-age adults, while 7.1 million people (11 per cent) are in persistent poverty; that is to say, they are in poverty now and have been in poverty for at least two of the previous three years (SMC 2020). In terms of the pandemic, the report says that almost half of Black African Caribbean households were in poverty compared with one in five White families. Moreover, BAME family members are between two and three times as likely to be in persistent poverty than people in White families. COVID-19 has made matters worse for many in poverty. Deep poverty is defined as being more than 50 per cent below the poverty line. In terms of this group, the report notes that since the pandemic, almost 65 per cent of those who were in deep poverty, but also in employment, have experienced negative labour change because of the virus; for example, reduced working hours or have been furloughed. This compares with 35 per cent of those who were employed and more than 20 per cent above the poverty line prior to the crisis. The report also finds that 20 per cent of those who are in deep poverty and previously employed have now lost their jobs, which is higher than other forms of poverty (SMC 2020: 5). Overall, SMC argues that around 26 per cent of all of those in deep poverty, irrespective of their status before the pandemic, have experienced a negative change in their employment status or earnings. Again, this figure is higher than other poverty groups. For example, the figure is

21 per cent for those living within 50 per cent below poverty line and 24 per cent for those living within 20 per cent above the poverty line (SMC 2020: 6).

Poverty and those struggling to make ends meet has other notable effects. To take one example, those in poverty and in lower income brackets will often experience higher levels of anxiety and concern about meeting everyday necessities like maintaining an adequate supply of food for the household. Research undertaken in the United States during the pandemic showed that four out of five respondents with an annual income below $20,000 reported that they suffered from food insecurity, which is an indication that a household has limited access to adequate food due to insufficient income, funds and/or resources, whereas only three people in ten on an annual income between $40,000 to $99,999 reported food insecurity (Schanzenbach and Pitts 2020: 4). By April 2020, the food insecurity rate for families with children stood at 34.5 per cent, which was almost three times the level predicted by previous surveys (Schanzenbach and Pitts 2020: 6). In another survey, 16.5 per cent of US households with children reported in June 2020 that it was sometimes or often the case that the children were not eating enough due to a lack of resources, which is five and half times the rate in 2018 (Bauer 2020). Food insecurity and hunger have therefore been adversely affected during the pandemic especially for those families in America on low wages, limited resources and with restricted access to credit (Bauer 2020).

It is a comparable story in the United Kingdom. In their 'State of Hunger Report', the food bank charity, the Trussell Trust, explored 'household-level economic and social condition of limited or uncertain access to adequate food' since the start of the pandemic. In their survey of people accessing their food banks, they found that just before the pandemic began in 2019/20 around 700,000 of UK households (2.5 per cent) used a foodbank, while 370,000 households, which included 320,000 children, were supported by a Trussell Trust food bank. During the first wave of the COVID-19 crisis, there was an increase of 24 per cent in the proportion of couples with children referred to a food bank (Trussell Trust 2021). The UK government's, Food Standards Agency, found that those families already experiencing food insecurity had now to cope with additional anxieties of trying to access extra funds to meet food shortages alongside other mounting problems. As the report notes: 'For many, food insecurity and Covid-19 were managed alongside other challenges: job insecurity/job loss, caring responsibilities, health/mental health issues, domestic violence, debt, and so on' (Connors et al. 2020: 2). Some who took part in the study showed signs of malnutrition, others were putting on weight even though they were eating less, while some respondents said they could no longer afford to buy certain types of food to combat food intolerances and manage their health in an appropriate and proper manner. There was also a significant increase in food bank usage, up by 10 per cent in June 2020 alone.

Class and Debt

The pandemic crisis has strengthened the relationship between class and debt. The United Kingdom once again provides an illustration. During the pandemic, some aspects of household debt actually decreased. Due in part to people not consuming as much due to successive lockdowns, some managed to pay back chunks of loans they had accumulated before the pandemic. In February 2021, for example, the Bank of England reported that UK households paid back £16.6 billion in consumer credit, the largest repayment on record. In December 2020, normally a time when consumer spending is high, net repayments on credit cards stood at £0.8 billion and then £0.1 billion on other forms of consumer credit. Annual rates subsequently fell further on both aspects to –16.2 per cent and –3.4 per cent, respectively. 'For credit cards', notes the Bank, 'this represents a new low' (Bank of England 2021). Unfortunately, a lack of consumer spending has negative effects for business. Another report published in February 2021 said that UK firms borrowed £35.5 billion in 2020 with a further £26 billion to be borrowed by the end of 2021. The amount borrowed in 2020 was £25 billion more on average than was borrowed across the previous five years (Luttig 2021).[3]

But just before the pandemic hit the United Kingdom, it was estimated that 3.2 million people were experiencing severe debt problems, while 9.8 million endured financial stress. A national poll survey taken in May 2020 found that 28 per cent of adults, which equates to about 14 million people, had experienced a direct negative affect on their income as a result of the virus. The survey found that those who are younger, female, who have childcare obligations and those in insecure work have been hardest hit during the pandemic by financial difficulties. Many of these people work in working-class occupations that have experienced tough conditions because of the virus – occupations like retail, catering, hospitality and wholesale. Of those living on an income of less than £30,000, 44

---

[3] Due to relatively low interest rates since 2008, corporations had already been borrowing heavily. One valuation discovered that corporate debt escalated from $3.3 trillion before 2008 to $6.5 trillion over a decade later (Roberts 2020).

per cent have fallen into arrears or borrowed to make ends meet when it comes to paying for everyday household goods, such as rent or utilities. This compares with 25 per cent of people earning £50,000–£60,000. By May, 4.6 million people negatively affected had accumulated £6.1 billion of arrears and debt, averaging £1,076 in arrears and £997 in debt per adult affected (StepChange 2020: 1). Debt is not, however, only a problem for ordinary people.

These problems are compounded by rising UK unemployment brought about by the pandemic. In August 2020, official data showed that nearly three-quarters of a million jobs had been lost from company payrolls since March. Hours worked also continued to fall, and regular pay fell by 0.2 per cent. More people had applied for benefits, and, since March 2020, the claimant count had risen by 116.8 per cent (ONS 2020g). More positively, vacancies were 30 per cent higher from June to August 2020 than the record low during April to June 2020 (ONS 2020g).

McNeil et al. (2020) further estimated that when the UK's Job Retention Scheme eventually closed, there could be a work shortage for nearly 3 million workers because of a continuing shortfall in consumer demand. Unemployment would then increase by 9 per cent. At best, 1.5 million workers could lose their jobs, while, at worst, 4 million might lose their jobs. Some 1 million jobs might never return. Working-class individuals – those who are employed in sectors and have no possession, control or legal title over the means of production – are especially vulnerable. Occupations in working-class sectors like hospitality, construction, support services, retail, entertainment and manufacturing would be hit hardest.

Encouragingly, McNeil et al. also suggest that 2 million of the vulnerable 3 million jobs could be protected if wage subsidies were extended. But a report issued in October 2021, based on a survey of 258 businesses, discovered that 46 per cent of respondents would make some redundancies over the next six months from September 2021, while a very high proportion of those surveyed expect to make redundancies in 12 months. The report observes:

> The research . . . indicates a very high correlation between organisations who were still using the furlough scheme during September and those that expect to make redundancies over the next 12 months. This suggests a very low level of confidence in employee job security for those employers who were still utilising the scheme at the conclusion. (Renovo 2021: 2)

Due to all of these circumstances, more people will likely be pushed into relying on debt to meet basic needs.

A similar situation can be found in the United States. In August 2020, the Federal Reserve reported that aggregate US household debt $34 billion in the second quarter of 2020, which added up to a 0.2 per cent decline, so that total US household debt was $14.27 trillion. Notably, credit card balances fell sharply during this period by $76 billion. Reflecting lower consumer spending during the pandemic, this was the steepest drop in card balances since the collection of this type of data (Center for Microeconomic Data 2020). Some, however, forecasted rising unemployment in the United States, with one study predicting that the highest rise would be around 30 per cent (Higginson et al. 2020), while another suggested that a 14 per cent unemployment rate would emerge by the end of 2020 (Jordan and Cunningham 2020). Numerous households would therefore be unable to pay off their accumulated debts, ensuring a wave of losses for the US-retail lending market. Higginson et al. (2020), in fact, suggested that 'an extended period of elevated losses, which could total an excess of $130 billion over the next two years', might be a possibility.

In saying this, the Bureau of Labor Statistics (BLS) released their October 2021 figures that claimed US unemployment was actually much less at 4.8 per cent of the population (Bureau of Labor Statistics October 2021). Nonetheless, the way in which the Bureau calculates unemployment is subject to some dispute by other organisations. The Ludwig Institute for Economic Prosperity argues that there should be estimates for a 'true rate of unemployment'. In their unemployment calculations, the BLS focuses on those individuals over sixteen years of age who have a job and are actively seeking work. For the Ludwig Institute, unemployment calculations should also include data on those who do not have a full-time job, but want one. Furthermore, the Ludwig Institute takes into account other factors when estimating unemployment levels, such as those in work but living on poverty wages (currently $20,000 or less per annum), and/or those who are on a reduced work-week that they do not want. When these other factors are taken into account, the Ludwig Institute calculate that the 'true' rate of unemployment is actually 23.9 per cent of the US population (Ludwig Institute for Economic Prosperity 2021).

Globally, the pandemic has highlighted debt relationships between the powerful Northern capitalist countries and those in the Southern sphere. One estimate currently puts global debt at around $277 trillion, with $52 trillion of this figure being added from 2016 to the end of September 2020. Those wielding power in the Northern hemisphere introduced the 'Debt Service Suspension Initiative' to help alleviate debt burdens under the pandemic for the seventy-seven least developed countries. Under the Initiative, the countries that qualify can suspend their debt interest repayments to 'official creditors', such as the World Bank and other nations that lend, until June 2021 (Smith 2021). Yet they still have to pay back interest to private lending companies, such as JP Morgan. While interest payments can be suspended from 'official creditors', these repayments are added to total outstanding debt. Unfortunately, to apply for this temporary debt relief could lead to the credit worthiness of the country in question being downgraded, which then increase future borrowing costs (Smith 2021).

CONCLUSION

COVID-19 has brought class relations to the forefront in society. Not only is this apparent in the ways in which the neoliberal and austerity state is using the pandemic as an opportunity to develop new outlets for financialisation, but also in how the crisis has made existing class relations more visible in society, and, indeed, how the crisis has exacerbated and worsened the tensions, problems and inequalities within and between classes. Class relations are, indeed, evident in a diverse array of pandemic social forms. This chapter has provided a background and broad overview to these COVID-19 class relations by placing them within their financialised, neoliberal and imperialist class forms. This is an advantageous approach to adopt because it both 'concretises' the discussion of alienation and social class groups explored in Chapter 3, and it shows how the pandemic has both strengthened and, in some ways, changed class relations embedded in financialisation, neoliberalism and imperialism.

In the next chapter, we start to explore productive global value chains run by major corporations within the remit of this neoliberal, financialised and imperialist formation. Productive capitalists obviously use the profits they make to invest in new labour (variable capital) and new technology (constant capital) in order to secure greater amounts of surplus value (cf. Mandel 1992: 17). In reality, though, even productive capitalists today increasingly look to make money from unproductive financialised practices. The chapter explores how competitive pressures these inherent crisis tendencies operate in some of the productive spheres of the economy. Chapter 7 is devoted to discussing platform 'gig' labour, and it will be shown in that chapter that platform labour is at present fairly rare in the productive sector when compared with commercial sectors. This is why for now we will not discuss in the next current chapter digital platform labour. Instead, we turn our attention to productive capital and productive labour in the digital workplace.

We therefore begin the next chapter by examining the productive digital labour process. We will see that in recent years, digital technology has helped to spread 'lean' production techniques and ideology throughout productive workplaces. The 'lean' in 'lean production' is concerned with harnessing the latest technology to ensure that less human effort, less manufacturing space, and less hours to produce a product or undertake certain workplace tasks than is and was typically the case in industrial societies. Unlike mass production, then, advocates of lean production 'set their sights explicitly on perfection: continually declining costs, zero defects, zero inventories, and endless product variety' (Womack et al. 1990: 13–14). In later chapters, it will also become apparent that lean techniques have also seeped into unproductive and non-labour digital labour processes. Lean work patterns focus on reducing a workforce to its core competences. Lean sets its sights on employing digital technology and automation to intensify work, albeit with an ideological chant of empowering workers with decision-making capabilities. Ideally, lean production also employs the latest technology to monitor the changing consumer tastes of customers in order to change production output as when it is required (see also Dyer-Witheford 2015: 51). However, the actual implementation of lean techniques is patchy, and often its contradictory nature of both intensifying and empowering workers opens up spaces for workers to resist lean restructuring.

Chapter 5

PRODUCTIVE DIGITAL WORK BEFORE AND DURING COVID-19

═══════

INTRODUCTION

In 2019, the World Bank published a report, *The Changing Nature of Work*. The report takes stock of how automation, or digitised labour as defined in Chapters 1 and 3, is impacting the world of work. While it touches on many different types of work, the report explores in detail the effects of automation on what might be termed as productive labour. Among other things, it makes some important claims about the productive sectors of the global economy; the sectors that create surplus value. It suggests that automation has become a more prominent feature of the manufacturing sector in recent years; manufacturing, of course, being a main area of the productive sphere of capitalism. Yet, the report continues, this has caused some anxiety in society. Automation and digitised labour, argue some, will take jobs away from 'real' people (World Bank 2019: 20). While manufacturing in strong Northern capitalist economies is declining, and while jobs in this sector are increasingly automated, the World Bank argues that the shift to services nevertheless establishes new types of jobs (Word Bank 2019: 28–9). Think about the rise of digital labour on digital platforms. These all require a new group of workers and employees, including skilled IT designers and technicians, who can operate, run and repair these platforms and interact with customers on them (World Bank 2019: 20). At the same time, the report continues, 'the share of industrial employment, primarily manufacturing, has remained stable in the rest of the world' (World Bank 2019: 6). In low-income countries, for instance, 10 per cent of the total labour force worked in the manufacturing sector between 1991 and 2017. Upper-middle-income countries saw an even higher figure of 23 per cent. In some developing countries, the numbers employed by the manufacturing sector also saw an overall increase. In Vietnam, there was a rise from 9 per cent in 1991 to 25 per cent in 2017. In all of these cases, the digitisation of labour is apparent across a range of jobs.

COVID-19 has turned upside down many of the more optimistic scenarios of digital labour and work. Before we come to some of these issues in the main body of the chapter, it is worth saying that even before the pandemic, a number of global governance bodies were already painting a less optimistic picture of automation than that of the World Bank. Writing for the IMF, Berg et al. (2018a) argue that automation has many negative consequences for workers. Wages can still fall in the short term for employees in certain sectors affected by automation, while increased competition between workers for the jobs that remain also negatively affects wages. Unskilled workers are particularly vulnerable to these changes. In their *World Economic Outlook* for 2018, the IMF note that overall investment in the global economy since the 2008 crisis has been sluggish and recovery has been slow. Relatively low investments in technology can partly explain this protracted activity. Looking at data concerned with investments in research and technology, the IMF argues that countries that experienced above-median output losses from 2008 to 2018 have generally registered falling investments in research and development compared with some competitors. Similar results are gained if one looks at data on investments in industrial robots. According to the IMF, the data, 'indicates that the average change in density – measured as robot shipments per thousand hours worked – during the post-crisis period was higher in countries that had smaller post-crisis losses in output' (IMF 2018: 77). An OECD study concluded that labour productivity in countries at the frontier of cutting-edge technology increased at an annual rate of 3.5 per cent in the manufacturing sector throughout the 2000s. In comparison, labour productivity in non-frontier manufacturing firms rose by only 0.5 per cent across the same period (McGowan et al 2015: 2).

In a widely cited report in the United States, Hicks and Devaraji suggest that while productivity per American worker has increased, many manufacturing companies are employing fewer workers. According to Hicks and Devaraji, 'the automation and information technology advances absorbed by these sectors over this time period' is a major reason why fewer workers are required in some manufacturing plants (Hicks and Devaraji 2017: 4). That is to say, and in the terms mapped out in Chapter 1, these companies have embarked on a digitisation process that employs greater amounts of digitised automated labour; the latter of which has replaced workers in some parts of the US economy. But there also another story. In this alternative narrative, other countries, most notably China, have used their cheap labour to attract, within their borders, major digital companies and some of their global production chains. Global trade has therefore caused major problems for the US economy and its manufacturing base, particularly the impact of cheaper labour costs from overseas competitors, and these factors account for America's declining productivity rather than the impact of automation (Nager 2017).

From this brief discussion, it is obvious that these pre-COVID-19 reports arrive at different conclusions about the impact of digital technology on the productive workforce: some positive, some not so positive. Critically, however, optimistic and pessimistic views on digital technology in *productive* workplaces present one-sided accounts of contradictory and dialectical processes at play in historically specific class relations. We know that at the heart of these processes is exploited alienated labour. Capital's thirst for exploited labour and the surplus value this labour produces is nevertheless subject to resistance by workers, and this class struggle feeds into the contradictions and uneven development of capital. The Trades Union Congress (TUC) in the United Kingdom, for example, note that digital technology has *the potential* to create better working conditions. UK GDP will could be 10 per cent higher by 2030 – a £200 billion boost – as a result of artificial intelligence. Correctly, the TUC further argues these technological improvements to the UK economy are highly contradictory and are dependent to a large degree on class divisions in the workplace. And this is where the TUC departs significantly from the likes of the IMF, World Bank and so forth. The TUC recognises that power relations between workers and management in the workplace are vital areas of concern. 'Technological change is not the only factor shaping the future of work in the UK. As we argue . . . technology is not destiny. The distribution of power in the workplace and beyond will be the critical determinant of the kind of future we face' (TUC 2018: 13).

Trade unions are, of course, pivotal in giving workers a voice in how technological advancements come to be applied to the workplace. Since the 1990s, though, trade unions have been involved in fewer and fewer workplace negotiations in the United Kingdom. In this chapter, we therefore explore how historically specific class relations are at play in the digitisation of productive labour and in the implementation of automated digitised technology in the productive workplace. As Chapter 4 argued, capitalisation, in the form of financialisation, has seeped into the productive sphere of major economies, and has done so through digital technology. This chapter discusses these points in detail, and also explains how COVID-19 has, in a short space of time, aggravated many of the problems that were already present in the productive sphere of the economy.

FINANCIALISATION, IMPERIALIST MANUFACTURING AND (DIGITAL) VALUE CHAINS

As noted in the previous section, there is some disagreement among economists and policy experts as to whether digital technology will create positive or negative outcomes for the workforce. In their report from the United States, Hicks and Devaraji (2017) argue that some of the highest growth in the American manufacturing sector was seen in computer and electronics products, which grew a staggering 829 per cent between 1998 and 2012, while there was a downturn in the manufacturing of minerals, fabricated metals, furniture, textiles, apparel, paper and plastics. Nager argues that by 2015, America had a trade deficit of $91.8 billion in the manufacture of advanced-technology products, with it exporting only 78.9 per cent of what it imports in this area (Nager 2017: 14).

The important point to observe is that digital technology reproduces the contradictory social relations of capitalism, albeit in new guises and forms. To understand this point in clearer terms, we need to analyse how the productive sectors of the economy have undergone a number of major transformations in the last few decades. The United Kingdom and the United States provide a useful analytical starting point through which to explore this issue. Between June 1978 and September 2017, the proportion of jobs in the United Kingdom accounted for by the manufacturing, and mining and quarrying sectors fell from 26.4 per cent to 7.8 per cent, while the proportion of jobs accounted for by the services sector increased from 63.2 per cent to 83.4 per cent (ONS 2018a: 14). The United States has witnessed a similar drop in the number of workers employed by industrial capitalists. According to Moody and Post (2014), the number of US production workers fell by roughly a third from over 12.5 million in 1994 to just over 8.4 million in 2013. 'Altogether, the industrial core of the working class, including goods production, transportation and warehousing, utilities and information, has fallen from 32 percent of the workforce in the 1980s to 21.4 percent of all production workers in 2010–13' (Moody and Post 2014: 298). But there have been peaks and troughs during this time. In 2018, for example, more manufacturing employment was generated for US workers than at any other point in the last two decades. A year later, the picture looked bleaker. 'Since January of 2019, the sector has added just 28,000 jobs, compared to 126,000 in the first six months of 2018' (Stettner and Novello 2019). Stettner and Novello also note that while corporate profits have been soaring, fewer people are now employed overall in manufacturing since the early 1990s. As we will see below, part of the still profitable fortunes of manufacturing rests in the ability of large productive firms to engage in imperialist practices and move part of their operations overseas to countries, especially to the Southern hemisphere, where costs are cheaper. But this is only part of the story. While it might be the case that fewer workers in dominant capitalist countries are now employed in manufacturing, there is nevertheless a greater level of exploitation of those who remain in productive sectors like manufacturing.

Before we delve further into these matters, we also need to note that for many years financial practices have been a staple diet for productive sectors of the economy. In the 1920s, Ford and General Motors were offering credit to their staff to buy their cars. Subsidiary companies called 'financial captives' enabled the company to facilitate car sales to consumers and, in the process, generate customer loyalty (Sinapi and Gagne 2016: 44). But the move towards financialisation of the economy has significantly altered and changed these more innocent practices in the productive sector of the economy. In the United States, the financial asset holdings of the manufacturing sector doubled from 25.1 per cent to 52.8 per cent of sales between 1980 and 2014 (Davis 2016: 124), while stock buybacks – the process by which managers of firms improve their stock market measure on the likes of share price and return on equity – has also increased. Shareholder value has therefore become an important consideration for managers of large productive corporations (Davis 2016: 131). That is to say, global competitive pressure in productive sectors has persuaded companies in these sectors to invest in the capitalisation of unproductive financialised enterprises.

Since the 1990s, car manufacturers have formed new intricate financial mechanisms, which are not necessarily related to manufacturing cars. Through its company the General Motors Acceptance Corporation (GMAC), for example, the financial subsidiaries of General Motors have become enmeshed in the likes of insurance, mortgage loans, financial investments and assets securitisation (Sinapi and Gagne 2016: 45). Established in 1919 to provide finance to customers of General Motors, by 2008 GMAC had obtained permission from the Federal Reserve to become a banking holding company. 'In the following year, its financing activities were extended to Chrysler's products and the Ally Bank was established, called Ally Financial since 2010. Also, in that year GM bought AmeriCredit, an important company in the segment of subprime loans to vehicle acquisition, for US$3.5 billion' (Borghi et al. 2013: 397). But it is not just General Motors who now play the financialisation game. Other car manufacturers – Toyota, Volkswagen, Ford, PSA and Renault – have all pursued similar financial strategies (Sinapi and Gagne 2016: 52–3; see also Bailey et al. 2010: 316; Froud et al. 2006).

Manufacturing operates on a hierarchical scale, and financialisation has deepened the stratified nature of global manufacturing production. Leading capitalist nations, led by the United States, have used their expertise in research, design, finance and so forth to bolster their dominant positions. To give one illustration, between 1980 and 2001, the United States dominated the global share of high-tech sectors, such as computers and office machinery and communication systems. During this period, they maintained a 32 per cent share of this industry, while Germany saw their share drop in half to 5 per cent and Japan's share fell by a third to 13 per cent (Panitch and Gindin 2012: 276). Relatively new financial devices have also enabled a wave of mergers and acquisitions to take place. From the 1990s onwards, there has been a tenfold increase in the net value of annual global acquisitions by the top 500 global corporations (Foster and McChesney 2012: 75). One UK report by Bell and Tomlinson (2018: 3) found that Britain's top 100 firms now account for 23 per cent of total revenue across British businesses, while the revenue streams in many other sectors, such as retail, are increasingly concentrated in fewer firms. The report also notes that the concentration of business in the United Kingdom has been accompanied by these firms 'making use of a relatively small amount of labour' (Bell and Tomlinson 2018: 4). For Moody (2007), the decentralisation of manufacturing production along value chains, and the re-engineering and reducing of the workforce by technology, has seen many manufacturing jobs disappear, while increasing the centralisation of control (Moody 2007: 31).

These trends enhance the corporate global power of leading firms. In terms of the US car industry during the 1990s, 'there was no longer a series of national automobile industries but rather a global oligopoly for automobile production, where five multinational firms . . . produced nearly half the world's motor vehicles, and the ten largest firms produced 70 percent of the world's motor vehicles' (Foster and McChesney 2012: 75). Moody makes similar observations, but also adds some important points. He notes that the big three US car manufacturers, Ford, Chrysler and General Motors, consolidated their production base and dominance by following the Japanese lean model in establishing three tiers of supply chains and introducing just-in-time schedules within them. Tier 1 suppliers make bigger and specialised component parts for cars, develop their own high-tech networked plants with the latest engineering and design skills, have greater influence with corporations, can adapt more flexibly to changes in technology because they have a more diverse range of competencies, and they offer higher wages for skilled labour. In 2012, twenty-nine Tier 1 companies were earning above $2 billion. Tier 1 firms also place downward pressure on Tier 2 and Tier 3 companies, which lead to many smaller firms in the supply chain eventually going bust or being submerged into the larger firms. 'By 2008–9 the top ten North American auto parts supplier firms controlled a third of the original equipment market that supplied assemblers. Continuing into 2015, mergers in the auto parts sector grew larger and larger, such as German-owned ZF's $12 billion purchase of TRW' (Moody 2017: 51). Uneven regional development has followed these trends. In the case of lower tier suppliers, their relatively weak position has further knock-on effects in terms of value capture. If they make less money, then less corporation tax can be collected, which then means less funds are generated by local government to meet local and regional needs (Pavlínek and Ženka 2016).

Corporate monopoly power also provides sustenance for imperialist global value chains (GVCs). The United Nations Conference on Trade and Development (UNCTAD) define GVCs in the following way: 'Raw material extracted in one country may be exported first to a second country for processing, then exported again to a manufacturing plant in a third country, which may then export it to a fourth for final consumption . . . Such cross-border production chains, which may comprise only two countries, a region or a global network, are commonly referred to as global value chains' (UNCTAD 2013: 1). Theoretically, mainstream analysis argues that different 'links' in GVCs gain competitive advantage to the extent that they produce competitive advantages through higher value-added economic activities. Examples of these forms of competitive advantage include 'product differentiation, brand reputation, industrial upgrading and customer relations' (Selwyn 2019: 75). As a result, firms that gain competitive advantages can then increase their costs to lower tier firms who wish to participate in these respective GVCs. Lower tier firms are willing to pay higher costs on the assumption they will reap rewards by having access to the latest innovations, and so on. But, as Selwyn notes, mainstream arguments fail to fully explain structurally embedded uneven development, relations of exploitation and inequality between workers in the Northern hemisphere and workers in the Southern hemisphere. According to mainstream GVC analysis, for example, workers in the Southern hemisphere receive on average lower wages than those in the North because there are low entry barriers and higher cost competition to these particular GVCs. Yet this 'cannot explain why workers employed in supplier firms within GVCs in the global South are often more productive than workers doing the same jobs in the global North, whilst earning only a fraction of the wage' (Selwyn 2019: 77). Marxist analysis, with its emphasis on exploitation and oppression, provides the theoretical tools to explain such global disparities with workers in productive GVCs.

In an age of corporate and monopoly capital, many 'intermediate' services that mediate goods to the individual consumer are centralised under the auspices of a corporate body (Mandel 1971: 386–7). This is even more pronounced today on a global scale. Manufacturing exports are becoming ever more fused with the service sector. According to UNCTAD, 'almost half (46%) of value-added inputs to exports is contributed by service-sector activities, as most manufacturing exports require services for their production' (UNCTAD 2013: iii). Crucially, GVCs increase the trade in 'intermediate goods', which are parts traded across the world used in production networks to assemble manufactured goods and products. East and Southeast Asian exporters, for instance, ensure that a high percentage of their exports are intermediate goods, which are then used in the exports of other countries (UNCTAD 2013: 13). Manufacturers, such as those in the auto industry, rely on global business in intermediate goods, and so it is no surprise that trade in intermediate goods is now twice as big as trade in final goods. Developed economies, in fact, rely ever more on intermediate import for their exports, which in turn add to the domestic exports of intermediate goods for developing countries (UNCTAD 2013: 13).

If we switch our attention to the production of digital products, the imperialist form of this trade is even more noticeable. Corporations outsource some of their production activities to an array of workforces and labour processes across the globe. In terms of the production of surplus value, a number of digital media companies draw upon the productive labour of workers in other countries to build its core products. China is often heralded as the main exporter of computers in the world. By 2009, its high-technology exports amounted to $376.9 billion, and this was the equivalent to 31.4 per cent of total exports (Hart-Landsberg 2013: 45). Digital tech giant, Apple, contracts out part of its production for goods like the iPod and iPhone to the Chinese electronic corporation, Foxconn. Foxconn also operates an assembly and shipment manufacturing process, drawing on the labour of thousands of Chinese workers, 24 hours per day, 365 days per year. Based in America, Apple deals with issues around branding, design, marketing, logos, copyrights and so on, while manufacturing Apple products occurs in China and elsewhere. Combined, all of these activities generate a global consumer class for Apple products. Foxconn is therefore one of Apple's major manufacturing branches and helps to generate the global working class by assembling Apple products (Ngai et al. 2016: 170). It employs about a million workers just in China, and the factory compounds of Foxconn alone employ between 50,000 and 400,000 workers, all labouring under military-style management methods (Ngai et al. 2016: 171).

Of course, while the component parts of, say, an iPhone might be produced in a huge factory like Foxconn, the actual manufacture of the major component and sub-component parts occur elsewhere in outsourced Chinese factories and in manufacturing plants in other East Asian countries. Furthermore, the production of supplementary component parts, such as semiconductor chips from silicon, plastic elements for iPhones, aluminium silicate glass, chemicals and epoxy, cardboard for containers and so on, occurs in China and in other East Asian countries like the Philippines. Divisions of labour on this global scale enable Apple to gain a monopoly share on the profits accruing through this global commodity chain (Clelland 2014: 83–4; Hart-Landsberg 2013: 33–8). As Ngai et al. observe: 'Apple's strength is well illustrated by its ability to capture an extraordinary 58.5 percent of the value of the iPhone. Particularly notable is the fact that labour costs in China account for the smallest share, only 1.8 percent or nearly US$10, of the US$549 retail price of the iPhone 4 (16GB model)' (Ngai et al. 2016: 169). In other words, Apple retain 58 per cent of the iPhone's sale price, which is more than any other firms in this supply chain.

Next in line to gain the biggest shares in sale price are major electronic firms like LG and Samsung who develop display and memory chips. They receive 5 per cent and 7 per cent, respectively, of final sale price (Kraemer et al. 2011: 4), while the smallest share goes to labour costs in China. Cheap labour and cheap land in China are therefore given to technological and digital companies that reside in other countries. Parts are sent to China, so that cheap Chinese labour can manufacture the computers, which are then exported to other parts of the world. While China therefore exports computers, it does so only in its capacity as a place to assemble computers rather than actually owning them. 'In sum, China's rise as an export powerhouse is primarily due to its position as the final assembly platform for transnational corporate cross-border production networks' (Hart-Landsberg 2013: 46). There is then some truth to the point that the sub-processes of a production chain are based in countries where costs, taxes, labour regimes and so on favour capital's interests. Global Northern populations are seen as consumers, while the global South populations are viewed as producers (Lauesen and Cope 2015: 3).

One further important factor of imperialism needs to be highlighted. Today, imperialism also operates through explicit force and unfree labour. According to LeBaron and Phillips:

> Common attributes of unfree labour include debt bondage, manipulation of contracts and credit, violence and threats of violence against workers

or their families, and the predatory overcharging of workers for services such as accommodation or recruitment fees. (LeBaron and Phillips
2019: 1)

As Crane et al. (2017) have noted, GVCs can, in some instances and in
some places, enlist workers through labour-market intermediaries like
temporary agencies, recruitment agencies, gangmasters and payroll providers. These intermediaries will also recruit workers from other labour-
market intermediaries. In productive industries like construction, it is
not uncommon to operate through these tiers in order to obtain labour
as and when required. Yet it is exactly this complexity in how labour-
market intermediaries behave and operate, along with the changing legal
status of many migrant workers around the world, which makes it difficult to assess when a company is employing forced and unfree labour.
    None of the discussion so far is to imply that productive workers in
GVCs are simply passive beings who do not react to being exploited.
The ability of these workers to 'resist' exploitative conditions is reliant
on local labour processes. In their study of Ethiopian GVCs, Oya and
Schaefer found a number of reasons for workers to engage in disruptive
workplace practices, particularly strikes. Broadly, low wages and wage-
setting systems are one prime cause for discontent among many workers
in productive GVCs, but other reasons why Ethiopian workers went on
strike included excessive working time, poor quality canteen food and
excessive negative treatment by the supervisory non-labour. 'Indirect'
forms of resistance by workers include leaving the workplace and not
returning, being absent, not taking up the opportunity to do overtime
and 'foot dragging' (Oya and Schaefer 2021: 5–6). Even so, COVID-
19 has highlighted what Lawreniuk (2020: 199) terms 'the exemplary
hyper-precarity of workers in global production networks', which we
now consider in more detail.

COVID-19 AND PRODUCTIVE (DIGITAL) VALUE CHAINS

COVID-19 has changed many of the processes outlined above. According
to the OECD (2020), the sectors most likely to be affected by the pandemic are service sectors, such as tourism, entertainment and restaurants,
primarily because these sectors were shut down for longer periods than
other sectors. Even so, the pandemic has many negative consequences
on the productive sectors of the economy. To begin to understand this
impact, let us look at the United Kingdom. Between March and April
2020, UK production output fell by a record 20.3 per cent, with manufacturing registering the sharpest decline and falling by 24.3 per cent.

Mining and quarrying fell by 12.2 per cent, electricity and gas by 9.5 per cent, and water and waste fell by 5.3 per cent. In manufacturing, the 24.3 per cent drop was headed by transport equipment, which fell by 50.2 per cent, followed by motor vehicles, trailers and semi-trailers, falling by a record 90.3 per cent (ONS 2020h). According to another report published in late May, a quarter of British manufacturing companies were planning to make some redundancies in the six months following the report's survey, with a further 45 per cent considering undertaking the same measure. Nearly 40 per cent of the companies surveyed thought it would take a year to return to normal trading conditions. Only a third of companies felt they would have all their staff back on the payroll once the pandemic had subsided. While 94 per cent of manufacturing companies said they were continuing to trade during the pandemic, only 11.7 per cent were operating at full capacity (Make UK 2020).

These developments have a negative impact on GVCs in seven interrelated ways. First, the United Nations Industrial Development Organization (UNIDO) estimated in April 2020 that lockdown measures in Northern economies had impacted on GVCs in Southern-based countries. This is not to deny that global production had already started to slow prior to the pandemic because of trade wars between China and the United States. But since the onset of the pandemic, UNIDO insist that supply chain disruptions in global manufacturing, alongside falling commodity prices, resulted, since early February, in a $50 billion drop in manufacturing production. Developing countries looked to lose nearly $800 billion in export revenue across 2020. Moreover, continues the report, developing countries will also experience a flight of capital due to volatility in global financial markets (UNIDO 2020).

Alarmingly, these changes could serve to exacerbate the worse tendencies in global value chains as noted above. Before the virus, as stated by the International Labour Organisation (ILO), 188 million working-age adults across the world were unemployed, while only 57 per cent of working adults had gained employment, or 3.3 billion people. A majority of these people were in low paid and informal work that gave them little protection against falling into poverty. Unsurprisingly, the pandemic aggravated these conditions. Global unemployment shot up. The ILO estimated for 2020 that the fall in working hours across the world was the equivalent to 305 million full-time jobs. About 38 per cent of the global workforce, or 1.25 billion workers, gain employment in high-risk sectors characterised by low pay, low skills and low social protection. These sectors include accommodation and food services, wholesale and retail trade, and repair of motor vehicles, real estate and, finally, manufacturing. All of these sectors experienced the worse labour market effects from the first stages of COVID-19 alongside declining production (ILO 2020a; see also below).

Secondly, the World Bank's *Global Investment Competitiveness Report 2019/2020*, presented an equally gloomy diagnosis of the world economy, with its analysis made just before and then during COVID-19. The report stated that before COVID-19, foreign direct investment (FDI) by major capitalist nations in developing countries had already started to dip. In the mid-2000s, FDI to developing countries stood at around 4 per cent of GDP of those countries, while by 2017–18, this had fallen to 2 per cent. A number of reasons account for this decline. Digital technologies have enabled investors to engage in other types of ventures, while protectionism through trade wars have eroded investor confidence. More than half of the 2,400 global business executives who took part in the report said they had experienced a decline in employment levels, firm productivity or investments as a result of protectionism (World Bank 2020b: 3–6). COVID-19 significantly worsened these conditions. For example, the World Bank found that, in 2020, the pandemic had adversely affected more than three-quarters of investors through demand- and supply-side channels. In a survey of foreign investors conducted in March–April 2020, the World Bank states:

> Nearly four in five MNEs (multinational enterprises) report reductions in revenues and profits over the past three months, on average by 40 percent . . . Demand has fallen sharply because of high uncertainty and precautionary behaviour of consumers, resulting in reduced consumer spending and corporate orders . . . The employment impacts are particularly likely to worsen: three in five businesses expect to have to reduce employment in the second quarter, on average by 25 percent. (World Bank 2020b: 7–8)

In May 2021, however, JP Morgan's global manufacturing index found that global manufacturing had strengthened in the second quarter of the year. Production increased at the fastest pace in over a decade and manufacturing production increasing for the tenth successive month. Total new orders and new export businesses, moreover, grew at the quickest rate since May 2010 (JP Morgan 2021). At the same time, a more recent World Bank report found that the pandemic had once again exacerbated many of the negative conditions in the productive sphere of the global economy. For example, COVID-19 reproduced in new ways uneven development between the most powerful capitalist nations and less powerful nations. In June 2021, the World Bank reported that global economic growth would 'accelerate' to 5.6 per cent during the year, mainly due to recoveries in the economies of the United States and

China. But the level of global GDP in 2021 is thought to be 3.2 per cent below pre-pandemic levels. Worryingly, the World Bank notes:

> Among low-income economies, where vaccination has lagged, growth has been revised lower to 2.9%. Setting aside the contraction last year, this would be the slowest pace of expansion in two decades. The group's output level in 2022 is projected to be 4.9% lower than pre-pandemic projections. Fragile and conflict-affected low-income economies have been the hardest hit by the pandemic, and per capita income gains have been set back by at least a decade. (World Bank 2021)

UNCTAD made a similar forecast. In their *World Investment Report 2020*, UNCTAD claimed that FDI would fall by up to 40 per cent in 2020, taking it down to below $1 trillion for the first time since 2005. FDI had been declining before COVID-19, but by the end 2021 the expected level of FDI was predicted to decline by 60 per cent from 2015 to reach less than $900 billion. However, UNCTAD also noted that large tech multinational enterprises (MNEs) had before the pandemic been purchasing successful start-up companies. Through these purchases, they had engaged in vertical integration, such as branching into retail markets and other service industries. 'The pandemic could reinforce the position of tech and digital companies with the growth of e-commerce solutions' (UNCTAD 2020: 7). A year later, UNCTAD reported that FDI flows to Europe had fallen by 80 per cent, while in North America the fall was estimated to be 42 per cent. Africa suffered a 16 per cent fall in FDI, while FDI flows to China increased by 6 per cent. However, Latin America and the Caribbean saw sharp declines in FDI by around 45 per cent (UNCTAD 2021: x–xi).

Cutbacks and downturns have therefore materialised in productive GVCs. UNCTAD notes that the pandemic has led to manufacturing being scaled down in the automotive, electronics and apparel (fashion and garment business) industries. This has seen reductions in production in different parts of the developing world in the Southern hemisphere. Nissan, for instance, reduced automotive production in Thailand, while apparel factories have been closed in Cambodia, Myanmar and Vietnam. UNCTAD also notes: 'The slowdown in manufacturing is expected to affect investment throughout 2020 and 2021. Announced greenfield investment in automotive production in the first quarter of 2020 fell by 67 per cent to $628 million and in computer and electronics by 36 per cent to $752 million as compared with the quarterly average of 2019' (UNCTAD 2020: 41). The ILO presents additional evidence of the devastating impact the virus has had on the global productive sectors. Falling consumer demand had by June 2020 placed 292 million jobs in manufacturing supply chains at high risk, with possible cuts in income, working hours or unemployment for these workers. Imported inputs in the manufacturing sector, for example, plastics, machinery, fabricated metals, suffered a 35 per cent disruption, which had adverse consequences on production. Those manufacturing sectors that have high or medium vulnerability for imported inputs also place workers in these sectors at risk – 255 million, or 68 per cent, of global manufacturing employment was thought at the time to be in danger (ILO 2020b).[4]

Thirdly, such is the complexity of supply and value chains that even before the pandemic struck, few, if any, CEOs of corporations actually had complete information to hand about their Tier 2 and Tier 3 suppliers. A global company like Volkswagen, for example, might have over a million suppliers located in different tiers. No senior managers of a corporation will know all of these suppliers. When the pandemic broke, this highly complex system was exposed and its convoluted nature laid bare. In February 2020, a report by the World Economic Forum found that the virus impacted on 90 per cent of the Tier 1 and Tier 2 suppliers of the Fortune 1000 multinational companies (Foster 2020: 7).

Fourthly, the pandemic has also exposed the uneven nature of risk assessments of supply and value chains. Pre-COVID, supply and value chains were assessed on factors such as whether goods and products would be delivered on time. Less was asked about cataclysmic events that might disrupt and disable supply and value chains or changing patterns of consumer behaviour through such events. To overcome this weakness, corporations have started to investigate and invest in technology that will build resilience in global chains, such as dashboards that can track and trace products moving through a chain (Free and Hecimovic 2020). Moreover, firms are beginning to look at whether corporate bodies should buy products from local suppliers, even though they might be more expensive, in order to find a balance between 'a lean, efficient supply chain that carries no fat (the ideal of just-in-time inventory regimes), but is susceptible to unexpected shocks, and an inefficient one that may be robust but expensive to maintain' (Free and Hecimovic 2020: 17).

Fifthly, COVID-19 has exposed the imperialist class relations embedded in supply and value chains. In one qualitative study of clothing supply chains in South Asian countries, interviewees from supplier com-

---

[4] UNCTAD does, however, sound a note of optimism in relation to some industries in the developing world. The digital economy in India, for example, might continue to attract investment through acquisitions. But as we will see below, COVID-19 has negatively affected suppliers in global supply and value chains.

panies said that during lockdown, major brands had exerted their power to cancel or postpone orders that had in fact been completed. The costs of COVID-19 are therefore switched to the suppliers, who had already paid overhead costs, labour and raw materials (Majumdar et al. 2020). Factory owners, who already operate on tight margins, are thereby left out of pocket and unable to pay their staff (Worker Rights Consortium 2020). Numerous workers at the end of these supply chains already exist on low wages with little prospect of managing to save money. Labour-intensive manufacturing sectors like the global garment industry, for example, employ a high proportion of female workers, who have been hit hard by falling demand for these products as well by turbulence and instabilities in the industry's supply chains brought about by the pandemic (ILO 2020a: 9).

Sixthly, exploitative relations in value and supply chains, though, are not only apparent in the Southern hemisphere. They are also readily apparent in Northern countries too. A case in point is apparel manufacturing in the United Kingdom. Regional differentiation characterises this productive sector in the United Kingdom. The East Midlands' apparel manufacturing hub in particular has been growing in terms of its above-average firm size compared with other regional hubs. Between 2008 and 2012, a number of these firms across the United Kingdom employed on average up to four people, while in the East Midlands 13 per cent of such firms employed between 20 and 99 people, and 2 per cent employed over 100 (Hammer et al. 2015). Employment rights in these factories are, however, often at breaking point, with limited or no employment contracts for workers, the under- or non-payment of wages, work conditions that put the health and safety of workers at risk, bullying and threats from managers, and little information given to workers about their rights (Hammer et al. 2015: 10). These extremely poor working conditions were once again found to be in operation during the pandemic, despite calls in 2019 for changes in the law to protect these vulnerable workers (ETI 2020). One report published in June 2020, found that a number of apparel manufacturing factories in Leicester, which also produced large volumes of clothes for the Boohoo fashion chain and corporation, were operating with limited COVID-19 working guidelines. For example, the factories were operating at full capacity with little social distancing, hand sanitiser or PPE. Lack of official inspections of these factories by the Health and Safety Executive is also common, enabling management to disregard COVID-19 regulations, and even telling workers who tested positive for COVID-19 not to inform other workers. Moreover, some workers in the factories reported being pressured by management to continue production even while owners claim they were furloughing staff (Labour Behind the Label 2020). Interestingly, there is some evidence to suggest that modern labour slavery initially decreased in some countries because of the pandemic. The charity, Unseen, dealt with 515 cases of labour exploitation across the United Kingdom during 2020, which was considerably lower than in previous years. Unseen claims that the 'lack of open venues' during the pandemic was the main reason for this decline (Unseen 2020).

Finally, digital platforms, according to Foster and Suwandi (2020), enable multinational corporations to maintain an at-a-distance regulation of different labour processes they are linked into. Indeed, upheavals in transport and shipment costs, particularly through the dominance of standardised containers, and a communication revolution, especially through the onset of fibre optic cables, cloud computing, the Internet and so on, have created an immense, complex, hierarchical and interrelated number of supply and value chains, which become almost impossible to disentangle and quantify, especially when a crisis of the magnitude of the pandemic suddenly erupts. 'When the novel coronavirus outbreak occurred in Wuhan in China, it was discovered that fifty-one thousand companies globally had at least one direct supplier in Wuhan, while five million companies had at least one two tier supplier there' (Foster and Suwandi 2020: 7). In the next section, we look in more detail at some of the digital workplace strategies that productive capitalists adopt in order to exploit productive labour.

EXPLOITATION AND THE LEAN PRODUCTIVE WORKPLACE

In terms of ideology, changes in the productive workplace are naturally caged in a rather cosy and unthreatening managerial language. Nowhere is this clearer than in the influential management ideology of lean production, which emerged during the 1970s as a new movement in the work landscape to save us from the dying embers of mass industrial production. Gaining prominence in 1970s Japan at the Toyota motor company, lean production is, in theory at least, predicated on multi-skilled workers at all levels of an organisation employing 'highly flexible, increasingly automated machines to produce volumes of products in enormous variety' (Womack et al. 1990: 13). Digital technology is therefore closely associated with lean production, but one further attractive aspect of lean production for some capitalists, managers and policymakers is the idea that products are created 'just-in-time'. This refers to the ability of an organisation to build products according to rapidly changing consumer preferences and tastes. In terms of machines, the thinking here is that businesses should invest in the latest digital technol-

ogy in order to develop a continuous flow of products to suit fluid consumer demands and tastes. In practice, this means that machines must
be adaptable and flexible enough to suit the rate of sales in a marketplace. 'The goal is to have raw materials, or parts and components from
your suppliers, enter one door and flow with hardly a pause as they are
assembled into finished goods' (Henderson and Larco 1999: 58). A lean
workforce is therefore one that is multi-skilled in the sense that individual workers can operate machines when they are running and can then
maintain machines when they are idle and even fix them when faults are
spotted. In terms of production efficiency, a study in 1989 estimated that
Japanese car manufacturers averaged only seventeen labour hours per
car, compared with twenty-five hours in US plants. And Japanese manufacturing maintained higher quality, 'with 50 percent fewer defects than
their American and European counterparts' (Babson 1995: 8).

'Quality' in production is also related to worker empowerment, and
this is an important point. For lean enthusiasts, empowerment through
digital technology can be achieved by equipping workers with a variety
of skills and tasks. And this makes perfect sense under a lean regime
because each worker can now undertake several tasks, which of course
cuts down the number of workers one must employ. Ideally, multi-skilled
workers are given a degree of autonomy and discretion to be inventive
and to solve problems in the workplace. Being inventive means, moreover, encouraging workers to move across workplace boundaries, to communicate with other workers, to initiate new projects and solve common
problems in a team. Lean managers thereby inspire fellow workers to
view an organisation as an integrated whole. By sharing knowledge
throughout a whole organisation, teamwork preferably 'builds up trust,
improves communications and develops interdependence' (Oakland
1989: 236).

Lean production is associated with the financialisation of the workplace because the pursuit of shareholder value implies restructuring a
company to ensure maximum financial returns and again the drastic
elimination of what is considered as waste. Lean production also stresses
that companies need to focus on their distinctive 'core competencies'
to remain competitive in their chosen markets and therefore relinquish
non-core activities, or at least parcel them out to other firms (Weil 2014:
50). But core competencies do not necessarily refer to physical or tangible properties. It is more often the case that they refer to underlying
skills, tacit knowledge, networks, specific emotions, brand identities and
so on, which help to produce successful products. Key to establishing
core competencies, then, is to off-load what is not required for financial success and restructure and exploit key capabilities. Lean logistics

naturally align themselves to core competencies because lean is founded on the belief that a business should only hold onto small batches of inventory to ensure any excess is eliminated.

The relationship between digital technology, lean and productive labour is crucial in discerning changes in the fortunes of employees in the workplace today, especially through the extraction of surplus value. Technology can compress and quicken up the turnover time of productive capital in order to procure larger quantities of surplus value. In those industries that require the exploitation of productive labour to gain profits, then investing in new technology will enable a capitalist to engage in product innovation, intensify labour and reduce costs of constant capital; for example, employing less machines but using them more efficiently (Smith 1997: 119–20; see also Carchedi 2011: 188; Smith 2000: 60; Umney 2018: 54–5). In lean times, every second of every minute is vital for capital in generating surplus value. Moody presents a useful illustration:

> The 2015 contract agreement between Ford and the United Auto Workers grants the company one minute less in break time for each hour worked each day by each of Ford's 53,000 unionised workers. That amounts to more than seven thousand extra hours per work per day for the entire workforce, the equivalent of almost four years for the company at no extra cost (Moody 2017: 16).[5]

These technological forms of exploitation are, in turn, refracted into earnings and income. One study, based on the years 2009–2014, found that while some UK professions, particularly those in finance, did relatively well in terms of real earnings, many others in productive sectors fared less well. In agriculture, for example, real average gross hourly pay fell by 16.6 per cent, while in the mining sector gross hourly pay fell by 15.1 per cent during this period, in construction it fell by 9.9 per cent, while manufacturing saw gross hourly pay fall by 7.7 per cent (Clarke and Greg 2018). These changes are also evident in the United States. Kristal (2013), for example, revealed that those who worked in American manufacturing, construction and transportation all saw on

---

[5] It should also be noted that in the unproductive world of e-commerce and retail, one will similarly find the latest range of automated technology, or digitised labour, being employed to reduce worker costs. Through automation, Amazon has managed to reduce the time to just one minute that a warehouse worker takes to take an item off the warehouse shelf to box it and then ship it. Robots and automated machines then take over and complete the task (McFarland 2016).

average decreases in respect to their share of national income – wages, salaries, fringe benefits, firms' profits, interest, rent and so forth. 'Since the mid-1970s, labour's share decreased by 14 percentage points in manufacturing, 10 percentage points in transportation, and five in construction' (Kristal 2013: 365; see also Kristal and Cohen 2016: 5). Intensive exploitation through the use of technology does not, then, necessarily translate into greater wages or income.

Importantly, productive capitalists have managed to increase the rate of exploitation, in part, by disciplining their respective workforce. Indeed, relative exploitation of a workforce, by introducing new technology, can also exist side-by-side with absolute exploitation underpinned by attacks on labour rights in the workplace and so forth (Gough 2003). Between 2004 and 2010 in European 'liberal' countries like the United Kingdom and Ireland, which have readily and radically transformed Keynesian demand management and welfare states to favour the free flow of capital over social rights and welfare entitlements (see Jessop 2010), there was a rise in jobs with high work intensity but low levels of empowerment of workers, especially among semi-skilled and non-skilled workers (Gallie and Zhou 2013: 139).

During the pandemic, these productive spheres of the economy have been considerably shaken by events. The Society of Motor Manufacturers and Traders (SMMT) found in their survey that in the four months of 2020, there was a 32 per cent decline in the global light vehicle market, while global shutdowns of assembly plants and car dealerships have negatively impacted on Tier 1, 2 and 3 suppliers. In the United Kingdom, car production dipped in April 2020 to its lowest level since the Second World War – down by 99.7 per cent (SMMT 2020). Unsurprisingly, this decline has heightened anxieties and stress among productive workers, as well as among workers in other unproductive sectors, such as retail. In their representative survey of 2,000 UK workers during the pandemic, Shaheen and Jesse (2020) found that almost half of their respondents 'somewhat' or 'completely' agreed with the statement that they are worried about their job because of coronavirus. One in four of the workers said they are only one month away from not paying their rent or mortgage if their income stopped, while a further 60 per cent are less than three months away. Dramatic declines in manufacturing lead in turn to increasing anxieties of workers in these manufacturing plants.

Predictably, the changes wrought by the virus have affected wages and incomes across many work sectors, including productive sectors. An ONS survey of UK earnings growth suggests that between February and April 2019 and February and April 2020, the construction sector saw negative earnings growth, estimated at a negative 1.8 per cent.

Manufacturing also saw very weak growth during this period at 0.1 per cent (ONS 2020i). Another study, which analysed data on self-reported earnings in February 2020 compared with April 2020, makes some interesting points. On average, the authors found that men working in the UK financial and insurance services sector experienced no loss of income. Manufacturing, construction, transport and storage – which are part of productive class relations – saw the largest fall in average earnings. A number of middle-class occupations, which have some autonomy over their working conditions, were less affected by the pandemic in terms of earnings. Social class once more takes on a number of guises here (Arnold and Jaccarini 2020).

It is important to observe that rising levels of exploitation were already noticeable in many productive workplaces before the pandemic. These rising levels appeared through other forms as well, such as increased stress levels of workers. In their quantitative and qualitative examination of the automotive plants, General Motors UK and Poland and BMW-UK and VW-Motors Poland, Stewart et al. (2016) discovered many similarities between how lean production was operationalised at these companies. Far from workers feeling liberated by so-called participation–collaboration with management in their work allocation and duties, many reported that lean techniques intensified their everyday work routines. Continuous technological improvement, a leitmotif of lean production, was employed by managers to get skilled workers to do other tasks for which they had limited training to undertake properly. At BMW-UK, one maintenance engineer complained that there was an expectation that all maintenance engineers would carry out other production operations when their normal workload was less busy. Yet, from the perspective of the engineers, managers had not invested in sufficient training for workers to carry out these additional repair tasks. Stewart et al. found similar sentiments being expressed by workers at GM-Poland. Both UK and Polish workers also spoke about how work had become intensified. Taken as a whole, lean routines unintentionally produced a collective worker experience of increased levels of stress, which would also often appear and manifest in physical disorders and ill-health (Stewart et al. 2016: 160; see also Krzywdzinski 2017).

In his comparative project of the United States, United Kingdom and Germany, which explored the role of supervisory non-labour in two branches of mechanical engineering (vehicle components and specialised high-speed machinery), Mason (2000) found that while German supervisors acquired more specialised supervisory training than their US or UK counterparts, there was by the late 1990s a recognition across all countries that more needed to be done in vocational training needs and requirements of supervisors. Despite these differences, supervisors were generally aware that their roles had significantly changed with the introduction of lean working techniques. For example, some supervisors noted that targets had become tighter and there was a continual pressure, especially with those plants using high-speed machinery, to improve the quality and performance of their products while having to compete on price as well. Day-to-day tasks, once core activities of supervisors, were handed to newly established 'team-leaders'. Even though Mason only hints at the following point, team-leaders now took on supervisory routines, while supervisors became co-opted into lean management ideology. In this instance, team-leaders had no ownership powers, but nevertheless enjoyed powers of control and supervision of labour in the workplace (cf. Carchedi 1991: 37–8). Arguably, then, the contradictory identity of team-leaders, being as they are on the frontline of productive labour, make them more attuned to the intensified effects of lean ideology. Digitised technology supports these new management class relations. In some productive workplaces, such as warehouse work, software can now rank individual effort of warehouse workers in some companies so that managers do not have to directly supervise them. Instead, warehouse employees internalise their own supervision via digital technology (Elliott and Long 2016; Moody 2007; Newsome et al. 2009).

Will the pandemic noticeably change any of these practices and processes? Coulter (2020) suggests that it will do. He argues that COVID-19 presents an opportunity for trade unions to engage in a corporatist pact with the government. He claims that this is already being played out to some extent in a number of countries. In the United Kingdom, for instance, the TUC have engaged constructively with the Conservative government and with employer representative organisations like the Confederation of Business Interests (CBI) to successfully advocate for social assistance for workers. On a number of occasions, the TUC and CBI have 'coordinated their messaging' and issued joint calls on a range of issues from protecting livelihoods to social distancing, while with the government, they have both helped to design the Job Retention Scheme. Coulter maintains that the crisis might yet open up more chances for social partnerships to flower between union, business and government. He is also aware that this prospect is still far off the British government's agenda. I would go further. From surveying some of the evidence in this chapter, it seems that so far the crisis surrounding COVID-19 has not led to any substantial challenge to neoliberal, financialised and lean work practices in the productive sectors of the economy. For now, then, COVID-19 has not been an opportunity to lower the rate of exploitation in the productive workplace. Indeed, as Shaheen and Jesse (2020) note, the pandemic presents an opportunity for companies to invest in digitised automated labour where possible to replace real labour. Under current neoliberal and financialised circumstances, in which trade unions and other workers' groups are still trying to rebuild their strength, then the crisis surrounding the virus might be used by businesses to lay-off people and replace them with technology. A global survey found that four in ten companies were going to bring forward plans to automate some work-related jobs in order to ensure they are 'pandemic proof' (Shaheen and Jesse 2020: 60).

CONCLUSION: CLASS RELATIONS, DIGITAL TECHNOLOGY AND GLOBALISATION

This chapter has argued that the contradictory circuits of global capital are still very much informed and mediated by the structural contradiction between capital and labour. As we have seen, for example, today's global trade is located in global value chains, which account for about 80 per cent of global trade (UNCTAD 2013: iii). Global value chains are dominated by major corporations in the Northern hemisphere, especially by US corporations. These global marketplaces are therefore based in *intra-firm trade* within a corporation's own specific global value chains (UNCTAD 2013: 17). Powerful corporations thus extend their dominance through these value chains. But the fact that the most powerful corporations are located in the most powerful economics starts to open up a conversation about how they come together to exploit and oppress less developed countries. As Suwandi and Foster (2016) explain, corporations, located as they mostly are in dominant capitalist countries, construct uneven socio-economic relations with the likes of factories in developing countries, which are mostly located in the Southern hemisphere. Dominant lead firms and corporations in the Southern hemisphere sub-contract out work to firms lower down the chain, creating distinctive local labour regimes subject to local control mechanisms.

For Ness (2016), this way of thinking about imperialism is intimately tied to the financial imperialism of the dominant capitalist interests in the global South, which, as we know, is supported through the power of the US state and its allies (Ness 2016: 44; see also Chapter 4, above). Lead firms, for example, monopolise a set of core competencies such as branding, mergers and acquisitions, and huge investments in IT hardware and software, enabling these firms to then outsource businesses to an array of other smaller companies within and outside their territorial borders, especially to smaller firms in the South (Selwyn 2015:

264–6). Once more, these processes are associated with a class-based and imperialist analysis, which relies on leading states competing to control and regulate global money. This class-based analysis is also useful because it reveals how imperialist relations, such as an increase in the importation of goods from less-developed countries, has reduced the bargaining power of what can be termed as productive labour in dominant capitalist countries and contributes towards lowering the wages of less skilled workers in these countries.

The chapter has also noted the role that management and supervisory 'non-labour' has played in these practices. It is possible to add to this discussion that business leaders generally share a collective resistance to the sort of welfare state intervention popular from 1945 to the mid-1970s. For example, it is common for some individual business leaders to assert their collective interests to governments in order to oppose state intervention which aims to regulate working conditions in ways favourable to labour (Philip et al. 2005). Strong national welfare state intervention is therefore discouraged by business leaders in favour of policies that help to move products more easily through a value chain. Problematically, this approach opens the way for corporate and multinational capital to ease its way into the lives of the global rural and urban poor, but without the necessary social and welfare protections for these populations (Neilson 2014: 59).

But lean production methods have also been transported into unproductive sectors and labour processes (see also Huxley 2015). Even so-called 'creative' and 'service' work has been subjected to fragmented, standardised and repetitive work routines. As we will see in more detail in the next two chapters, the creative and service sectors are often contrasted to industrialised work. Creatives are thought to be independent and high-skilled workers, often technologically savvy, who, through their soft skills (for example, imagination, knowledge, ideas), produce innovative outputs, experiences, art, public spectacles and so on. In reality, creatives can, however, be either productive workers or unproductive workers depending on whether they help to produce commodities with exchange-value. If we recall, productive labour is simply labour that 'creates or transforms use-values, thereby generating surplus value, and the labour power must be exchanged against capital' (Tregenna 2011: 288), which implies that productive labour does not necessarily have to produce a physical good to generate surplus value. Tregenna explores productive service commodities, which she claims are different to manufactured commodities insofar as 'the production and consumption of service commodities generally cannot be separated in time, or, in most cases, in space'. In manufacturing, there is a time lag between the production of a commodity and its consumption, whereas this is not necessarily the case with a service commodity (Tregenna 2011: 290).

Some service sectors will therefore contribute towards productive activities, while others will not (see also Chapter 6, below, for a more detailed analysis of the service sector). The same can be said of creative workers too. If their intellectual labour helps to produce commodities in order to accumulate surplus value, then creatives will experience in their own way the external global pressures of surplus value accumulation within their daily working lives. The next chapter starts to explore these lean and mean working conditions in relation mainly to unproductive commercial and financial sectors, while Chapter 7 explores these working conditions in the creative sectors.

Chapter 6

UNPRODUCTIVE DIGITAL WORK BEFORE AND DURING COVID-19

INTRODUCTION

As we noted in Chapter 2, one argument suggests we have entered a new informational and network economy predicated on 'knowledge generation, information processing, and symbol communication' (Castells 2000: 17). For Castells, technological networks are therefore an excellent illustration of the power of culture at work in today's society. While networks are 'complex structures of communication constructed around a set of goals that simultaneously ensure unity of purpose and flexibility of execution by their adaptability to the operating environment' (Castells 2009: 21), their common properties reside not in these structural characteristics as such, but in their cultural and communicative qualities (Castells 2009: 20; see also Lash 2002; Lash and Urry 1994). Other theorists similarly argue that we have witnessed a shift towards 'workerless factories' in which people conduct day-to-day work activities outside the confines of physical offices, and are assisted to do so by the likes of global information flows, high-technology, computerisation, tertiary occupations and flexible working hours. Some further argue that these 'cognitive' abilities accumulated inside and outside of work, associated with everyday cultural and social life, and 'interacting with automated and computerised . . . systems', are now '*directly productive of capital*' (Hardt and Negri 2009: 132–3; emphasis added). That is to say, everyday life, culture, creative and informational workplaces are today part thought to be 'productive' (see also Böhm and Land 2012; Fish and Srinivasan 2011; Fleming 2015).

This chapter, like the others, disputes some of these core ideas about the contemporary economy, and does so by drawing on arguments made throughout the book. First, we will challenge in this chapter the assertion that these relatively new workplaces can be automatically counted as being part of productive capital. Instead, many of the changes that have occurred in the digital workplace are mediated through, and following Mandel (1971), 'industrialised' ways of working in *unproductive commercial sectors*, which are founded on the 'mechanisation, standardisation, over-specialisation and parcellisation of labour' (Mandel 1971: 387). That is to say, the increasing rationalisation and standardisation of work, which is often similar to that found in Fordist factories, operates in unproductive circuits and sectors with an emphasis on decentralised work structures (Sawchuk 2013; Sweet and Meiksins 2008: Tomaney 1994).

Financialisation is often at the heart of these practices. Corporations, hedge funds, and other command and organising centres push forward investments in new 'industrial-like' methods to reduce perceived waste and inefficiencies in circuits of commercial capital. Today, this type of 'industrialisation' is frequently achieved through innovative but unproductive financialised forms of capitalisation. Certainly, investments in new technology have made some workplaces more 'aesthetic', 'branded', 'image-conscious' and 'networked', but these often operate in tandem with a certain logic and tendency of unproductive and industrialised capitalisation. In other words, 'cultural' and 'immaterial' factors of production are not necessarily productive and do not necessarily escape industrialisation techniques. Indeed, 'cultural' and 'immaterial' factors of production are best theorised as moments in the reproduction of the class relations of capitalism. In particular, they are moments in the reproduction of unproductive circuits of capital and the attempt of capital to escape the class contradictions embedded in productive capital by investing in unproductive circuits such as commercial, financial and rent circuits (Marx 1992). Whether we are talking about informational workers, or other occupational commercial groups, it is therefore important to analyse, at least to begin with, whether those working in these jobs are productive, unproductive or non-labour.

Marxist class analysis therefore provides a set of theoretical tools to understand the changing nature of many middle-class occupations in unproductive sectors. A common narrative found in many accounts of changing work practices, for instance, is that 'new' service jobs in commercial sectors provide more opportunities for the middle class to gain satisfying jobs, to gain advantages by adopting 'flexible' styles and modes of work, and become more upwardly mobile in terms of class. But while this might be true of some 'new' middle-class professions, it is certainly not true of numerous other middle-class professions. Intensified relations of oppression leading to less, not more, control in their respective labour process for some unproductive middle-class members has been one important means by which unproductive capitalists have tried to generate greater surplus profits (Pérez and Cifuentes 2020). The chapter will show that the pandemic has reproduced these class relations in new ways and forms. First, though, we say a little more about the unique nature of unproductive circuits of capital.

ONCE MORE ON UN/PRODUCTIVE CIRCUITS: THE CASE OF COMMERCIAL CAPITAL

Is it true to say, as some critics argue, that Marx simply dismissed 'unproductive' forms of capital and work? Arguably, Marx makes the opposite point, namely, that unproductive capital can be a vital moment for the completion of the circuit of productive capital. To illustrate this point further, let us momentarily think about commercial capitalists. For Marx, commercial capitalists are involved in the *movement* of industrial capital from the sphere of production to the sphere of circulation. So, '(c)ommercial capital . . . is nothing but the transformed form of a portion of this circulation capital which is always to be found on the market, in the course of its metamorphosis, and perpetually confined to the circulation sphere' (Marx 1991: 380).

At this level of analysis, then (which for now brackets out of the analytical picture the fact that, for example, commercial capitalists can also become directly involved in the production of industrial capital), commercial capitalists are primarily involved in the *circulation* and *distribution* of commodities created by productive industrial capital. As a result, commercial capital gains a relative degree of autonomy from industrial capital because it assumes 'the form of a specific business of its own, separate from the other functions of industrial capital . . .' (Marx 1991: 384). Productive capitalists who create surplus value sell their commodities to commercial capitalists because commercial capitalists reduce the circulation time of capital and speed up the realisation of surplus value for productive capitalists. Commercial capitalists are unproductive because they create no new value, but they reduce the costs of production for the productive capitalist (the commodity producer). This, therefore, lets the capitalist return more quickly to setting up a new production cycle (see Marx 1992: 134–6). Unproductive sectors like retail and finance are subsequently dependent on the productive sector insofar as they rely on the production of surplus value in order to make their own respective own profits (Wilkie 2011: 92; see also Beech 2015; Carchedi 2011; Mandel 1992). So, Marx does not dismiss unproductive activity quite so easily as some contemporary theorists suggest.

A number of further points can be made about the significance of commercial capital. First, the circuit of commercial capital generates its own crisis tendencies, which are nevertheless rooted in the crisis tenden-cies of industrial capital. Certainly, a retailer helps to facilitate the turn-over time of industrial capital. After all, a retailer purchases goods from an industrial capitalist and so contributes to the ability of an industrial capitalist to produce commodities in the first place. Commercial capital-ists are not, however, guided by direct production time and the turnover of surplus value. Given this, production time in the circuit of industrial capital appears as an external barrier to commercial capitalists, which commercial capitalists must seek to overcome. Commercial capitalists must also face the external barrier of the speed and volume of total individual consumption of goods and services. One route to overcome these barriers is through credit and finance. Gaining access to credit and finance enables commercial capitalists to purchase greater quantities of commodities from an industrial capitalist even if previous purchases of commodities have not yet been sold in the marketplace. Purchasing greater volumes of commodities through credit and finance implies that the commercial capitalist suddenly 'finds no barrier in production itself, or only a very elastic one' (Marx 1992: 419). For commercial capital, therefore, the rate of profit created in industrial capital appears as some-thing external to it, 'and this rate's inner connection with the forma-tion of surplus value is completely obliterated' (Marx 1992: 429). But this creates its own crisis tendency for commercial capital. For example, at certain points total stocks become too high because an increasing number of commodities are transformed into commercial capital and become autonomous of industrial capital (see Clarke 1994: 196).

Secondly, commercial capital generates no new surplus value. Commercial capitalists purchase commodities from industrial capital-ists, or work with already produced commodities, in order to participate 'in the general share-out of surplus value, but without . . . producing any part of it' (Mandel 1968: 189; see also Mandel 1971: 388; Wilkie 2011: 90). Commercial capital, therefore, generates profits through revenue rather than through the accumulation of surplus value (Foley 1986: 117; Jalée 1977: 64). However, commercial capital can help to establish an equalisation in the rate of profit, while, at the time, encourages other capitals to invest in areas where profits are highest, but not necessar-ily where the production of surplus value is at the maximum (Harvey 2013: 161). Problematically, then, commercial capital has a tendency to expand uneven development between different capitals.

Thirdly, commercial capital fashions a certain cultural outlook among commercial capitalists and labour. As we know, commercial capital is fixated on lessening the costs of the turnover time of industrial capital to gain a competitive share of already produced surplus value. Circulation costs are therefore a more prominent issue for a commercial capitalist than is the case for an industrial capitalist. After all, industrial capitalists relinquish part of their circulation costs to commercial capitalists. Circulation costs for the commercial capitalist therefore appear as the source of profits, and so the outlays on circulation appear as thoroughly productive for commercial capital (Marx 1991: 416). Commercial capitalists subsequently give precedence to the profitable circulation of goods and also the aptitude of specific consumer markets to absorb specific commodities (van der Pijl 1998: 53). Commercial capitalists are more likely than industrial capitalists, then, to spend a higher percentage of their costs, credit, finance and profits on the likes of advertising, branding and marketing in order to maintain a healthy level of consumer interest in their goods.

Finally, Marx further argues that much which goes under the heading of commercial labour is attached to 'basic skills, knowledge of commerce and languages, etc.', which 'are produced ever more quickly, easily, generally and cheaply . . . With few exceptions, therefore, the labour-power of these people is devalued with the advanced of capitalist production' (Marx 1991: 415). What Marx seems to be saying is that the skill set of commercial labour is rationalised and, in some respects, comes to be 'industrialised'. The commercial office congeals into 'a workshop', and with the rise of the industrialised mass production of commodities, the commercial capitalist must treat and measure circulation costs through 'industrialised' methods. Indeed, what is arguably 'new' and 'novel' today is how digital technology, often supported by financialised work practices, is being employed in unproductive sectors, including 'middle-class' work environments, in order to 'industrialise' day-to-day work tasks. Digitisation has enabled capital to expand forms of industrialisation and standardisation into commercial sectors, which also include some creative and service sectors. This involves setting automated and predetermined targets for employees in these sectors and breaking down individual discretion to minute detail of each employee. Each second of work-time is monitored and measured, with different types of data collected then compared with produced more data. This led Boes et al. to observe in terms of 'middle-class' work: 'If Taylorisation means detailed observation and measuring of work performance, refinement and a scientific approach to optimise work processes, the digital transformation might be interpreted as paving the way for a "Taylorism 2.0"' (Boes et al. 2017: 165).

The main point to make here is, of course, that capital has employed digitisation to increase certain aspects of industrialisation within a whole range of unproductive work, including those found in IT work, finance and so on, in its quest for greater profits, although not necessarily higher amounts of surplus value (Mandel 1971: 389). In my view, it is this theory of capitalisation and industrialisation that can help us make sense of changing class relations in a number of unproductive workplaces, as well as helping us to make sense of the more recent impact of coronavirus on these workplaces.

We now expand these theoretical points in more detail. We begin, first, by discussing the circuit of commercial capital, especially in the retail sector. We will see that the crisis tendencies and labour processes unique to commercial capital have been reconfigured in new ways by the pandemic. The chapter then outlines an alternative approach to thinking about unproductive classes, which stresses how these classes and their respective labour processes have been subject to capitalisation processes of industrialisation and standardisation. The chapter contends this is a more realistic way through which to analyse unproductive labour than some alternative approaches. Finally, the chapter suggests that despite the twin processes of industrialisation and standardisation, class struggles still erupt in the unproductive workplace between capital and labour.

UNPRODUCTIVE CLASS RELATIONS AND THE PANDEMIC

Under neoliberalism and financialisation, as we noted in Chapter 4, unproductive accumulation among corporations and other businesses has soared since the 1980s. The class attack on organised labour and welfare, which started in 1970s and really took hold in the 1980s, was accompanied by relatively low investments in the productive sphere, particularly manufacturing. In the United Kingdom, unemployment rose, but profits increased. Credit started to flow from liberalised financial markets to corporations, which enabled the latter to partake in takeovers and acquisitions and make their high returns despite employing less labour. Easy credit also opened up opportunities for corporations to invest in a wide range of unproductive sectors (Bonefeld et al. 1995: 59–62). Unproductive capital has therefore enjoyed huge injections of money since the 1980s. In the United Kingdom, for example, the service sector, which includes commercial sectors like wholesale retail, dominates the economy over manufacturing and other productive sectors. It was estimated in 2019 that the service sector, which includes commercial enterprises like retail, accounted for 80 per cent of UK gross domestic product. From 2008 to 2018, the year-on-year growth rate for the service sector was 1.6 per cent, which made it the best performing sector of the UK economy during this period. To put these figures in perspective, the production sector had a negative growth rate of 0.5 per cent, while construction grew by 1.3 per cent (ONS 2019).

Since COVID-19, many commercial and service sectors have been hit by the dramatic declines in trading. In the three months leading up to April 2020, it was estimated that the UK service sector experienced a record drop in growth of 9.9 per cent, with information and communication services falling in terms of growth by 13 per cent in April 2020 (ONS 2020j; 2020k). A later survey published by IHS Markit on 23 June 2020 found that UK measuring output of manufacturing and services output rose from 30.0 in May to 47.6. While a figure below 50.0 is thought to indicate a fall in activity, this rise was actually the highest since February and was a particularly notable rise from the very low figure of 13.8 during April at the height of the lockdown. At the same time, some retail and service sectors did not register this growth. Hotels, restaurants, new orders for cars and electrical goods were still performing poorly (Williamson 2020a). Still, official statistics on service sectors tend to conflate productive and unproductive service sectors together. From a Marxist viewpoint, this is problematic for the reasons already given. Therefore, it is important to try to extrapolate productive from unproductive services. A comprehensive examination is beyond the scope of this chapter. Indeed, it would require several chapters to trawl systematically through the relevant data. Retail, though, remains, to large extent, within the sphere of unproductive activities. Given this, retail is a helpful indicator of the state of unproductive activities during the pandemic.

The Centre for Retail Research said that during 2020, UK retail sales increased, although by only 0.3 per cent. Non-food retailers fared relatively poorly in this year with a decrease of 12.4 per cent in sales, whereas online retail sales shot up by 30.2 per cent (Centre for Retail Research 2021a). Another survey found that in the twelve weeks to 14 June 2020, UK supermarkets increased their take-home sales by 13.7 per cent. Large grocery businesses had particular successes, with Tesco's, for example, increasing their sales by 12.1 per cent. Over the four weeks to 14 June, online grocery sales rose by 91 per cent, while smaller convenience stores accounted for 14.7 per cent of all grocery sales during this period, which is noticeably higher than normal (McKevitt 2020). Data from other sources suggests that UK retail trade bounced back during May and June. In May, retail sales were increasing by 12 per cent, although still down by 13.1 per cent compared with February 2020 figures just before the onset of the pandemic. The amount of money spent online drastically grew in May and stood at 33.4 per cent as a proportion of all retailing (ONS 2020l). A different UK survey covering the week from 28 June to 4 July 2020, which was the third week that UK shops reopened after the first lockdown, found that the UK footfall, which measures the number of people going to UK high street stores, decreased 49.6 per cent year-on-year compared with a decrease of 53.4 per cent year on year for the previous week. UK footfall was still only half of what it was a year previously (BRC 2020). During July 2020, the UK retail sector increased by 3.6 per cent compared with a month earlier, and was 3 per cent higher than pre-pandemic levels in February. Clothing store sales came off worse in July 2020 in terms of sales, and were 25 per cent down on February sales. Food store sales and non-store retailing were still high even though they experienced monthly contractions of 3.1 per cent and 2.1 per cent, respectively. Online retail sales were down by 7 per cent in July, but, overall, online sales were still 50 per cent higher than in February 2020 (ONS 2020m).

Retail sectors in the United States also experienced a rebound in May 2020, up 17.7 per cent and amounting to $485.5 billion in total retail and food services sales. But this was still 6.1 per cent lower than the previous year's sales (Richter 2020). While activity in some retail sectors improved, overall, many remain closed and demand remains sluggish while unemployment is rising (Williamson 2020b). Furthermore, some forms of rent capital linked to the circuit of commercial capital have imploded. In the week ending in June, UK retailers paid only 36 per cent of third quarter rent compared with 41 per cent collected on the third quarter three months previously. Landlords of retail spaces have therefore lost large amounts of income, leading to one landlord, Intu, which owned several UK shopping centres, to go into administration. Before the pandemic, retail and shopping mall space had already been negatively impacted by less people going to stores to shop, preparing to buy goods online, and the pandemic has intensified this trend (Sidders 2020).

But before the pandemic struck, the UK retail sector had already been experiencing problems. One report, published in September 2019, analysed the changing patterns of UK retail high street jobs from 2011 to 2018. The report similarly found that between this period there was a net decline of 95,000 retail jobs. Furthermore, there was a net decline of 108,000 workers, or a 7 per cent fall, in sales and customer service occupations, which are jobs like sales assistants or retail check-out operators. This was a fall from 1.53 million to 1.42 million. Most of this decline comprised women at 75,000 (Wallace-Stephens and Lockey 2019: 4). Overall, 289,000 high street jobs were lost during this period, and of those jobs, 81 per cent employed women (RSA 2019). Since the pandemic, according to the Confederation of British Industry (CBI), from the start of 2020 up until August 2020, UK retail employment had fallen at the fastest rate since February 2009. Grocers, furniture and carpets, and non-store retailers were the only retail sectors that saw growth during this period. The CBI expected retail employment to suffer further falls in employment from the next quarter after August 2020 to be as low as −52 per cent in retail employment (CBI 2020a). Both before and during the pandemic, UK retail job losses have subsequently soared. From 2020 up until June 2021, it was estimated that 215,000 jobs will have been lost in the UK retails sectors, although it is also true to say that the UK retail sectors had been suffering large job losses for a number of years prior to the pandemic (Centre for Retail Research 2021b).

Generally, then, the pandemic has worsened what were already a number of fragile unproductive commercial sectors, such as retail. Working-class occupations have been some of the worse affected during the pandemic in these unproductive sectors. For example, the accommodation and food services sector, which has a high number of unproductive working-class positions, saw their turnover decrease by 52 per cent for the period 1 June to 14 June 2020, and the sector also had the second highest number of furloughed employees during this period standing at 67 per cent of its workforce (ONS 2020n). And, as we also noted in Chapter 4, accommodation and catering currently have the highest levels of in-work poverty in the United Kingdom with one in six of these workers living in poverty (JRF 2020), while another report estimated in 2018 that 42 per cent of retail workers were paid less than the real living wage set at £8.75 per hour (Wallace-Stephens and Lockey 2019).

These processes come to be refracted into other social issues that then impact on socio-economic issues such as the consumption of retail goods. To give one illustration, a report argues that lower-income households in the United Kingdom took on more debt during the lockdowns (see also Chapter 4). Income from financial assets and rental property, for instance, is dominated in the United Kingdom by those at the top end of the income distribution. In 2016–18, families in the top tenth of the net wealth distribution received 60 per cent of all financial investment income and 32 per cent of all rental income. Wealthy families can also use their wealth to reduce other costs.

> This means low-wealth households can therefore face lower living standards today partly *because* of their lower wealth. In 2016–18 the lowest-wealth fifth of households paid more than a quarter of their income in housing costs, whereas the highest-wealth fifth paid very little at all. (Bangham and Leslie 2020: 9)

In the context of the pandemic, these extra resources make a big difference. Those from wealthy backgrounds are more likely to have worked at home during the lockdowns and on average had savings of £4,700, which was two and half times the savings of £1,900 of a person in a shut-down part of the economy. Importantly, lower-income households have on average seen their savings decline each month during the lockdowns because they have to spend part of their savings on essential household items, and they are more likely to have taken on more debt during the crisis. For instance, a quarter of the second income quintile reported that they were taking on more consumer credit, which was twice as many compared with high-income families, and lower-income families were also more likely to draw on informal loans to make ends meet (Bangham and Leslie 2020: 9–10). In this respect, COVID-19 has deepened class divides for sections of the unproductive working class. Indeed, the report states that the workers in the 'shut-down' sectors, which account for 6.3 million people, are the lowest paid earning on average £348 per week and are employed in sectors like hotels, restaurants, wholesale and retail (Bangham and Leslie 2020: 61).

The main point is that class relations are very evident in this group of workers in respect to the neoliberal discipline of debt, credit and money on their everyday lives. And with more debt and less money to spend, the pandemic has contributed to a situation in which these consumer groups will have less money to buy from retail stores. In August 2020, the IHS Markit UK household finance index had dipped as consumers became more pessimistic about their spending power. The index fell from 41.5 in July to 40.8 in August. A figure below 50 signals a deterioration in household finances. The report also noted that less cash was available for households to spend, with less income received from employment, and, overall, households being more pessimistic about their job security and financial wellbeing over the next 12 months than at any time since April 2011 (IHS Markit 2020).

Technology is, naturally, key to disciplining unproductive labour and instilling new ideologies into their labour practices and processes. Way before the pandemic erupted, mobile media and digital technologies were being applied in innovative ways to monitor and regulate the unproductive labour process in subtle and not so subtle ways. These innovative ways of monitoring and regulating unproductive labour processes are also mediated through class relations and financialised management practices, which include attacking trade union rights in the workplace. Undoubtedly, however, some who work in unproductive circuits, such as the commercial circuit, might enjoy a degree of autonomy in how they work, but this has been constrained in recent years through the growth of the 'industrialisation' of their unproductive labour. It is to these issues that we now turn.

'INDUSTRIALISATION' AND STANDARDISATION IN THE DECENTRALISED WORKPLACE

One prominent argument suggests that informational and digital networks have generalised the Japanese 'lean', decentralised model of work to other workplaces. Castells (2000: 178–9) says that the Japanese model of manufacturing, which appeared during the 1960s, was based on doing away with vertical, rational bureaucracies associated with large corporate mass-production companies. Toyota has instead built a decentralised system, which, among other things, allows it to sub-contract out parts of its business to other firms when need be in order to respond flexibly to changing consumer tastes. And the decentralised structure of the organisation enables management to spread some decision-making powers down to workers and employees. Decentralised command and work structures, so the argument goes, have become embedded in organisations beyond car manufacturing plants and have moved into what we would term as unproductive workplaces. High-tech businesses, in particular, are thought to be run by outsourcing many functions and activities of core business away from a central office, and rely instead on distributed networking with different teams within and outside an organisation in order to work on specific projects. Team-based project work empower those colleagues and partners collaborating together to meet in a variety of locations, to self-organise in and around the project, and to act semi-autonomously of their central office (Lash and Urry 2013: 544–5; Urry 2007: 241–3). Team work fosters a horizontal type of interaction between colleagues and collaborators based, in part, on employees self-managing their projects to a certain degree (Fleming 2015: 36).

Certainly, some studies give empirical credibility to these claims of decentralisation in the contemporary unproductive workplace. Nowhere is this clearer than with the rise of a relatively new class of corporate and professional workers who work in what Kingma (2016) dubs as 'third workspaces'. 'First workspaces' can be said to constitute the home, while 'second workspaces' refer to the workplace. 'Third workspaces' are therefore in-between these two spaces: neither home nor the office. Kingma studied two Dutch organisations that hired out specialised, flexible workspaces to professionals, which were also equipped with a social and technological infrastructure to share knowledge and to socialise. The people who used these workspaces often consisted of 'highly educated knowledge workers with corporate contracts (and) self-employed individuals and mobile workers . . .' (Kingma 2016: 185). Digital technologies are crucial in how these workspaces were occupied by the professionals. Laptops, mobile phones and the like were employed by them to travel across these spaces. Unlike other spaces, however, workspaces were used by specific individuals for different work-related tasks, and some worked in them for a few hours a week, while others worked almost their whole week in them. For example, some professionals liked to spend periods of concentrated time doing work tasks like reading and writing in a workspace, while for others the opportunity to enter workspaces is a moment to move away from concentrated worktime. For many, workspaces provided a freedom to conduct work-related tasks in another place.

Kingma makes many astute observations, and the study presents a very useful account of new middle-class cooperative relationships in the digital workplace. Cooperation also implies establishing good working conditions in terms of technological efficiencies and interdependencies that move across spaces of private property. Nevertheless, two further points can be made. First, it is also true to say that under capitalism the cooperation and socialisation is dialectically fused with the profit motive. This does not imply that all work areas become productive, which is what some argue is the case, but certainly the tendency in capitalism is to ensure that the profit motive ensnares society, particularly through an 'industrialisation' and standardisation imperative. Secondly, industrialisation is also readily apparent in some of the most famous and powerful digital corporations operating in Northern countries. Staab and Nachtwey's case study of Amazon, the most famous online retail store, is instructive in this respect. Amazon builds but also purchases the latest digital technology to control and monitor its workforce. For example, it has invested in robots in order to digitise its labour. Robots pick products from Amazon warehouse shelves and then take them to the packing areas to be sent off to customers. Automated digitised labour in these warehouses is also complemented by digitisation strategies of the Amazon labour force. Smart cameras and barcodes are used by Amazon management to establish what in effect are lean strategies of extreme efficiency. To quote Staab and Nachtwey at length:

> The scanner system means that Amazon can monitor not only the exact location of all goods stored but also track its employees' activities – where they are, how many articles they handle in a given period of time, and how their performance compares to that of their co-workers. In performance review meetings with employees, management can draw on the symbolic power of 'objective' numbers provided by the digital control system in Amazon's warehouses, which allows precise assessment of individual employees' work. In the process of *industrialisation of service work*, no fundamental distinction is made between managing products and managing human labour. Barcodes are merely the visible emblem

of a digital control system that literally connects products and labour. (Staab and Nachtwey 2016: 467)

The industrialisation of work in these spheres is also noticeable in other unproductive labour processes. In his comparative study of the work–life balance at a 24/7 large private sector telecommunications organisation providing Internet support to customers, a large private retail outlet that opens from 6 am to 11pm, and a third sector organisation specialising in care through morning to evening hours seven days a week, Smith (2016) found a different and less socialised picture of working life for his respondents that differs significantly from Kingma's respondents, but which arguably shares many connections with Mandel's picture of 'industrialised' digital work. Smith interviewed a range of employees situated in different class positions, ranging from senior managers to store managers, and from administrators to shop assistants. In a neoliberal, highly competitive and deregulated marketplace that impacted on all three organisations, many employees spoke negatively of their work–life balance. At the telecommunications workplace, a senior manager connected the increasing competitive pressure to the need to 'give shareholders value for money' (cited in Smith 2016: 214). Senior managers were seen by other workers as being 'distant' to everyday working life, and they were thought to prioritise productivity targets over and above work–life needs like childcare. Call centre workers, moreover, did not experience flexibility, but instead had to endure changing shift patterns on an almost weekly basis, and work under IT systems that effectively 'Taylorise work and the company are attempting to reduce the duration of calls from 320 to 290 seconds, and seize "quick grabs" to maximise productive effort' (Smith 2016: 215). Similarly, workers at the retail store also endured Taylorised working conditions, with the expectation being that staff will scan 19.6 items on the checkout per minute. Managers, moreover, were subject to more intensified work patterns. Some retail managers worked over their contracted 45 hours per week, while others often had to be constantly available during evenings and weekend through IT and respond quickly to emails. Smith concludes that at these private business organisations, an 'employer-led' model of working life is dominant, 'with a reasserted management prerogative over working time and performance' (Smith 2016: 219). Interestingly, working practices at the third-sector care organisation were better, with managers more willing to create a work–life balance amenable to their staff. Importantly, though, industrialisation and standardisation were and are prevalent through a number of unproductive labour processes.

Even unproductive occupations in the financial banking sector, once lauded for their middle-class professional competence, are subject to these processes. In their study of UK bank workers across five banks, Laaser and Bolton (2017: 220) found a more disquieting picture. In the banking workplace, *quantitative* targets, associated with the likes of selling financial products to customers, stand in tension with the *qualitative* descriptors pursued by banks. For many bank employees, reaching management-set quantitative targets is believed by them to be the most important part of their job. The employees interviewed by Laaser and Bolton were more sceptical about certain qualitative descriptors. Indeed, some banks had introduced additional digitisation methods for management control and supervision in and around specific qualitative descriptors. Each worker was given a personalised balanced scorecard (BSC), which is a type of electronic monitoring of worker performance comprising data from Electronic Performance Management (EPM), which includes information on when employees log on and off, how long they spend with a customer and how many products they sell. EPM therefore present predetermined statistical results about employees to managers ranging from high achievers to underperformers. Qualitative targets, on the other hand, are inputted by management. Some bank employees felt that when they did not reach certain quantitative targets, then qualitative descriptors would be used by management to 'rank employees down'. Financialised banking practices, which are associated today with broader processes of unproductive financialised capitalisation, standardise the everyday working practices of these banking professionals (see also Movitz and Allvin 2017).

So, the idea that decentralised and horizontal workplaces are now the most important formation in the most profitable workplaces – a point made with force by many authors over the years – is only part of the story. Centralisation of control and surveillance, accompanied by types of almost Fordist-like industrialised standardisation of work practices, is apparent even at cutting-edge digital corporations. But unlike productive spheres such as manufacturing, 'industrialisation' and 'standardisation' of commercial and financial workplaces is more often than not entangled with branding exercises and with customer satisfaction. Monitored and regulated through a series of automated key performance indicators, for example, commercial employees in retail stores will be set a number of weekly targets, such as signing up customers for monthly payments for particular store products. Digitisation of labour is driven by automated anticipations built into the accumulated data about how many objects should be being sold per week, and so on. As these targets are mediated through data, there is a horizontal mode of governance here that is not necessarily predicated on managers directly supervising employees to reach targets. At the same time, retail stores, as part of the service sector, are also driven by symbolic and emotional labour, most famously through the words, 'customer satisfaction'. This, though, is a vertical mode of discipline, in which employees must be visibly seen to give excellent customer satisfaction. Yet this in itself can take time away from processing targets. For instance, an employee might have to take considerable time to assist a customer in showing them how to operate a product the customer has just purchased. But such emotional labour will not show up on coded database systems.

> Here, the two regimes of power in the store clash most clearly; control requires following the coded system, discipline requires ignoring the system and falling into a customer service role where the reward mechanisms are fuzzy, undefined and conventional rather than data-driven. (Evans and Kitchin 2018: 50; see also the study of a UK supermarket store by Mulholland 2009)

Given these digitalised managerial strategies in unproductive organisations, how do class struggles nevertheless emerge within them, and how do management try to contain and monitor what they will consider to be the worst excesses of class antagonisms that often appear in the form of trade union activism in and against management strategies? It is to these questions that we now turn.

CLASS STRUGGLES IN UNPRODUCTIVE WORKPLACE

The neoliberal and financialised restructuring of the contemporary unproductive workplace is often reliant on 'old-fashioned' management techniques to gain worker compliance to this restructuring. Notably, worker rights in the form of trade union power have frequently been attacked in this brave new world of work. Indeed, financialisation, lean and digital media has been combined in many workplaces not only to standardise work, but also to reorganise workers collective rights. Amazon provides an interesting illustration of these observations in practice. Before Amazon acquired it, for example, Whole Foods already enjoyed some notoriety among its workforce. In 2016, Whole Foods Market had hired Kulture Consulting, LLC, known as a union-busting company, in order to help Whole Foods maintain their 'non-union' status and try to ensure that worker disquiet about new digitised managerial practices were kept to a minimum (Hunt 2018; Peterson 2018). After Amazon acquired Whole Foods, some workers complained that conditions had actually worsened, with management more preoccupied than ever with increasing profits, homogenising stores, while cutting labour budgets (Butler, S. 2018).

Financialisation will also sometimes be used by management to install new and more rigorous anti-union practices. As we know, financialisation has helped to construct a new layer of financial top management. In effect, and starting in the 1980s, senior managers have become more adept at being active in financial devices and mechanisms, such as working the derivative markets, maximising shareholder value, being involved with and driving mergers and acquisitions, and so forth (Duménil and Levy 2011: 84; see also Bryan and Rafferty 2006). There is also a relationship here between financialisation and decreasing investments in innovation in some businesses. Venture capital especially wants quick returns, and so is generally not interested in 'the kind of patient long-term committed finance that is needed by uncertain innovation processes with long time horizons (Mazzucato 2013: 855).

Clark's analysis of the Automobile Association, now the AA, is useful in unravelling the connections in the unproductive service sector between financialised capitalisation, lean techniques and technology. In 2004, the AA was acquired by two private equity firms, and then in 2007 it was merged with Saga with its ownership renamed as Acromas Holdings. By 2014, Saga and the AA were demerged and then both were re-listed on the London Stock Exchange. A management team at the AA bought 70 per cent of the organisation with investment from the City fund managers. At all these major points from 2004 to around 2015, more debt was being loaded on the AA in order finance these processes and restructuring. On one level, the reason for taking on such debt is relatively simple to understand. Having a portfolio firm, in this case the AA, means that a company that owns the portfolio firm, in this case, Acromas Holdings, can off-set debts to it associated with the likes of loans, dividend payments, consultancy fees and so on. In this case, then, 'the AA was mined for returns to investors and shareholders and then charged for the direct and indirect costs of this appropriation of value' (Clark 2016: 243). By 2005, the new managers had de-recognised the GMB, which was the main trade union for AA employees, and instead created its own in-house union. Straightaway, the effects of this move were felt by the patrol staff. With the help of digitisation, human resources at the AA divided patrol staff in two: those whose performance met certain expectations and those whose performance did not meet these expectations. The former group were given a £2,000 bonus, while the latter group were offered £18,000 to leave or accept placement on an 'approval programme', which would lead to their instance dismissal if they did not attend the programme. Soon, 50 per cent of the patrol staff had left the

AA, with the £18,000 payment being considerably less than the £30,000 voluntary redundancy payment that the GMB achieved for its members (Clark 2016: 245).

But unproductive workers are not simply passive spectators in these changes to their working lives. Laaser and Bolten found in their case study of bank workers that some employees drew on pre-EPM bank narratives to create an image of workers who cared for one another and the wellbeing of fellow workers.

> Despite the undermining of caring relationships, pre-EPM bank workers' ethics of care goes beyond the assessment of current practices as unfair. Indeed, narratives indicate that bank workers search for ways to buffer the instrumentalisation of relationships at work by creating 'affective equality' . . . so that all can be involved in a cohesive workplace community. (Laaser and Bolten 2017: 223)

This basic observation – that even professional middle-class workers in the private sector can 'resist' standardised target-setting – shows the importance that even the professionalised middle class in financial settings can, in their own ways, 'politicise' their work context. Indeed, as Cleaver (2017: 217) notes, several financial unions have appeared in recent years that seek to get better pay and conditions for bank and other financial employees. The UNI Global Union, for example, seeks to represent individuals in 237 trade unions across the globe and in sectors ranging from commerce, finance and insurance, as well hairdressing, private care, security and IT. UNI is therefore a stark reminder that resistance to the de-skilling of middle class and professional occupations is palpable. This leads naturally to further considerations of class relations across the world.

This example leads to further broader political questions about how anti-union financialised and digital management strategies can be tackled and regulated. Certainly, during the pandemic, anti-union activity by management has had a detrimental impact on workers, including unproductive workers. As we know, a number of unproductive workers are employed in sectors that have low pay. For these workers, the pandemic could be used to entrench poor working conditions and poor bargaining power. Unions provide some protection under these circumstances. For example, strong unions can protect workers in unproductive industries from unfair dismissal, especially workers who have been furloughed, protect workers' income and argue that all workers require a living wage, and make it easier for workers to prove they have an increase risk from COVID-19 in their working conditions, which many unproductive workers do have (TUC 2020).

The pandemic has also been employed as an opportunity by some relatively new unions representing unproductive workers to engage in novel forms of organising and struggles in and against employers. For some time before the onset of the pandemic, Amazon workers in Europe had been organising against the working conditions they encountered at Amazon. This took a qualitative new turn during the week of 15 July 2019, when American Amazon workers joined with their European co-workers to stage work stoppages. This particular week was deliberately chosen because it coincided with Amazon's 'Prime Day' – a day on which Amazon has many bargain-priced goods to purchase in its online store. At a fulfilment centre in Shakopee, Minnesota, Amazon workers stopped working for six hours to protest against working conditions and the attempt by Amazon management to curb unionisation of its workforce. In Chicago, at the DCH1 delivery centre, which sorts out Amazon parcels before they are dispatched to Chicago residents, thirty Amazon workers gave a list of demands to management that included a pay rise, health insurance, clean water to drink, and decent air conditioning in the workplace due to the unbearable heat that workers had to endure (Burns 2019). What is particularly interesting here is that Amazon workers formed an autonomous union, DCH1 Amazonians United, to organise workers at their Amazon workplace. But more than this, DCH1 Amazonians United has successfully campaigned to ensure that part-time and temporary Amazon workers receive the right to paid time off (PTO) in the same way that full-time workers enjoyed this right. Specifically, the union showed that while the Amazon manual states that that all employees who work 20 hours per week or more are entitled to 'paid personal time' in the event of illness or other personal issues, this policy was not being followed in respect to part-time and temporary employees. Through a campaign that started in January 2020, DCH1 Amazonians United made sure that their fellow co-workers were aware of their rights, and the union launched a petition to gain publicity for their campaign.

These campaign strategies were strengthened during the pandemic because Amazon had been publicly rebuked from various quarters for suggesting that workers at its Whole Food chains place their PTOs into a pool, which would then be available for all workers. Moreover, the pandemic demonstrated that many workers in the United States were being failed by their employers in terms of adequate sick pay or sick leave. On 20 March 2020, Amazon confirmed that all part-time employees would be entitled to PTO (Amazonians United 2020a; Conley 2020). Also, in March 2020, Amazon workers and 10,000 Instacart workers staged walkouts in protest at a failure to receive basic protection at work during the pandemic. A 'national sickout' on 31 March then took place among some Whole Food workers, organised by the activism group Whole Worker, who felt aggrieved at the lack of protection in the Whole Food stores (Brown 2020).

The pandemic was then strategically used again by some US workers to further their workplace campaigns, but this time involved not only Amazon workers, but also gig and non-gig workers at Instacart, Whole Foods, Walmart, Target and FedEx. Taking advantage of the cultural and social significance of International Worker's Day on 1 May, a number of workers based in these companies walked off their jobs, some protested outside specific targeted stores, while others called in sick. Explicit in their reasons for staging the strike was the need for better protections and benefits during the pandemic, and a number of activist groups, such as Amazonians United, Target Workers Unite, Whole Worker and the Gig Workers Collective, joined the action (Medina 2020). The activism was brought together under the hashtag, #essentialworkersday, which relayed news about the action.

Some commentators have, however, been more critical of this action. Bond, for instance, notes: 'It is unclear how many people joined in the protests. Organizers said thousands of workers had pledged to participate. But the companies said the protests involved few employees, and they did not represent the views of most workers. Target said it was aware of less than 10 employees who participated. Amazon, Instacart, (and) Whole Foods . . . said their operations were not affected' (Bond 2020b). Even so, this pandemic activism is part of broader strategies to organise new types of digital labour. For Amazonians United, these are small local steps to think about and organise larger national worker strategies. The pandemic has given Amazonians United and its activism some national publicity in the United States, and have helped to make activist connections with other worker groups. They have also employed legal tactics, such as submitting unfair labour practice claims, to stop Amazon management from threatening work-based activists. In May 2020, Amazonians United joined with several similar groups across Europe to create Amazon Workers International to campaign for worker rights at Amazon. From these experiences, and a sense of dispossession and alienation, Amazonians United have developed organising advice, education, plans and programmes for workers at other Amazon sites and beyond. As Amazonians United note:

> Remember this crucial fact: a union is nothing more than you and your co-workers coming together to make change. By building the union together with our co-workers, we aim to have control over our

organization, our workplaces, and our lives, ensuring a future where we are respected as people and thrive together. Amazon bosses will do everything in their power to keep us separated and feeling powerless. But together we keep us safe. (Amazonians United 2020b)

The final chapter will look in more detail at some further possible union strategies in the wake of the pandemic. For now, however, we make some concluding observations about the arguments put forward in this chapter.

CONCLUSION

In the late 1980s, Lash and Urry (1987: 204) noted how major banks had escaped certain regulatory constraints and had built offshore money markets for the sale of dollars. A private money market subsequently became more prominent and influential across the globe, and one that was to some extent outside the 'normal' controls of nation-states. Finance was now 'disorganised' and operated along its own pathway and circuit at some distance from industry (Lash and Urry 1987: 207). Castells adds that communication networks have been key in strengthening these global financial flows. Communication networks enable billions of dollars in transactions to occur across the globe every few seconds. Technology, moreover, helps investors to number-crunch financial trans-actions and put into practice complex financial models, all of which helps to make financial calculations. Overall, Castells observes, capital flows have become increasingly autonomous of 'the actual performance of economies' (Castells 2000: 106). The 2008 global crisis was testament to this financialised progress. Deregulated economies, unfettered finance that can travel at astonishing speeds around the world through com-puter networks, 'and fed by relentless production of synthetic securities as the source of capital accumulation and capital lending' (Castells et al. 2012: 2; see also Castells 2011: 187–91), was at the root of the crisis.

There is much about finance and its role in unproductive sectors that is innovative in these accounts. But they also underestimate other vital factors at play across the world today. The chapter has demonstrated, for example, that financialised and neoliberal restructuring of unproduc-tive sectors can be regarded as a way in which businesses have attempted to cut costs, restructure class relations, and streamline their core func-tions in order to secure a slice of already produced surplus value; to increase their profits by 'realising as much of the surplus value expropri-ated during production into capitalists' profits as possible' (Wilkie 2011: 99; see also Mandel 1992: 49).

Digital technology similarly works alongside financialised capitalisation in further standardising and rationalising the unproductive labour process. 'Electronic calculating and accounting machines replace a multitude of office workers, clerks and book-keepers in banks and insurance companies. Self-service shops and automatic dispensing machines take the place of salesmen and shop-girls. The independent general medical practitioner is replaced by a polyclinic with affiliated specialists or by works doctors in big companies' (Mandel 1971: 385). Technology standardises many professional occupations in ways not always thought about by those who claim we live in qualitatively new 'informational', 'network', 'mobile', immaterial' times. In professional occupations, standardisation often intensifies the working lives of these professions, and, by so doing, brings to the fore the contradictory locations of these middle-class occupations. And as these contradictions become more apparent on a day-to-day level, then some even in management occupations find it difficult to simply follow past work obligations and their current rule-following organisational behaviour (Greenbaum 1998: 139).

The next three chapters addresses class relations in a distinctive set of labour processes: creative labour processes, so-called gig labour processes, and then public sector labour processes. What is noticeable about all these labour processes is that they can contain both productive and unproductive circuits of capital and labour. This means that they also contain unique configurations of class relations. We begin to explore these class relations in the next chapter by focusing on creative sectors and creative labour.

Chapter 7

CREATIVE INDUSTRIES AND CREATIVE CLASSES BEFORE AND DURING COVID-19

INTRODUCTION

It is generally acknowledged that one of the earliest attempts to define the creative industries was made by Tony Blair's 1997 New Labour government. The then newly established Department of Culture, Media and Sports (DCMS) founded a Creative Industries Task Force in order to map and measure the contribution of these sectors to the performance of the British economy and social and cultural life. The DCMS defines creative industries as, 'those activities which have their origin in individual creativity, skill and talent and which have the potential for wealth and job creation through the generation and exploitation of intellectual property' (DCMS 2020). In 1998, the DCMS Task Force produced its first report, and claimed that the UK's creative industries employed 1.4 million people and made about £60 billion a year for the economy (Flew 2012: 9; see also Schlesinger 2016: 192). In 2020, the DCMS estimated that by 2018 the creative industries had contributed £111.7 billion to the UK economy. Advertising, architecture, arts and antique markets, crafts, design, fashion, film and video, electronic games, music, performing arts, publishing, software and computer services, and television and radio are among those sectors listed by the DCMS as being part of the creative industries.

Creative industries are also said by some to be better equipped to weather economic storms because of an in-built flexibility in creative jobs and markets that enable these sectors to quickly adapt to changing circumstances. Indeed, a number of academics, politicians and policymakers optimistically claim that the creative industries represent a qualitatively different set of socio-economic practices to others, which are characterised by their greater immunity to the crisis tendencies of capitalism. One of the most well-known champions of the so-called creative class is the American public academic, Richard Florida. He argues that creative sectors – arts, film, music, museums, advertising, high-tech and financial services, legal firms, poets and so on – have laid the foundations for collaborative learning in specific regions and sectors. Indeed, economic value is built in to these sectors through creativity, according to Florida, and through that very intangible quality, 'ideas' (Florida 2012: 37). By working in clusters and teams, creatives generate new ideas, which alongside R&D, goods and services can be shared together with the aim of attracting capital investments to help these ideas grow into products that can then be brought to market. Knowledge and creative ideas therefore become a well of value (Florida 2012: 38).

This chapter scrutinises some of Florida's claims. Through different pieces of evidence, and by drawing on Marxist class analysis, three distinct arguments will be made. First, it will be suggested that while creative industries include both productive and unproductive circuits, evidence nevertheless suggests that contradictory middle-class positions are dominant within them. Secondly, however, it will be claimed that far from the optimistic picture painted by scholars and policymakers like Florida, many in the so-called creative classes operate through fragile and precarious working conditions and are employed on casual and temporary contracts subject to intensive labour practices and processes. Thirdly, COVID-19 has in some ways deepened these precarious working conditions and further exposed problems in the optimistic accounts of creative industries. But we start, first, by describing the basic arguments behind Florida's theory of the creative class.

RICHARD FLORIDA AND THE CREATIVE CLASS

Florida recognises the importance of the high growth rates of occupations in the service class, ranging from healthcare jobs, to office work, to food preparation. Traditional working-class jobs, covering the likes of production operations, maintenance and construction, have, according to Florida, declined to about a quarter of the US workforce (Florida 2012). For Florida, however, 'creatives' are more flexible in how they work than either the service class or working class, and this gives them advantages over other classes in the marketplace. To understand why this is the case, Florida first breaks down the creative class into a number of sub-groups. Super-Creative Core individuals include those working as scientists, university professors, poets and novelists, artists, entertainers, editors, cultural figures, think-tank researchers, architects, software programmers and analysts. Creative professionals are another group inside the creative class and include those employed in knowledge-intensive industries like high-tech companies, finance, legal and healthcare jobs, and business management. For Florida, these are people who engage 'in creative problem solving, drawing on complex bodies of knowledge to solve specific problems' (Florida 2012: 39).

Creatives are therefore paid to think on their own and to 'apply or combine standard approaches in unique ways to fit the situation, exercise a great deal of judgement, perhaps try something radically new from time to time' (Florida 2012: 39). Distinct to other classes, which are frequently based in bureaucratic workplace hierarchies, creative classes produce 'good ideas' through an entrepreneurial and non-vertical spirit (Florida 2012) and are 'paid to use their minds' (Florida 2012: 9) to generate economic value. A creative learning economy thus encourages different employees to work in 'teams' in knowledge and intelligence clusters. Important in this respect is the ability of these clusters to attract foreign direct investment (FDI). To achieve this creative clusters not only look to the nation-state for support, but also, and perhaps more importantly, seek to build region-states based on creativity. Region-states build competitive advantage to the extent that they mobilise ideas – continuous knowledge creation and knowledge workers. Ideally, this facilitates communication networks which link together people, information, R&D, goods and services on a global basis so that knowledge will replace physical labour as the main source of value. Driving creative clusters are the 'three Ts': technology, talent and tolerance (Florida 2012: 272). Creative people are attractive to areas and cities that invest in the latest innovation and technology within specific regions. Creatives are also drawn to places that welcome and develop talented people who have high skill levels, are ambitious, educated and display an entrepreneurial flair. Tolerance is founded on an appreciation of diversity in a workforce in terms of welcoming different cognitive styles among employees and appreciating demographic diversity in a workplace (Florida 2012: 232). Creatives move to places that embody all three Ts because these places are those that are most open to creative ideas.

Florida further argues that creatives have an additional advantage over other workers insofar as creatives can work 'flexibly'. Since the 2008 global crisis, for example, things have not gone well for those in the working class and service class. Just after the 2008 crisis, unemployment for the working class grew by 6.2 per cent to reach a total unemployment figure of 15.2 per cent, while unemployment for the service class reached a total of 9 per cent (Florida 2012: 50). Florida, though, further suggests that after the 2008 crisis, those in the creative class saw only a fractional rise in unemployment in their ranks. Creatives, according to Florida, are autonomous and flexible enough to take on additional projects to their 'normal' work in order to cultivate their creativity and thereby 'liberate' themselves during a crisis. Creatives like to operate in lean and flat labour market predicated on an ability to move and switch employers, to move between working for an employer, to work for themselves, and to work with other creatives in order to share and distribute knowledge with one another (Florida 2012: 277).

In making his arguments, however, Florida tends to homogenise creatives in the sense that he does not explore distinct differences between them in terms of the circuits of capital within which they operate – productive and unproductive circuits – and he tends not to be interested in the class power differences between creatives across and within creative industries. Some creatives, for example, will be located in managerial non-labour and so occupy different class locations to those creatives they manage. Overall, then, Florida does not analyse creative work through the class relations of capitalism. This leads to a number of distinct but also related problems with his analysis, and, by default, with similar celebratory viewpoints on the creative industries. Indeed, the pandemic has produced a crisis for the creative industries that in many respects is worse than other employment sectors. We now explore, in greater detail, these critical points.

CREATIVE INDUSTRIES BEFORE AND DURING COVID-19

As we know, Florida believes that creatives remained in far better socio-economic health after the 2008 global crisis than the traditional working class or the service class. We can add some figures here since the outbreak of the pandemic, at least in relation to the United Kingdom. In April 2020, employment levels in all fourteen UK service sectors that were measured, and which included wholesale retail and the motor trade, transport and storage, accommodation and food services, financial and insurance services, fell apart from public administration and defence. Eleven service sectors experienced their largest falls since records began in January 1997. To give some illustrations, accommodation and food service suffered a decline in growth of 88.1 per cent, information and communication declined by 13 per cent, while wholesale and retail trade and motor repairs fell by 27 per cent (ONS 2020k).

Yet many of those working in the UK's creative sectors have arguably fared even worse during the pandemic. In November 2020, it was stated that the arts, entertainment and recreation sectors had the highest proportion of its workforce on partial or full furlough leave at 34 per cent compared with an average of 9 per cent across all sectors. Furthermore, the UK's arts, entertainment and recreation sectors were the second highest recorded in which more than 50 per cent of its business had experienced a decline at this point due to the pandemic. Its figure stood at 72 per cent (ONS 2020n). The Broadcasting, Entertainment, Communications and Theatre Union (Bectu), found in their survey of 3,000 people working in the UK creative industries that around 50 per cent had been forced to borrow money during lockdown in order to survive, while only 33 per cent of people who said they are pay-as-you-earn (PAYE) freelancers reported they were furloughed, and 40 per cent of creatives, who were also a limited company, believed during lockdown they could qualify for the government self-employed support scheme (Bectu 2020).

Other studies demonstrate similar concerns for the UK's creative industries. Before the pandemic, the creative industries contributed £111.7 billion to the UK economy, and between 2017 and 2018 it grew by 7.4 per cent, while the UK economy as a whole on average grew by only 1.4 per cent. In 2019, the creative industries employed 2.1 million people, which was an increase of 34.5 per cent from 2011. Since the pandemic, it has been projected that the creative industries would have a combined £74 billion turnover loss in 2020 compared with 2019. There was also an estimated fall of 119,000 in employment in creative sectors alongside a drop of 287,000 in self-employed creative industry workers. Moreover, 38 per cent of creatives predicted an annual income fall of over 75 per cent during 2020, while 73 per cent of respondents predicted a fall of annual turnover of more than 50 per cent. UK design and fashion were, for example, predicted to lose £2 billion in revenue in 2020 compared with 2019; the craft sector was predicted to lose £513 million; museums, galleries and libraries were all said to lose about £743 million in turnover; the music industry was expected to lose £11 billion in turnover; while film, TV, video, radio and photography were all expected to lose £36 billion (Oxford Economics 2020). At the end of July 2021, it was reported that the creative arts and entertainment industries still had one of the highest percentages of its employees being furloughed at 34 per cent of its workforce. Photographic activities, another sector included by the UK government as being part of the creative industries, was even higher at 39 per cent (Coronavirus Job Retention Scheme statistics: 29 July 2021).

Clearly, then, the crisis surrounding COVID-19 is having a different impact on creatives than was arguably the case after the 2008 crash. Florida is, unsurprisingly, more than aware of the devastating consequences the pandemic has had on the creative sector. In fact, he has produced his own analysis of the impact of COVID-19 on American creative sectors. In the United States, Florida and Seman suggest that the pandemic has led to 'losses of 2.7 million jobs and more than $150 billion in sales of goods and services for creative industries nationwide, representing nearly a third of all jobs in those industries and 9 percent of annual sales' (Florida and Seman 2020: 3). What is less conspicuous in Florida's recent COVID-19 analysis is an analysis of the relationship between flexibility, the pandemic and creativity. Notably, the flexibility of the creative class, lauded in the past by Florida, now seems in our pandemic times to be a hindrance for some creatives. Indeed, Florida appears to underplay the precarious nature of creative employment and jobs. Freelancing creative work provides us with a way to develop this critical point about Florida's latest research.

Freelancing is a typical employment pattern for many who work in creative sectors, and some will do creative contract work alongside either other part-time salaried work or even other full-time work. Precarity in the creative sector might generate degrees of flexibility for creatives, but these hybrid types of employment can also prove a burden and hindrance when a crisis takes holds in society. For example:

> In Germany, over 6,600 cultural and creative self-employed persons surveyed during the Great Lockdown period experienced a drop in sales of over 30 percent and one in five expected sales losses of over 50 percent on annual sales . . . In the Netherlands, in the first quarter of 2020, 52.5 percent of the self-employed persons in the cultural and creative sector saw a decrease in turnover higher than the national average of 44.8 percent. The average amount of lost sales was EUR 5.6 thousand in the first quarter, while it increased by up to 8.7 thousand for 65 percent of the self-employed in the second quarter of the year. (IDEA Consult et al. 2021: 34)

COVID-19 has also shown that some income support policies and other government support measures have been inappropriate for those in these self-employed or hybrid employment creative categories. Creative professionals frequently lack access to these support mechanisms for a number of reasons. It is often difficult to estimate creative and cultural employment – some jobs might only be 'partially' creative', for instance – and so jobs in these sectors are sometimes missing in official government data, which then has negative effects in terms of gaining official government-led assistance during a crisis (Travkina and Sacco 2020). A study of the arts in Flanders found that some of the most vulnerable creative groups during the pandemic have been artists working on short-term contracts without professional status to count on. As well losing lots of income and revenue, these creatives could not access state support either (IDEA Consult et al. 2021: 35). Many of these hybrid employment practices are not recognised by governments and so those working in these areas have missed out on national social security schemes.

Creative and cultural industries are, furthermore, extremely varied and span 'not-for-profit and public institutions (for example, museums, libraries) to large for-profit players (for example, Netflix, Spotify)' (Travkina and Sacco 2020: 11). Creative and cultural businesses can therefore work from a whole variety of models, with many formed through tangible *and* intangible assets such as reputation or access to certain social networks. One study of the European creative and cultural sector found that the halting of creative and cultural events across Europe due to the pandemic, from festivals not going ahead to the closure of art galleries and heritage sites, meant that those working in these areas were denied vital business networking opportunities; opportunities that would normally lead to further job opportunities and income (IDEA Consult et al. 2021: 34). Problematically, lending bodies might then be reluctant to lend to a business during a moment of crisis whose assets are partly or mostly intangible (Travkina and Sacco 2020: 11).

A UK Parliamentary report, published on 23 July 2020, which looked at the impact of COVID-19 on the digital, media, culture and sports sectors, notes that just over 30 per cent of the workforce in the creative industries is self-employed compared with a UK average of 15 per cent, although levels of self-employment vary across the creative sector. The report presents evidence that many self-employed creatives will no longer be able to continue in their chosen profession because of financial pressures driven by the virus. Economic uncertainty under the current crisis for cultural freelancers include, 'declining income, uncertainty around maternity allowance or eligibility for mortgages, the inability to recoup money already spent on equipment, rehearsals and touring, and concerns about decreased work opportunities in the long term' (Culture, Media and Sport Select Committee 2020). The pandemic has dramatically shrunk the number of musical venues, for example, leading to 19 per cent of respondents to a survey by the Musicians' Union to say they were considering abandoning their careers as musicians. COVID-19 has, in addition, negatively affected the outreach and voluntary work conducted by many in the creative industries. Culture and creativity have long been seen as a major factor in regenerating communities and bringing communities together through cultural, education and heritage projects. Many of these initiatives are now thought to be under threat. The next section develops the foregoing observations by placing precarious creative conditions within an alternative class perspective to that offered up by Florida; a class perspective rooted in Marxist analysis.

THE CLASS NATURE OF CREATIVE WORK AND THE INDUSTRIALISATION OF CREATIVE INDUSTRIES

Trying to disentangle creative productive from unproductive creative work is an inherently tough task if one tries to use different frameworks employed by certain scholars, policymakers or governments. Indeed, a 2018 UNCTAD report on the global creative economy notes:

> Data for world trade in creative services are difficult to attain, because many countries do not report specifically on creative services, and only publish balance of payments data on broader service categories. (UNCTAD 2018: 10)

UNCTAD further observes that there is an inherent complexity of making clear distinctions and defining borderlines between a creative good which has been manufactured through mass production or which has been handmade, and between creative goods that are decorative or those which are functional, and so on (UNCTAD 2018: 13). UNCTAD therefore compiles data for all creative goods globally traded in art crafts, audio-visuals, design, digital fabrication, new media, performing arts, publishing and visual arts.

This is not to deny that class-based issues are absent from creative industries frameworks. For example, some earlier research in 2015 from the DCMS found that of the 1.9 million UK jobs classified as belonging to the creative industries, 1.7 million of them, or 91.9 per cent, were done by those in higher skilled and more 'advantaged groups' (DCMS 2016: 24), while more than half of the jobs at 59.9 per cent, were filled by people with degrees or equivalent compared with 32.7 per cent of all UK jobs (DCMS 2016: 14). From a Marxist perspective, many creatives could therefore be categorised through a range of contradictory middle-class positions. For example, some would own their own means of production, such as specialist IT equipment, and therefore be semi-autonomous of a capitalist firm even if they then entered into a contract with a capitalist firm to complete a contracted piece of 'creative' work. However, this still does not account for which particular creative work might at any one time be considered productive or unproductive. This crucial missing part of the creative story means it is difficult to gain a sense of exactly which creative sectors generate surplus value and which generate surplus profits. Even so, some reports do present an analysis of sorts on this issue. The 2018 UNCTAD report, for instance, suggests that developed economies such as the United States, Italy, the United Kingdom and France, design products like fashion, interior design and jewellery goods, all of which count for 54 per cent of creative goods export, while in developing economies such as China, Hong Kong, Singapore and Taiwan, these creative goods account for 70 per cent of their exported creative goods (UNCTAD 2018: 21). These are all commodities that have been produced to generate exchange-value and surplus value. Arguably, then, they can be counted as productive creative goods.

Florida, however, lacks an account of how systematic class relations mediate creative labour. Instead, Florida explores creative work through the lens of occupation, based in the skills and expertise that one possesses in the marketplace. He defines the 'highest order of creative work', for example, 'as producing new forms or designs that are readily transferable and widely useful' (Florida 2012: 38). In other words, super-core creatives are so-called because of their highly valued creative skills in the marketplace. Questionably, though, Florida roots his occupational theory in a type of economic reductionism. As he says: 'Class membership follows from people's economic functions' (Florida 2012: 37). Other socio-economic and socio-cultural attributes of a person, such as 'their social identities well as their cultural preferences, values, lifestyles, and consumption and buying habits', according to Florida, 'all flow from this' point about class membership. As a result, Florida operates with an all-embracing account of rather static single class categories in which a number of socio-economic and socio-cultural attributes for a person can simply be read off from their 'class membership'. For instance, the 'working class' in Florida's account become inserted in a small range of occupations, which include production, construction, and maintenance and repair. For Florida, then, there are no members of the working class in administrative and office work, or in sales and retail, and so on, because these occupations are delegated as being 'service sector' jobs and not working-class ones (Florida 2012: 402–3). Florida therefore has little to say about the basic class relationship in creative industries between capital and labour and the complex forms that class relations assume in different circuits of capital. As we know, for example, unproductive members of the working-class can be employed in the service sector, yet Florida tends to *distinguish* working-class occupations from service occupations.

Florida's insights on these issues are part of a wider difficulty in trying to analyse the creative industries. After all, 'creative industries' is a somewhat chaotic abstraction insofar as it bundles up a diverse array of jobs into this one category. It therefore soon becomes apparent that what might count as a 'creative' industry is sometimes difficult to grasp. To give one illustration, as well as measuring 'creative industries', the UK government also measures the 'cultural sector'. This sector is defined as 'those industries with a cultural object at the centre of the industry', and include the arts, film, TV and radio, photography, crafts, museums and galleries, library and archives, cultural education, and historic buildings and similar tourist attractions (DCMS 2020: 10). Notice, however, that many of the 'industries' included in the 'cultural sector' – film, TV, crafts, photography, museums, for example – are also those included in the DCMS' definition of 'creative industries'. Given this, it is not entirely clear where the creative industries end and the cultural sectors begin and vice versa.

Florida tries to overcome such problems by simply announcing that those in the creative class are those that employ ideas, whether this is through design, problem-solving, inventing a theorem or strategy, writing a song or a novel that is then sold and so on. They are people who are employed 'to think on their own, apply or combine standard approaches in unique ways to fit different situations, exercise a great deal of judgement, and perhaps even try something radically new from time to time' (Florida 2012: 39). Once again, however, this is a far too generic a description of the creative class. To begin with, all types of labour and work involve 'thinking' and thinking 'creatively'. And the so-called creative industries could not function without a huge working class operating 'behind-the scenes' through the likes of cleaning 'creative' offices, serving 'creatives' their food at lunchtimes, assembling creative products and so on (Dyer-Witheford 2015). O'Connor (2010: 47) goes as far as to say there is an absence of 'any empirical investigation' of 'creative occupations' in Florida's exploration. Instead, one discovers in Florida's account a conflation of different and often diverse occupations with one another under the rubric of 'the creative class'.

Theoretically, then, Florida's analysis lacks the necessary concepts through which one might gain a judicious understanding of 'creativity' in a capitalist society. Certainly, Florida discusses creative capacity, but, as Smith and McKinlay (2009: 6) observe, 'capacity' can also more abstractly refer to the 'capacity' that waged workers in the marketplace enjoy, or not, to sell their labour power to owners of production. Once one brings this labour process issue into the analytical framework, then further important concerns arise, especially those related to how 'creative capacity' is controlled and supervised in the workplace by managers. These labour process issues are unfortunately lacking in Florida's analysis. Most notably, many creative sectors operate through centralised and standardised labour processes, which constrain the flexibility of creative workers. But Florida does not possess adequate theoretical tools to explore this point in detail because he constructs a dualistic and linear historical view of working conditions rooted in his reductionist account of class. Historical working conditions in the United States can be comprehended, Florida tells us, through the binary opposition of industrial Fordist production versus flexible, post-Fordist creative production. For Florida, the 'high Fordist' factories of the 1960s and 1970s would often be defined, in part, through 'the squelching of creativity' on the factory floor. Rather than learn from the creative ideas of those working on the factory floor, who had developed a range of in-built knowledge and skills that were specific to the unique factory culture in which they worked, Fordist management would instead frequently impose ideas and knowledge onto workers. While Fordist managers might have 'considerable book knowledge', they therefore had 'little experience in the actual workings of the factory'. Managers would therefore propose new and complex ideas that regularly failed, 'and, at worse, brought production to a grinding halt' (Florida 2012: 33). Creative factories of today, by way of contrast, require workers who, at a minimum, can problem-solve, work in teams, contribute ideas towards solving tasks, and monitor and perhaps even programme computers within the factory (Florida 2012: 31).

Problematically, Florida assumes that the so-called 'creative factory' in our post-Fordist times will not be beholden to centralised management control mechanisms, but will, instead, open up opportunities for workers to take an active and creative part in the production of goods. A more critical approach, however, recognises that creative work can in fact be tied into 'Fordist-like' working methods of centralised control, which then negatively impacts on creative employment conditions. In terms of what can be called productive video-game production, as Woodcock notes, skilled creative game developers regularly find themselves positioned in heavily regulated and homogeneous work practices. Standardised software packages for employees to work on are frequently employed by game companies, but this limits the creative freedom of game designers, while the fragmentation involved in many game projects leads to de-skilling, insofar as each game worker needs only know their specialised task in designing a game rather than the whole game project. 'This makes it easier to outsource aspects of the game development process too' (Woodcock 2019: 79).

The study by Thompson et al. (2016) is instructive in this respect. They employ a labour process analysis and value chain analysis to analyse creative workers employed in the Australian digital mobile and console games industry. In Australia, Thompson et al., found that many games studios do not have the financial resources to produce games, which is why they depend on publishers and licence holders to gain access to these funding streams. Most publishers are located in the United States, and this means that independent games studios inhabit a minor place in a global value chain of games production. In a globally competitive market, developers have to jostle for work with other developers, trying to attract the attention of publishers, pitching new ideas, with pressures to under-budget and present ultimately unrealistic time schedules to publishers for the development of new games in order to win contracts. One knock-on effect of these working conditions is to make this creative work more fragmented and repetitious, with many forced into specialised tasks and a division of labour. Utilising their intellectual labour to transform the use-value of a product – for example, coding a digital game or animating digital characters – and by working within a capitalist value chain, game developers are subject to a highly managed and monitored labour process. Long hours, intensified pressures, many particularly larger projects being held hostage to the dictates of publishers higher up the value chain, with the end result of 'greater substantive subordination of creative producers to media giants' (Thompson et al. 2016: 329).

In my view, these work practices can be labelled as 'standardised creativity'. They illustrate what Wirsig and Compton (2017: 237) observe is a strategic dilemma at the heart of the contemporary creative digital workplace. Digital creatives are now supposed to be more 'entrepreneurial' in their outlook and in their actions when acquiring work through digital media. But, as the examples above testify, many of these creatives become complicit in fostering almost Fordist-like industrialised routines in their places of work, even while they recognise the potential harmful effects in doing so. In terms of class relations, these creatives might enjoy a degree of autonomy in how they work, but this has been constrained in recent years through the growth of financialised value chains and the 'industrialisation' of their unproductive labour. Florida does recognise that creative work can be embroiled in 'contingent employment relations' that give rise to moments of anxiety for creatives, such as tight work deadlines experienced by freelance creative workers (Florida 2012: 91). But Florida argues that these new work conditions in fact empower workers by handing them more control in their working lives. Skilled creatives leave permanent contract work to be 'liberated' from office politics, to be free of incompetent management, and because of a sense of inequity, for example, a sense of being constantly overworked, which often came from being tied to one firm (Florida 2012: 95). Nevertheless, not only does this account ignore how creative work in many sectors has become industrial-like, but it also ignores evidence that suggests many freelance creatives actually want to get permanent contracts at companies, and feel they have to engage in a constant cycle of competitive pressure to gain new contracts once their current one runs out (Vivant 2013).

Florida also seems to be reluctant to acknowledge any engrained class bias in many of the sectors associated with the creative industries, let alone productive and unproductive class processes. For example, one study found that in the United Kingdom, '(w)hile 34.7 per cent of the UK population aged 23–69 had a parent employed in a routine or semi-routine working-class occupation, the figure among those working in the (creative and cultural industries) is only 18 per cent' (O'Brien et al. 2016: 123). Such inequalities, as O'Brien et al. note further, are reinforced by uneven developments as certain major cities attract 'creatives' to the detriment of other cities. What O'Brien et al. could have legitimately added here is that uneven development is, more broadly, an essential and necessary feature of capitalism. Furthermore, there is evidence to suggest that some working in the creative industries internalise a neo-liberal resilience discourse, which then helps to justify and legitimate working in precarious conditions. Resilience has grown in importance in policy agendas. Broadly speaking, it refers to the awareness of risks in the world and therefore the ability to take pre-emptive action to off-set the worst case scenarios of these risks. To be resilient is therefore to adopt risk-adverse strategies to withstand any potential risks (O'Malley 2010). In their research on freelance cultural practitioners, Newsinger and Serafini suggest that a common theme from their interviews with these practitioners was the need for them to be resilient in the face of cut-backs to the arts under the austerity regime. Many of these practition-ers, like many creatives more generally, were on precarious temporary contracts, yet they spoke about their capability to adapt to an uncertain cultural labour market as being a strength and as making one 'resource-ful' in the marketplace. One artist described being 'blessed' when they embodied this type of resilience because it allowed them to 'thrive in a difficult environment'. For Newsinger and Serafini (2021: 603), this 'romantic resilience' in fact serves to ideologically support, in its own way, neoliberal austerity rather than challenge the 'trauma of post-crisis capitalism'.

CONCLUSION: HOW SHOULD CREATIVES BE SUPPORTED IN A POST-COVID-19 WORLD?

In his more recent writings, Florida does provide some recommenda-tions to help creatives during times of crises. In *The New Urban Crisis*, for example, Florida argues that one main way for cities to alleviate the poverty wrought about by the 2008 crash is to build institutions 'that unleash the creative energy of people and neighbourhoods . . .' (Florida 2018: 191). What people on lower incomes and in areas of poverty require is a basic infrastructure to support and set free their innate skills and creativity. In particular, they need time and resources, such as basic connectivity like functional roads, streets and public transport, which will encourage more economic activity, shops, services and other creative dynamisms to spring to life in certain areas (Florida 2018: 195). To construct this infrastructure, Florida insists it is important for the state and businesses to invest in societies to ensure decent social provisions are available to all to support them in tapping into their creative potential. Among other things, this means investing in public transport, affordable accommodation, a generous minimum wage, universal basic income, better overall wages for those working in service sector jobs, and empowering cities and communities through schemes such as devolving greater tax and fiscal authority power to cities and giving local representatives like city mayors new powers to coordinate large-scale investments in local infrastructures (Florida 2018: 208–26).

Since the onset of COVID-19, Florida has applauded the role that the US state has played in supporting those negatively affected by the pandemic. Self-employed creative workers have, for example, been able to tap into federal assistance. Longer term, however, Florida recommends that a 'bottom-up' strategy should be put in place that supports creatives and helps them to survive in a post-pandemic world. In practice, this would mean large-scale federalist support in terms of grants and other financial assistance alongside financial support from a variety of other organisations. 'It should be led locally by public–private partnerships of municipal governments, arts and cultural organizations, economic development and community groups, philanthropy, and the private sector, with support from government and philanthropy at the state and federal levels as well as large corporations' (Florida and Seman 2020: 21).

Florida's recommendations to sustain and strengthen the creative class during times of crisis therefore appear as arguments for both welfare state solutions and workfare state solutions. The welfare solution is outlined by Florida as a response to the 2008 global financial crisis. He appears to argue, in part, for a social democratic welfare state compromise, but without certain elements that once characterised the post-war welfare state settlement, such as a recognised role for trade unions to be involved in national bargaining over wages. The difficulty with this proposal is that it lacks a sufficient account of how neoliberalism and financialisation operate in global capitalism today. Indeed, there is little in *The New Urban Crisis* that explores financial capitalism and the neoliberal state. These contradictory dynamics of present-day

capitalism will then negatively impact the sort of welfare proposals suggested by Florida. Any major investments in cities today will be shaped
to some degree by the requirement to valorise capital. In practice, this
means that capital will eventually want to dominate any 'free' gifts, such
as affordable housing, which impinge on the essential principle of the
valorisation of capital. To 'dominate' here simply means that capital will
aim to transform free welfare gifts into commodity capital by incorpo-
rating them within the total social capital of the production and circulation of commodities and, ultimately, the ceaseless generation of profit
(Smith 2012: 175). We have already seen in Chapter 4 how capital
has sought to dismantle the post-war welfare state and subject various
welfare departments to financialised and neoliberal imperatives; points
we will address again in Chapter 9. There is no reason to expect, at least
under the current financialised form of globalisation, that Florida's recommendations would be spared the same fate as some current welfare
policies.

A post-welfare state solution (sometimes called a 'workfare state') is
also outlined by Florida as a response to the COVID-19 pandemic. He
appears to argue, in part, for the hollowing out of the welfare state in
which creatives look to the likes of public–private partnerships comprising private business, charities, community groups, governance agencies
(for example, quangos) and federalist government as a means to help
them and to actively support the creative economy. The difficulty with
this proposal is that it lacks a sufficient account of the contradictory
nature of the post-welfare state. For example, a post-welfare state is
often predicated on supply-side policies that place the responsibility of
employability on the shoulders of workers. This type of 'workfarism'
thus prepares people for the job market by making them more employable by, for example, equipping them with the right skills. As Florida
and Seman note, one important way that local economic organisations
can assist creatives during and after the pandemic is 'by developing skills
assessments and needs analysis, which would enable certain creative-
economy workers to use their talent and skills in other industries, such as
designers making masks' (Florida and Seman 2020: 22). Questionably,
though, these policies represent an individualistic solution to socio-
economic challenges. They also ignore the fact that capitalism operates
through uneven development, which means that some localities will have
a high number of resources and strong public–private partnerships that
creatives might tap into, while other localities will have relatively weak
and under-resourced public–private partnerships (Roberts 2014; see also
Chapter 9, below, which explores in more detail further contradictions
of the post-welfare workfare state).

Indeed, the signs so far during the current crisis would seem to demonstrate that the creative sectors are no less immune to the welfare state fallout from neoliberalism and, more recently, from the virus, than other sectors. Creative industries are in fact especially vulnerable during the pandemic because in order to survive many creative sectors rely on voluntary donations, volunteers, and state and local grants and subsidies. Due to the re-alignment of the state from welfare towards neoliberal workfare principles, alongside government cuts ushered in by a decade of austerity, many creative sectors have seen a cut in their government subsidies. The Arts Index Survey, carried out by the UK's National Campaign for the Arts, says that public funding for the arts per head of the population has fallen by 35 per cent since 2008, while local government funding is down 43 per cent since 2008. Contributions to the arts by business have also declined by more than a third since 2012, while philanthropic donations have dipped by 10 per cent in the last three years up until 2020. Funding of Arts Council England suffered a downward trend of 41 per cent from 2010 to 2018. Earned income by revenue-funded arts organisations per person, for example, box office sales, venue hires and catering, however, increased from 2012 to 2018 by 47 per cent, while employment in the cultural sectors rose by 21 per cent from 2011 to 2018, which is higher than UK average rise of employment at 10 per cent. The last two figures reveal that despite successive recent cutbacks, the arts and cultural sectors provide healthy returns and employment opportunities. Even so, these creative and cultural sectors have been particularly vulnerable during the pandemic because of, among other things, the drop in government funding. Without this support base, the UK's arts sector is now at risk (Arts Index 2020). Florida's diagnosis, while containing some rich insights, does not engage with these practical and ideological shifts in state funding. This gap is related, in turn, to Florida's lack of a systematic class analysis.

Chapter 8

DIGITAL LABOUR IN THE GIG ECONOMY BEFORE AND DURING COVID-19

INTRODUCTION

The UK's Royal Society for the encouragement of Arts, Manufactures and Commerce (RSA) says the gig economy is, 'the trend of using online platforms to find small jobs, sometimes completed immediately after request (essentially, on-demand) . . . Workers in the gig economy are sourcing one job at a time, but by logging into an app or clicking through to a website' (Balaram et al. 2017: 10). In this respect, gig work is the archetypal form of digital labour, which we defined in Chapter 1 and Chapter 3 as labour controlled and mediated by digital platforms. Naturally, there are many different varieties of gig work. Lehdonvirta (2017) makes a useful distinction between local and remote types of gig work. Local types of gig work might involve working for the delivery service, Deliveroo, whereas remote types of gig work involve being employed online for a certain period on projects via digital platforms. Remote gig work will also often require specific skills set such as programming skills. From July 2016 to June 2017, software development and technology remote gig work was the biggest category, which increased by 37 per cent during this time, with creative and multi-media the next largest category, followed by clerical and data entry work (Lehdonvirta 2017).

Gig work brings with it many positive employment opportunities, with flexibility in work being frequently touted. But many negative qualities of gig work are also apparent. According to the *New York Times*, the number of US jobs performed by part-time freelancers and part-time contractors – the sort of jobs found in the gig economy – grew from 20 million in 2001 to about 32 million by 2014. Interestingly, and unlike some other major media outlets, the *New York Times* argues that this rise has been engendered, in part, by the lean restructuring of major

US businesses and the contracting out many of their activities in order to focus on their 'core competencies'. Through outsourcing, private contractors have picked up these activities and jobs, often paying contract workers and freelancers per task rather than a regular hourly rate (Scheiber 2015). These new work conditions not only have negative consequences for the working class, but also create adverse work situations for the middle class. Hanauer and Rolf argue that during the period from 1950 to 1980, the US middle class could bank on having access to strong trade unions, health insurance, unemployment insurance, decent pensions, rising wages, decent and affordable education, overtime and sick pay and so on (Hanauer and Rolf 2015). Today, however, relatively stable work conditions have dissolved to be replaced for many middle-class members by short-term, task-based gig work, in which one combines two or three jobs in order to earn enough money to get by. Struggling to pay rent, decent education, health insurance and so on, will become the norm for many middle-class members. As expected, given these conditions, gig workers have been some of the workers hardest hit by COVID-19.

This chapter looks at some of the issues and controversies in and around the rise of platform and gig work, or what we will also term, 'digital labour'. While benefits of doing digital labour will be highlighted, we will also see that the increase in gig work is associated with the dominance of unproductive and precarious neoliberal markets, which, in our financialised world, are also supported and reinforced by imperialist value chains. More specifically, gig and platform digital labour represent a number of processes associated with capitalisation.

First, financial capitalists are attracted to funding opportunities in digital labour companies because they believe large and relatively easy profits are there for the taking. Gig work, however, also establishes new modes of managerial control and surveillance over workers, and takes the individualisation of work, especially the use of innovative types of emotional labour in order to gain and keep work, in new directions. As a result, certain aspects of class relations in the labour process are reconfigured through gig work.

Secondly, and related to the previous point, digital labour alters the employment contract between workers and employers. Being placed on temporary or self-employed contracts often means that gig workers are not granted the same work-related benefits as permanent workers. Precarious working conditions, as the chapter will show, are subsequently an ongoing issue for those working as digital labour. This is one of the main reasons that gig workers have been particularly affected by COVID-19.

Thirdly, the so-called 'new' phenomenon of gig work can reasonably be seen as being part of an ongoing process in which many workers take on multiple jobs after a crisis, such as the 2008 global crash or the crisis of the pandemic. What is novel today, as Moody (2017: 28) correctly observes, is that rather than looking for extra work in newspapers, people are turning instead to digital media as a means of finding new and additional sources of income.

Fourthly, gig and platform digital labour increases the number of people employed in unproductive socio-economic activities; at least in the Northern capitalist hemisphere. While short-term profits can be made through digital labour, the chapter will argue it is less clear that surplus value is being produced. Digital labour is prevalent in commercial and service sectors, yet, by-and-large, many of these sectors do not generate surplus value (cf. Moseley 2003: 161).

Fifthly, as we will come to appreciate, gig work extends and reconfigures imperialist social relations in developing countries in the Southern sphere of the world. Finally, however, the gig economy has generated new worker movements that engage in novel forms of class struggle in and against being digital labour and against managerial control of labour through platforms. And the crisis surrounding COVID-19 has been imaginatively used by these new movements to gain better gig employment conditions and rights. But before we discuss some of these critical points, we need, first, to map out in a little more detail the unique characteristics and properties of gig work.

DIGITAL GIG LABOUR AND CLASS RELATIONS

It is no easy task to define the gig or platform economy, let alone gain accurate figures of the number of workers in it. Forde et al. (2017) make a prescient observation here when they remark that most national statistical agencies do not systematically collect data on issues like costs and earnings on the platform economy, and research on gig work applies different methodologies, resulting in an assortment of estimates. Even so, we need to start with some definitions. Broadly speaking, then, platforms can be defined as digital structures and organisations that bring together different parties in order to interact with one another. They are, then, intermediaries that 'also come with a series of tools that enable their users to build their own products, services, and marketplaces' (Srnicek 2017: 43). Srnicek further observes that platforms are particularly good at collecting, extracting, recoding, organising and managing data of workers and users of platforms. Indeed, a major UK review of non-standard work notes: 'The gig economy tends to refer to people using apps to sell their labour' (Taylor et al. 2017: 25). In the United Kingdom, the House of Commons Work and Pensions Committee like-wise define the gig economy in similar terms:

> The term 'gig economy' is used to refer to a wide range of different types and models of work. A common feature of many of these is a reliance on intermediary digital platforms or apps to connect self-employed workers with work. Gig economy companies often operate in industries that have historically relied on self-employed workforces. New technology, however, enables them to operate on a scale which has substantial implications for the nature of work, the sectors in which they operate and the welfare state. (House of Commons Work and Pensions Committee 2017: 1)

Writing for the ILO, Berg et al. (2018) divide platform work into two broad categories. First, there is platform gig work associated with web-based jobs through which work-related tasks, such as IT work, are given to freelancers to complete for payment, and can be undertaken anywhere in the world – the remote gig workers alluded to in the introduction. Secondly, there is location-based platform gig work in which jobs are directly given to individuals to undertake tasks in specific spaces, such as offering a taxi service or household service.

Rinehart and Gitis (2015) add some important points about the gig economy. Gig work comprises 'mostly independent contractors and freelancers', such as agency temps, on-call workers, self-employed, con-tract workers, and part-time workers. The authors also note that the gig economy shares some similarities with practices in the sharing economy. For Rinehart and Gitis, the sharing economy operates when participants release the potential of underused assets for monetary or non-monetary benefits. Through decentralised networks and digital culture, partici-pants in other places can then contribute to developing these underused assets. Sharing models have become associated with gig workers through certain work platforms associated with well-known business brands like Uber, Lyft and Airbnb. Temporary work culture has therefore merged in different ways with the sharing ethos of online marketplaces. Similar to Rinehart and Gitis, Balaram et al. also connect the gig economy to sharing by distinguishing two types of platforms: asset-based platforms, predicated on whether one has an 'asset' like a spare room that can be advertised on a platform; and labour-based platforms, based on utilising one's skills or time via a platform (see also Unions NSW 2016).

Gig work can therefore be characterised as non-standard employment. Normally, non-standard is divided into four categories. First, is tempo-rary employment where individuals are employed for specific periods of time to complete a number of tasks. Secondly, there is part-time work, that is, individuals being employed on fewer hours than the average. Next, temporary agency work, which is work that involves work arrangements through multiple parties. Finally, disguised employment is often used by employers to evade certain work-related legal requirements, and so an employer might be 'masked' by hiring workers through a third party (ILO 2016). Gig work is temporary work and can also be part-time and based on zero hours contracts. Normally, gig work is found through a platform, with the platform acting as an agency to locate a gig worker with an employer. Platforms are attractive investments for corporations because once initial outlays have been paid to set one up, a platform is then opened up to third parties to add content to it, and do so freely. 'This stimulates network effects whereby value increases geometrically as the extensive range of products and services expands market share' (Howcroft and Bergvall-Kåreborn 2019: 23).

To get a sense of what sort of jobs are popular on labour-based platforms, it is instructive to briefly take stock of the global crowdsourcing and labour-based marketplace website, Freelancer.com. With 52 million registered users, Freelancer.com enables employers to post jobs online. Freelancers then bid for these jobs. In 2018, work related to creating and designing websites and online content was Freelancer.com's biggest jobs growth area, with the category, 'writing', increasing by a massive 537.5 per cent. Other growing online content areas include 'academic writing', 'blog writing', 'search engine optimization writing', '2D animation' and 'After Effects', which is a visual effects and motion graphics piece of software (Freelancer.com 2021). From March 2020 and for the rest of that year, when the first lockdown started in many countries, eight out of the ten fastest growing jobs were app development and website development. Overall, a record 2.1 million jobs were posted on Freelancer in 2020 (Freelancer.com 2021). In their face-to-face survey with 8,000 UK gig workers, Balaram et al. estimate that there are currently around 1.1 million UK workers who can be classified as gig workers. They discovered that 59 per cent, over half of respondents in their survey, worked in professional, creative or administrative services, such as copyediting, graphic designers and data entry, and gained such work through platforms like PeoplePerHour and Upwork. Next, they found that around 33 per cent of gig workers gained skilled work like plumbing and who sourced jobs through platforms like MyBuilder and RatedPeople. Finally, driving and delivery services made up around 16 per cent of the UK gig workforce, with platforms like Uber and Just Eat serving this group of workers. Another study published in June 2019, based on an online survey of 2,235 UK residents between the ages of 16 and 75, found that the number of people in the United Kingdom working for online platforms at least once a week has doubled from 4.7 per cent of the adult population to 9.6 per cent. Platform workers are more likely to be young, with 31.5 per cent aged 16–24 and 28.7 per cent aged 25–34. Most people who did gig work reported undertaking more than one type of platform employment.

> Simplifying this picture by aggregating categories into four main types shows that the largest category, at 7.8 per cent of the adult population, is online work. This is followed, at 5.4 per cent, by work involving the provision of services in other people's homes. Third in order of importance, at 5.1 per cent, is driving and delivery work, followed, at 3.5 per cent by running errands (Statistical Services and Consultancy Unit 2019: 17).

Schwellnus et al. (2019), however, estimate that a relatively small number of people – between 1 and 3 per cent of total employment – work for the global gig economy. One of the reasons why they arrive at a smaller figure is because they have a narrower definition of what constitutes the gig economy; for example, they rule out other areas of the sharing economy as forming part of the gig economy. Accordingly, they define the gig economy as, 'two-sided digital platforms that match workers on one side of the market to customers (final consumers or businesses) on the other side on a per-service ("gig") basis' (Schwellnus et al. 2019: 6). Deliberately, then, Schwellnus et al. (2019) exclude platforms based on one-sided business-to-customer platforms, and two-sided platforms, such as Airbnb, which are not intermediaries for labour (in the case of Airbnb, it acts as an intermediary for accommodation).

From reading some of the literature, it therefore appears that different results about the extent and size of the gig economy can be obtained depending on the definition of gig work that is applied. Most studies agree, however, that gig work is relatively new and is connected with the rise of digital platforms. At present, though, few studies on the gig economy reflect on the class composition of this digital labour. This is unsurprising. As we can see, there are several different ways of defining gig workers. Different reports on the gig economy, moreover, often only vaguely refer to class-relevant groupings, let alone linking these to critical issues like class oppression and class struggle in the gig workplace. As Joyce (2020) notes, many studies share a reluctance to analyse these relatively new forms of work to the primary contradiction of capitalism, namely, the continuous separation of labour from the means of production. So, while the following observations I now make on the relationship between the gig economy and social class are rather sketchy, they do, I think, provide some sort of guide on class-based characteristics of gig work.

First, platforms are means of production owned and controlled by digital corporations, who themselves employ a large number of people and who gain investment from large financial investors. Those who find work on these platforms do not, then, own and control these platforms, and so on this ground alone, specific class relations are evident in platform gig work. Gig work, though, attracts a number of different workers, some who gain more autonomy and payments than others. Professional and creative gig workers sell their labour-power, but also possess specialist skills, for example, specialist IT skills, which give them some autonomy over their working conditions and wages (Balaram et al. 2017). They often have a high degree of professional knowledge and competence and, according to Howcroft and Bergvall-Kåreborn (2019), they are closely aligned to the traditional self-employed. In terms of class, we can designate them as occupying semi-autonomous middle-class positions. Similarly, those skilled in certain trades, such as building, plumbing or car maintenance, will own their own tools and can also find work on platforms (see also Sutherland et al. 2020). In this instance, we might say that these individuals are acting as small businesses using a platform to hire out their trade skills to those that require them in much the same way that they would do so without a platform. They therefore appropriate their own labour time as profit and thus have some possession and control over their labour process. There are other gig workers, however, who have little control, possession or legal rights over their means of production. We discuss some examples of these gig employees below, but for now we can note that these are working-class gig operatives who are often located in online and contracted task platform labour that revolve around fragmented, Taylorist conditions with high levels of digital management control (see also Howcroft and Bergvall-Kåreborn 2019: 26; Forde et al. 2017). Platform workers in certain service sectors, like taxi services, or those doing micro-tasks paid at piece rates are illustrations of working-class gig workers.

It also needs to be borne in mind that the platform economy and gig work can, in theory at least, be both productive and unproductive. Indeed, it has the potential to design new and more efficient communication networks between productive and unproductive sectors (OECD 2016: 1). Elsewhere, the OECD suggests that important digital advancements, such as the Internet-of-Things (IoT), which refers to the 'ecosystem' connected through devices and sensors that share data and information with one another and channel this data and information to everyday applications and services, will be able to effectively and harmoniously bring together different sectors of the economy like health, education, transport and manufacturing (OECD 2017: 19). Such digital advancements make it easier for machines to transmit mobile data to other machines, ensuring not only that data flows more easily between productive and unproductive sectors, but that productive sectors can take advantage of apps and platforms to employ gig workers. In terms of productive sectors, then, Srnicek (2017: 65) argues that these latest technological developments enable major manufacturers to develop an 'industrial internet'; a specific process in which sensors and computer chips are embedded into the production process and trackers that are then connected through the internet. Industrial platforms therefore have the ability to connect 'sensors and actuators, factories and suppliers, producers and consumers, software and hardware' (Srnicek 2017: 67). Corporaal and Lehdonvirta (2017) suggest there are advantages for corporations to use platform freelancers. It gives them easy and flexible access to specialised skills and expertise, can reduce transaction costs of a contract, and eliminates conventional hiring processes. There are different work-related projects that freelancers can work on that include customer service, admin work, software development, and design and creative projects.

But while some productive sectors will employ gig and platform labour (see Chapter 5), it is probably true to say that at this moment in time, the unproductive sectors benefit most from gig work. For example, the JP Morgan report estimates that the biggest sector of gig work in the United States lies in transportation. The study found that between 2013 and 2018, transportation platforms, which include taxi services, delivery and moving, have grown to dominate the platform economy in terms of both numbers of participants and transactions. Indeed, by March 2018, transportation accounted for as many transactions as the other three major platform sectors of non-transport work, selling and leasing (Farrell et al. 2018: 3). Corporaal and Lehdonvirta also note: 'In most of the cases that we studied, firm adoption of platform sourcing was still at a relatively nascent stage' (Corporaal and Lehdonvirta 2017: 21). Similarly, Freelancer.com says that on their site, jobs associated with industrial design had fallen in 2018 by 60 per cent to 1,256, manufacturing jobs had fallen by 59.7 per cent to 1,808, while materials engineering had fallen by 57.7 per cent to 654 jobs (Freelancer.com 2019). With their narrower definition of the gig economy, Schwellnus et al. (2019) go further and suggest that 'in manufacturing, natural resources and a broad range of services industries, including public services, there is thus far no gig economy platform activity' (Schwellnus et al. 2019: 9). In other words, sectors like manufacturing that create a mass of surplus value in the global economy do not at present employ nearly as many gig or platform workers – digital labour – as is the case with unproductive sectors.

In terms of managerial non-labour, and this will be a point developed in the next section, digital labour provides a degree of flexibility for managers supervising contractual relations with gig workers (Berg et al. 2018b: 3). For instance, managers at platform-based companies can operate through an at-a-distance policy with their gig workers. Lots of platform-based companies function with a 'ratings' system, whereby the performance of individual gig workers is 'rated' online by customers. Rating workers in this way means that these companies no longer require normal HR-led peer and performance review mechanisms. Instead, they off-load this responsibility to the workers. As De Stefano (2016: 5) notes, such companies shift and outsource many functions of customer care to workers. Digital technology allows platform-based companies to create algorithms that act as automated management commands, while other platforms that deal in assigning micro-tasks to workers can automatically evaluate 'correct' solutions to problems in allocated tasks as they arise.

So-called 'algorithmic management' therefore includes factors like the continuous tracking of workers' performance, automated decision-making about tasks and evaluations of client feedback. These workers are therefore deprived 'of opportunities for feedback or discussion and negotiation with their supervisor, as would be typically the case in offline jobs' (Berg et al. 2018b: 9). Unsurprisingly, much that goes under the rubric of algorithmic management leaves little room for negotiation between management and workers. Indeed, a recent study that explored labour experiences in Australia of 'on-demand-work' for platform app companies, Deliveroo and UberEATS, found that management of these companies have developed obscure and hybrid bureaucratic forms of control of workers. Selected information is withheld from workers during their work. Addresses of customers, for example, are only revealed on the app once a delivery worker has picked up the order at a restaurant, which means that workers do not know exact locations between order pickup and customer location before they start a particular work task. Furthermore, management employs vague metrics which many workers do not fully understand. While most knew that management would give 'priority bookings' to those workers who provided a 'reliable service', it was less clear to them how exactly management, at an everyday level, made decisions about how the changing threshold of algorithmic ratings of workers actually function. Obscurity was, nevertheless, a useful device for management because it meant workers would try to second guess how these management decisions operated and so the workers responded in ways that normalised a certain 'customer-oriented mind-set' and 'the creation of a "techno-normative" control' over their digital labour process (Veen et al. 2020: 398)

Now that we have sketched out some of the class relations found in gig work, we need to start to analyse these in more critical detail, and relate them to a number of issues and points raised in previous chapters, including exploring some of the affects that COVID-19 has had on gig work. One place to start this discussion is through a common argument advanced that says gig work has unleashed a new type of flexibility in the workplace. Many welcome this development. For example, the RSA's report into gig work and the Taylor Review (2017) of modern working practices in the United Kingdom, argue that atypical work patterns and trends, such as part-time work, agency work, self-employment, temporary work, zero hours contracts, multi-jobs and gig economy work, present many benefits, such as the flexibility to set their own work schedule around other commitments in their everyday lives and the ability to gain more freedom and control over work (Balaram et al. 2017: 22, 35; Taylor et al. 2017: 95). Balaram et al., for instance, found that 53 per cent of their respondents were drawn to gig work because it provides them with greater flexibility. Yet, while Balaram et al. and Taylor et al. make some astute observations about this issue, there is also a sense that there is much missing in their respective analyses, not least a class-based and labour process account. It is to these issues that we now turn.

CLASS AND CONTROL IN THE GIG LABOUR PROCESS BEFORE AND DURING COVID-19

Some well-known policy studies, such as the Taylor Report, tend to downplay gig work and its relationship to new types of management control. 'Flexibility' gained from gig work can after all provide workers with a sense of 'freedom' over their work, which is beneficial. 'Platforms present individuals with greater freedom over when to work, and what jobs to accept or decline, than most other business models' (Taylor et al. 2017: 37). MBO Partners, a business located in the United States dedicated to matching independent professionals to enterprise organisations, provides an illustration to support Taylor et al.'s point. In their 2018 report, MBO claim that 4.8 million professionals in America would describe themselves as 'digital nomads'. For MBO, digital nomads are usually freelancers, independent contractors, self-employed, and are likely to be younger and male (although one-third are female), who enjoy the freedom to travel between countries, sometimes for years, sometimes for short periods, in order to work on projects via the Internet. These are typically creative professionals (writers, designers, editors and so forth), IT professionals, marketing professionals and ecommerce professionals, who enjoy working remotely and through short-term contracts to complete projects (MBO Partners 2018: 2). However, three distinct criticisms can be made of these optimistic pictures.

First, I doubt most would disagree that some types of gig work offer many opportunities to some. But as is the case in the 'real' world of work, gig work is mediated through different labour processes and different work experiences. Let us momentarily explore the issue of flexibility in order to expand on this point. Some studies of gig workers gain what seem at first glance to be similar results on the question of flexibility to those of the RSA and Taylor Reports. Lehdonvirta (2018) conducted a number of qualitative interviews with workers for three different platforms: Mechanical Turk sources online piecework for employers, such as transcribing receipts and classifying images; CloudFactory likewise finds pieceworkers for various online work, but also encourages its workers to meet a minimum earnings target, as well as a maximum earnings cap in order to ensure that there is enough work available for all its workers; MobileWorks applies algorithms to assign tasks to workers based on their skills, and employs managers to recruit pieceworkers, train them and then resolve any problems that might arise. But Lehdonvirta's study also provides subtly different results on the question of flexibility in the gig economy to those found in the RSA and Taylor Reports. Lehdonvirta approaches this issue, in part, within the domain of respective platform *labour processes*. He therefore explores matters such as the amount of *control* gig workers have during their employment for their respective platform employer (Lehdonvirta 2018: 14). In the case of workers at CloudFactory, flexible working is combined with sharing conversational time with fellow workers so that workers can then collectively discuss issues like coordinating work time around their own needs as employees. Lehdonvirta found that at the more individualised Mechanical Turk, workers were often less successful at coordinating time around their own needs because, in one sense at least, they did not enjoy the formal discussions of the type experienced by CloudFactory workers, but relied more on informal chat forums with fellow workers to gain advice and tips about temporal work structures.

Secondly, broadly positive accounts of gig work tend to underplay class relations in the gig labour process. For example, many who take on digital work in the unproductive sector have to transform themselves into an entrepreneurial individual who can try to anticipate and pre-empt 'job opportunities' in the gig marketplace (cf. Martin 2002: 78). One way to gain this financialised subjectivity in the world of gig work is through the soft and intangible character trait of the 'reputation' to complete gig work tasks to a high standard. Gaining 'reputation' in this sense, though, is fraught with difficulties. Schörpf et al.'s study of creative gig workers is instructive here. For these creatives, crowdsourcing platforms have become a key place for some creative gig workers to win work contracts. Two types of crowdsourcing platforms are particularly relevant. Bid-based platforms enable employers to post up jobs so creative workers can bid for them, while contest-based platforms allow creative workers to upload examples of their work to entice an employer who has posted up a specific job. Each platform will, in addition, expect creative workers to upload a profile of their past work experience and a portfolio, along with results of platform tests they complete on the platform including their proficiency in English. Yet, once jobs are gained, these workers then often face punishing schedules to finish them on time. After all, their 'reputation' is on the line, and to demonstrate a degree of flexibility they have to ensure that they are always on call to their employer, work long hours in a relatively short time period, blur the boundaries between work and leisure by being prepared to work during asocial hours to finish the project on time, and so forth. For Schörpf et al., therefore, maintaining a creative 'reputation' also represents modes of control (Schörpf et al. 2017: 106; for analysis of soft managerial control in Uber, see Rosenblat and Stark 2016; Stanford 2018).

Yet 'soft' managerial control can operate differently across classes. For example, in their study of the professional platform, Upwork, Sutherland et al. (2020) discovered that some of the middle-class professional freelancers on this platform would 'learn' strategies to gain high reputations. For example, one person interviewed told Sutherland et al. that he took a number of short-term, low-paying jobs in order to gather positive online reviews. Importantly, Sunderland et al. argue that while a platform for professionals like Upwork does have some similar algorithmic management techniques as found in companies like Uber, there is also a vital difference. '(D)ue to the more complicated and knowledge-intensive nature of online freelancing, (professional) gig workers typically enjoy a higher level of agency in connecting with clients and determining their own work' (Sutherland et al. 2020: 470). That is to say, these professional middle-class gig workers had more semi-autonomous control over their working conditions than other gig workers working for different platforms.

Thirdly, reports, like the Taylor Review, tend to discuss platforms in neutral terms as if platforms do not belong to corporations. Similarly, MBO note that, 'corporations large and small are expected to hire more remote workers – both independent and traditional – in the coming years' (MBO Partners 2018: 3). Corporations are depicted here as impartial global entities whose role is to simply 'hire more remote workers'. As we will see in the next section, this rather whimsical picture blocks out of view class-based politics and corporate power towards different 'remote' workers across the globe. For now, we can simply agree with the International Workers of the World GB (IWGB), who argue that it is clearly wrong to suggest that many gig companies are simply platforms. Uber is not only a 'platform', but is instead a transportation service that employs an app to conduct its business (IWGB 2017: 34–5).

These three points are all vital issues to address especially when we directly focus on digital gig labour and COVID-19. Precarity is associated with much that goes under the label of gig work, and with precarity comes related negative work themes such as limited rights in the workplace. Gig workers are often placed in the category of insecure work because gig work is contract-based. Jaccarini and Krebel (2020) note that before the pandemic hit the United Kingdom, unemployment was not high, and yet, at the same time, 5.1 million workers were in low paid and insecure work, which includes gig work and zero hours contracts. Before COVID-19, 30 per cent of these workers had reported that they could not manage if they lost one month of their household income. And while insecure work reached its highest level in 2013 at 19 per cent of the UK workforce, it has remained high ever since (Jaccarini and Krebel 2020). Since the pandemic, a large percentage of workers in 'atypical work' – temporary work, zero hours work and the like – have lost their main job or were furloughed. For example, almost one-fifth of temporary workers in the United Kingdom have lost their main job, while 31 per cent of workers with variable hours have lost their main job or have been furloughed (Gardiner and Slaughter 2020). One survey published in late March 2020 of 1,400 gig workers found that the majority who took part in the study initially had no income because of the pandemic, while a minority at 23 per cent had some money saved. Around 70 per cent felt dissatisfied with the support provided by the company they worked for. Over half of the gig workers said they had lost their jobs, while over 25 per cent had their hours cut (Moulds 2020).

Another survey of sixty-four platforms, however, reports that around 25 per cent of them provided financial assistance to their workers when the pandemic started. Frequently, this was the equivalent of two weeks salary, with the level of salary based on the level of activity with the platform pre-COVID (Scarpetta et al. 2020: 6). The charity, Fairwork, analysed how gig platforms have been building support mechanisms for their workforce during the pandemic. Fairwork conducted a survey of 191 platforms across forty-three countries and enquired into their working conditions under COVID-19 in respect to fair pay, fair conditions, fair contracts, fair management and fair representation. The authors found that of those surveyed, only 10 per cent of the platform companies paid their employees any pay loss compensation, even though this was the most important issue for workers. Most of the platform companies argued that their workers were independent contractors, which would then lessen the impact on the companies to pay sickness benefits. But 60 per cent of the companies did say they were providing personal protective equipment for their employees (Fairwork 2020).

As with any crisis, these job losses have taken a contradictory form. The pandemic has actually led to a surge in sales and an increase in employment opportunities for some digital corporations. In one month from March to April, Amazon employed 100,000 extra workers to cope with increased demand during the lockdown, while in mid-April it announced it was to hire a further 75,000 people. Amazon also increased its wages by $2 per hour, and increased its overtime pay (Romano 2020). COVID has, moreover, shown how many different gig workers have been 'essential' to normal day-to-day living under the pandemic. One only has to think about how 'at risk' groups, the elderly and other groups have relied heavily on gig workers to deliver food to them to appreciate this observation (Cherry and Rutschman 2020). Meanwhile, other well-known giants of the gig world have suffered badly under the pandemic. Uber, for example, initially experienced an 80 per cent drop in its business because of the virus. In early May, Uber announced it was laying off 14 per cent of its workforce, or 3,700 full-time employees, and then two weeks later announced it was going to lay off a further 3,000 employees. In April, Lyft announced it was laying off nearly 1,000 employees (Hawkins 2020).

But is it also possible to detect underlying long-term trends in respect to the gig economy? For example, while gig work is a notable and relatively new feature of the present-day capitalist economy, is it also reasonable to argue that gig work represents a new development in work-related practices which nevertheless share commonalities and similarities with older and more conventional tendencies of labour markets? We now explore these questions.

GIG WORK AND INSECURE LABOUR MARKETS

One important insight from the RSA report is its observation that there is a corresponding rise in the number of people undertaking gig work in the United Kingdom and the number of people taking up self-employed work. Certainly, self-employment has increased in the United Kingdom. The ONS reports that the number of self-employed people swelled from 3.3 million people (12 per cent of the labour force) in 2001 to 4.8 million (15.1 per cent) in 2017 (ONS 2018a). Since the 2008 Great Recession, the ONS shows that self-employment in the United Kingdom has continued to grow, and since 2014 self-employment jobs represents a larger share of total employment growth than its share of overall employment. Up until 2018, self-employment contributed to around one-third of total UK employment growth. Interestingly, the ONS also states that the main rise in self-employment from 2001 to 2016 occurred with individuals who work with a partner or for themselves, while those who are self-employed but also hire employees has actually fallen over this period. Self-employed people who work for themselves or with a partner constitute around 4 million workers, whereas in 2001 they numbered 2.4 million workers, and it is these workers who would seem to fit the characteristics of a self-employed gig worker.

Still, while recognising a link between self-employment and the gig economy, the RSA does not attach these figures to wider employment trends over time. What the RSA does note is that since the financial crisis of 2008, self-employment in the United Kingdom has increased, which is true enough. However, if this data is merged with data on employment trends per se over a longer time period, then we can start to present a significantly different picture of the UK gig economy. Figures suggest that for the United Kingdom the lowest employment rate was actually in 1983 and stood at 65.6 per cent. During this time, Britain was in the middle of a recession. Employment increased in the years after 1983, but as expected there are dips at various other points in time. For instance, the employment rate decreased again from 1990 until a low point in April 1993 when it stood at 68.3 per cent. Before the pandemic, the employment rate next started to decline again in May 2008, reaching a low point of 70.1 per cent in August/October 2011 (ONS 2018b).

What is the significance of these trends? As Moody notes, one important detail here is that the emergence of the so-called 'gig economy' actually represents a long-standing cycle of multiple job-holding 'that happened to be accompanied by an as yet marginal rise in those seeking work through the Internet rather than newspaper want ads, old-fashioned employment agencies, or vanishing state employment services' (Moody 2017: 28). In particular, the rise in temporary work comes about during and after an economic recession. At these moments, employment rates decline as more people lose their jobs or firms just stop hiring new people. We see this during the pandemic. Not only have unemployment levels increased (see Chapter 4), but the number of people looking for temporary work has also risen. One survey in August 2020, noted that the United Kingdom saw the fastest rate increase in the supply of temporary workers in over twenty years of data collection on this area, which was driven mostly by redundancies coming from the pandemic (KPMG and REC 2020).

De Stefano (2016) makes a similar observation. He notes that the 'extreme flexibility' evident in gig work has been part of a wider casualisation process of the labour market for some time now. Zero hours and 'hire' and 'fire' have been the mainstay for large numbers of the workforce. At the more extreme end of this development, suggests De Stefano, has been the 'demutualisation of risks' in which employers use 'disguised employment relationships' so that they can escape labour and social security obligations towards their workforce. Instead, such obligations and their accompanying risks are simply passed on to their workers (De Stefano 2016: 7). Likewise, Peticca-Harris et al. (2020) argue that some types of gig work (they interviewed Uber taxi drivers) provide a temporary space for individuals seeking employment opportunities in precarious jobs markets in their journey to eventually gaining permanent jobs. In this respect, continue Peticca-Harris et al. (2020: 53), gig work is not only a 'platform of precarity' for these people, but can also act as a platform 'of opportunity'.

Once all these points are acknowledged, it should come as less a surprise that gig work is often used by employees to top up earnings gained from more traditional types of employment. For their 2018 report, researchers at JP Morgan tracked supply-side participation and earnings through the US platform economy. They identified 38 million payments directed through 128 different online platforms to 2.3 million families participating in the platform economy between October 2012 and March 2018. Importantly, the report notes: 'Platforms are not replacing traditional sources of family income. Among those who have participated in the Online Platform Economy at any point in a year, average platform earnings represent roughly 20 percent of total observed take-home income in any month of that year' (Farrell et al. 2018: 4). During the pandemic, evidence similarly exists that suggests that more people have taken up gig work opportunities in order to top up lost income or to find new work after unexpectedly losing their job. One study of food couriers in Poland found that opportunities to make what was considered by the couriers to be satisfactory amounts of money during the pandemic was relatively high. This was because food orders had increased, and with more orders came greater levels of pay (Polkowska 2021).

For these reasons, van Doorn (2017) quite rightly argues that those platforms that support gig work should be seen as 'platform labour intermediaries', which act like temporary staffing agencies. Similar to temporary staffing agencies, platform labour intermediaries therefore reconstitute labour relations and the nature of work in line with a neoliberal and financialised sensibility. To expand a little, the last decade or so has seen an increase in what is commonly known as the 'temporary staffing industry' (TSI). Designed initially to provide temporary cover for absent staff, the TSI has grown through the years and now covers a wide variety of industries and occupations. Yet as it has grown and now operates in the public sector in areas such as nursing and education as well as the private sector, the TSI industry has also been used as one way to attack certain employment benefits, union rights and general rights in the workplace. Employers therefore like TSI practices for these reasons, and this is complemented in their eyes by lower regulatory costs (Peck and Theodore 2007: 190). For van Doorn, therefore, platform and gig work operate as relatively new types of labour intermediaries, which have helped to restructure labour relations. Not only is this the case in terms of reclassifying the status of platform and gig workers as independent contractors, and who thereby enjoy less rights in the workplace than permanent employees, but also by increasing the fungible and superfluous nature of the workforce. For van Doorn, platforms that employ labour anticipate a constant churn and turnaround of employees – 'a "surplus population" of underemployed gig workers' (van Doorn 2017: 904) – so that many workers become invisible to customers and to one another.

Another notable commonality of gig work to other types of work can be found in relation to imperialism, especially imperialist value chains. Like some other types of work, gig work often operates in varying degrees in imperialist value chains. At the same time, and again like other workforces, those working in the gig economy have engaged in a class offensive in and against their employers and employment conditions both before and during the pandemic, most noticeably by forming trade unions. We now turn to look at these issues.

CLASS STRUGGLES OVER FINANCIALISED AND IMPERIALIST GIG WORK

Class relations in gig work operate through financialisation. Uber is a particularly good illustration of how capitalisation, financialisation and gig work function together. As Stanford observes: 'Intense investor excitement in "hot new prospects," combined with the capacity of flexible financial markets to generate purchasing power to pay for large and speculative financial placements, has made the owners of Uber fantastically wealthy – on paper, at least' (Stanford 2018: 28). Financial investors have laid bets on the future of Uber, and anticipate that Uber will be profitable in its different ventures at some point soon. But things do not always go to plan for financial investors. Unexpected crises like that unleashed by the pandemic can have adverse consequences for digital companies like Uber, as already noted.

Financialisation, however, also operates in the gig economy through imperialist value chains. Shestakofsky's case study of a San Francisco tech start-up called AllDone is instructive in this respect. AllDone seeks to bring together buyers and sellers of services, such as house cleaning, wedding photography and so on. Launched in early 2010, over 600 service categories were represented on AllDone, and its expansion was rapid. By June 2013, more than 250,000 sellers had signed up to its site. The company would eventually be valued at $1 billion in the financial marketplace. According to Shestakofsky, at the start of their set-up executives soon realised that there was a 'machine lag' between what they imagined AllDone could achieve and the actuality of what the firm was realistically accomplishing. In order to overcome this machine lag, the executives employed the computational labour of Philippine workers, 'who performed repetitive information-processing tasks to complement software infrastructure' (Shestakofsky 2017: 383). AllDone executives also employed people in the Las Vegas area who, through their emotional labour, could reassure users as to the robustness and accessibility of their software. Soon, AllDone attracted more venture capital funding, with one venture capital firm pumping in $12 million.

AllDone therefore usefully illustrates how gig work is often connected globally through imperialist and financial value chains. More broadly, low wages and low levels of control over working conditions are reproduced in gig work that is especially evident in Southern countries like India, Malaysia, Nigeria, the Philippines and Vietnam. Naturally, there are many who take on gig work in these countries who are content with their wages and the additional skills they gain while doing the work. Graham et al. (2017) discovered examples of people working on digital platforms in places like the Philippines under these favourable conditions. But Graham et al. found many other examples of professionals working in the gig economy who secured less generous benefits. A female worker from Ho Chi Minh City, who was an ex-banker with a degree in economics, often took on low skilled and low wage gig work. One platform job, for instance, involved labelling images for 8 hours per day. Precarious working conditions were also evident in some of the gig work she undertook. For instance, she initially agreed an hourly rate of US$8 with one of her employers, only for the employer to lower the rate to US$6 due to the project 'not going well'. The project was then subsequently discontinued without any notice. Subsequently, this particular worker had moved from a professional middle-class occupation in the banking sector, to a working-class occupation with little control or possession over the means of production. In terms of workplace bargaining, then, these conditions present many gig workers in Southern countries with a feeling of being 'disempowered', especially since employers are often located in the North in countries like the United States, making face-to-face bargaining over wages a near impossibility (Graham et al. 2017: 153).

But two additional factors mark out gig workers in these chains. First, gig workers are often inserted into precarious global value chains, while, secondly, gig workers are not in most cases embedded in a labour process that brings workers together in one shared space. They are, instead, included in a delinked labour process of individual workers who might share their collective experiences with other online workers, but arguably only a few will meet face-to-face with fellow gig workers (Graham and Anwar 2019; see also Callaghan and Thompson 2001). Perhaps unsurprisingly, then, gig work can create new modes of alienated labour. Some who work for platform companies do menial, repetitive and simple tasks like checking online surveys or tagging online images (Webster 2016: 59), while being paid at cheaper than normal rates, 'without any of the associated social protection or moral obligation' (Bergvall-Kåreborn and Howcroft 2014: 221). One survey conducted for the ILO (De Stefano 2016), found that 40 per cent of respondents reported they regularly worked seven days a week and 50 per cent indicated that they had worked for more than 10 hours during at least one day in the past month. 'Low pay coupled with the need to work resulted in workers spending long hours online' (Berg and De Stefano 2017).

Ideologically speaking, and as Irani (2015) observes, advocates of platform employment opportunities suggest that gig work is in fact 'innovative', 'creative' and 'valuable' forms of digital labour, which is conducted through 'free collaboration' in non-hierarchical global networks of peer production – the so-called sharing economy (Irani 2015: 735; see also Crouch 2019: 6). This, of course, is a fetishised view of gig work because it focuses on 'equal' and 'free' market transactions between individual gig workers and 'individual' capitalist employers. It thereby mystifies underlying oppressive social relations between both (see Marx 1988: 164–5; see also Crompton and Gubbay 1980: 12).

Despite these oppressive social relations, gig workers nevertheless engage in collective action in and against platform management in a variety of countries. For Wood and Lehdonvirta (2021), platforms possess unique coordinating mechanisms in the job market. Platforms can allocate tasks, set prices for different jobs, collect data and so on. Moreover, platforms manage membership accounts and enforce rules and regulations for its members. Therefore, platforms reduce management costs as well as other costs such as those relating to information, still exert control over labour, govern labour demand for a plethora of jobs and so on (Wood and Lehdonvirta 2021: 9–10). Through interviews with remote gig workers, Wood and Lehdonvirta discovered that respondents were willing to assert their work rights against what they considered to be client micromanagement by threatening to exit working relationships with certain clients. Some remote gig workers who employed this tactic would also encourage other fellow remote gig workers to employ similar tactics if need be. But while this gave some remote gig workers a degree of autonomy in the workplace, they were also subject to the rules and regulations of the platform from which they received work. Still, Wood and Lehdonvirta found that these similar experiences and relations of antagonism towards platforms actually brought remote workers together through sets of shared interests.

> In fact, findings suggested widespread support for unions, despite the fact that almost none of the informants had any previous experience of organised labour, and that the informants had little certainty as to how unions could function in a gig economy. A clear theme was the hope that a union could rebalance the freelancers' subordinated relationship with the platform. (Wood and Lehdonvirta 2021: 27)

It is little surprise, then, that recent years have seen gig workers organising themselves through both conventional and new collective organisations. In October 2018, for example, representatives from different courier and delivery platform worker organisations, and arriving from across Europe and from the United States, met in Brussels and founded the Transnational Federation of Couriers (TFC). The summit lasted two days and activists discussed struggles and strategies in and around gaining greater rights and worker representation in their respective digital employment. TFC was democratically established at the summit with the aim to create global campaign networks for couriers. Key discussions included, first, ways to organise courier activism, such as the use of rallies, assemblies strikes, disconnections, pickets and occupations; secondly, debates about whether platform couriers are freelance or employed workers; and thirdly, how algorithms manage and control the work that platform couriers do (Alter Summit 2018).

Cant and Mogno (2020) argue that what is unique about the class struggle of TFC is that it is building a global worker union based on collective activism around similar worker experiences. Many workers' experiences are, of course, qualitatively different from one another. Think for moment of the issue discussed in the previous chapter of the different experiences of productive workers in global value chains. Workers in the Northern hemisphere, in countries like the United States and United Kingdom, have noticeably distinct work-related experiences to those in the Southern hemisphere in countries like the Philippines. For Cant and Mogno, however, platform workers such as courier and delivery workers globally share very similar experiences and platform capitalists often adopt the same business model. This has therefore generated spaces of commonality among courier and delivery platform workers across the globe; for instance, the common experience of waiting for work to come in via apps, working for piece rates and using self-communicating digital media to discuss among one another and across nation-states rights in their workplace and pay and conditions. The TLC emerged in these conditions and has since engaged in a number of campaigns, not least expressing solidarity with migrant platform workers, compiling a list of data concerning delivery workers killed doing their job in order to campaign for better safety at work, and helping to organise direct action for local disputes between courier and delivery workers and the platforms for which they work (Cant and Mogno 2020).

Other cases of platform workers from different countries coming together to fight for their rights are readily apparent. In 2017, the United Private Hire Drivers (UPHD) was formed in the United Kingdom, which serves as a union for app-based drivers. It arose from the legal challenge brought by two drivers in 2016 against Uber. The drivers claimed they were not self-employed while working for Uber, but were in fact legally employed by Uber and so deserved legally recognised workplace rights and protections. In January 2020, representatives and members of UPHD and the IWGB, along with other representatives from twenty-three countries, met in London to discuss strategies and share information about action against platform operators. From this conference was born the International Alliance of App-Based Transport Workers (IAATW). One specific point to emerge from the conference was the need for activists across countries to pool together data and information to gain a more nuanced understanding of how apps operate to regulate and control platform drivers (Varghese 2020). The long-established GMB union in Britain managed as well to secure a deal for Hermes' self-employed couriers. The deal is a collective bargaining agreement between GMB and Hermes to support certain workplace rights of the self-employed couriers, including the right of couriers to take holiday pay and have guaranteed earnings (GMB 2019). Independent worker centres have also emerged, mostly in the United States, to provide advice, resources and social services to a wide range of workers in distinct geographical locations. The centres in particular provide support for those in non-standard forms of work and who face obstacles in forming unions in their workplaces (Johnston and Land-Kazlauskas 2018: 16).

COVID-19, and the crisis surrounding it, has also provided avenues for these workers to take their collective action further, and extend their activism across workers' unions. UPHD, for example, launched a campaign in April 2020 to force the British government to introduce safety measures for Uber and other platform drivers after the death of an Uber driver from coronavirus. UPHD noted that while Uber and other operators had provided free or discounted travel to NHS staff, it had not provided basic measures to prevent risk of infection to drivers. For UPHD, this amounted to corporate negligence and government and regulatory failure to tackle an industry-wide problem of worker rights abuse (UPHD 2020). On 10 June, the IWGB in the United Kingdom organised a virtual strike of its medical courier members. Specifically, the strike was called because some medical couriers were going to be made redundant by an NHS contractor, the Doctors Laboratory. According to IWGB, the Doctors Laboratory was not only going to make some medical couriers redundant during the pandemic, but it had also failed to maintain certain health and safety measures, including maintaining adequate PPE, social distancing and regular Covid-19 testing for couriers that enter wards to collect coronavirus samples (IWGB 2020).

CONCLUSION

Given the fact that the gig economy supports neoliberal and financialised labour markets, then one should not be too shocked to learn that many governments have made only tentative moves to regulate gig work. In the United Kingdom, for example, the Conservative government in December 2018, and following the Taylor Report, released their *Good Work Plan* with policy recommendations to employment practices. Many of the policy proposals contained in the *Plan* have since been made into law. Among other proposals, agency workers now have a right to receive a document from their employer that sets out clearly information about work assignments, and after twelve weeks service in one assignment, agency workers can expect wages comparable with permanent employees. Moreover, the threshold to request a right to be consulted at work about issues in an organisation was reduced from fifty employees putting in such a request to management to a minimum of fifteen employees. If an employer engages in aggregated breach of contract, they can now face a penalty of up to £20,000, whereas it used to £5,000 (Good Work Plan 2018).

However, these changes only go so far, and do not change the critical issues we have discussed about gig work. As the TUC points out, to really tackle the problems in gig work, a further set of policies are required. They advocate five in particular:

- a ban on zero-hours contracts and bogus self-employment;
- decent rights for all workers and the return of protection against unfair dismissal;
- all workers should enjoy the same basic rights as employees, including redundancy pay and family-friendly rights;
- new rights so that workers can be protected by a union in every workplace;
- new rights for workers to bargain through unions for fair pay and conditions across industries (Sharp 2019).

The TUC has been consistent in campaigning for these rights. Before the publication of the *Good Work Plan*, the TUC was arguing that insecure workers needed more protection. According to a TUC report published in 2017, there are around 3.2 million people in the United Kingdom that face insecurity at work. Insecurity at work includes zero hours contract workers, agency workers, seasonal workers and low paid self-employed workers (TUC 2017: 8–9). Zero hours contract workers and self-employed workers are the fastest growing groups of insecure workers in the United Kingdom. Of these insecure jobs, it is women who account for the largest increase at 58 per cent within them. Moreover, 'Black, Asian and minority ethnic workers are over a third more likely than white workers to be in temporary or zero-hours work ... Black workers in particular face insecurity at work, and are more than twice as likely as white workers to be in temporary and zero-hours work' (TUC 2017: 9; see also Moody 2017: 37–8).

In other words, both in the United States and the United Kingdom, greater levels of low-paid and insecure working-class jobs are being taken by BAME groups as well as by women. This point relates to the arguments made in Chapters 1 and 3, which stated that class relations are formed through economic, political and cultural processes, identities and relationships. So, while the productive working class based in the likes of manufacturing jobs has declined since the 1980s, the unproductive working class based in places like the gig economy has risen. Still, platform workers have demonstrated great resolve and tenacity in mobilising other workers and building collective representative bodies and unions to campaign for greater platform work rights. This has been achieved, in part, by platform workers, like courier workers, using limited resources to form alliances with other worker bodies and unions. UPHD, for example, is affiliated to the IWGB. Platform workers have likewise been successful in mounting public campaigns around a variety of issues, not least more recently issues related to the pandemic, and, in the process, maintaining media profiles that are often favourable towards their plight. Sometimes, the public profile these campaigns attract has translated into government action setting minimum standards for employment protection for platform workers (Vandaele 2018).

Insecure work, however, also operates in hospitality jobs like restaurants, along with residential care, the education sector and the public sector. Indeed, the next chapter examines in greater detail how the public sector has been steadily marketised and privatised. This has reproduced greater levels of insecure work in its ranks, while, correspondingly, digital technology has been at the forefront in pushing these changes in labour processes in the public sector.

Chapter 9

DIGITAL WORK IN THE STATE AND PUBLIC SECTOR BEFORE AND DURING COVID-19

INTRODUCTION

The UN's E-government Survey 2018 placed the United Kingdom at number four in providing government information and services through the Internet (UN 2018). Arguably, part of the UK's success is associated with the steady growth of e-government in delivering public services for well over two decades (Coleman 2004; Roberts 2014). Since 2011, for instance, the UK government has been keen to introduce Agile ICT development in the public sector. Briefly, Agile is based on the belief that working software can be applied in the public sector so that those working in public services can respond quickly to changes in society, collaborate with public service 'customers' and 'citizens', and, in the process, reduce the need to publish documents (Michaelson 2013: 296–7). Agile is predicated on applying both digitised labour (or automation) and the digitisation of labour in UK public services.

There are currently a number of illustrations of Agile at work in the UK's public sector. University College Hospital in London has started to employ artificial intelligence to analyse appointments for MRI scans, with the intention to detect 90 per cent of patients who would fail to attend hospital appointments. Failure to keep hospital appointments, which then disrupts clinical management and other resources, currently costs the NHS £1 billion per year. An algorithm has therefore been developed that computes non-linear and complex interactions between many variables concerning hospital data. Machine-learning is thus coupled with large-scale complex and rich data, which can be applied to the specific case of hospital appointments. 'Complex models', according to Nelson et al., therefore 'not only predict attendance, enabling targeted intervention, but also prescribe it by matching detailed appointment and patient characteristics' (Nelson et al. 2019: 1). A more controversial example

192

of the use of Agile in the United Kingdom has been the introduction of Universal Credit (UC). Aiming to bring a raft of existing benefits in the United Kingdom, such as unemployment benefit and housing benefit, under one payment system in order to make the benefit system more streamlined and to give greater incentives to those on benefits to get back into the workplace, the introduction of UC has fallen way behind its intended introduction into the welfare infrastructure. Rather than its intended roll out in 2017, it is now estimated that it will be eventually fully working by 2022 (Butler, P. 2018).

UC has been dogged by an array of blunders and problems, not least in its use of Agile technology to get it up and running. Millions have been spent on just the design and development of software required to get UC to function, and further millions have been spent integrating a raft of services for UC to work properly. Contracts have been handed out to procure service providers to do this work, and to maintain and monitor the infrastructure over the years. Digital expansion is also intended to equip claimants with a degree of digital literacy because all communications about benefits will be online. Michaelson (2013) argues, however, that this has potential negative consequences for those who will need to claim UC, because many in this social group have relatively low IT skills compared with other social groups in society. Far from streamlining and making the benefit system leaner, UC has moreover so far already been embroiled in IT system failure. As The Guardian reported in 2013, a national auditor's report found that UC had not been good value for money. Up until the end of April 2013, most of its money had been spent on building IT programs, and of this £303 million, £34 million had to be written off due to IT problems and malfunctions (Watt et al. 2013).

The pandemic has exposed these problems to a wider public. The first point to note here is that the virus initially pushed a huge number of people into the category of claimant unemployment. Claimant unemployment is a combination of claimants on Jobseeker's Allowance and claimants on Universal Credit who are in the category of 'searching for jobs'. In the United Kingdom, according to the ONS, this figure rose to 2.8 million people in May 2020, a massive increase of 1.6 million from two months previously in March 2020. Moreover, the number of job adverts and vacancies noticeably fell. From March to May 2020, UK vacancies saw the largest quarterly fall since 2001, which was the year when the ONS began to collect this data. During the first three months of the lockdown, from March to May 2020, there were an estimated 476,000 vacancies in the United Kingdom. This was 342,000 fewer vacancies than in the previous quarter from December 2019 to February 2020 (ONS 2020i). Under these circumstances, the flaws in UC become more pronounced. One defect of UC is that it has a disproportionate negative impact on Black and Ethnic Minority (BAME) groups. As we know from previous chapters, some BAME groups are in the lower income levels or in poverty, and so it will be especially difficult for them to cover for basic costs if there is a delay in payments (Sandhu 2016; see also Baraki 2020). Other evidence suggests that between 430,000 and 560,000 who were eligible for UC assistance at the start of the pandemic did not apply. Around 220,000 of these people who believed they were eligible did not want to claim, with the 'perceived hassle of claiming' (59 per cent) being the most common reason given, but with 27 per cent saying they did not claim because of 'benefit stigma'. About 280,000–390,000 did not claim UC because they wrongly believed they did not qualify for UC assistance (Geiger et al. 2021).

This sorry tale of Agile and UC provides us with some of the themes that will be discussed in this chapter. We will see that the state and public sector produces a novel set of tensions in terms of digital labour, digitisation of labour and digitised labour. By marketising and privatising the welfare state, and by using automated digitised labour and developing new routes to the digitisation of public sector work, there has been a struggle between managers and different segments of public sector workers over whether state labour can be transformed into more profitable and capital-intensive types of labour. Or, more specifically, financialisation and neoliberalism have made an attempt to introduce a type of unproductive capitalisation of the public sector labour process. Staying with the United Kingdom, there has been a concerted effort by successive governments since the early 1980s to contract out much of the public sector to private companies, which, as we will see, is still occurring under the pandemic. This, then, is an attempt to transform the public sector into mostly unproductive profitable avenues for capital. Technology is employed by private companies to achieve these goals. Many of the private companies who take charge in the running of the public sector are not, however, based in productive capital, but are, instead, found in unproductive areas of the economy, such as in hedge funds, which bid to take over and run certain public sector operations.

Occasionally, struggles between public sector workers and managers will be focused on whether some public sector departments can be transformed into exploitable productive spheres, but more often than not, these struggles revolve around the increased economic oppression of public sector workers by unproductive private companies who take over and manage public sector work. In fact, previous research by labour process scholars shows that public sector workers, including those in working-class and middle-class locations, are more willing than those employed in the private sector to challenge and resist managerial control over their work mainly because they embody 'non-capitalist' logics in how they see and perform their work-related duties. As a result, some newer management strategies linked with financialisation often fail in the public sector due to more successful strategies of class struggle waged by public sector employees (Pérez and Cifuentes 2020). We will see examples of these struggles below, but it is also true to say that the pandemic made many of these struggles more visible to the public.

In discussing these points, the chapter will also concentrate on a number of important issues around co-production, digital work and lean ideology in the public sector. More precisely, it will underline a number of contradictions, dilemmas and tensions in the use of digital technology and digital media in the move to privatise the welfare state, and it will flag up the class struggles that emerge in and around these changes. These are all vital points to make because they focus our attention on how public sector work is being subject to greater levels of economic oppression through the entrenchment of unproductive capital in its everyday practices. We start, first, by examining some aspects associated with the hegemonic project of the neoliberal capitalist state, which will provide us with much-needed theoretical tools to apply to a number of empirical public sector contexts.

THE LEAN, FINANCIALISED, WORKFARE STATE AND COVID-19

Noordegraaf (2016) argues that it is important to avoid simple dualisms that posit the professionalism of public sector employees as being undermined by 'managerialism'. In fact, some go further and insist that a digital network society has brought new opportunities for people to become 'co-creators' of state and public policies. According to Castells, we now live in an age of 'networked individualism' in which 'individuals build their networks, on-line and off-line, on the basis of their interests, values, affinities, and projects' (Castells 2001: 131). 'Thick' sociability, associated with nation-states and a sense of belonging within close-knit communities, has therefore been replaced in a network society by 'thin' sociability' based around specific policy projects and multi-layered networks that bring together a whole host of 'partnership' arrangements between community organisations, public sector bodies, private business and voluntary organisations. As a result, 'the kind of political culture and political communication advanced by good governance is premised on the identification of policy projects and the creation of policy publics' between a variety of groups and interests (Bang and Esmark 2009: 17).

Community groups, as part of a partnership network with others, enjoy some freedom to help to co-create a specific local policy. As a result, where political and power asymmetries exist between groups in a policy network, these can nevertheless be balanced out because these imbalances are not an inherent feature of political authority (see Bang and Esmark 2007).

Yet, while it is true that certain types of power between groups in civil society and the state might be alleviated or lessened at specific points in time, it is nevertheless problematic to make the stronger claim that an 'asymmetry' is somehow atypical of aspects of political authority. The capitalist state is in fact best viewed as a concentration of force and as a strategic relation of powers. Capitalist accumulation is a global social relation. Capital annihilates space and time and seeks to conquer the world. Capital is at the same time mediated through the power of property rights and money. Globally, capital must ensure that both these powers – property rights and money – are imposed in different countries. Social relations allied to and connected with property rights and money therefore arise in civil society and then come to be enforced, governed and regulated through law and the state, or, more precisely, through legal forms of the person, property and contract. Money is also made legal tender by the state (Clarke 1988: 127). Under capitalism, therefore, the 'economic' and the 'political' separate from one another, and the 'political' fragments into a multiplicity of national states, which nevertheless are connected together through global forms of money and global political bodies. 'The relation of the national state to capital is a relation of a nationally fixed state to a globally mobile capital' (Holloway 1995: 126). Thus, the class character of the state is founded in both money and the state as being the complementary forms of existence of capital-in-general (Clarke 1988: 125).

Money and the state do not, however, share a passive relationship with one another. State and legal forms gain their identities at particular points in time through the reproduction of capital. So, a crisis in a dominant capitalist accumulation strategy at a particular point in time – such as the 2008 global crisis of financialised accumulation strategies – is also potentially a crisis in the particular form of the state at a particular point in time – such as a potential crisis of the neoliberal state. And as a moment of capital, the state is also a moment of class struggle. The capitalist state therefore not only seeks to organise a consensual basis applicable for a specific capitalist accumulation strategy, it also seeks to galvanise support for its own basis of socio-political representation. If this is the case, then the state is not a coherent and substantive institution as such. It is, rather, a condensation of class forces, projects and strategies which endeavour to modify and influence the balance of class and social forces in society as a whole. The state, then, is both a site of class struggle and a site for class struggle – it is a strategic battlefield (Poulantzas 2000). As such, the state does not possess its own autonomous power, but rather acts as a centre and exercise for classes and groups to build and win support for specific hegemonic socio-political projects (Gramsci 1986).

The hegemonic state project that has since the 1980s become dominant, at least in the most powerful capitalist societies, is a neoliberal workfare state (see also Chapter 4). A workfare state can broadly be defined as the subordination of welfare benefits to the performance of labour in the economy. This is supplemented by a variety of measures to make labour flexible in the market place and to subordinate social policy to economic global competitiveness, the privatisation of public services, permanent innovation and new modes to discipline labour, such as curbing trade union rights in the workplace. Jessop is clear that the workfare state assumes a number of forms depending upon specific institutional arrangements and different path dependencies. While liberal strategies pursued by the US and UK governments might be said to be the most well-known workfare strategy, there also exist neo-corporatist strategies (based upon, for instance, high taxation for social investment), neo-statist strategies (based upon, for instance, state-regulated competition and state auditing of public–private sectors), and neo-communitarian strategies (based, for instance, upon the empowerment of voluntary organisations, fair trade and social cohesion) (Jessop 2002: 259–67).

The move towards workfare has impacted on the state and public sector. In the United Kingdom, for example, over recent decades there has been a substantial marketisation of public services. This involves the imposition of free market forces onto and into public services, including the commercialisation of public services and public sector workers by, for example, giving public sector contracts to private business, making public services compete with one another for resources through market mechanisms, treating service users as 'consumers', and ensuring that business interests have a prime place and role in determining public policy making (Whitfield 2006: 7). Since 2010, those managing UK public services have also had to endure severe funding cutbacks under the auspices of 'austerity'. As the Institute for Fiscal Studies notes, departmental spending in the United Kingdom was more than £40 billion lower in 2018–19 than in 2009–10. Some departments, like the Ministry of Justice and the Department for Environment, Food and Rural Affairs, have seen a reduction of around 40 per cent (IFS 2019).

Neoliberal state hegemony has therefore made it easier for unproductive forms of capitalisation to become embedded in the UK's public services. Private companies and corporations that have hospitality, food, security and cleaning services, as well as a whole raft of other functions, have taken over and now run these amenities in many public services. Many of these private firms are also based overseas. As Whitfield observes, 'markets and the procurement process led to increased competition between employers on staffing levels, working practices and terms and conditions, and in a globalising economy, where different parts of the service will be produced' (Whitfield 2006: 135). Financialisation of public services has subsequently taken on a variety guises in recent years. Privately led and managed joint venture companies that take control of some public sector services enjoy their own accounting and reporting mechanisms, is just one illustration of these practices (Whitfield 2012). These, though, are often opaque financial mechanisms that lack proper public scrutiny. The Carillion scandal, which became a public talking point in the United Kingdom in late 2017 and early 2018, is instructive here. Carillion was a multinational construction service, and held many contracts with the UK government on outsourced public services. Carillion also made millions by selling off many buildings it had netted through such deals with government, including £200 million after 2010. Purchasers of Carillion projects were in many cases offshore funds that paid no UK corporation tax. Ominously, Carillion also accumulated huge debts through these and other purchases of large companies. By 2017, its financial edifice started to buckle as the debts were exposed and seen as being hugely risky. In January 2018, Carillion went into liquidation (ESSU 2018).

COVID-19 has provided new opportunities for private companies to take on more public sector and NHS contracts. By February 2021, there were thirty-eight strategic suppliers bidding to manage and run a variety of public sector policy areas. These strategic suppliers included well-known public brands like Microsoft, IBM, Serco, Capital, as well as less well-known brands like Amey. In 2020, strategic suppliers won 165 contracts worth £737 million out of the 2,500 contracts from the UK government's COVID response. While this represented only 3.5 per cent of the total value of the COVID response contracts, strategic suppliers nevertheless took control of major government initiatives, such as the test and trace programme (Tussell 2020). Pandemic opportunities for private companies to gain public sector contracts also extends globally. One study estimated that governments around the world spend around $13 trillion per year on public contracts for goods, services and works. Of this figure, over $10 trillion is spent by sixteen countries, including

China, the United States, Japan, Germany, the United Kingdom, Brazil, the Netherlands, Russia and Spain. Very few of these contracts – only 2.8 per cent of them, in fact – are published openly. Crisis-forms surrounding COVID-19 have presented new openings for companies to win public sector contracts. Between January and July 2020, governments around the world paid out around $100 billion in COVID-19-related contracts. At the same time, the report argues that the pandemic has demonstrated the ineffectiveness and impervious nature of procurement in terms of best deals for taxpayers for their public services. In the words of the report:

> Around the world, governments needing to respond quickly and efficiently to the emergency often struggled under archaic and ineffective systems. Buyers and suppliers failed to connect, and in many cases, governments weren't able to respond to a scarce market with skyrocketing costs and inexperienced suppliers. Coordination was limited, with different parts of government competing with each other. (OCP 2020: 3; see also the discussion below on the NHS in the UK)

The pandemic has, moreover, delivered benefits for former public utilities that are now privately run franchises. Take the UK railway system. It has been successively privatised since the 1990s, starting in 1993 with the Conservative government's Railways Act that separated train infrastructure from train operators. Like many public sector privatisation schemes, the state still subsidises private rail companies in a number of ways. One report published in 2013, for example, found that since 2003 and up until 2013 passenger numbers on trains have gone up along with fares for train-operating companies, yet Network Rail, which owns and manages the majority of rail networks in Britain, had seen its revenue from track charges from train operating companies actually decline in real terms during this period from £1.7 billion to £1.6 billion. So, Network Rail was indirectly subsiding the train-operating companies through their low track charges (Bowman et al. 2013: 24–5).

Privatisation also increased 'cash leakages' from railways; for instance, when money and funds are diverted from the train-operating companies to banks and shareholders. In particular, privatisation launched private sector debt and equity into the UK railway system, and the start of interest-bearing capital buying up railway debt, and so on. Cash leakages in the industry therefore grew under privatisation. 'Between 1995/96 and 2002/03, for example, the dividend and interest payments of the rail companies totalled £5.5 billion, while (train-operating companies) have paid a total of £1.5 billion in dividends since privatisation' (Jupe and Funnell 2017: 859). The pandemic has reproduced these subsidised practices in new ways. Research from the National Union of Rail, Maritime and Transport Workers (RMT) suggested that train operators stand to make almost £500 million from the COVID crisis thanks to British state subsidies. These appear in two forms. First, the government's Emergency Measures Agreement entailed, among other things, the British state giving train operators about £231 million in operating profits over 12 months. Secondly, the state agreed to pay the lease charges that train operators normally pay to rolling-stock companies. This amounts to another £241 million. These funds therefore leaked out of the public purse into private profit (RMT 2020). Later, we will also explore how the private sector has been key in gaining contracts in the NHS both before and during the pandemic.

In many respects, the fact that the workfare state encourages the public sector to work closely with private businesses is compatible with a lean agenda. Lean ideology encourages the public sector to build partnerships with the private and voluntary sectors. This, in turn, has inspired a large range of experimentations in how lean might be adopted in the public sector (Bateman et al. 2018). Lean ideology likewise encourages experimentation with similar managerial buzzwords; 'knowledge management' comes to mind here. Associated with the fashionable ideals that we now live in a 'knowledge economy' and 'network society', knowledge management seeks to find, support, and then creatively develop an organisation's 'tacit' and explicit knowledge in order to gain competitive advantage. Each organisation or firm contains pools of individual and collective knowledge, and the role of management is to recognise these different types of knowledge, many of which go unnoticed, and to make them explicit and function productively through flexible knowledge networks (Hong and Ståhle 2005; Pan and Leidner 2003). For Bilton (2007: 56), knowledge management is an attempt to 'leverage' a firm's internal knowledge base, 'to make the tacit knowledge explicit and available, and to ensure that the firm builds on its accumulated memories and experiences'. This is why, continues Bilton, managers need to move from a person-centred view of knowledge creativity to a system-centred view so that managers can tap into, and in the process help to develop, the 'ideas and talents' spread across knowledge networks (Bilton 2007: 59).

It is in this context that New Public Management (NPM) has become influential in 'rethinking' the role of the public sector. NPM theorists believe that the public sector must be more business-like in its approach, while, at the same time, it stresses the importance of 'citizen engagement and user involvement should occur at all phases of a (public) service lifecycle' (Osborne et al. 2012: 142). This is particularly noticeable in terms of digital technologies. Osborne et al. suggest that when in the past new technologies have been introduced into the public sector this has been for operational purposes – for example, to rationalise service delivery. Yet digital technologies also have a great potential to enhance and develop strategic priorities of public services, particularly around user engagement. New technologies can, for instance, help to build holistic integration of internal and external environments that improve communication with its citizens and communities. These changes can also build trust with users and communities in terms of updating them on how public services are fulfilling promises made, and demonstrating that public services do genuinely care about the welfare of users and communities (Osborne et al. 2012: 144).

At the heart of such strategic commitments should be a dedication to the principle of co-production between public services and its users. In the sections below, we will explore in more detail co-production of public sector services. For now, we can note one problem in particular. By empowering a formalised contract culture in public service delivery based on business-led customer–client relationships, the workfare state unintentionally creates new contradictions and dilemmas in how it tries to embed NPM and digital media in the public sector. Research from Cloud Industry Forum (CIF) found that 40 per cent of public sector organisations lack the necessary skills to adapt to digital transformation, and that 41 per cent of public service organisations lack the internal skills required to migrate to cloud-based solutions and fixes to and for their work. The research stressed that one difficulty with this organisational lag in skills lies with the unique nature of the UK state and public services sector. The public sector, the research suggests, has contracted out large parts of its ICT base to system integrators (SIs) in the private sector. In the words of the Chief Executive of CIF: 'This reliance on SIs, combined with the cutbacks imposed by years of austerity, has left many public sector organisations without the necessary skills and staff in-house to confidently adapt to new approaches to ICT such as the cloud' (CIF 2017).

Digital corporations can find many profitable roles, schemes and work opportunities within this contradictory public sector environment. A recent study for the UK trade union, GMB, found that from 2015 to 2019, Amazon has been steadily making inroads into Britain's public service delivery (Tussell 2019). The report claims that across this period, Amazon won forty contracts from the UK public sector. In the space of one year alone during 2018, Amazon gained £50 million in contracts from central and local government bodies. Most of the contracts won by Amazon were for their cloud-hosting services, which public sector bodies can purchase through Amazon Web Services subsidiary. Still, the report's authors also note that Amazon is expanding its reach into the UK public sector through other marketplace routes, particularly through its retail business. For example, in July 2018, Amazon signed a deal with the Yorkshire Purchasing Organisation's (YPO) Digital Marketplace Platform. YPO procures public sector products and services – for example, it can give local authorities access to regional and national providers for apprenticeships – and this new deal has enabled Amazon to create an online 'one-stop shop' for public bodies to purchase an array of products (Tussell 2019). Some local authorities have also started to integrate and automate their services with smart machines linked through the voice-activated assistant, Amazon Alexa. One illustration of this innovation in public service delivery comes in the guise of Aylesbury Vale District Council in Buckinghamshire, England. In October 2017, the council launched a new 'skill' for Alexa. This permits residents who own an Alexa-enabled device to access selected information on the council and its services through simple voice commands. Currently, residents can ask for various information, including who are the political leaders of the council, council tax payment options and what items can go in recycling bins. There is also the option to book assisted waste collections (Aylesbury Vale District Council 2017). As we will see below, the pandemic has also offered up new opportunities to private business to gain yet more public sector contracts.

This hollowing out of public services to private contractors has also been accompanied by a dramatic diminution in funds for local authorities, which has been intensified by austerity. Once more, this has noticeable negative outcomes on the ability of local authorities to successfully tackle the fallout from the pandemic. One study in June 2020, found that out of 151 upper tier councils in England, 131 did not have sufficient funds to compensate for the increased costs and reduced income due to COVID-19. Councils with high levels of deprivation will suffer the most in terms of funding per person, which will deepen already precarious income public authority streams because of ten years of austerity (Billingham 2020). A later study, in August 2020, found that mounting costs for local authorities, for example, increasing funds required to buy PPE, rising overheads to implement social distancing in a range of services, increased expenses to provide extra support for vulnerable groups in localities, and loss of money from the likes of non-tax income, meant that councils were facing an in-year pressure to find an extra £7.2 billion to cover lost income and higher expenses. While the UK government provided councils with £4.8 billion additional general purpose and specific grant funding, and while other pots of money were available to councils, it was estimated at the time that there was still a gap of at least £2 billion across local authorities that needed to be somehow plugged (Ogden and Phillips 2020). A report published in July 2020 by the House of Commons Public Accounts Committee noted that it had taken evidence from the Local Government Association, which represents the interests of local authorities. The Association informed the Committee that many local authorities were already anticipating funding shortfalls and taking steps to make possible in-year cuts to vital local services which, somewhat ironically, were originally supposed to be helping residents through the crisis (House of Commons Public Accounts Committee 2020).

For these reasons, several local authorities have been forced to increase their cash borrowing. In April 2020, it was estimated that the public sector had borrowed £89 billion in cash terms. A year previously, this figure stood at a £7 billion surplus, and the last time there was a peak in public sector cash borrowing was in April 2009, when the figure stood at £11 billion. So, public sector cash borrowing is the highest at any point in the forty years of collecting the data (Emmerson and Stockton 2020). According to the Office for Budget Responsibility, the UK government could have spending pressures on average of around £10 billion over the next three years because of the effects of COVID on society. Health budgets alone could be around an extra £7 billion per year, which includes extra resources required for ongoing vaccination programmes and physical and mental health issues (OBR 2021: 8). Such figures, of course, might provide the UK government with further ammunition to ensure austerity keeps on playing a key role in policy decision-making and for local authorities to keep borrowing. For example, some research suggests that despite a recovery of sorts for some sectors in the UK economy in July 2021, the cash size of the economy will actually be 3 per cent smaller than pre-pandemic levels. Given this decrease alongside other issues, one forecast suggests that while the current budget deficit will improve by £30 billion in 2021–22, there is still limited space for the Chancellor in the medium term to spend extra on public services. Indeed, if the Chancellor wishes to stick with current spending plans, then that will in effect mean spending up to £17 billion less on public services than planned before the pandemic (Emmerson et al. 2021). For example, some suggested that the Chancellor would set out to 'fix the public finances', which is typical government austerity speak, with plans to scale back still further funds for 'non-protected' public services like transport (Button 2021). In his October 2021 budget, for example, the Chancellor gave extra funds mainly to support social care, while 'unprotected' government departments, such as Transport and Work and Pensions, will see further cuts (The Resolution Foundation 2021: 2).

Interestingly, the rapid contracting out of public services to the private sector has also been accompanied by a noticeable decline in living standards for many public sector workers. To get to grips in more detail with these specific issues and problems in an age of lean, marketised and neoliberal public services, we need to focus on the changing class relations in the public sector.

CLASS RELATIONS AND LEAN LABOUR PROCESSES IN THE PUBLIC SECTOR

As we know from previous chapters, lean production is associated with class politics and the emergence of new class layers. In terms of non-labour, lean theorists argue that there needs to be a management class that will take hold and transform the public sector. According to Holmemo and Ingvaldsen, some lean theorists often conceive 'middle managers' as relics from the past, holding up progress towards implementing a more flexible, dynamic, flatter and 'de-layered' organisational hierarchy. Ideologically, then, lean methods are said to reduce public sector costs by being more efficient, eliminating waste and engaging in a process of continuous improvement (Holmemo and Ingvaldsen 2015). Other champions of the lean agenda think that managers can act as guardians of change in an organisation while providing a degree of stability as these changes are put into practice. Digital technologies can be employed by managers to push forward these lean strategies. Using digital networks to create horizontal links between different work teams in an organisation, as well as establishing collective learning, is one illustration (see also Hong and Ståhle 2005).

In practice, however, new contradictions and dilemmas in and around class relations emerge when implementing lean methods in the public sector's different labour processes. In their own study of lean transformations in five Norwegian public sector organisations, Holmemo and Ingvaldsen (2015) discovered that some of the difficulties encountered in pushing through these transformations emerged within a number of problematic relationships within management groups. Middle managers had different roles and responsibilities in these organisations, but one role was to coordinate the work of other employees. During the process of lean implementation, this group generally was not included in adopting lean processes. Top managers, those who control the organisation, normally sponsored lean programmes and spoke in glowing terms at external events about the benefits of lean methods. The actual implementation and execution – that is, those who controlled and monitored lean – was given to operational managers who worked with lean

consultants. These different class relations within management produced some positive results – for example, there were some successes
in introducing lean techniques into these organisations – but they also
produced many negative results. One particular problem was the relative
absence of top managers in helping to embed lean techniques in their
own organisations, believing this was the job of operational managers.
Meanwhile, middle managers did not think they should be involved in
pushing forward new lean methods, believing instead that this was the
role of operational managers. As a result, there was a gap between top
managers trying to push forward lean techniques from above with no
real coordination from below via middle managers. In this example, we
see how managers combine different ways of working in order to protect
their own class identity. Middle managers mainly still retained their local
working expertise and knowledge about how to operate within specific
public sector contexts, and to deal with particular issues, while top managers were aware of the need to incorporate in their daily practices a new
managerial ethos in how they work. In the same organisation, then, a
hybrid set of managerial ideas can be found to operate side-by-side (see
also Döring et al. 2015). Other studies of public sector workers have
similarly demonstrated how managers have gradually been located into
the 'new middle class' by having to assume more supervisory and control
roles over and above other workers. In this respect, managers are moved
away from being part of the 'collective worker' (see Carter et al. 2011;
2014).

Under lean regimes, it is perhaps therefore unsurprising that far from
feeling 'creative', public sector workers feel the opposite: stressed and
anxious. Indeed, some evidence suggests that lean, stress and bullying
often go hand-in-hand. During a period of lean restructuring, spaces
often open for managers to exploit and harass those being managed.
Lean restructuring, for example, highlights the need for employees to be
taken out of their 'comfort zones', to experience new and more flexible
work routines, to be prepared to take on new tasks and so on, all of
which can heighten the anxiety of employees (Corbett 2013: 423). Such
lean changes often make employees fearful that their work is slowly
being degraded.

An interesting study by Taskin and van Bunnen that illustrates this fear
examines the introduction in a public sector department of knowledge
management in human resources (HRs). Managers in this department
had initiated major public sector reforms along knowledge management principles, which included codifying various types of knowledge.
Through digitisation, knowledge is bundled up and sorted into distinctive 'repositories'. By capturing and storing knowledge in this way, it

can then be sorted and shared among employees to teach 'best practices' about various issue to a workforce. At this particular HR department, knowledge around specific HR practices, such as payroll, career development and recruitment procedures, were entered into a knowledge repository with the intention of eradicating waste, avoiding discretion on tasks and ensuring that the tasks were accessible and transparent. Moreover, these new initiatives were implemented with a view to creating a single database of reliable information for staff, to be more client-focused and more professional in how daily HR tasks were being administered. According to Taskin and van Bunnen, however, many employees felt they were losing specialised knowledge. 'De-skilling' was a theme that emerged, linked with the formalisation and standardisation of knowledge. 'For most of them … knowledge has become fragmented into short and easy-to-understand sentences, which makes knowledge accessible only through limited training' (Taskin and van Bunnen 2015: 165). Some employees, moreover, felt that they now collaborated through initiative and learning-on-the-job with their colleagues to a lesser degree because their work was simplified and because managers gained greater control over their work (see also Moore and Hayes 2018).

While managers act more and more as controllers, through databases, of the activities of front-line public sector workers, it is still nevertheless possible for managers, unions and front-line workers to try to work as a team to ensure certain values of care and justice are maintained in and against 'the individualising mantras of NPM and neoliberalism' (Baines et al. 2014: 447–8). Similarly, Taskin and van Bunnen also found in their study of the Belgian public sector organisation that employees did display points of resistance to the introduction of the new knowledge management regime. Some colleagues withheld knowledge from managers, and some colleagues simply gave false information to project leaders for the digital repository.

In the public sector, managers, particularly those who have 'dual roles' as practitioners and managers, often develop a degree of scepticism towards lean principles, which then lends itself to a type of resistance against lean ideology. In their case study of a hospital, McCann et al. (2015) focus on the introduction of consultants to train middle managers at the hospital about the benefits of lean working practices, and how to implement these practices across different hospital departments and divisions. One key discursive theme here was that lean would lead to an overall 'improvement' in the way that day-to-day business was carried out at the hospital. Training events also enlisted other slogans, such as 'Satisfied Staff', to legitimise lean ideas to middle managers. Newsletters featuring successful lean initiatives in the hospital were circulated to staff, and were also placed on their intranet. While some middle managers at first welcomed lean principles into their daily lives, others, particularly those who occupied dual-class roles as both clinicians and managers, were sceptical. And as the complexities and realities of trying to adopt lean principles into the day-to-day life of a working hospital became apparent through time, the very concept of 'lean' was stretched by trainers and employees, so that 'almost anything that was felt to be effective or "good" was said to be "lean"' (McCann et al. 2015: 1568). One senior consultant who was also a manager told the researchers that part of the problem here lay with the complexity of a working hospital. Unlike an office, which has a more predictable and steady working life, hospitals contain a high level of contingency. Lean, therefore, soon dropped out of favour in the hospital. Interestingly, McCann also note that lean did not lead to an intensification or fragmentation of work for the hospital's workforce. This, then, is an example, noted in the introduction, in which middle-class public sector workers resisted certain management lean control strategies being imposed on them. The next section will show how these problems and modes of resistance also cause dilemmas and tensions in terms of how users might co-create and become prosumers of public services.

NEW PUBLIC MANAGEMENT AND PROSUMERS OF PUBLIC SERVICES BEFORE AND DURING COVID-19

For Osborne et al., co-creation and co-production has many advantages. It can unlock tacit and 'sticky' knowledge that service users possess to improve services. 'Here, the service organisation proactively seeks to uncover, understand and satisfy "latent (or future) needs", rather than simply reacting to existing or currently expressed needs – as has invariably been the case with public services' (Osborne et al. 2012: 146). For these reasons, some argue that co-production in the public sector should not be confused with similar, although noticeably different, forms of governance in the public sector. So-called 'collaborative governance', for example, is premised on organised stakeholders working together to provide solutions to problems and dilemmas in public sector services. But this type of collaboration tends to underplay the role that 'lay actors' – community members, service users, citizens and so forth – might play in generative innovative recommendations to ongoing problems. Politicians and policymakers have therefore increasingly moved towards co-production because 'it may help them to understand and meet unfulfilled social needs, mobilise societal resources, expand the reach of public organisations to social domains where they have no leverage, facilitate integrated service delivery and coordinated governance, stimulate public innovation, build joint ownership over public policy solutions, and increase democratic legitimacy' (Torfing et al. 2021: 3). Dunleavy et al. (2005) add that NPM has started to be surpassed by 'digital-era governance' (DEG) in local government. Digital technologies encourage a holistic approach to policy agendas by linking together and reintegrating different components and units. It also opens up opportunities to take back some activities and ventures into the public sector which had initially been privatised and for ordinary users of public services to have an active input into how these services might be delivered.

As I have noted elsewhere (Roberts 2014), the claim that co-creation and co-production has surpassed NPM in fact, albeit implicitly, constructs ideal-typical models between different approaches to the public sector. In reality, digital media and co-production can work together with NPM to further and strengthen neoliberalism and workfarism in the public sector. One characteristic of NPM is the application and design of new automated information systems in order to quantify outputs related to targets. Indeed, the increasing dependence on computers is directly related to the quantification of the accountability, efficiency and effectiveness of public services. Yet this type of audit culture based on variables such as 'service users seen' often miss key qualitative measures of outcomes for 'service users' (Gillingham and Graham 2016: 193). NPM also underlines the importance for public services to be accountable, and this can be achieved when public sector workers use information systems that record service user case activity. While containing obvious benefits, it is also the case that such recorded information can end up being so voluminous as to be almost impossible to digest. Moreover, information systems subject practitioners to potential new modes of surveillance and control in the workplace, ensuring that public sector practitioners feel they are ensnared in an electronic mode of performance management that takes away their discretion when dealing with users (Gillingham and Graham 2016: 193–6; see also Mearns et al. 2015).

These problems rebound and are refracted into the work carried out by some in the public sector. One study of frontline service workers in northern regions of England focused on how these workers used the Internet and social media in their work with young people aged between 14 and 18 years old who lived in socially and economically deprived areas. Popular social media platforms like Facebook and YouTube had been brought into this frontline work to help with some administration, communication and evaluative needs. For instance, some frontline workers had started to experiment with social media in encouraging young people to become co-creators in a youth unemployment campaign

(Mearns et al. 2015: 196). However, austerity cuts to the public sector had placed real constraints on what these workers might deliver to their young clients. All interviewees on the practitioner side also reported that Internet and social media activity could not replace the importance of face-to-face meetings with young people. Moreover, frontline workers stated that they received little national or local government guidance on how best to use the Internet and social media in their jobs, which again created a number of strategic dilemmas and tensions for them in their everyday work routines. For instance:

> Practitioners had to determine what they should and should not be uploading and downloading, when and how to gain informed consent and how to ensure the security of photographs, text or video which often included details of the young people with whom they had contact. (Mearns et al. 2015: 199)

In this instance, social media blurred boundaries between institutional public sector norms and the everyday lives of clients (in this case, the lives of young people); boundaries that were once thought to be separate.

Crucially, it needs to be borne in mind that those who use and rely on the public sector will never be 'customers' in the conventional business sense of that term. Users of the public sector are people with specific and often complex social needs and requirements. They consume social services out of necessity and not through what might be consider 'choice' as is applied in the business world. Moreover, the state still funds these services to a large degree (Sturgeon 2014). To illustrate these points further, we turn once more to the example of the NHS. Indeed, the NHS is a particularly good example because it has been subject to major neoliberal reforms over the last three decades or so, many of which have been justified as a means to 'empower' its users and 'clients'. Furthermore, the digitisation of NHS labour and work has been at the forefront of these changes.

By the early to mid-1980s, under Margaret Thatcher's government, administrative reforms were already being pushed on to the NHS. The Griffith proposals, implemented in 1984, sought to empower centralised management structures in the NHS and focus the attention of the NHS towards applying commercial initiatives in terms of the NHS estate. Key buzzwords like 'efficiency' and 'cost-effectiveness' guided the proposals, which in reality meant more and ongoing budget cuts to the NHS. At this point in time, the NHS had already experienced a drop of around 2 per cent in hospital revenues, and the Griffith proposals effectively outlined further areas and measures for more cuts to be made (Illife 1985).

Under the New Labour governments of 1997–2008, successive rounds of contracting-out the NHS continued apace. Private Finance Initiatives grew steadily, enabling private businesses to build and maintain NHS hospitals, while primary care reforms allowed the private sector to run some clinical services (see Aldred 2007). In 2006, for instance, New Labour under Tony Blair granted control of NHS Independent Sector Treatment Centres to eleven private companies, which included Netcare from South Africa, Interhealth Care Services from Canada and Capio from Sweden (Whitfield 2006: 109). Yet the procedures around how private companies won NHS contracts were frequently vague, often being based in social and personal networks between various 'partners', with important information about how contracts were being awarded not being properly scrutinised. This 'structural secrecy' did in some instances help to 'produce a mutually reinforcing process, contributing to "group think" and discouraging the raising of concerns and challenges' (Sheaff 2017: 537).

Under the Conservative and Liberal Democrat Coalition Government, which took power in 2010, the Health and Social Care Act was passed in 2012. The Act introduced 207 Clinical Commissioning Groups (CCGs) made up of local GPs, which replaced Primary Care Trusts and Strategic Health Authorities. CCGs were instructed to make sure a range of clinical services were put out for competitive tender. No longer having a duty to provide a health service, the Secretary of State for Health instead gave this responsibility to local and central government. 'Public Health was taken out of the NHS . . . (and) NHS Foundation Trusts are no longer obliged to provide particular aspects of healthcare' (Niechcial 2020). Then, in 2014, the government introduced Sustainability and Transformation Plans for the NHS with the stated aim of integrating NHS services, having greater emphasis on prevention, and putting communities and patients in control of their health. In reality, and under the auspices of austerity, the NHS has been constrained in the way it operates, having to implement a raft of changes within very tight deadlines (Hudson 2018).

More NHS medical staff today currently deliver medical care through digital technologies, there has been an increase in health promotion through ICTs, a greater number of patients have digital devices implanted in them for healthcare reasons, and new information systems help to monitor and keep records on and about patients (Lupton 2014a: 1345). All these innovations enable NHS users to become prosumers of their healthcare and services. But while these new technologies provide the NHS with many positives, observes Lupton, they can also cause problems. Technologies designed to monitor patients in their own homes do often give patients a sense of control over their bodies, and they mean that patients can stay in the comfort and familiarity of where they live while being monitored. Studies also demonstrate that patients can become frustrated with these technologies, seeing them as difficult to use, creating additional anxiety if they do not function properly, and give people a feeling that they are being constantly monitored and therefore lack a degree of privacy (Lupton 2014a: 1351–2). In these neo-liberal and financialised circumstances, in which medical care is longer confined to physical meetings between healthcare workers and patients, public sector health 'e-professionals' are empowered at the expense of traditional health professionals (Noordegraaf 2016: 796).

NHS patients are increasingly being seen as prosumers in other ways too. Private companies have for a number of years been designing and rolling out healthcare platforms and apps, such as HealthTap. Once integrated into a healthcare system like the NHS, these platforms collect vast amounts of data about patients, and, indeed, patients are encouraged to share information about their daily routines in relation to their specific illness so that it can then be analysed by the appropriate medical team. Many of these platforms also encourage patients to share their thoughts and feelings about their illness within a specified electronic community. Spin-off websites operate in more commercial ways, and use the data received from patients in more commercial ways, such as selling and targeting adverts on the sites. Yet, notes Lupton, 'patients themselves are rarely encouraged to participate in the design of websites . . . or in the design, analysis and writing phases of research studies using their data' (Lupton 2014b: 865).

For all the talk about digital technology making patients feel like they are co-producing their own healthcare, research also suggests that different groups of NHS users often feel they have not been fully consulted about changes to their healthcare, nor have they been given degrees of 'control' over their healthcare. Healthcare professionals also often find health plans are full of jargon and difficult to follow, and they sometimes share with patients that overall healthcare aims and goals are lost to a world of saving money and financial efficiencies (Hudson 2018: 421). Co-producing knowledge and practices between NHS users (or 'prosumers' of NHS services) and managers therefore starts to buckle under these conditions. Given, then, the complexity of the working life of a hospital, and given the broader added pressures of trying to work through various constraints and pressures within the UK NHS, not least continual contracting out of services to the private sector and the increasing marketisation of the NHS, it is perhaps no wonder that Hudson found many NHS employees simply ignored lean practices, which were then quietly and slowly dropped by management.

Interestingly, we have witnessed some of these dilemmas and tensions in the NHS during COVID-19. Continuing privatisation of the NHS has had a detrimental impact in tackling the virus. In 2006, the procurement arm of the NHS, known as NHS Logistics, was outsourced to a private German firm called DHL in a contract worth £22 billion. DHL then worked with its US healthcare specialists, Novation, in order to ensure the NHS supply chain was subject to lean processes. While DHL finally lost their contract to another private firm in 2018, the Conservative government introduced their Procurement Transformation Programme in 2017 with the aim of centralising and dividing up the NHS procurement process so that more parts of it could be outsourced. When the pandemic started, it soon became apparent that this privatised procurement system could not cope with providing enough PPE for NHS staff. Companies were accused of ripping off the NHS, with one supplier offering PPE at 825 per cent of the normal price (Hall et al. 2020: 5–7).

As Hall et al. argue, the main problem in trying to get enough PPE during the crisis lay with the fragmented outsourced procurement system imposed on the NHS. Indeed, up until the pandemic, the NHS had eleven different outsourced procurement segments, each of which procured different medical and non-medical goods and equipment, and each of which is managed by a different contractor. Each contractor, however, does not locate medical supplies themselves, but obtains them through a catalogue and then orders the required supplies from contractors listed in the catalogue, and they often order bulk supplies to save money. With such a complex layered system, it was not surprising to see that during the pandemic many PPE goods and products ordered fell below expected standards (Hall et al. 2020: 11–12).

Unlike the neoliberal slant on co-production of health services, Hall et al. also document NHS co-production during the pandemic based on networks of solidarity about the social good that the NHS provides. To give just two examples, Cheltenham Hackspace, a community workspace where people get access to tools to produce goods, came together to make 2,000 PPE face shields for NHS workers, while Helping Dress Medics delivered 8,000 scrubs to newly qualified medical staff who could not get hold of them from usual suppliers (Hall et al. 2020: 29). The pandemic crisis has therefore opened up some alternative perspectives on how cooperative relationships might be created in the present and in the future. COVID-19 has, for instance, demonstrated the need for new trusting relationships to be built between different users, community groups and those working in the NHS (Beresford et al. 2021: 159).

At the same time, however, co-production operates within the strategic constraints of the workfare state. Crisis narratives have therefore been generated by neoliberal policy thinkers and politicians to be used as a strategic opportunity for the development and furthering of hollowed out welfare practices and processes. In a report, the British Medical Association (BMA) is highly critical of the NHS procurement system especially in times of crisis, and warns against '"just in time delivery systems and lean inventories" working against maintenance of stockpiles required for use at times of surges in demand and disruptions of supply' (BMA 2020: 3). Furthermore, the BMA notes that some of the private firms who, during the pandemic, have been awarded new NHS contracts already have tarnished records of working with the NHS. Capita, for instance, was awarded a contract in March 2020 to assist with returning health workers in England to help with NHS work during the pandemic. According to the BMA, Capita has been slow in completing some tasks around this contact, with the swiftest completions taking four weeks. As a result, some returning NHS doctors who wished to help combat the virus were not allocated to NHS teams. Capita's track record in taking on past NHS contracts, though, has not been without its problems. In May 2018, it was reported that Capita's management of its Primary Care Support services contract, which it had won in 2015, led to 148,000 active patient records being wrongly archived (BMA 2020: 9). For this and other reasons, NHS England subsequently eventually fined Capita £5.3 million for poor performance (Practice Business 2018).

CONCLUSION

Even under financialisation and neoliberalism, the state and other non-private bodies have been vital in supporting the public infrastructure. The COVID-19 pandemic illustrates this point. One study argues that public funding from 2000 onwards accounted for about 97 per cent of the money required over time for the research and development to produce the Oxford/AstraZeneca COVID-19 vaccine. Funds came from a variety of public sources and include overseas government funders, especially the EU, the UK government and charities, such as major charitable organisations like the Wellcome Trust (Cross et al. 2021).

But this chapter has been concerned to map out some of changing class relations in the public sector, and how they are related to different technological forms and media. As noted, the capitalist state and public sector is a strategic battlefield between different class forces and relations embedded in socio-political agendas and strategies. In the strategic battlefield of the neoliberal state, those who work in the public sector must also contend with an array of issues and problems, from austerity, to audit cultures and target setting, to changing strategic state policies, to gaining basic training in employing effectively the latest digital technology and digital culture in everyday work practices. Furthermore, some public sector personnel have been co-opted into managerial control positions and have thus made a transition from 'labour' to 'non-labour'. These often create added pressures and workloads on those working in the public sector. Yet such targets 'reflect a management-employer relationship divorced from the service user' (Martin 2018: 31). Co-production and co-creation of local policy with 'service users' thereby becomes subordinated to the pressures of performance targets.

Lean in the public sector also emphasises a management-based approach, or 'new public management (NPM)', towards policy issues, which aims to cut costs rather than actively engage policy users (Martin 2018: 33). For NPM theorists, governments should take on a more business-led role, while business should take on a more government-led role in providing and developing social policies (Box et al. 2001). At an abstract level of analysis, namely, that of the reproduction of capital, we might say that NPM is part of a broader movement by neoliberalism to try to make what it sees as 'idle capital' in the public sector into profitable forms of unproductive financial capital (see Mandel 1971: 406).

At a more concrete and everyday level of understanding, there has been, and indeed there is, a variety of ways that the public sector learns about lean, and then starts to implement lean strategies. 'Fashion-setting actors', like management gurus, academic researchers and consultants, can all act as 'organic intellectuals' in pushing forward the lean ideology into the state. Politicians and local government officials likewise push forward lean strategies into the public sector, and public sector actors can be influenced to adopt lean by colleagues working in the public sector in other regions (Madsen et al. 2017). In our pandemic age, however, the marketisation and privatisation of the public sector has drained it of resources to combat the virus at local and regional levels as fully as might once have been the case. Cuts to public services, for example, have pushed local councils in the United Kingdom to rely ever more on the performance of their local economies to gain income. Between 2009/10 and 2018/19, the Ministry of Housing, Communities and Local Government had an 86 per cent cut in its spending. A crisis of the magnitude of COVID-19 inevitably places enormous pressure on public services, but it has placed 'unsustainable pressure' on local authorities, particularly those authorities located in deprived and working-class areas. So much is this the case that some public authorities in the North, such as Leeds and Liverpool, were considering issuing section 114 notices, 'which is essentially local authority bankruptcy' (Johns 2020: 4).

The chapter has also shown that digital technologies are often introduced to implement lean techniques, but which then inadvertently feed into the problems of lean transformations and in many respects make them worse. For instance, digital media has the potential to empower 'clients' of public sector services. Sure enough, digital technology makes it easier for 'clients' to lodge complaints about a particular service delivery. Even so, 'the autonomy of many human service professionals has been reduced through attempts to codify and categorise the competencies they require to complete their work and to quantify and measure the outcomes of professional intervention' (Dutil et al. 2007: 83). Not only is it the case that the digitisation of everyday work-related tasks occurs in the public sector, but there is also an attempt to digitise public sector labour and to automate it where possible. This can lead to standardisation in service delivery along with greater efficiency in financialised target-setting. Decision-making is increasingly handed over to smart machines, ensuring that human discretion over particular cases is diminished, and the 'voice' of clients gets lost in an increasing digital bureaucracy (Bannister and Wilson 2011). Moreover, studies suggest that adopting lean in the public sector can be piecemeal, or it can even stall, be rejected or just ignored, because, among other things, implementing lean is time-consuming and even stifling in an age when the public sector is under enormous pressures because of factors like austerity and neoliberalism (Madsen et al. 2017).

Chapter 10

CONCLUSIONS: TOWARDS A POST-COVID-19 POLITICS OF CLASS STRUGGLE

INTRODUCTION

During the latter half of the 1990s, many commentators in media outlets, policy circles and governments around the world suggested we were entering a 'new economy'. The new economy was, and is, said to be based on new technological advancements like the Internet and digital modes of technology. When the new economy was taking off many commentators, policy advisers and politicians greeted these economic developments in an extremely positive manner. We know, too, that many academics also sought to show that we live in 'new times' of informational labour and networked subjectivities in which capitalism gains profits through every nook and cranny of society. Of course, we could go even further back in history. In the early 1970s, the futurologist and sociologist, Daniel Bell, argued that dominant capitalist societies were in the midst of a transformation from industrial societies to post-industrial societies. Comprising a service sector with professional white-collar workers, post-industrial societies employed information and knowledge to establish new cooperative relations among and between people. For example, information networks provided greater mechanisms for participation in public affairs by making it easier for people to gather information about public issues (Bell 1999: 128–9).

Unsurprisingly, many have been sceptical of such declarations. Mosco (2004), for instance, does much to debunk some of the hyperbole surrounding contemporary forms of communication and its impact on society. He reminds us of the exhilaration felt by many commentators of the day with the arrival of everyday technologies like electricity, the telegraph, radio, TV. Some observers in the 1920's United States genuinely believed that direct democracy would spring from radio's accessibility and mass appeal. In the words of one commentator, radio had dispensed

216

with the 'political middlemen' by forcing politicians to speak their mind 'fully, candidly, and *in extenso*' (cited in Mosco 2004: 129). Just as some analysts today herald technological advances as having the potential to change politics as we know it, so some commentators in the 1920s saw radio as bringing about a social revolution unshackled by the prevailing social order.

Mosco's point, of course, is that a type of 'technological hype' has been prevalent throughout modern history. Similarly, we have seen throughout the book that while digital technologies have brought us many benefits, they are still nevertheless ensnared in the same basic contradictions and dilemmas identified by Marx in the nineteenth century. Rapid innovative technological developments across the globe are still subsumed under the weight of external competitive pressure and the need to quicken up cycles of accumulation. The necessity to overproduce subsequently quickens in pace. In this final concluding chapter, we therefore take stock of the arguments put forward throughout the book, and, in particular, assess their relevance for building political strategies to overcome neoliberalism. We will see that different political strategies follow on from different standpoints taken on our current socio-economic terrain. Marxist value theory leads to quite different political conclusions than the idea, advanced by theorists like Hardt and Negri, that we live in qualitatively new decentred, informational and networked times.

WHITHER MARX'S THEORY OF VALUE FOR THE DIGITAL AGE?

This book has partly been a defence of Marx's theory of value, and his account of class politics that arises from this theory. Yet we noted early on in the book that many contemporary leftist critics are today sceptical about this theory of value. In particular, it is frequently said that digital technology and new types of digital work have rendered Marx's value theory as being somewhat outdated. Hardt and Negri are arguably two of the most current influential proponents of this view. In their own words:

> In the newly dominant forms of production that involve information, codes, knowledge, images, and affects, for example, producers increasingly require a high degree of freedom as well as open access to the common, especially in its social forms, such as communication networks, information banks, and cultural circuits. Innovation in Internet technologies, for example, depends directly on access to common code and information resources as well as the ability to connect and interact with others in unrestricted networks. (Hardt and Negri 2009: ix–x)

We have reached a point, then, when social and economic production is grounded in 'the common'. A surplus is therefore no longer generated solely by wage relationships, and neither are class struggles determined by wage relationships. Struggles over the common, such as common knowledge created by the Internet, are at a minimum at least as important as struggles over wage relations, 'because in the common is embedded the value necessary for rigorous social reproduction' (Hardt and Negri 2009: 287). In other words, 'the rate of surplus value . . . to rewrite Marx's definition, is the expression of the level of exploitation by capital on not only the labour-power of the worker but also the common powers of production that constitute social labour-power' (Hardt and Negri 2009: 288). Capital must subsequently move beyond the factory walls and engage in a never-ending process of 'capitalisation' across society as whole (Hardt and Negri 2000: 227).

As the book has argued throughout, however, Marx himself talks about capitalisation in relation to financial capital, but, of course, his observations are intrinsically related to his value theory. We know that many types of capitalisation are generated by capital to realise greater profits through unproductive accumulation. Digital technology is a key element for capital in mining new sources of unproductive labour. Capital engages in unproductive accumulation because wells of surplus value start to run dry. Yet, by rejecting Marx's value theory, some progressive theorists, like Hardt and Negri, rob us of a full critique of contemporary capitalism and present an ambiguous analysis of contemporary capitalism. For example, Hardt and Negri argue that exploitation is now located in numerous 'non-factory' spheres of social life; for example, in social media websites. To make this claim, however, one must conflate the exploitation of productive labour, based in the extraction of surplus value, with the oppression of unproductive labour, based in the extraction of surplus labour. Making this conflation enables some critical theorists to then argue that so-called 'free labour' of social media users acts as a type of 'productive labour' for capital. We have seen, though, that this belief is mistaken. 'Free labour' is not usually productive, nor does it, in most cases, create surplus value.

But the idea that unproductive labour, particularly that found in digital networks, is now the source of exploitation leads further to one-sided political strategies and programmes, which aim to overcome capitalist exploitation and oppression. According to Hardt and Negri, in the past era of industrial societies, the 'working class' would fight to ensure 'the stability of the direct wage and the indirect wage (that is, welfare)' (Hardt and Negri 2017: 189). That is to say, the proletariat would fight for better wages within the confines of the workplace itself, which would be supported through welfare rights too. In the times in which we now live, they continue, workers engage in 'struggles around a social wage of citizenship' (Hardt and Negri 2017: 190) throughout a variety of spaces in society beyond the closed walls of workplaces. This, then, is a struggle for a democratic 'commons' – 'a common organized against the capitalist appropriation of social life, against private property and its markets . . .' (Hardt and Negri 2017: 245).

While making many astute and true observations, Hardt and Negri's political programme has the unfortunate and unintended consequence of constructing a dualism between what they say is an 'industrial' political strategy of favouring the 'productive labour' of industrial manufacturing with its enclosed workplace and a 'post-industrial' political strategy of favouring 'reproductive social labour' that spreads across society as a whole, whether this is in the office, at home, a café, at a university, going for a walk and so on. What this dualistic political standpoint overlooks, however, is that neoliberal and financial capitalism has sought to increase surplus value and surplus profits *by intensifying the normal working day and attacking the direct workplace wage at the same time that it gains profits through the 'social wage'*. In other words, exploitation and oppression in the paid workplace is still a dominant method employed by capitalists to extract a surplus from their workforce (Carchedi 2011: 234–5). Let us momentarily explore empirical data around this claim.

Despite soaring corporate profits, the wages of workers in the United States have not grown significantly. Inflation-adjusted hourly wages under Trump were lower than under the Obama regime. Growing on average per year at just 0.3 per cent under Trump, this figure stood at 1.1 per cent during the Obama era. Much of the tax gains enjoyed by corporations will simply go to shareholders (Olorunnipa and Chandra 2018). More broadly, wages and incomes for many groups have stalled and stagnated from the financial crisis of 2008 up until the onset of the pandemic. In their *Global Wage Report 2018/19*, the ILO suggested that global wage growth was at that point the lowest since 2008. Global wage growth in real terms declined from 2.4 per cent in 2016 to 1.8 per cent in 2017, while in the advanced G20 countries, these figures stood at 1.7 per cent in 2015 and 0.4 per cent in 2017. Some Eastern European countries, however, experienced a wage recovery of sorts. Yet, notes the ILO, over the period 1999–2017, labour productivity increased more rapidly than wages in fifty-two high-income countries. The ILO continues:

> Possible explanations for subdued wage growth include slow productivity growth, the intensification of global competition, the decline in the bargaining power of workers and the inability of unemployment statistics

to adequately capture slack in the labour market, as well as an uncertain economic outlook which may have discouraged firms from raising wages. (ILO 2018: xiii)

Another report finds that in the United States, households experienced an increase in real annual median income for a third year in a row. Median household income was $61,372 in 2017, a 1.8 per cent increase from the 2016 median of $60,309 in real terms. Nevertheless, the report goes on to note that 'the real median earnings of men and women working full-time, year-round each decreased from their respective 2016 medians by 1.1 percent' (Fontenot et al. 2018: 1). Interestingly, more US citizens left part-time work and went into full-time work. 'The number of men and women full-time, year-round workers increased by 1.4 million and 1.0 million, respectively, between 2016 and 2017, continuing a shift from part-time, part-year work status to full-time, year-round work status' (Fontenot et al. 2018: 10). As John Cassidy (2018) notes in *The New Yorker*, the discrepancy between rising household incomes and yet stagnant wages can therefore be solved when one looks at hours worked. More Americans across the class spectrum are simply working longer hours to make ends meet.

The Bureau of Labor Statistics nevertheless estimates that in the first quarter of 2019, the average weekly wages for US citizens had increased to $1,184, which represents a 2.8 per cent increase over the year (Bureau of Labor Statistics 2019). Of course, different measurements often give different pictures on these issues. Before 2013, for instance, the US Census Bureau used to estimate median household income through different measures. By 2014, the Census Bureau were asking different questions to households about their earning and income, and these new questions generally raised median household income by about 3.2 per cent. If one goes by the pre-2013 measurements, though, then the picture is very different. As one analyst from the US Census Bureau observed: '(T)he 2017 median household income is not statistically different from the pre-recession estimate for 2007 or the year with the highest estimated median household income, 1999' (Waddington 2018: 4). In other words, Americans, including middle income Americans, have seen their income nosedive since the 2008 financial crash. Indeed, according to two other analysts, the only group that has seen marginal gains since 2008 are those in the top 10 per cent. In 2017, the 95th percentile income was $237,034, which is 3.9 per cent higher than the median household income of $61,372. In their words: 'Altogether, from 2000–2017, the median income for non-elderly households (those with a head of household younger than 65 years of age) fell from $71,577 to $69,628, a decline of $1,949, or 2.7 percent. In short, the last three years should not make us forget that incomes for the majority of Americans have experienced a lost 17 years of growth' (Gould and Wolfe 2018). In the United States, the federal minimum wage has similarly lost its value over the last decade or so. Standing at $7.25, the federal minimum wage has not been increased since July 2009. With rising costs over the years, the minimum wage had therefore lost 21 per cent of its value up until 2021 (Zipperer 2021).

It is a similar story for those living in the United Kingdom. In one of their reports, the Institute for Fiscal Studies shows that median annual earnings have dropped from £23,327 in 2017. Since 2008, this represents a decrease of 3.2 per cent from when average wage was £24,088. As in the United States, the report finds that average UK household incomes are higher than in 2008, even though wages have fallen. 'Median real household income has risen from £24,300 to £25,700 (a 6 per cent rise) since 2008'. 'But', the report continues, 'had incomes continued to grow at the same rate as the decade before the crisis, average household income would now be £29,900 – £4,200 higher than it actually is' (Cribb and Johnson 2018). And, perhaps inevitably, when wages stagnate, people turn to debt to maintain their spending power. In recent years, for example, UK household consumers have pushed their finances into deficit for the first time since the credit boom of the 1980s. In 2018, the ONS observed that UK households saw their outgoings surpass their income for the first time in nearly thirty years, and households became net borrowers for the first time since 1988. On average, each household spent £900 more than they received in income. This totalled almost £25 billion. To fund this shortfall, households borrowed more or used more of their savings. Overall, households took out nearly £80 billion in loans in 2017, but only deposited £37 billion in UK banks (ONS 2018c). As we saw in Chapter 4, we know that many households have started to pay off their debt since the pandemic, but debt is still nevertheless a problem with over £60 billion in debt on credit cards alone reported in June 2020. One UK charity estimated in January 2021 that of those surveyed, 45 per cent of those who had experienced an 'income shock' because of the pandemic have had to borrow to make up this loss, while 2.4 million are in 'problem debt' and 2.8 million have used high-cost credit to make ends meet (StepChange 2021). Just before the pandemic, the Living Wage Foundation (2019) discovered in 2019 that 1.2 million UK public sector workers are not earning the real living wage of £9.00 per hour across Britain and £10.55 in London. This means that 20 per cent of all low paid workers in the United Kingdom now work in the public sector. Since the pandemic, many have seen their earnings decline.

In the second half of 2020, for example, 49 per cent of employed UK workers, about 13.5 million people, faced a real fall in their earnings. Some forecasts suggest that real earnings will be 4.3 per cent below pre-pandemic forecasts by 2025 (Slaughter 2021).

One of the main reasons to explain labour's declining share of national income distribution is due to the relative weakness in the collective bargaining power of labour trade unions; a point conceded by the ILO's 2018 report cited above. Under neoliberalism and financialisation, a number of governments have actively pushed forward anti-union legislation. In the case of the United Kingdom, a restructuring of employment relations and union rights, including the dismantling of collective bargaining between employers and trade unions, and legislation after legislation restricting strike activity, has been underway since the early 1980s. After gaining power in 2010, the Conservatives passed further legislation to make union activism and union support even more difficult. For example, they reduced the consultation period for redundancies from ninety to forty-five days, removed fixed-term workers from collective dismissal rights, and made legal redress for unfair dismissal tougher by bringing in fees of £250 for making a claim and a further £950 for having the claim heard (Grimshaw et al. 2017). The Trade Union Act 2016 made it mandatory that at least 50 per cent of members who are entitled to vote do vote for action by a trade union before the outcome of the vote is valid. Relentless attacks on the public sector have also weakened trade union power in these places of employment (Barradas 2019: 387). A report by UNCTAD, argues that since the 1980s, and in nearly all regions and in almost every country, the share of national income falling in the laps of labour has declined even when the profit share has increased. 'In developed countries this redistribution has been generally larger and occasionally extreme (with 10 per cent or more of GDP transferred from workers to capitalists in Australia, Italy and Japan), but the trend has been visible in developing countries as well . . .' (UNCTAD 2019: 42). In the opinion of the report, key underlying reasons for the redistribution of income from workers to capitalists include, 'decreasing unionization rates, the erosion of social security, growing market concentration and the spread of outsourcing through global value chains' (UNCTAD 2019: 42).

Financialisation has led to an increase in short termism in companies and a rise in individualised employment relations. In the United Kingdom, large and some medium-sized companies seek to gain profits from realising financial value rather than producing goods and services. Declining manufacturing and the rise in the service industries have also seen a move away from stable workplace relations and spending money in human capital (Grady 2017: 278). Again, the relatively simple point to make here is that financial and neoliberal capitalism has engaged in an offensive against the representatives of labour; this is not new to the capitalist armoury, but is a continuation of its attack on the rights of labour over many years. The data, therefore, seems to complicate Hardt and Negri's dualistic picture of 'old' versus 'new' capitalistic practices, and suggests that class struggles, socio-political activism and strategies in and against capital must indeed be attuned to old *and* new plans of resistance. After all, the 'normal' capitalist attacks on the wages of labour are also evident in terms of digital work, as we will now see.

CAPITAL'S DIGITAL OFFENSIVE AGAINST LABOUR

The diminution of trade union rights and the re-organisation of legal protection in favour of employers can be seen most tellingly in digital labour and gig work. In UK law, when people perform work, they are classified under three main categories. An employee works for an employer and subsequently there is an understanding between both about the nature of the employee's work duties for the employer. Employees also enjoy full employment rights. Next, there is an independent contractor who has their own business and is employed by clients or customers to carry out specific work for a period of time. They pay their own taxes and have no employment rights. Finally, there is an intermediate category, called a 'limb b' worker, or just 'worker', who while self-employed nevertheless carries out their work as part of another person's business. A 'worker' is therefore subject to the control, rules and regulations of an employer, and because of this stipulation, he or she, as a paid worker, should enjoy some employment rights, such as trade union rights, minimum wage, paid holidays, and employer pension contributions (IWGB 2017: 5). Given these categories, reports like the Taylor Review (see Chapter 8) often argue that there is a trade-off between employment law and flex ibility for atypical workers such as those found in the gig economy. If the likes of gig workers want to maintain their flexibility, then current employment law needs to change in order to catch up with these employment trends. As critics argue, though, there should be no trade-off here insofar as current employment law should simply be enforced to ensure that 'flexible' gig workers also receive their legal employment rights. For unions like the IWGB and TUC, the real problem is exactly the point that current employment law is often not being enforced by the state. The main issue, then, is not so much that gig workers require new regulations to safeguard their new worker identities. Rather, one of the main issues is that many platform employers simply ignore or flout existing laws. And there is no reason to believe that these employers will not try to overcome new laws when push comes to shove (IWGB 2017: 21).

This is a particularly important point to make because many platform organisations do in fact operate like 'normal' employers. Take the example of Airtasker. If there is a household task that you cannot bear the thought of doing, such as assembling a new wardrobe, then Airtasker is a platform that lets you list the job you want done, which then allows others to place a bid to undertake the work for you. Reviews of previous work done by people allows customers to judge somebody before employing them, and Airtasker takes a 15 per cent fee for handling the transaction cost between customer and worker. Already successful in other countries like Australia, and claiming to undertake 1.4 million jobs there per year, Airtasker also raised over $30 in 2017 to launch its platform in the United Kingdom (Lunn and Collinson 2018). In Australia, trade unions nevertheless believe that while Airtasker classifies workers as independent contractors, thereby denying these very same workers are not entitled to normal employment rights in Australia, Airtasker in reality acts as an employer. After all, it controls who can perform and gain work on its platform, it acts as an arbitrator in disputes between customers and workers, it provides limited insurance coverage, it maintains the right to remove workers from its platform and thereby restrict work for them, and so on. The competitive nature of trying to get work via the Airtasker platform implies that many workers under-price their labour, and often do not even get a minimum wage, and workers also have to pay for their own leave, compensation insurance and so on. In terms of workers' compensation insurance, Airtasker has no uniform third-party injury insurance cover for job posters. Moreover, no proper licences are required by workers who do trades work, such as electrical work. As UnionsNSW notes:

> This raises concerns as to what, if any, warranty is provided by Airtasker to ensure qualified workers are matched to appropriate work to mitigate possible workplace accidents or unlicensed work being undertaken. (Unions NSW 2016: 9)

What these examples point towards is the continuation of work practices that have been noticeable at least since the mid-1980s. Montalban et al. (2019) note that what seems to be a new 'uberisation' of a wage-labour relation associated with 'platform capitalism' in fact represent older work practices than at first appear. During the 1980s, financialised companies started to outsource areas of their production to suppliers while passing on stock options and huge wages to CEOs and increasing their returns to shareholders. 'These new practices accelerated the end of the historical compromise between top management and unions and replaced it with a compromise between shareholders and managers pitted against unions and low-skilled employees' (Montalban et al. 2019: 9). In Chapter 5, we also noted how car manufacturers have been 'financialised' for many years now, while in other chapters we have analysed the increasing financialisation of work practices in the public sector and in other unproductive sectors. Since the 2008 crisis, financialised working methods have continued apace, but have also been complemented by temporary work practices associated with digital labour and the platform economy. So, for Montalban et al., the platform economy represents the next stage of an ongoing process of individualisation and flexibilisation of the labour force.

Digital technology, for example, has been at the forefront of changing class relations in the productive sectors of the economy, and, in particular, attacking the rights of productive labour. Kristal (2013) argues that digital technology in US manufacturing sectors has led to the automation of many work-related tasks and has helped to downsize and replace jobs once undertaken by blue-collar unionised workers. Moreover, 'computer technology is linked to skill polarization in the workforce, which may have undermined workers' solidarity, thereby reducing the likelihood of working-class cohesion and solidarity' (Kristal 2013: 382; see also Livingstone and Scholtz 2016).

Given these issues, one can argue that Hardt and Negri's views that the class relation between capital and labour has been usurped by new antagonistic relations again overstate changes that have occurred in the global economy across the last fifty years or so. Indeed, the 'old' divisions between capital and labour are still very much with us. This can be appreciated at an empirical level of understanding in respect to trade unions and digital technology. Trade unions have over time been weakened, both by declining membership, but also by state legislation and attacks by employers that have sought to limit union power and influence. Neoliberal fondness for 'flexible labour markets' often means in reality diminishing rights for workers to engage in collective bargaining over the likes of wages and democratic accountability of managers. Digital technology has been at the forefront of the capitalist offensive against unions. Kristal and Cohen (2015), for instance, found that from the early 1970s to 1997, the 'computerisation', or 'digitisation', of work in the productive sectors of manufacturing, transportation and construction industries, operated in tandem with a diminishing role for trade unions in wage bargaining with employers and managers in these sectors. Wage inequality subsequently increased between productive workers and managers and owners. Digitisation and computerisation of the labour process is one main reason, therefore, for the decline in productive labour's share of the national income. Evidence suggests, in fact, that national trade union strength based on strong trade union density is often associated with high levels of influence in workplace representation, as Nordic countries demonstrate (Gallie and Zhou 2013: 130), and high-performance workplaces work best when employees and workers are unionised and adopt concessionary wage bargaining with management (Bryson et al. 2005).

Strong trade unions in the workplace therefore benefit a wide variety of workers, including productive workers, in terms of gaining better workplace conditions, higher wages, more accountable managers and so forth. Another study from the IMF finds that de-unionisation and a weakening of the bargaining power of trade unions is associated with the vast increase in income of capitalist classes, particularly corporate managers and shareholders. In other words, weak trade unions are an important factor in the rise of income inequality across social classes (Jaumotte and Buitron 2015). To attack union rights in the workplace is therefore a key mechanism at the disposal of capitalists in order to weaken the power of productive workers, limit class struggle, and boost relative and absolute exploitation. Kristal further argues that a decline in union density in industrial sectors corresponds to a decline in national income going to those sectors. 'In manufacturing, union regression explains almost the entire decline in labour's share. The 20 percentage-point in manufacturing industries from 1978 to 2002 depressed labour's share by 8.4 percentage points' (Kristal 2013: 376).

Despite the attack on trade unions, there are many instances when organised activism by workers has blunted the power of management and the latter's ability to control the geographical mobility of capital and working conditions in productive plants. Köhler and Begega (2016) explore a case study of the American multinational corporation Tenneco in Gijón, Spain. In early September 2013, the 221 employees of Tenneco were notified that their production plant, which manufactured shock absorbers and exhausts for the automobile industry, was about to be closed and relocated to Eastern Europe. Furthermore, corporate management was increasingly bypassing local management structures and imposing competitive benchmarking between different workplaces within MNCs across (and within) countries and industries. This gave corporate management extra leverage to threaten local workers with plant relocation if need be. In reaction, the workers occupied the plant, and soon the local and regional media, along with the regional administration, were portraying the case as being unfair and unjust towards the workers. Workers also employed legal tactics against Tenneco. An audit report was also published in November 2013 that rejected the arguments made for closing down the plant. The report had been demanded by the workers. At the same time, a local representative in the European Parliament took up the cause of the workers, while local community support for the workers grew dramatically, which included organising a local rally, attended by around 10,000 people, in support of the workers in October 2013. Activism in and around the closure lasted for about eight months, after which the corporate management cancelled the decision to relocate the plant. As Köhler and Begega (2016) observe, the workers were victorious not just because they galvanised a number of key allies in their activism, but also because they built a case around the social injustice of management deciding to relocate the plant and a failure by local managers to negotiate fairly on issues concerning restructuring, redundancies and so on. Productive labour is not passive when it comes to questions about financialised restructuring.

Since the onset of the pandemic, there has been an even greater need for trade unions. In the United Kingdom, for instance, advice from government and industry has been sought from trade unions on different COVID-related issues. More ordinary workers have joined trade unions and online devices have encouraged a whole range of employees from other industries to join unions. Union online events have similarly attracted hundreds to watch and be involved in union activities and activism. One event organised by the National Education Union in January 2021, for instance, 'was attended, in its entirety, by over 100,000 people, with over 400,000 watching some part of it' (Bettington 2021: 76). Given the organising capacity of trade unions, they should therefore be guaranteed a place on participatory bodies and so-called co-creative forums in the public sector and in all workplaces. As we saw in Chapter 9, co-creative forums in the public sector often become the means for management to articulate financialised and neoliberal hegemony. Trade unions, however, can and should try to use the crisis surrounding COVID-19 as a means to gain greater participatory rights to sit on such forums and to play an active role in them. This will then install a form of 'active participation' in which service users, public employees and their representative organisations – trade unions for employees and community organisations for users – all meet to discuss relevant issues with management. Within these discussions, the reality of factors impacting the workplace and service delivery in question must be discussed. For example, the realities of the impact financialisation, including its contradictions, dilemmas and problems, must be discussed. It should therefore be argued that 'public employee/trade union and user/community organisation participation in the planning, design, and delivery benefits the quality of services, jobs innovation and the effectiveness of services' (Whitfield 2020: 347).

To give one illustration, the pandemic has highlighted the predatory nature and limitations of the financialisation of public services. The pandemic therefore opens up a space to discuss this issue. Evidence demonstrates, for instance, that outsourcing public services to private companies has negative consequences on pay, terms and conditions for outsourced workers. 'Analysis ... found that across six key metrics, including hours, pay, job tenure and qualifications, workers in the public sector had better standards than those performing the same jobs in the private or voluntary sector' (TUC 2021b). In creating a public sphere around this issue, there is an opportunity to generate a wider discussion in society at large concerning intensification of work, lower wages, and the impact of these issues on other social spheres of life beyond the workplace. As we know, these are issues that cut across many different social classes and different socio-cultural identities. Campaigns around increases minimum wages, for instance, serve to bring together important social, political and cultural issues in the workplace and beyond. So, according to Zipperer, a move towards a $15 national minimum wage would see the wages of 32 million workers increase. It would also:

> (I)ncrease the earnings of nearly one in three Black workers (31%) and one in four Hispanic workers (26%). It would also raise the wages of 19 million front-line and essential workers. By helping to ensure decent pay, a national $15 minimum wage by 2025 would lift up to 3.7 million people out of poverty, including 1.3 million children. (Zipperer 2021)

A real democratic public sphere in the workplace must therefore be created that can start to address issues about how to de-commodify social life from neoliberalism and financialisation. This, at least, is a tentative step towards building a post-capitalist public sphere that incorporates both socio-political and socio-economic aspects of democracy in the workplace.

But if this is the case, then how should we adapt and develop a political strategy to challenge this neoliberal and financialised way of working? Indeed, what political strategy might challenge neoliberalism more broadly in society, not only in the sphere of work, but also in the spheres of politics, ideology, culture and so forth? It is to this question we now turn.

TOWARDS A POST-COVID-19 PROGRESSIVE AGENDA: THE NECESSITY TO TAKE STATE POWER

Hardt and Negri argue that to be effective, a social movement must engage in a constant process of building networks of ongoing organisational activity (Hardt and Negri 2017: 20–1). Hardt and Negri's focus of attention is on those global movements of loosely connected activist groups that emerged in the late 1990s, and which communicated together through digital networks and campaign on specific issues like environmentalism, social justice and poverty. A more recent illustration is the Occupy Movement. The Occupy protests started on 17 September 2011 in New York City by campaigners and protestors buoyed by the Arab Spring and the camp-out movements in Spain, and were swept along by anger at the 2008 financial crisis, spread across the world and brought together activists from conventional social and political organisations in local communities. Like global social movements, the Occupy Movement was organised around horizontal networks, it arranged its campaigns through a variety of social and political issues with no domineering political perspective, and it employed new media to create image events and to publicise activism at both local and global levels. At the same time, the Occupy Movement was aware of the need to galvanise support from local residents and from existing and ongoing campaign and groups in local communities.

In such instances, according to Hardt and Negri, protestors were, and are, motivated 'to weave together political, economic, and social liberation; redefining constituent power as continuous processes of transformation; and promoting and constitutionalising a plurality of diverse social subjectivities ... through critiques of inequality, privatisation, and the powers of finance' (Hardt and Negri 2017: 35). Above all else, these movements show that leaders within them make tactical decisions but will always defer to the strategic autonomy and cooperation of the movements themselves. In practice, this implies that traditional forms of centralised leadership as found, for example, in state and parliamentary institutions are to be rejected in favour of alternative administrative forms 'that immanently organise the collective, democratic decision-making of the entire population' (Hardt and Negri 2017: 134). One concrete example they give to illustrate this new organisational structure from below is that of social unionism. In this type of organisation, social movements join together with labour unions in order to campaign for a whole array of rights in society. Social unionism therefore moves beyond the traditional workplace and traditional areas of trade union issues. Social unionism therefore operates with the idea that the whole of social life is 'an enormous factory of social production and reproduction, or more precisely, it is a space produced in common' (Hardt and Negri 2017: 149).

Like the new economy and creative industries thesis, the idea that politics is now informed through a new network type of engagement sounds convincing. Indeed, many of Hardt and Negri's observations do set out and describe important changes that have occurred to the public sphere and their relationship with the state. As is the case with many such approaches, however, there are problems with their arguments. These are noticeable in terms of Hardt and Negri's suggested political strategies for progressive and leftist social movements. According to them, the state must be smashed. As the state is 'an instrument of class rule insofar as it stands above and rules over society', then to smash the state means 'destroying that gap' and creating institutions that represent genuine democratic decision-making (Hardt and Negri 2017: 134). Laudable as this proposal is, though, it seems to ignore social and political cultures in societies. For example, Marsh (2011) detects a conservative notion of responsibility that has been prevalent in British culture for many years dominated by political hierarchal governance rather than networks. Moreover, a participatory culture is a staple characteristic of British political culture, but it is one that underlines the importance of periodic elections yet downplays any other kind of active citizenry. Taking these points on board, we need to take seriously such political cultures. Left-wing forces cannot simply ignore the likes of parliamentary cultures, for example. Hardt and Negri are, of course, aware that there have been attempts by some social movements of late to capture state power. Syriza in Greece is one notable instance of this type of politics. Formed in 2004 as a coalition of leftist groups and including socialists, green activists, feminist activists, and a variety of other workers' and community groups, Syriza had a number of successes in Greek general elections until it became the main opposition party in 2012, eventually forming a government in the 2015 general election. But because Syriza failed to maintain their immanent links with progressive and leftist Greek social movements, and soon became a social democratic government held hostage to the neoliberal ideals of the EU rather than a socialist one (Panitch and Gindin 2018: ch. 4). Hardt and Negri are generally dismissive of this type of parliamentary movement politics. For them, it represents a form of populism: 'constant lip service to the power of the people but ultimate control and decision-making by a small clique of politicians' (Hardt and Negri 2017: 23). But while Syriza ended in failure and Greece has had to endure yet more failed neoliberal policies, does it necessarily follow that those partnerships between social movement politics and parliamentary parties are doomed to failure?

The United Kingdom provides an interesting comparison with Greece, and to a number of other EU countries as well. Della Porta (2015) argues that since the 2008 financial crisis, several conditions have emerged that opened up spaces for social movements to move successfully into parliamentary politics. These conditions included the post-crisis conditions of each country; increasing institutional distrust by large sections of the population in each country with an established two-party system; the failure of centre-left parties to address new and old issues, and questions about social justice in each respective country; the organisational weakness of traditional parties based on factors such as corruption and declining memberships; the ability of new movement parties to make links with already established party organisational structures, such as being active participants in European social forums, while some members of established political parties left to join new movement parties; and increasing electoral successes of movement parties at national and European levels (Della Porta et al. 2017: 184–8). In the case of the United Kingdom, however, the traditional two-party system has been used by movement activists to advance their aims and goals. Specifically, a left-wing social movement, Momentum, emerged in 2015 during the election of the left-wing politician Jeremy Corbyn, as leader of the Labour Party. According to some of its founders, Momentum was originally conceived to bring together social movements in civil society, trade unions, constituency Labour Party groups and the Parliamentary Labour (Klug et al. 2016: 37).

Momentum therefore represents a movement that is situated firmly within a mainstream parliamentary party. This gives Momentum, as a social movement, a somewhat different identity to other European movement parties like Syriza in Greece, Podemos in Spain and M5S in Italy. For example, unlike their European counterparts, Momentum was created to support the election of the seasoned left-wing politician, Jeremy Corbyn, as leader of the long-established parliamentary political machine, the Labour Party. Labour Party membership soon grew to over 500,000. As a result, the Labour Party became fused to a social movement, while a social movement gained access to established state structures and established and embedded institutional party mechanisms in local communities and civil society more generally. It also meant that organisations that directly represented workers, like large trade unions, became part of this reinvigorated Labour Party. In this way, the Labour Party under Corbyn was *potentially* in a better position than other leftist parliamentary groups in Europe because they had in their hands the mechanisms to develop socialist policies and explore 'how' they might actually implement them in dialogue with social and political movements 'from below'.

Before we follow Hardt and Negri and try to smash the state, we therefore need to harness state capacities and transform them in new socialist directions, such as democratic planning and collective property rights (Panitch and Gindin 2018: 93). Among other things, this further implies building alliances with social movements like Momentum and other progressive and leftist civil society movements and forging alliances with workers' organisations, such as established trade unions. Certainly, during the 2017 general election, the new socialist policies of Corbyn made substantial electoral gains for Labour and led to a hung Parliament. During that election, Corbyn managed to get Labour its largest vote since 2005 and closed a twenty-four-point deficit with the Conservatives. Momentum helped to mobilise the increased mass base of Labour members, and, through innovative uses of digital media, community campaigns and door-to-door canvassing, contributed towards building a reinvigorated left-wing politics in the United Kingdom (Sunkara 2017).

Unfortunately, two years later in the December 2019 general election, Labour suffered a catastrophic defeat. There are a number of reasons for this defeat, but undoubtedly Brexit looms large. Unlike 2017, Corbyn had by 2019 been boxed into a hybrid mixture of leave and remain positions, promising a second referendum if elected. As Watkins perceptively notes, the outcome of this new Brexit standpoint, which was developed by different factions in the Labour Party, was to make Labour appear to some of its 'natural' voters in working-class areas (areas that had voted to leave the EU) like it was endorsing 'a functionally conservative position', in the sense that Corbyn and Labour now seemed to represent the 'Remainer elite' to these voters (Watkins 2020: 16). In the years between the 2017 election and the 2019 election, moreover, both liberal and conservative mainstream media launched scathing attacks on Corbyn in and around a number of issues, while sections of the Labour Parliamentary Party voiced numerous criticisms of Corbyn and his leadership team. Researchers at Loughborough University, for example, found that press hostility to Labour in 2019 was more than double than that identified in 2017, while negative press towards the Conservatives halved (Deacon et al. 2019). If anything, the Labour leadership had subsequently underestimated the extent to which certain powers in British society were willing to forge together temporary hegemonic blocs to stop an avowedly socialist politician like Corbyn from gaining power. At the same time, Labour needed to draw on its newly enlarged membership base and resources to mobilise working-class communities as well as its urban and metropolitan communities (Cant 2019). Arguably, Labour had more success with the latter communities than the former ones. However, this underlines the importance of drawing on state resources and instruments to establish links and build alliances with a variety of groups in civil society.

CONCLUSION: CAPITALISM IS STILL CRISIS

Central to way that capitalism operates is a class relation forged through the constant dispossession of labour from the means of production. In the words of Marx:

> (T)he result of the process of production and realisation is, above all, the reproduction of new production of the *relation of capital and labour itself, of capitalist and worker*. This social relation, this production relation, appears in fact as an even more important result of the process than its material results. And more particularly, within this process the worker produces himself as labour capacity, as well as the capital confronting him, while at the same time the capitalist produces himself as capital as well as the living labour capacity confronting him. Each reproduces itself, by reproducing its other, its negation. (Marx 1973: 458)

A Marxist theory of digital technology, labour and work, must therefore begin with the premise that the labour process is part and parcel of the capitalist mode of production and the creation of surplus value through alienated labour (see Gough 2003). The capitalist mode of production comprises a contradictory unity between forces and relations of production; between the production of use-values and the production of surplus value. This contradictory unity is powered by alienated labour and its endless dispossession from the means of production.

In our capitalist world today, subjects are still treated as abstract social entities in the manner described by Marx in *Capital*. Globalisation has extended and intensified the mechanisms in which every object potentially becomes a commodity to be exchanged. More than ever, people's concrete differences – their use-values – have been transformed into the same abstract homogeneous entity of being commodities. People with real needs and real moral worth and everyday ethical sensibilities are of no immediate value to capital. Capital is still only interested in 'free legal subjects' mediated through a minority who can own and control the means of production, on the one hand, and a majority who can freely dispose of their labour, on the other hand. As Albritton observes, under this ideological schema subjects are radically decentred, 'since such a subject is simply a collection of opportunistic profit-making capacities without any centre or inner connectedness' (Albritton 2007: 50). Each person is not seen as being inextricably tied to an antagonistic and moral social relation, but is thought by capital as existing merely as a de-socialised individual to be economically exploited or oppressed (Marx 1988: 280).

Capitalism, however, develops unevenly because at the heart of how it functions is a contradiction between the satisfaction of human needs through the production of use-values versus the inherent requirement to exchange goods for profit and, hence, for goods to possess exchange-value. A good is thus produced, but a seller will not know if that very same good will be exchanged for another good. Buyer and seller remain there-fore separate from one another. This atomistic relationship is deepened through money, which, while acting as a universal means of exchange, also exacerbates the division between buyer and seller because it is an abstract measure of all commodities and so treats people as isolated 'things'. As commodity relationships develop and extend into capitalist relationships, an external competitive pressure is then placed on each producer to develop their productive forces and capacities without taking note of the conditions under which this occurs. Technological innovation is always the main way for capitalists to remain competitive because it creates the conditions for relative surplus value to occur (Smith 2000).

To expand their production, capitalists must also have access to finance, particularly credit. But credit is a contradictory mechanism. Credit helps to drive a greater competitive intensity among capitals. Credit likewise helps to expand the purchase of consumer goods. But credit also subordinates social life to the power of money and reproduc-tion of capital, and credit potentially expands the power of unproduc-tive capital and labour (Clarke 1988). Sooner or later the limits of the market can no longer be so readily overcome by credit, or by other finan-cial mechanisms, and a crisis erupts. 'In these crises there breaks out an epidemic that, in all earlier epochs, would have seemed an absurdity, the epidemic of overproduction . . . The productive forces at the disposal of society no longer tend to further the development of the conditions of bourgeois property' (Marx and Engels 1964: 12). In turn, the uneven development of capitalism is pushed to greater lengths so that, eventu-ally, rising prices and rising wages place the profits of expanded com-modity producers under increasing pressure. If credit is swelled further, inflation will ensue. The limits of the market will suddenly assert them-selves and the economy will nose-dive into crisis. Over-accumulation of capital appears as debt, and the overproduction of commodities leads to the devaluation and destruction of productive capital (Clarke 1990/91: 460–3; see also Foster 2000).

Marx's theory makes connections between underlying class relations and everyday experiences of workers in their daily labour processes where they experience the likes of 'lengthening the working day, intensifying labour and displacing labour with machinery . . .' (Albritton 2007: 67). Marx's value theory therefore provides crucial insights for political practice. First, it uncovers the 'motor' of capitalist exploitation, which lies in alienated labour. Secondly, it shows that exploitation is a contradictory, crisis-ridden process, subject to continual change. Finally, value theory demonstrates how exploitation functions and, hence, it lays the groundwork for us to think of ways to overcome it (Elson 1979: 171). For Marx, then, seemingly separate social processes – for example, monetary relations and labour process relations – are one-sided reflections of an exploitative, political and social unity. By demonstrating the underlying alienated 'essence' that connects capitalist society together, but which also tears it apart, Marx can then examine how the contradictions of capitalism push capital to move beyond its immediate abstract forms to reproduce itself into an array of everyday class processes and workplaces.

BIBLIOGRAPHY

Albritton, R. (2007). *Economics Transformed*, London: Pluto.

Aldasoro, I and Ehlers, T. (2018). 'Global Liquidity: Changing Instrument and Currency Patterns', *BIS Quarterly Review*, September: 17–27.

Aldred, R. (2007). 'Closed Policy Networks, Broken Chains of Communication and the Stories Behind an "Entrepreneurial Policy": The Case of NHS Local Improvement Finance Trust (NHS LIFT)', *Critical Social Policy*, 27(1): 139–51.

Alston, P. (2020). 'The Parlous State of Poverty Eradication', *Human Rights Council*, 2 July, available at: https://chrgj.org/wp-content/uploads/2020/07/Alston-Poverty-Report-FINAL.pdf, last accessed 23 July 2020.

Alter Summit (2018). 'Transnational Couriers' Assembly #riders4rights', available at: http://www.altersummit.eu/home/article/international-couriers-declaration, last accessed 25 June 2020.

Amazonians United (2020a). 'Amazonians United Wins PTO for all Amazon Workers', *Medium*, 22 March, available at: https://medium.com/@dch1united/amazonians-united-wins-pto-for-all-amazon-workers-f17e6ffbb192, last accessed 2 June 2020.

Amazonians United (2020b). 'How Amazon Workers are Organizing for the Long Haul', *Labor Notes*, 11 May, available at: https://labornotes.org/2020/05/how-amazon-workers-are-organizing-long-haul, last accessed 2 June 2020.

Anderson, T (2020). 'As the State Sails Communities, Mutual Aid Projects are Working to Meet People's Needs Across the UK', *The Canary*, 17 May, available at: https://www.thecanary.co/feature/2020/05/17/as-the-state-fails-communities-mutual-aid-projects-are-working-to-meet-peoples-needs-across-the-uk, last accessed 30 May 2020.

Andrew, A., Catton, S., Dias, M. C., Farquharson, C., Kraftman, L., Krutikova, S., Phimister, A. and Sevilla, A. (2020). 'How are Mothers and Fathers Balancing Work and Family under Lockdown?' Institute for Fiscal Studies,

27 May, available at: https://ifs.org.uk/publications/14860, last accessed 15 July 2021.

Antunes, R. (2013). *The Meanings of Work*, Chicago: Haymarket.

Appelbaum, E. (2020). 'CEPR Statement on New Labor Department Guidance Allowing Risky Private Equity Investments in Workers' 401(k) Accounts', *CEPR*, 4 June, available at: https://cepr.net/cepr-statement-on-new-labor-de partment-guidance-allowing-risky-private-equity-investments-in-workers -401k-accounts, last accessed 16 June 2020.

Arnold, S. and Jaccarini, C. (2020). 'Who's Losing Income During the Pandemic?' *New Economics Foundation*, 14 June, available at: https:// neweconomics.org/2020/06/whos-losing-income-during-the-pandemic, last accessed 23 June 2020.

Arts Index (2020). *Arts Index 2007–2018*, National Campaign for the Arts, June, available at: https://www.theguardian.com/culture/2020/jun/08/triple -whammy-of-funding-cuts-has-left-uk-arts-vulnerable-report?CMP=Share _iOSApp_Other, last accessed 30 June 2020.

Atzeni, M. (2010). *Workplace Conflict*, London: Palgrave.

Aylesbury Vale District Council (2017). 'AVDC Launches "Skill" for Amazon's Alexa', 12 October, available at: https://www.aylesburyvaledc.gov.uk/news /avdc-launches-%E2%80%98skill%E2%80%99-amazon%E2%80%99s -alexa, last accessed 20 September 2019.

Babson, S. (1995). 'Lean Production and Labor: Empowerment and Exploitation', in S. Babson (ed.), *Lean Work*, Detroit, MI: Wayne State University Press.

Baeck, P. and Reynolds, S. (2020). 'Smart Cities during COVID-19', 24 April, available at: https://www.nesta.org.uk/blog/smart-cities-during-covid-19, last accessed 2 July 2020.

Bailey, D., de Ruyter, A., Michie, J. and Tyler, P. (2010). 'Global Restructuring and the Auto Industry', *Cambridge Journal of Regions, Economy and Society* 3(3): 311–18.

Baines, D., Charlesworth, S., Turner, D. and O'Neill, L. (2014). 'Lean Social Care and Worker Identity: The Role of Outcomes, Supervision and Mission', *Critical Social Policy* 34(4): 433–53.

Balaram, B., Warden, J. and Wallace-Stephens, F. (2017). *Good Gigs: A Fairer Future for the UK's Gig Economy*, RSA: London.

Banaji. J. (2011). *Theory as History*, Chicago: Haymarket.

Banet-Weiser, S. and Castells, M. (2017). 'Economy is Culture', in M. Castells (ed.), *Another Economy is Possible*, Cambridge: Polity.

Bang, H. (2005). 'Among Everyday Makers and Expert Citizens', in J. Newman (ed.), *Remaking Governance*, Bristol: Policy Press.

Bang, H. and Esmark, A. (2007). 'Introduction: A Critical Look at Contemporary

Publics', in H. Bang and A. Esmark (eds.), *New Publics With/out Democracy*, Copenhagen: Samfundslitteratur Press.

Bang, H. and Esmark, A. (2009). 'Good Governance in Network Society: Reconfiguring the Political from Politics to Polity', *Administrative Theory and Praxis* 31(1): 7–37.

Bangham, G. and Leslie, J. (2020). *Rainy Days*, The Resolution Foundation, June, available at: https://www.resolutionfoundation.org/app/uploads/2020 /06/Rainy-Days.pdf, last accessed 2 July 2020.

Bank of England (2021). 'Money and Credit – December 2020', 1 February, available at: https://www.bankofengland.co.uk/statistics/money-and-credit /2020/december-2020, last accessed 13 July 2021.

Bannister, F. and Wilson, D. (2011). 'O(ver)-Government?: Emerging Technology, Citizen Autonomy and the Regulatory State', *Information Polity* 16(1): 63–79.

Baraki, B. (2020). *Universal Credit in the Time of Coronavirus*, New Economics Foundation, June, available at: https://neweconomics.org/uploads/files/UC -briefing-FINAL.pdf, last accessed 25 June 2020.

Barradas, R. (2019). 'Financialization and Neoliberalism and the Fall in the Labor Share: A Panel Data Econometric Analysis for the European Union Countries', *Review of Radical Political Economics* 51(3): 383–417.

Bateman, N., Radnor, Z. and Glennon, R. (2018). 'Editorial: The Landscape of Lean across Public Services', *Public Money and Management* 38(1): 1–4.

Batty, M., Bricker, J., Briggs, J., Holmquist, E., McIntosh, S., Moore, K., Nielsen, E., Reber, S., Shatto, M., Sommer, K., Sweeney, T. and Henriques, A. V. (2019). 'Introducing the Distributional Financial Accounts of the United States', *Finance and Economics Discussion Series 2019-017*, Washington: Board of Governors of the Federal Reserve System, available at: https://doi .org/10.17016/FEDS.2019.017, last accessed 20 June 2019.

Bauer, L. (2020). 'About 14 Million Children in the US Are Not Getting Enough to Eat', *The Hamilton Project*, 9 July, available at: https://www.hamiltonpr oject.org/blog/about_14_million_children_in_the_us_are_not_getting_enou gh_to_eat?utm_source=newsletter&utm_medium=email&utm_campaign= newsletter_axiospm&stream=top, last accessed 13 August 2020.

Bauman, Z. (2000). *Liquid Modernity*, Cambridge: Polity.

Beatty, C. and Fothergill, S. (2016). 'The Uneven Impact of Welfare Reform: The Financial Losses to Places and People', Centre for Regional Economic and Social Research, Sheffield Hallam University.

Beech, D. (2015). *Art and Value*, Chicago: Haymarket.

Bell, D. (1999). *The Coming of Post-Industrial Society*, New York: Basic Books.

Bell, T. and Tomlinson, D. (2018). *Is Everybody Concentrating? Recent Trends in Product and Labour Market Concentration in the UK*, London: The

Resolution Foundation, available at: https://www.resolutionfoundation .org/app/uploads/2018/07/Is-everybody-concentrating_Recent-trends-in-pr oduct-and-labour-market-concentration-in-the-UK-1-1.pdf, last accessed 9 September 2018.

Beresford, P., Farr, M., Hickey, G., Kaur, M., Ocloo, J., Tembo, D. and Williams, O. (2021). 'Co-production in Emergency Responses and the "New Normal"', in P. Beresford, M. Farr, G. Hickey, M. Kaur, J. Ocloo, D. Tembo and O. Williams (eds.), *COVID-19 and Co-production in Health and Social Care, Research, Policy and Practice*, Bristol: Policy Press.

Berg, J. and De Stefano, V. (2017). 'It's Time to Regulate the Gig Economy', *Speri: Sheffield Political Economy Research Unit*, available at: http://speri.de pt.shef.ac.uk/2017/04/17/its-time-to-regulate-the-gig-economy, last accessed 3 February 2018.

Berg, A., Buffie, E. F. and Zanna, L-F. (2018a). *Should We Fear the Robot Revolution? (The Correct Answer is Yes)*, IMF Working Paper 18/116, available at: https:/www.imf.org/en/Publications/WP/Issues/2018/05/21/Sho uld-We-Fear-the-Robot-Revolution-The-Correct-Answer-is-Yes-44923, last accessed 2 February 2019.

Berg, J., Furrer, M., Harmon, E., Rani, U. and Silberman, M. S. (2018b). *Digital Labour Platforms and the Future of Work: Towards Decent Work in the Online World*, Geneva: International Labour Organization.

Bergvall-Kåreborn, B. and Howcroft, D. (2014). 'Amazon Mechanical Turk and the Commodification of Labour', *New Technology, Work and Employment*, 29(3): 213–23.

Berry, C., Macfarlane, L. and Nanda, S. (2020). *Who Wins and Who Pays? Rentier Power and the Covid Crisis*, IPPR, 13 May, available at: http://www .ippr.org/research/publications/who-wins-and-who-pays, last accessed 16 June 2020.

Bettington, P. (2021). *Work in 2021: A Tale of Two Economies*, Centre for Labour and Social Studies, May, available at: http://classonline.org.uk/docs /Work-in-2021-CLASS-v7.pdf, last accessed 16 July 2021.

Billingham, Z. (2020). *Why the Government Needs to Pay Up before Levelling Up*, Centre for Progressive Policy, 23 June, available at: https://www.prog ressive-policy.net/publications/why-the-government-needs-to-pay-up-before -levelling-up#_ftn1, last accessed 10 July 2020.

Bilton, C. (2007). *Management and Creativity*, Oxford: Blackwell.

Blanden J., Crawford, C., Fumagalli, L. and Rabe, B. (2021). *School Closures and Children's Emotional and Behavioural Difficulties*, Institute for Social and Economic Research, May, available at: https://www.iser.essex.ac.uk/files/ news/2021/school-closures/school-closures-mental-health.pdf, last accessed 15 July 2021.

Blundell, R., Dias, M. C., Joyce, R. and Xu, Xiaowei (2020). *COVID-19 and*

Inequalities, Institute for Fiscal Studies, 11 June, available at: https://www
.ifs.org.uk/inequality/covid-19-and-inequalities, last accessed 16 June 2020.

Boes, A., Kämpf, T., Langes, B. and Lühr, T. (2017). 'The Disruptive Power of
Digital Technology', in K. Briken, S. Chillas and M. Krzywdzinski (eds.),
The New Digital Workplace, London: Routledge.

Böhm-Bawerk, Eugen von (1949). 'Karl Marx and the Close of His System', in
P. Sweezy (ed.), *Karl Marx and the Close of His System*, Clifton: Augustus
M. Kelley.

Böhm, S. and Land, C. (2012). 'The New "Hidden Abode": Reflections on
Value and Labour in the New Economy', *Sociological Review* 60(2): 217–40.

Boltanski, L. and Chiapello, E. (2003). *The New Spirit of Capitalism*, London:
Verso.

Bond, S. (2020a). 'Apple and Google Build Smartphone Tool to Track COVID-
19', *npr*, 10 April, available at: https://www.npr.org/sections/coronavirus
-live-updates/2020/04/10/831912284/apple-and-google-build-smartphone
-tool-to-track-covid-19, last accessed 27 May 2020.

Bond, S. (2020b). '"We're Out There" So Protect Us, Protesting Workers Tell
Amazon, Target, Instacart', *npr*, 1 May, available at: https://www.npr.org
/2020/05/01/849218750/workers-walk-off-jobs-demand-safer-working-con
ditions, last accessed 2 June 2020.

Bonefeld, W. (2010). 'Abstract Labour: Against its Nature and on its Time',
Capital and Class 34(2): 257–76.

Bonefeld, W. (2014). *Critical Theory and the Critique of Political Economy*,
London: Bloomsbury.

Bonefeld, W., Brown, A. and Burnham, P. (1995). *A Major Crisis? The Politics
of Economic Policy in Britain in the 1990s*, Farnham: Dartmouth.

Borghi, R. A. Z., Sarti, F. and Macedo, M. A. (2013). 'The "Financialized"
Structure of Automobile Corporations in the 2000s', *World Review of
Political Economy* 4(3): 387–409.

Bowman, A., Folkman, P., Froud, J., Johal, S., Law, J., Leaver, A., Moran, M.
and Williams, K. (2013). *The Great Train Robbery: Rail Privatisation and
After*, CRESC: Public Interest Report, available at: https://www.tuc.org.uk
/sites/default/files/tucfiles/The_Great_Train_Robbery_7June2013.pdf, last
accessed 30 July 2020.

Box, R. C., Marshall, G. S., Reed, B. J. and Reed, C. M. (2001). 'New Public
Management and Substantive Democracy', *Public Administration Review*
61(5): 608–19.

Boyer, R. (1988). 'Wage/Labour Relations, Growth, and Crisis: A Hidden
Dialectic', in R. Boyer (ed.), *The Search for Labour Market Flexibility*,
Oxford: Clarendon Press.

Boyer, R. (1990). *The Regulation School*, New York: Columbia University Press.

Boyle, M-E. and Silver, I. (2005). 'Poverty, Partnerships, and Privilege: Elite Institutions and Community Empowerment', *City and Community* 4(3): 233–53.

Braverman, H. (1974). *Labor and Monopoly Capital*, New York: Monthly Review Press.

Brenner, R. (1998). 'The Looming Crisis of World Capitalism', *Solidarity* November/December, available at: https://solidarity-us.org/atc/77/p871, last accessed 1 September 2017.

Brewer, M., Corlett, A., Handscomb, K., McCurdy, C. and Tomlinson, D. (2020). *The Living Standards Audit 2020*, The Resolution Foundation, available at: https://www.resolutionfoundation.org/app/uploads/2020/07/living-standards-audit.pdf, last accessed 22 July 2020.

British Chamber Commerce (BCC) (2020). *Quarterly Recruitment Outlook: Q2 2020*, available at: https://www.britishchambers.org.uk/media/get/BCC%20QRO%20Q2%202020.pdf, last accessed 21 July 2020.

British Council for Offices (BCO) (2020). 'Majority of Workers Plan a Return to the Office, but Home Working is Here to Stay', 5 October, available at: http://www.bco.org.uk/News/News46982.aspx, last accessed 12 October 2020.

British Medical Association (BMA) (2020). *The Role of Private Outsourcing in the COVID-19 Response*, 23 July, available at: https://www.bma.org.uk/media/2885/the-role-of-private-outsourcing-in-the-covid-19-response.pdf, last accessed 31 July 2020.

British Retail Consortium (BRC) (2020). 'UK Footfall Recovery Remains Sluggish', 7 July, available at: https://brc.org.uk/news/corporate-affairs/uk-footfall-recovery-remains-sluggish, last accessed 10 July 2020.

Broadcasting, Entertainment, Communications and Theatre Union (Bectu) (2020). 'Half of Creative Freelancers Borrowing Money to Survive COVID-19 Crisis', 15 May, available at: https://bectu.org.uk/news/half-of-creative-freelancers-borrowing-money-to-survive-covid-19-crisis, last accessed 30 June 2020.

Brown, A. (2020). 'No Masks and Uncertain Sick Leave: New York Whole Foods Delivery Workers Say Amazon is Failing to Protect Them', *The Intercept*, 31 March, available at: https://theintercept.com/2020/03/31/coronavirus-amazon-whole-foods-strike, last accessed 2 June 2020.

Bruns, A. (2008). *Blogs, Wikipedia, Second Life and Beyond*, New York: Peter Lang.

Bryan, D. and Rafferty, M. (2006). 'Financial Derivatives: The New Gold?' *Competition and Change* 10(3): 265–82.

Brynjolfsson, E., Horton, J., Ozimek, A., Rock, D., Sharma, G. and Ye, H. Y. T. (2020). 'COVID-19 and Remote Work: An Early Look at YS Data', May, available at: https://www.brynjolfsson.com/remotework, last accessed 23 July 2020.

Bryson, A., Forth, J. and Kirby, S. (2005). 'High-involvement Management Practices, Trade Union Representation and Workplace Performance in Britain', *Scottish Journal of Political Economy* 52(3): 451–91.

Bureau of Labor Statistics (BLS) (2019). 'News Release 21 August', available at: https://www.bls.gov/news.release/pdf/cewqtr.pdf, last accessed 23 September 2019.

Bureau of Labor Statistics (BLS) (2021). 'News Release', 8 October, available at: https://www.bls.gov/news.release/pdf/empsit.pdf, last accessed 1 November 2021.

Burke, M. (2020). 'End the Policy of Putting Profits before People', *Socialist Economic Bulletin*, 16 April, available at: https://www.socialisteconomic bulletin.net/2020/04/end-the-policy-of-putting-profits-before-people, last accessed 16 June 2020.

Burns, R. (2019). 'Angry about Low Pay and Sweltering Heat, These Amazon Warehouse Workers are Organizing', *In These Times*, 19 July, available at: http://inthesetimes.com/working/entry/21971/amazon-workers-chicago-pri me-day-jeff-bezos-organize, accessed 2 June 2020.

Butler, P. (2018). 'Universal Credit: What is It and What Exactly is Wrong with It?' *The Guardian*, 25 January, available at: https://www.theguardian.com /society/2018/jan/25/universal-credit-benefits-scheme-iain-duncan-smith, last accessed 2 August 2018.

Butler, S. (2018). 'Amazon Offsetting Pay Rise by Removing Bonuses, Union Says', *The Guardian*, 3 October, available at: https://www.theguardian.com /technology/2018/oct/03/amazon-offsetting-pay-rise-by-removing-bonuses -union-says?CMP=Share_iOSApp_Other, last accessed 16 February 2019.

Button, D. (2021). 'Make Government Spending Matter', New Economics Foundation, 10 March, available at: https://neweconomics.org/2021/03/ma king-government-spending-matter, last accessed 20 July 2021.

Cahill, D. (2014). *The End of Laissez-Fare?* Cheltenham: Edward Elgar.

Callaghan, G. and Thompson, P. (2001). 'Edwards Revisited: Technical Control and Call Centres', *Economic and Industrial Democracy* 22(1): 13–37.

Callinicos, A. (1987). 'The "New Middle Class" and Socialist Politics', in A. Callinicos and C. Harman (eds.), *Essays on Class Structure*, London: Bookmarks.

Campbell, D. (2019). 'How WeWork Spiralled from a $47 Billion Valuation to Talk of Bankruptcy in Just 6 Weeks', *Business Insider* 28 September, available at: https://www.businessinsider.com/weworks-nightmare-ipo?r=US& IR=T, last accessed 1 October 2019.

Cant, C. (2019). 'Understanding Our Defeat', 18 December, *Notes from Below*, available at: https://notesfrombelow.org/article/understanding-our-defeat, last accessed 9 March 2020.

Cant, C. and Mogno, C. (2020). 'Platform Workers of the World, Unite! The Emergence of the Transnational Federation of Couriers', *South Atlantic Quarterly* 119(2): 401–11.

Capgemini (2019). *Capgemini World Wealth Report 2019*, available at: https://worldwealthreport.com/resources/world-wealth-report-2019, last accessed 10 June 2020.

Carchedi, G. (1977). *On the Economic Identity of Social Classes*, London: Routledge & Kegan Paul.

Carchedi, G. (1991). *Frontiers of Political Economy*, London: Verso.

Carchedi, G. (2011). *Behind the Crisis*, Leiden: Brill.

Carchedi, G. and Roberts, M. (2018). 'The Long Roots of the Present Crisis: Keynesians, Austerians, and Marx's Law', in G. Carchedi and M. Roberts (eds.), *World in Crisis*, Chicago: Haymarket Books.

Carroll, W. (2010). *The Making of a Transnational Capitalist Class*, London: Zed Books.

Carter, B., Danford, A., Howcroft, D., Richardson, H., Smith, A. and Taylor, P. (2011). 'Lean and Mean in the Civil Service: The Case of Processing in HMRC', *Public Money and Management* 31(2): 115–22.

Carter, B., Danford, A., Howcroft, D., Richardson, H., Smith, A. and Taylor, P. (2014). '"They Can't be the Buffer Any Longer": Front-line Managers and Class Relations under White-Collar Lean Production', *Capital and Class* 38(2): 323–43.

Cassidy, J. (2018). 'Ten Years after the Start of the Great Recession, Middle-Class Incomes Are Only Just Catching Up', 13 September, *The New Yorker*, available at: https://www.newyorker.com/news/our-columnists/ten-years-after-the-start-of-the-great-recession-middle-class-incomes-are-only-just-catching-up, last accessed 9 November 2018.

Castells, M. (1983). *The City and the Grassroots*, Berkeley, California: University of California Press.

Castells, M. (2000). *The Rise of the Network Society*, 2nd edn., Oxford: Blackwell.

Castells, M. (2001). *The Internet Galaxy*, Oxford: Oxford University Press.

Castells, M. (2009). *Communication Power*, Oxford: Oxford University Press.

Castells, M. (2016). 'A Sociology of Power: My Intellectual Journey', *Annual Review of Sociology* 42: 1–19.

Castells, M. (ed.) (2017). *Another Economy is Possible*, Cambridge: Polity.

Castells, M., Caraça, J. and Cardoso, G. (2012). 'The Cultures of the Economic Crisis: An Introduction', in M. Castells, J. Caraça and G. Cardoso (eds.),

Aftermath: The Cultures of the Economic Crisis, Oxford: Oxford University Press.

Center for Microeconomic Data (2020). *Quarterly Report on Household Debt and Credit: Q2, 2020*, August, available at: https://www.newyorkfed.org /medialibrary/interactives/householdcredit/data/pdf/HHDC_2020Q2.pdf, last accessed 12 August 2020.

Centre for Retail Research (2020a). *Retail Forecast 2021–2022*, available at: https://www.retailresearch.org/retail-forecast.html, last accessed 9 July 2021.

Centre for Retail Research (2020b). *The Crisis in Retailing: Closures and Job Losses*, available at: https://www.retailresearch.org/retail-crisis.html, last accessed 9 July 2021.

Chandler, M. (2020). 'Lockdown Surge for Library Membership and E-book Loans', *The Bookseller*, 5 May, available at: https://www.thebookseller.com /news/member-surge-and-205-e-book-lockdown-lending-rise-change-librari es-long-term-1201874, last accessed 28 May 2020.

Chartered Institute of Personnel and Development (CIPD) (2020). *FSTE 100 CEO Pay in*

2019 and During the Pandemic, August, available at: https://www.cipd.co.uk /Images/ftse-100-executive-pay-report_tcm18-82375.pdf, last accessed 9 August 2020.

Cheng, J. and Wessel, D. (2020). 'What is the Repo Market, and Why Does It Matter?' *Brookings*, 28 January, available at: https://www.brookings.edu/bl og/up-front/2020/01/28/what-is-the-repo-market-and-why-does-it-matter, last accessed 12 June 2020.

Cherry, M. A. and Rutschman, A. S. (2020). 'Gig Workers as Essential Workers: How to Correct the Gig Economy beyond the COVID-19 Pandemic', *ABA Journal of Labor and Employment Law* 1: 11–16, available at: https://www .americanbar.org/content/dam/aba/publications/aba_journal_of_labor_em ployment_law/v35/number-1/gig-workers-as-essential.pdf, last accessed 12 July 2021.

Choonara, J. (2017). 'A Class Act: Erik Olin Wright in Perspective', *International Socialism* 154, available at: http://isj.org.uk/a-class-act-erik-olin-wright-in -perspective, last accessed 5 June 2017.

Christian Aid (2020). *Building Back with Justice: Dismantling Inequalities after COVID-19*, July, available at: https://www.christianaid.org.uk/sites/defa ult/files/2020-07/building-back-justice-covid19-report-Jul2020_0.pdf, last accessed 31 July 2020.

Clark, I. (2016). 'Financialisation, Ownership and Employee Interests under Private Equity at the AA, Part Two', *Industrial Relations Journal* 47(3): 238–52.

Clarke, S. (1979). 'Socialist Humanism and the Critique of Economism', *History Workshop Journal* 8: 137–56.

Clarke, S. (1988). *Keynesianism, Monetarism and the Crisis of the State*, Aldershot: Edward Elgar.

Clarke, S. (1990/91). 'The Marxist Theory of Overaccumulation and Crisis', *Science and*

Society 54(4): 442–67.

Clarke, S. (1991a). *Marx, Marginalism and Modern Sociology*, London: Macmillan.

Clarke, S. (1991b). 'Overaccumulation, Class Struggle and the Regulation Approach', in W. Bonefeld, and J. Holloway (eds.), *Post-Fordism and Social Form*, London: Macmillan.

Clarke, S. (1992). 'What in the F. . .'s Name is Fordism?' in N. Gilbert, R. Burrows and A. Pollert (eds.), *Fordism and Flexibility*, London: Macmillan

Clarke, S. (1994). 'The Value of Value: A Review of *Rereading Capital*', in S. Mohun (ed.), *Debates in Value Theory*, London: Macmillan.

Clarke, S. (2001). 'Class Struggle and Global Overaccumulation', in R. Albritton, M. Itoh, R. Westra and A. Zuege (eds.), *Phases of Capitalist Development*, London, Macmillan.

Clarke, S. and Greg, P. (2018). *Counting the Pennies: Explaining a Decade of Lost Pay Growth*, London: Resolution Foundation, available at: https://www.resolutionfoundation.org/publications/count-the-pennies-explaining-a-decade-of-lost-pay-growth, last accessed 2 August 2019.

Cleaver, H. (2017). *Rupturing the Dialectic*, Edinburgh: AK Press.

Clelland, D. A. (2014). 'The Core of the Apple: Dark Value and Degrees of Monopoly in Global Commodity Chains', *Journal of World-Systems Research* 20(1): 82–111.

Clement, W. and Myles, J. (1995). *Relations of Ruling: Class and Gender in Postindustrial Societies*, Montreal and Kingston: McGill-Queen's University Press.

Cloud Industry Forum (CIF) (2017). 'Public Sector IT Shortages Puts Brakes on Digital Transformation of Government Services', 16 November, available at: https://www.cloudindustryforum.org/content/public-sector-it-skills-shortages-puts-brakes-digital-transformation-government-services, last accessed 18 March 2018.

Coleman, S. (2004). 'Connecting Parliament to the Public via the Internet: Two Case Studies of Online Consultations', *Information, Communication and Society* 7(1): 1–22.

Collins, C., Ocampo, O. and Paslaski, S. (2020). *Billionaire Bonanza 2020: Wealth Windfalls, Tumbling Taxes, and Pandemic Profiteers*, Institute for

Policy Studies, available at: https://ips-dc.org/wp-content/uploads/2020/04/Billionaire-Bonanza-2020.pdf, last accessed 4 June 2020.

Collins, C. and Ocampo, O. (2021). 'Global Billionaire Wealth Surges $4 Trillion over Pandemic', Institute for Policy Studies, 31 March, available at: https://ips-dc.org/global-billionaire-wealth-surges-4-trillion-over-pandemic, last accessed 13 July 2021.

Collinson, A. (2020). 'The New Class Divide: How Covid-19 Exposed and Exacerbated Workplace Inequality in the UK', TUC, 18 May, available at: https://www.tuc.org.uk/blogs/new-class-divide-how-covid-19-exposed-and-exacerbated-workplace-inequality-uk, last accessed 14 October 2021.

Confederation of British Industry (CBI) (2020a). 'Sharp Fall in Retail Employment – With Worse Yet to Come', 25 August, available at: https://www.cbi.org.uk/media-centre/articles/sharp-fall-in-retail-employment-with-worse-likely-to-follow, last accessed 10 September 2020.

Conley, J. (2020). 'Amazon Warehouse Workers Win Fight for Paid Time Off as Company Condemned for "Reckless" Labor Practices', *Common Dreams*, 23 March, available at: https://www.commondreams.org/news/2020/03/23/amazon-warehouse-workers-win-fight-paid-time-company-condemned-reckless-labor, last accessed 2 June 2020.

Connors, C., Malan, L., Canavan, S., Sissoko, F., Carmo, M., Sheppard, C. and Cook, F. (2020). *The Lived Experience of Food Insecurity under COVID-19*, July, available at: https://www.food.gov.uk/sites/default/files/media/document/fsa-food-insecurity-2020_-report-v5.pdf and at: https://www.food.gov.uk/research/research-projects/the-covid-19-consumer-research, last accessed 13 August 2020.

Corbett, M. (2013). 'Cold Comfort Firm: Lean Organisation and the Empirical Mirage of the Comfort Zone', *Culture and Organization*, 19(5): 413–29.

Coronavirus Job Retention Scheme statistics: January 2021, available at: https://www.gov.uk/government/statistics/coronavirus-job-retention-scheme-statistics-january-2021/coronavirus-job-retention-scheme-statistics-january-2021#furloughing-by-sector-at-30-november-and-provisional-figures-for-31-december, last accessed 15 July 2021.

Coronavirus Job Retention Scheme statistics: 1 July 2021, available at: https://www.gov.uk/government/statistics/coronavirus-job-retention-scheme-statistics-1-july-2021/coronavirus-job-retention-scheme-statistics-1-july-2021#main-points, last accessed 15 July 2021.

Coronavirus Job Retention Scheme statistics: 29 July 2021, available at: https://www.gov.uk/government/statistics/coronavirus-job-retention-scheme-statistics-29-july-2021/coronavirus-job-retention-scheme-statistics-29-july-2021, last accessed 31 July 2021.

Corporaal, G. F. and Lehdonvirta, V. (2017). *Platform Sourcing: How Fortune 500 Firms are Adopting Online Freelancing Platforms*, Oxford: Oxford Internet Institute, available at: https://www.oii.ox.ac.uk/publications/platfo

rm-sourcing.pdf, last accessed 9 March 2018.

Coulter, S. (2020). 'All in it Together? The Unlikely Rebirth of Covid Capitalism', *Political Quarterly* 91(3): 534–41.

Crane, A., LeBaron, G., Allain, J. and Behbahani, L. (2019). 'Governance Gaps in Eradicating Forced Labor: From Global to Domestic Supply Chains', *Regulation and Governance* 13(1): 86–106.

Cribb, J. and Johnson, P. (2018). '10 Years On – Have We Recovered from the Financial Crisis?' *Institute for Fiscal Studies* 12 September, available at: https://www.ifs.org.uk/publications/13302, last accessed 2 November 2021.

Crompton, A. (2019). 'Inside Co-production: Stakeholder Meaning and Situated Practice', *Social Policy and Administration* 53: 219–32.

Crompton, R. and Gubbay, J. (1980). *Economy and Class Structure*, London: Macmillan.

Cross, S., Rho, Y., Reddy, H., Pepperrell, T., Rodgers, F., Osborne, R., Eni-Olotu, A., Banerjee, R., Wimmer, S. and Keestra, S. (2021). 'Who Funded the Research Behind the Oxford-AstraZeneca COVID-19 Vaccine?' preprint paper, available at: https://www.medrxiv.org/content/10.1101/2021.04.08 .21255103v1.full.pdf, last accessed 9 July 2021.

Crouch, C. (2019). *Will the Gig Economy Prevail?* Cambridge: Polity.

Culture, Media and Sport Select Committee (2020). *Impact of COVID-19 on DCMS Sectors: First Report*, available at: https://publications.par liament.uk/pa/cm5801/cmselect/cmcumeds/291/29102.htm, last accessed 19 August 2020.

D'Arcy, C. and Gardiner, L. (2017). *The Generation of Wealth: Asset Accumulation Across and Within Cohorts*, The Resolution Foundation, available at: https://www.resolutionfoundation.org/app/uploads/2017/06 /Wealth.pdf, accessed 10 June 2020.

Davis, L. E. (2016). 'Identifying the "Financialization" of the Nonfinancial Corporation in the U.S. Economy: A Decomposition of Firm-level Balance Sheets', *Journal of Post Keynesian Economics* 39(1): 115–41.

Davis, M. (2020). *The Monster Enters: COVID-19, Avian Flu and the Plagues of Capitalism*, London: OR Books.

Dayen, D. (2020). 'How the Fed Bailed Out the Investor Class Without Spending a Cent', *The American Prospect*, 27 May, available at: https://prospect.org /coronavirus/how-fed-bailed-out-the-investor-class-corporate-america, last accessed 18 February 2020.

Deacon, D., Goode, J., Smith, D., Wring, D., Downey, J. and Vaccari, C. (2019). 'General Election 2019: Report 5 7 November to 11 December, 12 December, available at: https://www.lboro.ac.uk/news-events/general-elec tion/report-5, last accessed 9 March 202).

DeCambre, M. (2019). 'U.S. Consumer Debt is Now Above Levels Hit during

the 2008 Financial Crisis', *MarketWatch* 25 June, available at: https://www
.marketwatch.com/amp/story/guid/771B18E2-92A9-11E9-9D89-429213C
87F49?__twitter_impression=true, last accessed 2 July 2019.

DeFilippis, E., Impink, S. M., Singell, M., Polzer, J. T. and Sadun, R. (2020).
'Collaborating during Coronavirus: The Impact of COVID-19 on the Nature
of Work', NBER Working Paper No. 27612, July, 1–32, available at: https://
www.nber.org/papers/w27612, last accessed 20 August 2020.

Della Porta, D. (2015). *Social Movements in Times of Austerity*, Cambridge:
Polity.

Della Porta, D., Fernández, J., Kouki, H. and Mosca, L. (2017). *Movement
Parties against Austerity*, Cambridge: Polity.

Dellot, B., Mason, R. and Wallace-Stephens, F. (2019). *The Four Futures of
Work*, March, RSA, Action and Research Centre, available at: https://www
.thersa.org/globalassets/pdfs/reports/rsa_four-futures-of-work.pdf,   last
accessed 20 July 2020.

Department of Culture, Media and Sport (DCMS) (2016). *Official Statistics:
Key Findings*, 20 June, available at: https://www.gov.uk/government/statis
tics/creative-industries-2016-focus-on/key-findings, last accessed 31 July
2021.

Department of Culture, Media and Sport (DCMS) (2020). *DCMS Sectors
Estimates 2018*, 5 February, available at: https://assets.publishing.service
.gov.uk/government/uploads/system/uploads/attachment_data/file/959053
/DCMS_Sectors_Economic_Estimates_GVA_2018_V2.pdf, accessed 31 July
2021.

De Stefano, V. (2016). *The Rise of the 'Just-in-Time Workforce': On-Demand
Work, Crowdwork and Labour Protection in the 'Gig-Economy'*, Geneva:
International Labour Office, available at: https://www.ilo.org/wcmsp5/gro
ups/public/---ed_protect/---protrav/---travail/documents/publication/wcms
_443267.pdf, last accessed 14 February 2017.

Dhillon, A. S. (2020). 'The Politics of Covid-19: The Frictions and Promises of
Mutual Aid', *Red Pepper*, 4 May, available at: https://www.redpepper.org
.uk/the-politics-of-covid-19-the-frictions-and-promises-of-mutual-aid, last
accessed 28 May 2020.

Döring, H., Downe, J. and Martin, S. (2015). 'Regulating Public Services: How
Public Managers Respond to External Performance Assessment', *Public
Administration Review* 75(6): 867–77.

Drezner, D.W. (2010). 'Will Currency Follow the Flag?' *International Relations
of the Asia-Pacific* 10(3): 389–414.

Drucker, P. (1993). *The Practice of Management*, New York: HarperCollins.

du Gay, P. (ed.) (1997). *Production of Cultures, Cultures of Production*,
London: Sage.

Duggan, W. (2020). 'Latest E-Commerce Market Share Numbers Highlight

Amazon's Dominance', *Yahoo Finance*, 4 February, available at: https://finance.yahoo.com/news/latest-e-commerce-market-share-185120510.html, last accessed 9 August 2020.

Duménil, G. and Levy, D. (2011). *The Crisis of Neoliberalism*, Cambridge, MA: Harvard University Press.

Dunleavy, P., Margetts, H., Bastow, S. and Tinkler, J. (2005). 'New Public Management is Dead: Long Live Digital-era Governance', *Journal of Public Administration Research and Theory* 16: 467–94.

Dutil, P. A., Howard, C., Langford, J. and Roy, J. (2007). 'Rethinking Government–Public Relationships in a Digital World: Customers, Clients, or Citizens?' *Journal of Information Technology and Politics* 4(1): 77–90.

Dwyer, P. (2002). 'Making Sense of Social Citizenship: Some User Views on Welfare Rights and Responsibilities', *Critical Social Policy* 22(2): 273–99.

Dyer-Witheford, N. (2015). *Cyber-Proletariat*, London: Pluto.

Eadicicco, L. (2020). 'Apple Just Hit a $2 Trillion Market Cap and it's Proof that its Master Plan to Keep Users Locked into the IPhone Ecosystem is Working', *Business Insider*, 19 August, available at: https://www.businessinsider.com/apple-2-trillion-company-market-value-stock-powerful-iphone-ecosystem-2020-8?r=US&IR=T, last accessed 11 September 2020.

Elliott, C. S. and Long, G. (2016). 'Manufacturing Rate Busters: Computer Control and Social Relations in the Labour Process', *Work, Employment and Society* 30(1): 135–51.

Elson, D. (1979). 'The Value Theory of Labour', in D. Elson (ed.), *Value: The Representation of Labour in Capitalism* London: CSE Books.

Emmerson, C. and Stockton, I. (2020). 'Cash Borrowing by the Public Sector was £89 Billion in April 2020, Far More than in Any Previous Month on Record', Institute for Fiscal Studies, 22 May, available at: https://www.ifs.org.uk/publications/14857, last accessed 20 August 2020.

Emmerson, C., Stockton, I. and Zaranko, B. (2021). 'What Does the Changing Economic Outlook Mean for the Spending Review?' Institute for Fiscal Studies, 21 July, available at: https://ifs.org.uk/publications/15542, last accessed 29 August 2021.

Epstein, G. and Jayadev, A. (2005). 'The Rise of Rentier Incomes in OECD Countries: Financialization, Central Bank Policy and Labor Solidarity', in G. Epstein (ed.), *Financialization and the World Economy*, Cheltenham: Edward Elgar.

Esmark, A. and Bang, H. (2007). 'A Critical Look at Contemporary Publics', in H. Bang and A. Esmark (eds.), *New Publics with/out Democracy*, Frederiksberg: Samfundslitteratur.

Ethical Trading Initiative (ETI) (2020). 'Working Conditions in the Leicester Garment Industry', available at: https://www.ethicaltrade.org/issues/company-purchasing-practices/working-conditions-leicester-garment-industry, last accessed 25 October 2021.

European Services Strategy Unit (ESSU) (2018). 'Carillion Made £500m in Revenue from Selling PFI Projects and Netted Annual Returns of Up to 39%', 28 January, available at: https://www.european-services-strategy.org .uk/news/2018/carillion-made-500m-in-revenue-from-selling-pfi-projects-a nd-netted-annual-returns-of-up-to-39, last accessed 4 March 2018.

Evans, L. and Kitchin, R. (2018). 'A Smart Place to Work? Big Data Systems, Labour, Control and Modern Retail Stores', *New Technology, Work and Employment* 33(1): 44–57.

Fairwork (2020). *The Gig Economy and Covid-19: Looking Ahead*, Oxford, available at: https://fair.work/wp-content/uploads/sites/97/2020/09/COVID -19-Report-September-2020.pdf, last accessed 13 July 2021.

Farr, M. (2018). 'Power Dynamics and Collaborative Mechanisms in Co-production and Co-design Processes', *Critical Social Policy* 38(4): 623–44.

Farrell, D., Greig, F. and Hamoudi, A. (2018). *The Online Platform in 2018: Drivers, Sellers, and Lessors*, London: JP Morgan Chase Institute, available at, https://www.jpmorganchase.com/corporate/institute/document/institute -ope-2018.pdf, last accessed 1 December 2018.

Featherstone, M. (1991). *Consumer Culture*, London: Sage.

Felstead, A. and Reuschke, D. (2020). 'Homeworking in the UK: Before and During the Lockdown', *WISERD Report*, Cardiff: Wales Institute of Social and Economic Research, August, available at: https://wiserd.ac.uk/sites/de fault/files/documents/Homeworking%20in%20the%20UK_Report_Final _3.pdf, last accessed: 22 September 2020.

Fine, B. (1998). *Labour Market Theory: A Constructive Reassessment*, London: Routledge.

Fine, B. (2001). *Social Capital versus Social Theory*, London: Routledge.

Fine, B. (2013). 'Financialization from a Marxist Perspective', *International Journal of Political Economy* 42(4): 47–66.

Fish, A. and Srinivasan, R. (2011). 'Digital Labor is the New Killer App', *New Media and Society* 14(1): 137–52.

Fisher, E. (2012). 'How Less Alienation Creates More Exploitation? Audience Labor on Social Network Sites', *tripleC* 10(12): 171–83.

Fitzgerald, S. W. (2012). *Corporations and Cultural Industries*, Lanham, MD: Lexington Books.

Fleming, P. (2015). *The Mythology of Work*, London: Pluto.

Flew, T. (2008). *New Media*, 3rd edn., Oxford: Oxford University Press.

Flew, T. (2012). *The Creative Industries*, London: Sage.

Florida, R. (2012). *The Rise of the Creative Class*, updated edn, New York: Basic Books.

Florida, R. (2018). *The New Urban Crisis*, London: Oneworld.

Florida, R. and Seman, M. (2020). *Measuring COVID-19's Devastating Impact on America's Creative Economy*, Metropolitan Policy Program at Brookings, Washington, DC, available at: https://www.brookings.edu/research/lost-art-measuring-covid-19s-devastating-impact-on-americas-creative-economy, last accessed 8 July 2021.

Foley, D. K. (1986). *Understanding Capital*, Cambridge, MA: Harvard University Press.

Folkman, P., Froud, J., Johal, S. and Williams, K. (2007). 'Working for Themselves? Capital Market Intermediaries and Present Day Capitalism', *Business History* 49(4): 552–72.

Fontenot, K., Semega, J. and Kolla, M. (2018). *Income and Poverty in the United States: 2017*, Current Population Reports, September, United States Census Bureau, available at: https://www.census.gov/content/dam/Census/library/publications/2018/demo/p60-263.pdf, last accessed 5 May 2018.

Forbes (2018). 'United States', available at: https://www.forbes.com/places/united-states, last (accessed 2 August 2019.

Forde, C., Stuart, M., Joyce, S., Oliver, L., Valizade, D., Alberti, G., Hardy, K., Trappmann V., Umney, C. and Carson, C. (2017). *The Social Protection of Workers in the Platform Economy*, Brussels: Policy Department A of the European Parliament.

Forsgren, N. (2020). *Octoverse Spotlight: An Analysis of Developer Productivity, Work Cadence, and Collaboration in the Early Days of COVID-19*, 6 May, available at: https://github.blog/2020-05-06-octoverse-spotlight-an-analysis-of-developer-productivity-work-cadence-and-collaboration-in-the-early-days-of-covid-19/#thirdtheme, last accessed 27 May 2020.

Foster, J. B. (2000). 'Monopoly Capital at the Turn of the Millennium', *Monthly Review* 51(11): 1–14.

Foster, J. B. (2020). 'COVID-19 and Catastrophe Capitalism', *Monthly Review* 72(2): 1–20.

Foster, J. B. and Magdoff, F. (2009). *The Great Financial Crisis*, New York: Monthly Review Press.

Foster, J. B. and McChesney, R. (2012). *The Endless Crisis*, New York: Monthly Review Press.

Foster, J. B. and Suwandi, I. (2020). 'COVID-19 and Catastrophe Capitalism', *Monthly Review Press* 7(2): 1–20, available at: https://monthlyreview.org/2020/06/01/covid-19-and-catastrophe-capitalism, last accessed 25 October 2021.

Free, C. and Hecimovic, A. (2020). 'Global Supply Chains after COVID-19: The End of the Road for Neoliberal Globalisation?' *Accounting, Auditing and Accountability Journal*, early view, available at: https://www.emerald.com

/insight/content/doi/10.1108/AAAJ-06-2020-4634/full/html, last accessed 9 October 2020.

Freelancer.com (2019). 'Freelancer.com Reveals the Fastest Growing Online Jobs in 2018', available at: https://s3.amazonaws.com/press.freelancer .com/Freelancer.com%20reveals%20the%20fastest%20growing%20 online%20jobs%20in%202018.pdf, last accessed 15 March 2019.

Freelancer.com (2021). 'Record Number of Online Jobs in 2020, Freelancer .com's Fast 50 Reports', 12 January, available at: https://s3.amazonaws.com /press.freelancer.com/Media%20Release_FLN_Fast%2050%20Q4%2020 20.pdf, last accessed 13 July 2021.

Frey, C. B. and Osborne, M. A. (2013). 'The Future of Employment: How Susceptible are Jobs to Computerisation?' Oxford Martin School Working Paper No. 7.

Freudenberger, E. (2020). 'Programming through the Pandemic', *Library Journal*, 22 May, available at: https://www.libraryjournal.com/?detailStory= Programming-Through-the-Pandemic-covid-19, last accessed 28 May 2020.

Froud, J., Johal, S., Leaver, A. and Williams, K. (2006). *Financialization*, London: Routledge.

Fuchs, C. (2014a). *Social Media*, London: Sage.

Fuchs, C. (2014b). *Digital Labour and Karl Marx*, London: Routledge.

Fuchs, C. (2016). *Critical Theory of Communication*, London: University of Westminster Press.

Fuchs, C. (2019). 'Karl Marx in an Age of Big Data Capitalism', in D. Chandler and C. Fuchs (eds.), *Digital Objects, Digital Subjects*, London: University of Westminster Press.

Fuchs, C. (2020). *Communication and Capitalism: A Critical Theory*, London: University of Westminster Press.

Fuchs, C. and Sevignani, S. (2013). 'What is Digital Labour? What is Digital Work? What's their Difference? And why do These Questions Matter for Understanding Social Media?' *tripleC* 11(2): 237–93.

Gallie, D. and Zhou, Y. (2013). 'Job Control, Work Intensity and Work Stress', in D. Gallie (ed.), *Economic Crisis and the Quality of Work*, Oxford: Oxford University Press.

Galvagno, M. and Dalli, D. (2014). 'Theory of Value Co-creation: A Systematic Literature Review', *Journal of Service Theory and Practice* 24(6): 643–83.

Gardiner, L. and Slaughter, H. (2020). 'The Effects of the Coronavirus Crisis on Workers', *The Resolution Foundation*, 16 May, available at: https://www .resolutionfoundation.org/publications/the-effects-of-the-coronavirus-crisis -on-workers, last accessed 18 June 2020.

Gartman, D. (1983). 'Structuralist Marxism and the Labor Process: Where Have the Dialectics Gone?' *Theory and Society* 12: 659–69.

Gauntlett, D. (2011). *Making is Connecting: The Social Meaning of Creativity, from DIY and Knitting to YouTube and Web 2.0*, Cambridge: Polity.

Geiger, B. B., Scullion, L., Summers, K., Martin, P., Lawler, C., Edmiston, D., Gibbons, A., Ingold, J., Robertshaw, D. and de Vries, R. (2021). *Non-take-up of Benefits at the Start of the COVID-19 Pandemic*, Welfare at a Distance, April, available at: https://62608d89-fc73-4896-861c-0e03416f9 922.usrfiles.com/ugd/62608d_602f7840f4114361a4dbf6d007d3825b.pdf, last accessed 9 July 2021.

Gere, C. (2008). *Digital Culture*, 2nd edn, London: Reaktion Books.

Gereffi, G. (2014). 'Global Value Chains in a Post-Washington Consensus World', *Review of International Political Economy* 21(1): 9–37.

Gillingham, P. and Graham, T. (2016). 'Designing Electronic Information Systems for the Future: Social Workers and the Challenge of New Public Management', *Critical Social Policy* 36(2): 187–204.

GitHub (2020). *GitHub Productivity Report: Finding a Balance between Work and Play*, available at: https://octoverse.github.com/static/github-octoverse -2020-productivity-report.pdf, last accessed 10 August 2021.

GitHub (2021). Website available at: https://github.com/about, last accessed 10 August 2021.

GMB (2019). 'Hermes and GMB in Groundbreaking Gig Economy Deal', 4 February, available at: https://www.gmb.org.uk/news/hermes-gmb-groundb reaking-gig-economy-deal, last accessed 29 July 2020.

Good Work Plan (2018). Available at: https://assets.publishing.service.gov.uk/gov ernment/uploads/system/uploads/attachment_data/file/766187/good-work- plan-printready.pdf, last accessed 29 July 2020.

Gough, J. (2003). *Work, Locality and the Rhythms of Capital*, London: Routledge.

Gould, E. and Wolfe, J. (2018). 'Household Income Growth Slowed Markedly in 2017 and was Stronger for Those at the Top, while Earnings Declined Slightly', *Economic Policy Institute*, 12 September, available at: https://www .epi.org/blog/household-income-growth-slowed-markedly-in-2017-and-was -stronger-for-those-at-the-top-while-earnings-declined-slightly, last accessed 14 October 2018.

Grady, J. (2017). 'The State, Employment, and Regulation: Making Work not Pay', *Employee Relations* 39(3): 274–90.

Graham, M. and Anwar, M. (2019). 'The Global Gig Economy: Towards a Planetary Labour Market?' *First Monday* 24(4), available at: https://journa ls.uic.edu/ojs/index.php/fm/article/view/9913/7748, last accessed 7 August 2019.

Graham, M., Hjorth, I. and Lehonvirta, V. (2017). 'Digital Labour and Development: Impacts of Global Digital Labour Platforms and the Gig Economy on Worker Livelihoods', *Transfer* 23(2): 135–62.

Gramsci, A. (1986). *Selections from Prison Notebooks*, London: Lawrence & Wishart.

Grant, M. (2017). 'The Risks in Central-Bank Balance Sheets Are Clear', *Bloomberg*, 7 December, available at: https://www.bloomberg.com/opinion /articles/2017-12-07/the-risks-in-central-bank-balance-sheets-is-clear-mark -grant, last accessed 7 February 2018.

Greenbaum, J. (1998). 'The Times They are A'Changing: Dividing and Recombining Labour Through Computer Systems', in P. Thompson and C. Warhurst (eds.), *Workplaces of the Future*, London: Macmillan.

Greenstein, T. (2011). 'The Fed's $16 Trillion Bailouts Under-reported', *Forbes*, 20 September, available at: https://www.forbes.com/sites/traceygreenstein /2011/09/20/the-feds-16-trillion-bailouts-under-reported/#52d9a53626b0, last accessed 1 August 2017.

Grimshaw, D., Johnson, M., Keizer, A. and Rubery, J. (2017). 'The Governance of Employment Protection in the UK: How the State and Employers are Undermining Decent Standards', in A. Piasna and M. Myant (eds.), *Myths of Employment Deregulation*, Brussels: ETUI.

Haasch, P. (2020). 'Coronavirus Tests, Homelessness, and Solo Births: People are Posting Their Real-life COVID-19 Woes on TikTok', *Insider*, 20 March, available at: https://www.insider.com/coronavirus-video-tiktok-social-dis tancing-college-birth-hospitals-prom-dorms-2020-3, last accessed 28 May 2020.

Hall, D., Lister, J., Hobbs, C., Robinson, P., Jarvis, C. and Mercer, H. (2020). 'Privatised and Unprepared: The NHS Supply Chain', *We Own It*, available at: https://weownit.org.uk/sites/default/files/attachments/Privatised%20and %20Unprepared%20-%20The%20NHS%20Supply%20Chain%20Final .pdf, last accessed 25 June 2020.

Hall, S. (2009). 'Financialised Elites and the Changing Nature of Finance Capitalism: Investment Bankers in London's Financial District', *Competition and Change* 13(2): 173–89.

Hamilton, D., Asante-Muhammad, D., Collins, C. and Ocampo, O. (2020). *White Supremacy is the Pre-existing Condition: Eight Solutions to Ensure Economic Recovery Reduces the Racial Wealth Divide*, Institute for Policy Studies, available at: https://ips-dc.org/wp-content/uploads/2020/06/RWD2 020-June19-Final.pdf, last accessed 13 August 2020.

Hammer, N., Plugor, R., Nolan, P. and Clark, I. (2015). *A New Industry on a Skewed Playing Field: Supply Chain Relations and Working Conditions in UK Garment Manufacturing*, Leicester and London: University of Leicester and CSWEF, Ethical Trading Initiative, available at: https://www2.le.ac.uk /offices/press/for-journalists/media-resources/Leicester%20Report%20-%2 0Final%20-to%20publish.pdf, last accessed 11 July 2020.

Hanauer, N. and Rolf, D. (2015). 'Shared Security, Shared Growth', *Democracy*

Summer (37), available at: https://democracyjournal.org/magazine/37/sha red-security-shared-growth/?page=all, last accessed 3 March 2017.

Haque, Z., Becares, L. and Treloar, N. (2020). *Over-exposed and Under-protected: The Devastating Impact of COVID-19 on Black and Ethnic Minority Communities in Great Britain*, Runnymede, August, available at: https://www.runnymedetrust.org/uploads/Runnymede%20Covid19%20 Survey%20report%20v2.pdf, last accessed 10 August 2020.

Hardt, M. and Negri, A. (2000). *Empire*. Cambridge, MA: Harvard University Press.

Hardt, M. and Negri, A. (2004). *Multitude: War and Democracy in the Age of Empire*, New York: Penguin.

Hardt, M. and Negri, A. (2009). *Commonwealth*, Cambridge, MA: Harvard University Press.

Hardt, M. and Negri, A. (2017). *Assembly*, Oxford: Oxford University Press.

Hart-Landsberg, M. (2013). *Capitalist Globalization*, New York: Monthly Review Press.

Harvey, D. (2005). *Neoliberalism: A Brief History*, Oxford: Oxford University Press.

Harvey, D. (2013). *A Companion to Marx's Capital, Volume 2*, London: Verso.

Harvey, D. (2014). *Seventeen Contradictions and the End of Capitalism*, London: Profile.

Harvey, D. (2017). *Marx, Capital and the Madness of Economic Reason*, London: Profile Books.

Hawkins, A. J. (2020). 'Uber Lays Off 3,000 More Employees in Latest Round of COVID-19-Inspired Cuts', *The Verge*, 18 May, available at: https://www .theverge.com/2020/5/18/21262337/uber-layoff-3000-employees-covid-19 -coronavirus, last accessed 24 June 2020.

Hay, C. (1996). 'Narrating Crisis: The Discursive Construction of the "Winter of Discontent"', *Sociology* 30(2): 253–77.

Heath, A. (2017). 'Snap has Spent $352 Million on Acquisitions this Year – Here are All of the Startups it's Bought So Far', *Business Insider* 12 November, available at: http://uk.businessinsider.com/history-of-snapchats-acquisitions -and-their-prices-2017-11, last accessed 12 September 2018.

Hedges, C. (2021). 'The American Rescue Plan Does Not Address the Deep-Rooted Inequality Killing Us', *Common Dreams*, 12 March, available at: https://www.commondreams.org/views/2021/03/12/american-rescue-plan -does-not-address-deep-rooted-inequality-killing-us, last accessed 13 July 2021.

Henderson, B. A. and Larco, J. L. (1999). *Lean Transformation*, Richmond, VA: Oaklea.

Hennelly, B. (2018). 'A Decade after Lehman Brothers, U.S. is still a Stucknation',

Salon, 15 September, available at: https://www.salon.com/2018/09/23/a-decade-after-lehman-brothers-u-s-is-still-a-stucknation, last accessed 15 January 2019.

Hern, A. (2018). 'Microsoft is Buying Code-sharing Site GitHub for $7.5bn', *The Guardian*, 4 June, available at: https://www.theguardian.com/technology/2018/jun/04/microsoft-is-buying-code-sharing-site-github-say-reports?CMP=Share_iOSApp_Other, last accessed 23 July 2018.

Hicks, M. J. and Devaraji, S. (2017). *The Myth and the Reality of Manufacturing in America*, Muncie, IN: Ball State University Center for Business and Economic Research, available at https://conexus.cberdata.org/files/MfgReality.pdf, last accessed 15 December 2017.

Higginson, M., Jacques, F. and Malik, N. (2020). 'What Next for US Credit-card Debt?' McKinsey and Company, 13 May, available at: https://www.mckinsey.com/industries/financial-services/our-insights/what-next-for-us-credit-card-debt, last accessed 12 August 2020.

Holloway, J. (1992). 'Crisis, Fetishism, Class Composition', in W. Bonefeld, R. Gunn and K. Psychopedis (eds.), *Open Marxism, vol. 2: Theory and Practice*, London: Pluto.

Holloway, J. (1995). 'Global State and the National State', in W. Bonefeld and J. Holloway (eds.), *Global Capital, National State and the Politics of Money*, London: Palgrave.

Holmemo, M. D-Q. and Ingvaldsen, J. A. (2015). 'Bypassing the Dinosaurs? – How Middle Managers Become the Missing Link in Lean Implementation', *Total Quality Management and Business Excellence* 27(11/12): 1332–45.

Hong, J. and Ståhle, P. (2005). 'The Coevolution of Knowledge and Competence Management', *International Journal of Management Concepts and Philosophy* 1(2): 129–45.

Horton, R. (2020). 'Offline: COVID-19 is not a Pandemic', *The Lancet*, 396 (26 September): 874.

House of Commons Public Accounts Committee (2020). *Whole of Government Response to COVID-19: Thirteen Report of Session 2019–20*, 23 July, London: House of Commons, available at: https://committees.parliament.uk/publications/2024/documents/19531/default, last accessed 31 July 2020.

House of Commons Work and Pensions Committee (2017). *Self-Employment and the Gig Economy: Thirteenth Report of Session 2016–17*, 21 May, London: House of Commons, available at: https://publications.parliament.uk/pa/cm201617/cmselect/cmworpen/847/847.pdf, last accessed 5 March 2018.

Howcroft, D. and Bergvall-Kåreborn, B. (2019) 'A Typology of Crowdwork Platforms', *Work, Employment and Society* 33(1): 21–38.

Hudson, B. (2018). 'Citizen Accountability in the "New NHS" in England', *Critical Social Policy* 38(2): 418–27.

Hunt, M. (2018). 'Whole Food Hired Far-Right Wing Activist as Union Buster', *Medium*, June 8, available at: https://medium.com/@MatthewTHunt/whole-foods-hired-far-right-wing-activist-as-union-buster-dd46bee7c854, last accessed 23 September 2018.

Huws, U. (2014). *Labor in the Global Digital Economy*, New York: Monthly Review Press.

Huws, U. (2019). *Labour in Contemporary Capitalism*, London: Palgrave.

Huxley, C. (2015). 'Three Decades of Lean Production: Practice, Ideology, and Resistance', *International Journal of Sociology* 45(2): 133–51.

IDEA Consult, Goethe-Institut, Amann, S. and Heinsius, J. (2021). *Research for CULT Committee – Cultural and Creative Sectors in post-Covid-19 Europe: Crisis Effects and Policy Recommendations*, European Parliament, Policy Department for Structural and Cohesion Policies, Brussels, available at: https://www.europarl.europa.eu/RegData/etudes/STUD/2021/652242/IPOL_STU(2021)652242_EN.pdf, last accessed 9 July 2021.

IHS Markit (2020). 'IHS Markit UK Household Finance Index™: Strains on Household Finances Intensifies in August', IHS Markit, 17 August, available at: https://www.markiteconomics.com/Public/Home/PressRelease/99aa1031515d4f8b85729bd31a9ec90a, last accessed 19 August 2020.

Illife, S. (1985). 'The Politics of Health Care: The NHS under Thatcher', *Critical Social Policy* 5(14): 57–72.

Independent Workers' Union of Great Britain (IWGB) (2017). *Dead on Arrival: The IWGB's reply to the Taylor Review on Modern Employment Practices*, available at: https://iwgbunion.files.wordpress.com/2017/07/iwgb-response-to-taylor-review1.pdf. last accessed 19 August 2017.

Independent Workers' Union of Great Britain (IWGB) (2020). 'Covid-19 Couriers First Key Workers to Strike during Pandemic Following Victimisation by NHS Contractor TDL', 10 June, available at: https://iwgb.org.uk/post/covid19-medical-couriers-strike, last accessed 25 June 2020.

Innes, D. and Schmuecker, K. (2021). 'JRF Spring Budget 2021 Analysis', Joseph Rowntree Foundation, 4 March, available at: https://www.jrf.org.uk/report/jrf-spring-budget-2021-analysis, last accessed 20 July 2021.

Institute for Fiscal Studies (IFS) (2019). 'The Outlook for the 2019 Spending Review', 11 February, available at: https://www.ifs.org.uk/publications/13854, last accessed 11 March 2019.

Institute for Public Policy Research (IPPR) (2018). *Prosperity and Justice: A Plan for the New Economy*, IPPR, available at: https://www.ippr.org/files/2018-10/cej-final-summary.pdf, last accessed 10 June 2020.

International Labour Organisation (ILO) (2016). *Non-standard Employment Around the World*, available at: https://www.ilo.org/wcmsp5/groups/public/---dgreports/---dcomm/---publ/documents/publication/wcms_534326.pdf, last accessed 23 June 2020.

International Labour Organisation (ILO) (2018). *Global Wage Report 2018/ 19*, available at: https://www.ilo.org/wcmsp5/groups/public/---dgreports/---dcomm/---publ/documents/publication/wcms_650553.pdf, last accessed 5 February 2019.

International Labour Organisation (ILO) (2020a). *Policy Brief: The World of Work and COVID-19*, June, available at: https://www.ilo.org/wcmsp5/grou ps/public/@dgreports/@dcomm/documents/genericdocument/wcms_748428 .pdf, last accessed 19 June 2020.

International Labour Organisation (ILO) (2020b). *Policy Brief: COVID-19 and Global Supply Chains: How the Job Crisis Propagates across Borders*, available at: https://www.ilo.org/wcmsp5/groups/public/---dgreports/---inst /documents/publication/wcms_749368.pdf, last accessed 8 October 2020.

International Monetary Fund (IMF) (2018). *World Economic Outlook 2018*, Washington, DC: IMF, available at https://www.imf.org/en/Publica tions/WEO/Issues/2018/09/24/world-economic-outlook-october-2018, last accessed 2 February 2019.

International Monetary Fund (IMF) (2020a). *Global Financial Stability Report: Markets in the Time of COVID-19*, April, Washington, DC: IMF, available at: https://www.imf.org/en/Publications/GFSR/Issues/2020/04/14/global-fin ancial-stability-report-april-2020, last accessed 4 June 2020.

International Monetary Fund (IMF) (2020b). *World Economic Outlook Update*, June, available at: https://www.imf.org/en/Publications/WEO/Issu es/2020/06/24/WEOUpdateJune2020, last accessed 20 July 2020.

International Monetary Fund (IMF) (2020c). *Global Financial Stability Update*, June, available at: https://www.imf.org/en/Publications/GFSR/Issues/2020 /06/25/global-financial-stability-report-june-2020-update, last accessed 20 July 2020.

International Monetary Fund (IMF) (2021). *World Economic Outlook*, April, available at:
https://www.imf.org/en/Publications/WEO/Issues/2021/03/23/world-economic -outlook-april-2021, last accessed 13 July 2021.

Irani, L. (2015). 'The Cultural Work of Microwork', *New Media and Society* 17(5): 720–39.

Jaccarini, C. and Krebel, L. (2020). 'Tackling Insecure Work is Vital to Any Meaningful Recovery from Crisis', *New Economics Foundation*, 19 June, available at: https://neweconomics.org/2020/06/why-tackling-insecure-work -is-an-important-part-of-any-meaningful-recovery-from-crisis, last accessed 23 June 2020.

Jackson, T. (2020). 'The Sovereign Fed', *Dissent*, 16 April, available at: https:// www.dissentmagazine.org/online_articles/the-sovereign-fed, last accessed 12 June 2020.

Jalée, P. (1977). *How Capitalism Works*, New York: Monthly Review Press.

Jaumotte, F. and Buitron, C. O. (2015). 'Power from the People: The Decline in Unionization in Recent Decades has Fed the Rise in Income at the Top', *Finance and Development* 52(1): 29–31.

Jessop, B. (2002). *The Future of the Capitalist State*, Cambridge: Polity.

Jessop, B. (2008)..*State Power*, Cambridge: Polity.

Jessop, B. (2010). 'From Hegemony to Crisis? The Continuing Ecological Dominance of Neoliberalism', in K. Birch and V. Mykhnenko (eds.), *The Rise and Fall of Neoliberalism*, London: Zed.

Jessop, B. (2015), 'Variegated Capitalism and the Political Economy of Austerity', in R. Westra, D. Badeen and R. Albritton (eds.), *The Future of Capitalism After the Financial Crisis*, London: Routledge.

Jessop, B. (2019). 'Ordoliberalism and Neoliberalization: Governing Through Order or Disorder?' *Critical Sociology* 45(7/8): 967–81.

Johns, M. (2020). *10 Years of Austerity: Eroding Resilience in the North*, IPPR, June, available at: https://www.ippr.org/files/2020-06/10-years-of-austerity .pdf, last accessed 23 July 2020.

Johnston, H. and Land-Kazlauskas, C. (2018). 'Organizing On-Demand: Representation, Voice, and Collective Bargaining in the Gig Economy', *Conditions of Work and Employment Series*, No. 94, International Labour Office.

Jones, K. (1982). *Law and Economy*, London: Academic Press.

Jordan, P. and Cunningham, E. (2020). 'Our Path to "New Normal" in Employment? Sobering Clues from China and Recovery Scores for US Industry', Ash Center for Democratic Governance and Innovation, Harvard Kennedy School, July, available at: https://ash.harvard.edu/files/ash/files/us _china_covid_policy_brief_7.6.2020_01.pdf?m=1594842725, last accessed 12 August 2020.

Jordan, T. (2015). *Information Politics*, London: Pluto.

Jordan, T. (2020). *The Digital Economy*, Cambridge: Polity.

Joseph Rowntree Foundation (JRF) (2020). *UK Poverty 2019/20*, available at: https://www.jrf.org.uk/report/uk-poverty-2019-20, last accessed 10 June 2020.

Joyce, R. and Xu, X. (2020). 'Sector Shutdowns during the Coronavirus Crisis: Which Workers are Most Exposed?' Institute for Fiscal Studies, 6 April, available at: https://ifs.org.uk/publications/14791, last accessed 15 July 2021.

Joyce, S. (2020). 'Rediscovering the Cash Nexus, Again: Subsumption and the Labour–Capital Relation in Platform Work', *Capital and Class* 44(4): 541–52.

JP Morgan (2021). 'Global Manufacturing Upturn Accelerates with Firmer Growth of Production, Demand and Employment', available at: https://

www.markiteconomics.com/Public/Home/PressRelease/822c6852695d468
7bd06239011648b80, last accessed 15 July 2021.

Jubilee Debt Campaign (2020). *IMF Loans Bailing Out Private Lenders During the COVID-19 Crisis*, July, available at: https://jubileedebt.org.uk/wp-con tent/uploads/2020/07/IMF-bailouts-briefing_07.20.pdf, last accessed 21 July 2020.

Jupe, R. and Funnell, W. (2017). '"A Highly Successful Model"? The Rail Franchising Business in Britain', *Business History* 59(6): 844–76.

Khan, L.M. (2017) 'Amazon Bites Off Even More Monopoly Power', *New York Times*, 21

June, available at: https://www.nytimes.com/2017/06/21/opinion/amazon-who le-foods-jeff-bezos.html?ref=opinion&referer=https://www.newamerica.org /open-markets/articles/amazon-bites-even-more-monopoly-power/ (accessed 08/09/17).

Kicillof, A. and Starosta, G. (2007). 'On Materiality and Social Form: A Political Critique of Rubin's Value-Form Theory', *Historical Materialism* 15(3): 9–43.

Kiely, R. (2005). *Empire in the Age of Globalisation*, London: Pluto.

Kiely, R. (2010). *Rethinking Imperialism*, London: Sage.

Kingma, S. F. (2016). 'The Constitution of "Third Workspaces" in between the Home and the Corporate Office', *Work, Technology and Society* 31(2): 176–93.

Kivinen, M. (1989). 'The New Middle Classes and the Labour Process', *Acta Sociologica* 32(1): 53–73.

Klein, N. (2020). 'Screen New Deal', *The Intercept*, 8 May, available at: https:// theintercept.com/2020/05/08/andrew-cuomo-eric-schmidt-coronavirus-tech -shock-doctrine, last accessed 27 May 2020.

Klug, A., Rees, E. and Schneider, J. (2016). 'Momentum: A New Kind of Politics', *Renewal* 24(2): 36–44.

Köhler, H-D. and Begega, S. G. (2016). 'Tenneco-Gijón: A Case of Local Worker Resistance Against a Global Player', in V. Pulignano, H-P. Köhler and P. Stewart (eds.), *Employment Relations in an Era of Change*, Brussels: ETUI.

Kotz, D. (2015). *The Rise and Fall of Neoliberal Capitalism*, Cambridge, MA: Harvard University Press.

KPMG and REC (2020). 'Staff Appointments Drop at Much Weaker Pace in July', 6 August, available at: https://home.kpmg/uk/en/home/media/press-re leases/2020/08/kpmg-and-rec-uk-report-on-jobs.html, last 20 August 2020.

Kraemer, K. L., Linden, G. and Dedrick, J. (2011). 'Capturing Value in Global Networks: Apple's iPad and iPhone', available at: http://economiadeservicos .com/wp-content/uploads/2017/04/value_ipad_iphone.pdf, last accessed 12 April 2015.

Kristal, T. (2013). 'The Capitalist Machine: Computerization, Workers'

Power, and the Decline in Labor's Share within U.S. Industries', *American Sociological Review* 78(3): 361–89.

Kristal, T. and Cohen, Y. (2015). 'What Do Computers Really Do? Computerization, Fading Pay-Setting Institutions, and Rising Wage Inequality', *Research in Social Stratification and Mobility* 42 (December): 33–47.

Krzywdzinski, M. (2017). 'Automation, Skill Requirements and Labour-Use Strategies: High-Wage and Low-Wage Approaches to High-Tech Manufacturing in the Automotive Industry', *New Technology, Work and Employment* 32(3): 247–67.

Kutter, A. and Jessop, B. (2015). 'Culture as Discursive Practice: Combining Cultural Political Economy and Discursive Political Studies in Investigations of the Financial Crisis', in B. Jessop, B. Young and C. Scherrer (eds.), *Financial Cultures and Crisis Dynamics*, London: Routledge.

Laaser, K. and Bolton, S. (2017). 'Ethics of Care and Co-worker Relationships in UK Banks', *New Technology, Work and Employment* 32(3): 213–27.

Labour Behind the Label (2020). *BooHoo and COVID-19*, June, available at: https://labourbehindthelabel.net/wp-content/uploads/2020/06/LBL-Boohoo-WEB.pdf, last accessed 11 July 2020.

Lange, A-C., Lenglet, M. and Seyfert, R. (2016). 'Cultures of High-frequency Trading: Mapping the Landscape of Algorithmic Developments in Contemporary Financial Markets', *Economy and Society* 45(2): 149–65.

Langley, P. (2014). 'Equipping Entrepreneurs: Consuming Credit and Credit Scores', *Consumption, Markets and Culture* 17(5): 448–67.

Lapavistsas, C. (2013). *Profiting Without Producing*, London: Verso.

Lash, S. (2002). *Critique of Information*, London: Sage.

Lash, S. (2011). *Intensive Culture*, London: Sage.

Lash, S. and Urry, J. (1987). *The End of Organized Capitalism*, Cambridge: Polity.

Lash, S. and Urry, J. (1994). *Economies of Signs and Space*, London: Sage.

Lash, S. and Urry, J. (2013). 'Book Review Symposium: Response to Reviewers of *The End of Organized Capitalism*', *Work, Employment and Society* 27(3): 542–6.

Lauesen, T. and Cope, Z. (2015). 'Imperialism and the Transformation of Values into Prices', *Monthly Review Press* 67(3): 1–13.

Lawreniuk, S. (2020). 'Necrocapitalist Networks: COVID-19 and the "Dark Side" of Economic Geography', *Dialogues in Human Geography* 10(2): 199–202.

Lazonick, W. and O'Sullivan, M. (2000). 'Maximizing Shareholder Value: A New Ideology for Corporate Governance', *Economy and Society* 29(1): 13–35.

LeBaron, G. and Phillips, N. (2019). 'States and the Political Economy of Unfree Labour', *New Political Economy* 24(1): 1–21.

Legal and General (2020). *The Isolation Economy*, May, available at: https://www.legalandgeneralgroup.com/media/17835/lg_isolationeconomy_repor t2_rbg_final.pdf, last accessed at 28 May 2020.

Lego Foundation (2020). 'The LEGO Group and the LEGO Foundation Support Children and Families Impacted by COVID-19', 30 March, available at: https://www.legofoundation.com/en/about-us/news/the-lego-group -and-the-lego-foundation-support-children-and-families-impacted-by-covid -19, accessed 28 May 2020.

Lehdonvirta, V. (2017). 'The Online Gig Economy Grew 26% over the Past Year', 10 July, available at: http://ilabour.oii.ox.ac.uk/the-online-gig-econo my-grew-26-over-the-past-year, last accessed 3 March 2018.

Lehdonvirta, V. (2018). 'Flexibility in the Gig Economy: Managing Time on Three Online Piecework Platforms', *New Technology, Work, and Employment* 33(1): 13–29.

Leslie, J. and Shah, K. (2021). *(Wealth) Gap Year*, The Resolution Foundation, available at: https://www.resolutionfoundation.org/app/uploads/2021/07 /Wealth-gap-year.pdf, last accessed 15 July 2021.

Lichten, E. (1986). *Class, Power and Austerity*, South Hadley, MA: Bergin & Garvey Publishers.

Liimatainen, K. (2018). 'London Leads Widening U.K. Wealth Gap since Financial Crisis', *Bloomberg*, 1 September, available at: https://www.bloom berg.com/news/articles/2018-08-31/london-leads-widening-u-k-wealth-gap -since-financial-crisis, last accessed 14 January 2019.

Lipietz, A. (1988). 'Reflections on a Tale: The Marxist Foundations of the Concepts of Regulation and Accumulation', *Studies in Political Economy* 26 (Summer): 7–36.

Living Wage Foundation (2019). 'Low Pay Spotlight: Public Sector Workers', 28 February, available at: https://www.livingwage.org.uk/news/low-pay-sp otlight-public-sector, last accessed 23 March 2019.

Livingstone, D. W. (1983). *Class Ideologies and Educational Futures*, Lewes: Falmer Press.

Livingstone, D. W. and Scholtz, A. (2016). 'Reconnecting Class and Production Relations in an Advanced Capitalist "Knowledge Economy": Changing Class Structure and Class Consciousness', *Capital and Class* 40(3): 469–93.

Lucio, M. M. and Stewart, P. (1997). 'The Paradox of Contemporary Labour Process Theory: The Rediscovery of Labour and the Disappearance of Collectivism', *Capital and Class* 62 (Summer): 49–77.

Ludwig Institute for Economic Prosperity (2021). 'Rate of True Unemployment', available at: https://www.lisep.org/tru, last accessed 1 November 2021.

Lunn, E. and Collinson, P. (2018). 'Boring Chore? Airtasker or TaskRabbit Could Help – At a Price', *The Guardian*, 10 March, available at: https://www.theguardian.com/money/2018/mar/10/boring-chore-airtasker-or-task rabbit-could-help-at-a-price?CMP=Share_iOSApp_Other, last accessed 10 June 2018.

Lupton, D. (2014a). 'Critical Perspectives on Digital Health Technologies', *Sociology Compass* 8(12): 1344–59.

Lupton, D. (2014b). 'The Commodification of Patient Opinion: The Digital Patient Experience Economy in the Age of Big Data', *Sociology of Health and Illness* 36(6): 856–69.

Luttig, V. (2021). 'By the End of 2021, UK Firms will have Borrowed Over £60bn Through the Pandemic', 8 February, available at: https://www.ey.com/en_uk/news/2021/02/by-the-end-of-2021-uk-firms-will-have-borrowed-over-p60bn-through-the-pandemic, last accessed 13 July 2021.

Madsen, D. Ø., Risvik, S. and Stenheim, T. (2017). 'The Diffusion of Lean in the Norwegian Municipality Sector: An Exploratory Survey', *Cogent Business and Management* 4(1): 1–25.

Majumdar, A., Mahesh, S. and Sinha, S. K. (2020). 'COVID-19 Debunks the Myth of Socially Sustainable Supply Chain: A Case of the Clothing Industry in South Asian Countries', *Sustainable Production and Consumption* 24: 150–5.

Make UK (2020). *Manufacturing Monitoring 19 May 2020*, available at: https://www.makeuk.org/insights/publications/manufacturing-monitor-290 52020, last accessed 19 June 2020.

Mandel, E. (1968). *Marxist Economic Theory*, London: Merlin Press.

Mandel, E. (1971). *Late Capitalism*, London: New Left Books.

Mandel, E. (1992). 'Introduction', in K. Marx, *Capital*, vol. 2, London: Penguin.

Mandel, E. (1995). *Long Waves of Capitalist Development*, London: Verso.

Mansell, R. and Javary, M. (2004). 'New Media and the Forces of Capitalism', in C. Sparks and A. Calabrese (eds.), *Toward a Political Economy of Culture: Capitalism and Communication in the Twenty-First Century*, London: Rowman & Littlefield.

Marsh, D. (2011). 'Late Modernity and the Changing Nature of Politics: Two Cheers for Henrik Bang', *Critical Policy Studies* 5(1): 73–89.

Marte, J. (2019). 'Recession Watch: What is an "Inverted Yield Curve" and Why Does It Matter?' *The Washington Post*, 14 August, available at: https://www.washingtonpost.com/business/2019/08/14/recession-watch-what-is-an-inverted-yield-curve-why-does-it-matter, last accessed 12 June 2020.

Martens, P. and Martens, R. (2020). 'Wall Street's Financial Crisis Preceded COVID-19: Chart and Timeline', *Wall Street on Parade*, 1 May, available

DIGITAL, WORK, CLASS

at: https://wallstreetonparade.com/2020/05/wall-streets-financial-crisis-pre ceded-covid-19-chart-and-timeline, last accessed 12 June 2020.

Martin, D. (2018). 'Lean in a Cold Fiscal Climate: The Public Sector in an Age of Reduced Resources', *Public Money & Management* 38(1): 29–36.

Martin, R. (2002). *The Financialization of Daily Life*, Philadelphia: Temple University Press.

Marx, K. (1969). *Theories of Surplus Value, Part 1*, Moscow: Progress Publishers.

Marx, K. (1972). *A Contribution to the Critique of Political Economy*, New York: International Publishers.

Marx, K. (1973). *Grundrisse*, London: Pelican.

Marx, K. (1988). *Capital*, vol. 1, London: Pelican.

Marx, K. (1991). *Capital*, vol. 3, London: Penguin.

Marx, K. (1992). *Capital*, vol. 2, London: Penguin.

Marx, K. and Engels, F. (1964). *The Communist Manifesto*, London: Monthly Review Press.

Mason, G. (2000). 'Production Supervisors in Britain, Germany and the United States: Back from the Dead Again?' *Work, Employment and Society* 14(4): 625–45.

Mason, P. (2015). *PostCapitalism*, London: Allen Lane.

Mathur, P. and Thorne, J. (2020). 'Facing Crisis, Venture Capitalists Follow a New Script', *PitchBook*, 2 June, available at: https://pitchbook.com/ne ws/articles/coronavirus-forces-venture-capitalists-to-follow-new-script, last accessed 16 June 2020.

Mazzucato, M. (2013). 'Financing Innovation: Creative Destruction vs. Destructive Creation', *Industrial and Corporate Change* 22(4): 851–67.

MBO Partners (2018). *A State of Independence in America Research Brief: Digital Nomadism: A Rising Trend*, available at https://s29814.pcdn.co/wp -content/uploads/2019/02/StateofIndependence-ResearchBrief-DigitalNoma ds.pdf, last accessed 15 March 2019.

McCann, L., Hassard, J. S., Granter, E. and Hyde, P. J. (2015). 'Casting the Lean Spell: The Promotion, Dilution and Erosion of Lean Management in the NHS', *Human Relations* 68(10): 1557–77.

McChesney, R. W. (2013) *Digital Disconnect*, New York: The New Press.

McFarland, M (2016). 'Amazon Only Needs a Minute of Human Labor to Ship Your Next Package', *CNN Business*, 6 October, available at: https://money .cnn.com/2016/10/06/technology/amazon-warehouse-robots/index.html, accessed 9 August 2020.

McGimpsey, I. (2017) 'Late Neoliberalism: Delineating a Policy Regime', *Critical Social Policy* 37(1): 64–84.

McGowan, M. A., Andrews, D., Criscuolo, C. and Nicoletti, G. et al (2015). *The Future of Productivity*, Paris: OECD, available at: https://www.oecd.org/eco/OECD-2015-The-future-of-productivity-book.pdf, last accessed 2 February 2019.

McKevitt, F. (2020). 'UK Online Grocery Growth Clicks Up as Lockdown Trends Continue', Kantar, 23 June, available at: https://www.kantar.com/inspiration/fmcg/uk-online-grocery-growth-clicks-up-as-lockdown-trends-continue, last accessed 2 July 2020.

McNally, D. (2011). *The Global Slump*, Oakland, CA: PM Press.

McNeil, C., Jung, C. and Hochlaf, D. (2020). *Rescue and Recovery: COVID-19, Jobs and Income Security*, August, available at: https://www.ippr.org/files/2020-08/rescue-and-recovery-august20.pdf, last accessed 17 August 2020.

Meadway, J. (2021). *Bidenomics: The Economic Strategy of the Biden Administration*, Progressive Economy Forum, June, available at: https://progressiveeconomyforum.com/publications/bidenomics-the-economic-strategy-of-the-joe-biden-administration,last accessed 13 July 2021.

Mearns, G. W., Richardson, R. and Robson, L. (2015). 'Enacting the Internet and Social Media on the Public Sector's Frontline', *New Technology, Work and Employment* 30(3): 190–208.

Medina, D. A. (2020). 'As Amazon, Walmart and Others Profit amid Coronavirus Crisis, Their Essential Workers Plan Unprecedented Strike', *The Intercept*, 28 April, available: https://theintercept.com/2020/04/28/coronavirus-may-1-strike-sickout-amazon-target-whole-foods, last accessed 2 June 2020).

Megaw, N. (2020). 'Lloyds Sets Aside Another £2.4bn to Cover Potential Bad Loans', *Financial Times*, 30 July, available at: https://www.ft.com/content/a6c44d6f-28f0-47e2-bfca-b880f28fbfd5, last accessed 31 July 2020.

Meil, P. and Kirov, V. (2017). 'Introduction: The Policy Implications of Virtual Work', in P. Meil and V. Kirov (eds.), *Policy Implications of Virtual Work*, London: Palgrave.

Mian, A., Straub, L. and Sufi, A. (2020). 'The Saving Glut of the Rich and the Rise in Household Debt', CESifo Working Paper No. 8201, March, available at: https://www.cesifo.org/DocDL/cesifo1_wp8201.pdf, last accessed 12 August 2020.

Michaelson, R. (2013). 'Is Agile the Answer? The Case of UK Universal Credit', in Y. K. Dwivedi, H. Z. Henriksen and D. Wastell and R. De' (eds.), *Grand Successes and Failures in IT: Public and Private Sectors*, London: Springer.

Mirowski, P. (2013). *Never Let a Serious Crisis Go to Waste*, London: Verso

Mirwoski, P. and Doherty, A. (2020). 'How Neoliberalism Will Exploit the Coronavirus Crisis: An Interview with Philip Mirwoski', *Tribune*, 18 May, available at: https://tribunemag.co.uk/2020/05/how-neoliberalism-will-exploit-the-coronavirus-crisis, last accessed 26 May 2020.

266

Mohi-uddin, M. (2020). 'Renminbi Strength Foretells Dollar's Decline', *Financial Times*, 1 October, available at: https://www.ft.com/content/0534f14b-20c0-4206-83fd-77f98be6326d, last accessed 5 October 2020.

Montalban, M., Frigant, V. and Jullien, B. (2019). 'Platform Economy as a New Form of Capitalism: A Régulationist Research Programme', *Cambridge Journal of Economics* early view: 1–20.

Montgomerie, J. (2018). 'Debt Dependence and the Financialisation of Everyday Life', in J. McDonnell (ed.), *Economics for the Many*, London: Verso.

Moody, K. (2007). *U.S. Labour in Trouble and Transition*, London: Verso.

Moody, K. (2017). *On New Terrain*, Chicago: Haymarket.

Moody, K. and Post, C. (2014). 'The Politics of US Labour: Paralysis and Possibilities', in L. Panitch and G. Albo (eds.), *The Socialist Register 2015: Transforming Classes*, London: Merlin Press.

Moore, S. (2011). *New Trade Union Activism*, London: Palgrave.

Moore, S. and Hayes, L. J. B. (2017). 'The Electronic Monitoring of Care Work—The Redefinition of Paid Working Time', in P. Moore, M. Upchurch and X. Whittaker (eds.), *Humans and Machines at Work: Dynamics of Virtual Work*, London: Palgrave.

Moraitis, A. B. and Copley, J. (2017). 'Productive and Unproductive Labour and Social Form: Putting Class Struggle in its Place', *Capital and Class* 41(1): 91–114.

Mosco, V (2004). *The Digital Sublime*, Cambridge, MA: MIT Press.

Moseley, F. (1992). 'The Decline of the Rate of Profit in the Postwar US Economy: Is the Crisis Over?' *Capital and Class* 16(3): 115–30.

Moseley, F. (2000). 'The New Solution to the Transformation Problem: A Sympathetic Critique', *Review of Radical Political Economics* 32(2): 282–316.

Moseley, F. (2003). 'Marxian Theory of the Decline of the Rate of Profit in the Postwar Economy', in R. Westra and A. Zuege (eds.), *Value and the World Economy Today*, London: Palgrave.

Moulds, J. (2020). 'Gig Workers among the Hardest Hit by Coronavirus Pandemic', *World Economic Forum*, 21 April, available at: https://www.weforum.org/agenda/2020/04/gig-workers-hardest-hit-coronavirus-pandemic, last accessed 24 June 2020.

Movitz, F. and Allvin, M. (2017). 'Changing Systems, Creating Conflicts: IT-Related Changes in Swedish Banking', in K. Briken, S. Chillas, M. Krzywdzinski and A. Marks (eds.), *The New Digital Workplace: How Technologies Revolutionise Work*, Houndmills: Palgrave Macmillan.

Mulholland, K. (2009). 'Life on the Supermarket Floor: Replenishment Assistants and Just-in-Time Systems', in S. C. Bolton and M. Houlihan (eds.), *Work Matters*, London: Palgrave.

Murray, P. (2011). 'Avoiding Bad Abstractions', *Critique of Political Economy* 21(September): 217–48.

Nager, A. (2017). 'Trade vs. Productivity: What Caused U.S. Manufacturing's Decline and How to Revive It', *Information Technology and Innovation Foundation*, February, available at: http://www2.itif.org/2017-trade-vs-pro ductivity.pdf, last accessed 13 September 2019.

Naisbitt, B., Boshoff, J., Holland, D., Hurst, I., Kara, A., Liadze, I, Macchiarelli, C., Mao, X., Juanino, P. S., Thamotheram, C. and Whyte, K. (2020). 'The World Economy: Global Outlook Review', *National Institute Economic Review*, 253 (August): 35–87.

National Council for Voluntary Organisations (NCVO) (2020). *Impact on the Charity Sector during Coronavirus: Research Report June 2020*, available at: file:///C:/Users/hsstjmr/AppData/Local/Temp/1/1coronavirus-impact-sur vey-report-june-2020.pdf, last accessed 2 September 2020.

National Union of Rail, Maritime and Transport Workers (RMT) (2020). *Profiting at the Times of Crisis*, 21 July, available at: https://www.rmt .org.uk/news/publications/profiteering-at-a-time-of-crisis-rmt-report, last accessed 30 July 2020.

Neilson, J. (2014). 'Value Chains, Neoliberalism and Development Practice: The Indonesian Experience', *Review of International Political Economy* 21(1): 38–69.

Nelson, A., Herron, D., Rees, G. and Nachev, P. (2019). 'Predicting Scheduled Hospital Attendance with Artificial Intelligence', *npj Digital Medicine* 2(26): 1–7.

Ness, I. (2016). *Southern Insurgency*, London: Pluto.

Newsinger, J. and Serafini, P. (2021). 'Performative Resilience: How the Arts and Culture Support Austerity in Post-crisis Capitalism', *European Journal of Cultural Studies* 24(2): 589–605.

Newsome, K., Thompson, P. and Commander, J. (2009). 'The Forgotten Factories: Supermarket Suppliers and Dignity at Work in the Contemporary Economy', in S. C. Bolton and M. Houlihan (eds.), *Work Matters*, London: Palgrave.

Ngai, P., Yuan, S., Yuhua, G., Huilin, L. U., Chan, J. and Selden, M. (2016). 'Apple, Foxconn, and Chinese Workers' Struggles from a Global Labor Perspective', *Inter-Asia Cultural Studies* 17(2): 166–85.

Niechcial, J. (2020). 'The NHS is Being Systematically Dismantled by Privatisation', *We Own It*, 4 June, available at: https://weownit.org.uk/bl og/nhs-being-systematically-dismantled-privatisation, last accessed 25 June 2020.

Nielsen Book (2020). 'Reading Increases in Lockdown', 13 May, available at: https://nielsenbook.co.uk/wp-content/uploads/sites/4/2020/05/Press-Release _Covid-Tracker_wave-1-1.pdf, last accessed 28 May 2020.

Noordegraaf, M. (2016). 'Reconfiguring Professional Work: Changing Forms of Professionalism in Public Services', *Administration and Society* 48(7): 783–810.

Norfield, T. (2013). 'Derivatives, Money, Finance and Imperialism: A Response to Bryan and Rafferty', *Historical Materialism* 21(2): 149–68.

Oakland, J. S. (1989). *Total Quality Management*, Oxford: Butterworth-Heinemann.

O'Brien D., Laurison, D., Miles, A. and Friedman, S. (2016). 'Are the Creative Industries Meritocratic? An Analysis of the 2014 British Labour Force Survey', *Cultural Trends* 25(2): 116–31.

O'Connor, J. (2010). *The Cultural and Creative Industries: A Literature Review*, 2nd edn, Newcastle: Creativity, Culture and Education, available at: https://www.creativitycultureeducation.org//wp-content/uploads/2018/10/CCE-lit-review-creative-cultural-industries-257.pdf, last accessed 9 September 2020.

Office for Budget Responsibility (OBR) (2021). *Financial Risk Report*, July, available at: https://obr.uk/docs/dlm_uploads/Fiscal_risks_report_July_2021.pdf, last accessed 9 July 2021.

Office for National Statistics (ONS) (2018a). *Trends in Self-Employment*, available at: https://www.ons.gov.uk/employmentandlabourmarket/peopleinwork/employmentandemployeetypes/articles/trendsinselfemploymentintheuk/2018-02-07, last accessed 27 February 2018.

Office for National Statistics (ONS) (2018b). *UK Labour Market: January 2018*, available at: https://www.ons.gov.uk/employmentandlabourmarket/peopleinwork/employmentandemployeetypes/bulletins/uklabourmarket/january2018, last accessed 20 March 2018.

Office for National Statistics (ONS) (2018c). *Making Ends Meet: Are Households Living Beyond their Means?* available at: https://www.ons.gov.uk/economy/nationalaccounts/uksectoraccounts/articles/makingendsmeetarehouseholdslivingbeyondtheirmeans/2018-07-26, last accessed 17 October 2018.

Office for National Statistics (ONS) (2019). *Services Sector, UK: 2008–2018*, available at: https://www.ons.gov.uk/economy/economicoutputandproductivity/output/articles/servicessectoruk/2008to2018, last accessed 2 July 2020.

Office for National Statistics (ONS) (2020a). *Coronavirus and Homeworking in the UK: April 2020*, available at: https://www.ons.gov.uk/employmentandlabourmarket/peopleinwork/employmentandemployeetypes/bulletins/coronavirusandhomeworkingintheuk/april2020, last accessed 23 July 2020.

Office for National Statistics (ONS) (2020b). *Coronavirus and the Social Impacts on Great Britain: 19 June 2020*, available at: https://www.ons.gov.uk/peoplepopulationandcommunity/healthandsocialcare/healthandwellbeing/bulletins/coronavirusandthesocialimpactsongreatbritain/19june2020, last accessed 23 July 2020.

Office for National Statistics (ONS) (2020c). *Coronavirus and the Social Impacts on Great Britain: 22 May 2020*, available at: https://www.ons.gov .uk/peoplepopulationandcommunity/healthandsocialcare/healthandwellb eing/bulletins/coronavirusandthesocialimpactsongreatbritain/22may2020 #unity-kindness-and-equality, last accessed 30 May 2020.

Office for National Statistics (ONS) (2020d). *Labour Market Overview, UK:* available at: https://www.ons.gov.uk/employmentandlabourmarket/people inwork/employmentandemployeetypes/bulletins/uklabourmarket/july2020, last accessed 15 September 2020.

Office for National Statistics (ONS) (2020e). *Coronavirus (COVID-19) Related Deaths by Occupation, England and Wales: Deaths Registered Up to and Including 20 April 2020*, available at: https://www.ons.gov.uk/peoplepopu lationandcommunity/healthandsocialcare/causesofdeath/bulletins/coronavir uscovid19relateddeathsbyoccupationenglandandwales/deathsregisteredupto andincluding20april2020#men-and-coronavirus-related-deaths-by-occupa tion, last accessed 18 June 2020.

Office for National Statistics (ONS) (2020f). *Coronavirus (COVID-19) Roundup, 27 April to 1 May 2020*, available at: https://www.ons.gov.uk/pe oplepopulationandcommunity/healthandsocialcare/conditionsanddiseases /articles/coronaviruscovid19roundup27aprilto1may2020/2020-05-01, last accessed 18 June 2020.

Office for National Statistics (ONS) (2020g). *Labour Market Overview, UK: August 2020*, available at: https://www.ons.gov.uk/employmentandlabour market/peopleinwork/employmentandemployeetypes/bulletins/uklabourma rket/august2020, last accessed 12 August 2020.

Office for National Statistics (ONS) (2020h). *Index of Production, UK: April 2020*, available at: https://www.ons.gov.uk/economy/economicoutputandp roductivity/output/bulletins/indexofproduction/april2020, last accessed 19 June 2020.

Office for National Statistics (ONS) (2020i). *Labour Market Overview, UK: June 2020*, available at: https://www.ons.gov.uk/employmentandlabourmar ket/peopleinwork/employmentandemployeetypes/bulletins/uklabourmarket /june2020#unemployment, last accessed 23 June 2020.

Office for National Statistics (ONS) (2020j). *Index of Services, UK: April 2020*, available at: https://www.ons.gov.uk/economy/economicoutputandproduc tivity/output/bulletins/indexofservices/april2020, last accessed 2 July 2020.

Office for National Statistics (ONS) (2020k). *Coronavirus and the Impact on Output in the UK Economy: April 2020*, available at: https://www.ons.gov .uk/economy/grossdomesticproductgdp/articles/coronavirusandtheimpact onoutputintheukeconomy/april2020#services-industries, last accessed 30 June 2020.

Office for National Statistics (ONS) (2020l). *Retail Sales, Great Britain: May 2020*, available at: https://www.ons.gov.uk/businessindustryandtrade/reta

ilindustry/bulletins/retailsales/may2020#online-retail-sales, last accessed 3 July 2020.

Office for National Statistics (ONS) (2020m). *Retail Sales, Great Britain: July 2020*, available at: https://www.ons.gov.uk/businessindustryandtrade/retai lindustry/bulletins/retailsales/july2020, last accessed 9 September 2020.

Office for National Statistics (ONS) (2020n). *Coronavirus and the Economic Impacts on the UK: 19 November 2020*, available at: https://www.ons.gov .uk/businessindustryandtrade/business/businessservices/bulletins/coronaviru sandtheeconomicimpactsontheuk/latest#workforce, last accessed 9 August 2021.

Office for National Statistics (ONS) (2021), *Coronavirus (COVID- 19) and the Different Effects on Men and Women in the UK, March 2020 to February 2021*, available at: https://www.ons.gov.uk/people populationandcommunity/healthandsocialcare/conditionsanddiseases/arti- cles/coronaviruscovid19andthedifferenteffectsonmenandwomenintheukmar ch2020tofebruary2021/2021-03-10, last accessed 9 August 2021.

Ogden, K. and Phillips, D. (2020). *COVID-19 and English Council Funding: How are Budgets Being Hit in 2020–21?* Institute for Fiscal Studies, August, available at: https://www.ifs.org.uk/uploads/R-174-COVID-19%20and %20English-council-funding-how-are-budgets-being-hit-in-2020%E2%80 %9321.pdf, last accessed 20 August 2020.

O'Leary, T. (2020a). 'Record Low Growth and Worse to Come. Boris Johnson is Not "Deficit-Financing Growth"', *Socialist Economic Bulletin*, 12 March, available at: https://www.socialisteconomicbulletin.net/2020/03/record-low -growth-and-worse-to-come-boris-johnson-is-not-deficit-financing-growth, last accessed 19 October 2021.

O'Leary, T. (2020b). 'Government Policy is Responsible for the Decimation of Jobs', *Socialist Economic Bulletin*, 10 July, available at: https://www.socialis teconomicbulletin.net/2020/07/government-policy-is-responsible-for-the-de cimation-of-jobs, last (accessed 21 July 2020.

O'Leary, T. (2021). 'Why Sunak and Biden are not Keynes, Corbyn or McDonnell', *Socialist Economic Bulletin*, available at: https://www.socialis teconomicbulletin.net/2021/03/why-sunak-and-biden-are-not-keynes-corb yn-or-mcdonnell, last accessed 13 July 2021.

Olorunnipa, T. and Chandra, S. (2018). 'American's are Making Less Money Despite Trump's Promises', *Bloomberg*, 28 August, available at: https:// www.bloomberg.com/news/articles/2018-08-28/trump-s-promises-to-forgo tten-man-undercut-by-wage-stagnation, last accessed 7 November 2018.

Olsen, E. K. (2015). 'Unproductive Activity and Endogenous Technological Change in a Marxian Model of Economic Reproduction and Growth', *Review of Radical Political Economics* 47(1): 34–55.

O'Malley, P. (2010). 'Resilient Subjects: Uncertainty, Warfare and Liberalism', *Economy and Society* 39(4): 488–509.

Open Contracting Partnership (OCP) (2020). *How Governments Spend: Opening Up the Value of Global Government Procurement*, available at: https://www.open-contracting.org/wp-content/uploads/2020/08/OCP2020 -Global-Public-Procurement-Spend.pdf, last accessed 4 September 2020.

Organisation for Economic Cooperation and Development (OECD) (2016). *Automation and Independent Work in a Digital Economy (Policy Brief on the Future of Work)*, Paris: OECD Publishing, available at: https://www.oe cd.org/els/emp/Policy%20brief%20-%20Automation%20and%20Indepen dent%20Work%20in%20a%20Digital%20Economy.pdf, last accessed 12 November 2018.

Organisation for Economic Cooperation and Development (OECD) (2017). *OECD Science, Technology and Industry Scoreboard 2017: The Digital Transformation*, Paris: OECD Publishing, available at: https://read.oecd -ilibrary.org/science-and-technology/oecd-science-technology-and-industry -scoreboard-2017_9789264268821-en#page1, last accessed 12 November 2018.

Organisation for Economic Cooperation and Development (OECD) (2020a). *OECD Labour Force Statistics 2010–2019: International Comparisons*, available at: https://read.oecd-ilibrary.org/employment/oecd-labour-force-st atistics-2020_5842cc7f-en#page1, last accessed 31 July 2021.

Organisation for Economic Cooperation and Development (OECD) (2020b). *World Economic Outlook 2020*, Paris: OECD Publishing, available at: https://www.oecd-ilibrary.org/sites/0d1d1e2e-en/index.html?itemId=/conte nt/publication/0d1d1e2e-en, last accessed 16 June 2020.

Organisation for Economic Cooperation and Development (OECD) (2021). *OECD Economic Outlook, Interim Report September 2021: Keeping the Recovery on Track*, available at: https://www.oecd-ilibrary.org/sites/490d 4832-en/index.html?itemId=/content/publication/490d4832-en&_ga=2.15 0260854.1584332532.1635867643-1320167406.1635867643#section-d1 e530, last accessed 2 November 2021.

Osborne, S. P., Radnor, Z. and Nasi, G. (2012). 'A New Theory for Public Service Management? Toward a (Public) Service-Dominant Approach, *American Review of Public Administration* 43(2) 135–58.

Oxfam (2020). *The Hunger Virus: How COVID-19 is Fuelling Hunger in a Hungry World*, 9 July, available at: https://oxfamilibrary.openrepository .com/bitstream/handle/10546/621023/mb-the-hunger-virus-090720-en.pdf ;jsessionid=718BC83FC778D2D7C33A946D4A5B2B95?sequence=1, last accessed 25 July 2020.

Oxford Economics (2020). *The Projected Impact of COVID-19 on the UK Creative Industries*, Creative Industries Federation, 17 June, available: https://www.creativeindustriesfederation.com/publications/report-projec ted-economic-impact-covid-19-uk-creative-industries, last accessed 30 June 2020.

Oya, C. and Schaefer, F. (2021). 'The Politics of Labour Relations in Global Production Networks: Collective Action, Industrial Parks, and Local Conflict in the Ethiopian Apparel Sector', *World Development* 146: 1–13.

Pan, S. L. and Leidner, D. E. (2003). 'Bridging Communities of Practices with Information Technology in Pursuit of Global Knowledge Sharing', *Journal of Strategic Information Systems* 12: 71–88.

Panitch, L. and Gindin, S. (2009). 'The Current Crisis: A Socialist Perspective', *Studies in Political Economy* 83(1): 7–31.

Panitch, L. and Gindin, S. (2012). *The Making of Global Capitalism*, London: Verso.

Panitch, L. and Gindin, S. (2018). *The Socialist Challenge Today: Syriza, Sanders, Corbyn*, London: Merlin.

Pavlínek, P. and Ženka, J. (2016). 'Value Creation and Value Capture in the Automotive Industry: Empirical Evidence from Czechia', *Environment and Planning A* 48(5): 937–59

Peck, J. and Theodore, N. (2007). 'Flexible Recession: The Temporary Staffing Industry and Mediated Work in the United States', *Cambridge Journal of Economics* 31(2): 171–92.

Perez, C. (2009). 'The Double Bubble at the Turn of the Century: Technological Roots and Structural Implications', *Cambridge Journal of Economics* 33(4): 779–805.

Pérez, P. and Cifuentes, L. (2020). 'The Service Industry, Private-sector Employment and Social Class in Chile: New Developments from Labour Process Theory', *Critical Sociology* 46(3): 443–61.

Peterson, B. (2017). 'GitHub, the "Facebook for Programmers", has Quietly Built Up an Enterprise Business that Accounts for Half its $200 Million in Sales', *Business Insider*, 12 October, available at: http://uk.businessinsider .com/githubs-enterprise-service-brings-in-half-its-200-million-in-sales-2017 -10, last accessed 23 July 2018.

Peterson, H. (2018). '"Seeing Someone Cry at Work is becoming Normal": Employees Say Whole Foods is Using "Scorecards" to Punish Them', *Business Insider*, 1 February, available at: https://www.businessinsider.com /how-whole-foods-uses-scorecards-to-punish-employees-2018-1?r=UK, last accessed 12 June 2018.

Peticca-Harris, A., deGama, N. and Ravishankar, M. N. (2020). 'Postcapitalist Precarious Work and those in the "Driver's" Seat: Exploring the Motivations and Lived Experiences of Uber Drivers in Canada', *Organization* 27(1): 36–59.

Pfeiffer, S. (2017). 'The Vision of "Industrie 4.0" in the Making – a Case of Future Told, Tamed, and Traded', *NanoEthics* 11(1): 107–21.

Philip, B., Harvie, D. and Slater, G. (2005). 'Preferences, Power, and the Determination of Working Hours', *Journal of Economic Issues* 39(1): 75–90.

Platt, L. and Warwick, R. (2020). *Are Some Ethnic Groups More Vulnerable to COVID-19 than Others?* Institute for Fiscal Studies, 1 May, available at: https://www.ifs.org.uk/inequality/chapter/are-some-ethnic-groups-more-vulnerable-to-covid-19-than-others/?fbclid=IwAR2D22FC_8pfEse2IWcqFa_lBwTwFDXbIE-rop1CMwyXTZWNtGtzQIrGmPk, last accessed 18 June 2020.

Plender, J. (2017). 'Snap and the 21st Century Governance Vacuum', *Financial Times*, 22 February, available at: https://www.ft.com/content/1c618f6a-f45b-11e6-8758-6876151821a6, last accessed 12 September 2018.

Polkowska, D. (2021). 'Platform Work during the COVID-19 Pandemic: A Case Study of Glovo Couriers in Poland', *European Societies* 23(S1): S321–31.

Postigo, V. (2014). 'The Socio-technical Architecture of Digital Labor: Converting Play into YouTube Money', *New Media and Society* 18(2): 332–49.

Potts, J., Cunningham, S., Hartley, J. and Ormerod, P. (2008a). 'Social Network Markets: A New Definition of the Creative Industries', *Journal of Cultural Economy* 32(3): 166–85.

Potts, J., Hartley, J., Banks, J., Burgess, J., Cobcroft, R., Cunningham, S. and Montgomery, L. (2008b). 'Consumer Co-creation and Situated Creativity', *Industry and Innovation* 15(5): 459–74

Poulantzas, N. (1978). *Classes in Contemporary Capitalism*, London: Verso.

Poulantzas, N. (2000). *State, Power, Socialism*, new edn., trans. P. Camiller, London: Verso.

Practice Business (2018). 'NAO Report Shows "Scandalous" Failings in Capita's Delivery of GP Services, says BMA', 17 May, available at: https://practicebusiness.co.uk/nao-report-shows-scandalous-failings-in-capitas-delivery-of-gp-services-says-bma, last accessed 31 July 2020.

Public Library News (2020). Available at: https://www.publiclibrariesnews.com, last accessed 28 May 2020.

Ratto, M. and Boler, M. (2014). 'Introduction', in M. Ratto and M. Boler (eds.), *DIY Citizenship*, Cambridge, MA: MIT Press.

Redfield & Wilson (2020). 'Clear Majority of British Workers Believe Working from Home Increased Their Productivity', Redfield & Wilson Strategies, 27 July, available at: https://redfieldandwiltonstrategies.com/clear-majority-of-uk-workers-believe-working-from-home-increased-their-productivity, last accessed 20 August 2020.

Renovo (2021). *Life after Furlough: Employer and Employee Perspectives on the Threat of Redundancy*, October, available at: https://renovo.uk.com/wp-content/uploads/2021/10/Life-after-Furlough-Report.pdf, last accessed 1 November 2021.

Resolution Foundation, The (2021). 'The Boris Budget', 28 October, available at: https://www.resolutionfoundation.org/publications/the-boris-budget, last accessed 2 November 2021.

Richter, F. (2020). 'US Retail Sales Rebound after Historic Slump', *Statista*, 16 June, available at: https://www.statista.com/chart/21760/monthly-retail-sales-in-the-united-states, last accessed 2 July 2020.

Rigi, J. (2014). 'Foundations of a Marxist Theory of the Political Economy of Information: Trade Secrets and Intellectual Property, and the Production of Relative Surplus Value and the Extraction of Rent-Tribute', *tripleC* 12(2): 909–36.

Rigi, J. and Prey, R. (2015). 'Value, Rent, and the Political Economy of Social Media', *Information Society* 31(5): 392–406.

Rinehart, W. and Gitis, B. (2015). 'Independent Contractors and the Emerging Gig Economy', *American Action Forum*, 29 July, available at: https://www.americanactionforum.org/research/independent-contractors-and-the-emerging-gig-economy/#_edn1, last accessed 5 March 2018.

Ritzer, G. (2014). 'Prosumption: Evolution, Revolution, or Eternal Return of the Same?' *Journal of Consumer Culture* 14(1): 3–24.

Ritzer, G. and Jurgenson, N. (2010). 'Production, Consumption, Prosumption: The Nature of Capitalism in the Age of the Digital "Prosumer"', *Journal of Consumer Culture* 10(1): 13–36.

Roberts, J. M. (2004). 'What's "Social" about "Social Capital"?' *British Journal of Politics and International Relations* 6(4): 471–93.

Roberts, J. M. (2009). *The Competent Public Sphere*, London: Palgrave.

Roberts, J. M. (2014). *New Media and Public Activism*, Bristol: Policy Press.

Roberts, M. (2016). *The Long Depression*, Chicago: Haymarket Books.

Roberts, M. (2020). 'Pandemic Economics', *International Socialism*, 167, 13 July, available at: https://www.ons.gov.uk/employmentandlabourmarket/peopleinwork/employmentandemployeetypes/bulletins/uklabourmarket/latest, last accessed 15 September 2020.

Robinson, J. (1977) 'The Labor Theory of Value', *Monthly Review* 29(9): 50–59.

Robinson, W. I. (2017). 'Debate on the New Global Capitalism: Transnational Capitalist Class, Transnational State Apparatuses, and Global Crisis', *International Critical Thought* 7(2): 171–89.

Romano, B. (2020). 'Amazon Adds 75,000 Job Openings on Top of the 100,000 it Already Filled in a Month', *TechXplore*, 14 April, available at: https://techxplore.com/news/2020-04-amazon-job-month.html, last accessed 25 June 2020.

Rosenblat, A. and Stark, L. (2016). 'Algorithmic Labor and Information Asymmetries: A Case Study of Uber's Drivers', *International Journal of Communication* 10(27): 3758–84.

Rotta, T. (2018). 'Unproductive Accumulation in the USA: A New Analytical Framework', *Cambridge Journal of Economics* 42(5): 1367–92.

Rotta, T. and Teixeira, R. (2016). 'The Autonomisation of Abstract Wealth: New Insights on the Labour Theory of Value', *Cambridge Journal of Economics* 40(4): 1185–201.

Roubini, N. (2020). 'Reports of the Dollars Demise are Greatly Exaggerated', *MarketWatch*, 25 August, available at: https://www.marketwatch.com/sto ry/nouriel-roubini-says-reports-of-the-dollars-demise-are-greatly-exaggerat ed-11598282130, last accessed 5 October 2020.

Royal Society for the Encouragement of Arts, Manufactures and Commerce (RSA) (2019). 'What are the Jobs of the Future?' 30 December, available at: https://www.thersa.org/about-us/media/2019/289000-high-street-jobs-lo st-in-last-decade-as-new-analysis-reveals-winners-and-losers-of-2010s, last accessed 10 July 2020.

Rubin, I. I. (1994). 'Abstract Labour and Value', in S. Mohun (ed.), *Debates in Value Theory*, London: Macmillan.

Rubin, I. I. (2008). *Essays on Marx's Theory of Value*, Delhi: Aakar Books.

Rushe, D. (2018). 'Netflix Valuation Breaks $100bn for First Time', *The Guardian*, 22 January, available at: https://www.theguardian.com/media/20 18/jan/22/netflix-valuation-breaks-100bn?CMP=Share_iOSApp_Othe, last accessed 14 April 2018.

Ryan, S. (2018). 'Sheldon Adelson Cuts $30 Million Check to House Republicans, Received $670 Million in Tax Breaks from GOP Bill', *Paste*, 10 May, available at: https://www.pastemagazine.com/articles/2018/05 /sheldon-adelson-cuts-30-million-check-to-house-rep.html, last accessed 15 February 2019.

Saad-Filho, A. (2002). *The Value of Marx: Political Economy for Contemporary Capitalism*, London: Routledge.

Sandhu, K. (2016). 'Universal Credit and Impact on Black and Minority Ethnic Communities', *Race, Equality Foundation: Better Housing Briefing 27*, June, available at: https://raceequalityfoundation.org.uk/wp-content/uploa ds/2017/11/Better-Housing-27-Universal-Credit.pdf, last accessed 25 June 2020.

Sawchuk, P. H. (2013). *Contested Learning in Welfare Work*, Cambridge: Cambridge University Press.

Sayers, S. (2011). *Marx and Alienation*, London: Palgrave.

Scarpetta, S., Broecke, S. and Lane, M. (2020). 'What Have Platforms Done to Protect Workers During the Coronavirus (COVID-19) Crisis?' *OECD*, 21 September, available at: https://read.oecd-ilibrary.org/view/?ref=136_13 6534-6kmopirex5&title=What-have-platforms-done-to-protect-workers-du ring-the-coronavirus-%28COVID-19%29-crisis%3F&_ga=2.76272341.11

53316983.1626090374-1924597945.1625760160, last accessed 12 July 2021.

Schanzenbach, D. W. and Pitts, A. (2020). *Estimates of Food Insecurity during the COVID-19 Crisis: Results from the COVID Impact Survey, Week 1(April20–26, 2020)*, Institute for Policy Research Rapid Research Report, 13 May, available at https://www.ipr.northwestern.edu/news/2020/food-in security-triples-for-families-during-covid.htm, last accessed 13 August 2020.

Scheiber, N. (2015). 'Growth in the "Gig Economy" Fuels Work Force Anxieties', *New York Times*, 12 July, available at: https://www.nytimes.com /2015/07/13/business/rising-economic-insecurity-tied-to-decades-long-trend -in-employment-practices.html, last accessed 3 March 2018.

Schlesinger, P. (2016). 'The Creative Economy: Invention of a Global Orthodoxy', *Les Enjeux de L'information et de la Communication* 17(2): 187–205.

Scholz, T. (2013). 'Introduction: Why Does Digital Labour Matter Now?' in T. Scholz (ed.), *Digital Labour: The Internet as a Playground*, London: Routledge.

Scholz, T. (2017). *Uberworked and Underpaid*, Cambridge: Polity.

Schörpf, P., Flecker, J. and Schönauer, A. (2017). 'On Call for One's Online Reputation – Control and Time in Creative Crowdwork', in K. Briken, S. Chillas and M. Krzywdzinski (eds.), *The New Digital Workplace*, London: Routledge.

Schutz, E. A. (2011). *Inequality and Power*, London: Routledge.

Schwellnus, C., Geva, A., Pak, M. and Veiel, R. (2019). 'Gig Economy Platforms: Boon or Bane?' OECD Economics Department Working Papers No. 1550: 1–33, available at: http://www.oecd.org/officialdocuments/publicdisplaydo cumentpdf/?cote=ECO/WKP(2019)19&docLanguage=En, last accessed 13 July 2019.

Scott, M., Braun, E., Delcker, J. and Manancourt, V. (2020). 'How Google and Apple Outflanked Governments in the Race to Build Coronavirus Apps', *Politico*, 15 May, available at: https://www.politico.eu/article/google-apple -coronavirus-app-privacy-uk-france-germany, last accessed 27 May 2020.

Selwyn, B. (2015). 'Commodity Chains, Creative Destructive and Global Inequality: A Class Analysis', *Journal of Economic Geography* 15(2): 253–74.

Selwyn, B. (2019). 'Poverty Chains and Global Capitalism', *Competition and Change* 23(1): 71–97.

Shaheen, F. and Jesse, R. (2020). *Coronavirus and the Workers Emergency: Labour Market Realities 2020*, CLASS, 17 May, available at: http://classon line.org.uk/pubs/item/coronavirus-and-the-workers-emergency-labour-mar ket-realities-2020, last accessed 23 June 2020.

Shaikh, A. M. and Tonak, E. A. (1994). *Measuring the Wealth of Nations*, Cambridge: Cambridge University Press.

Sharp, C., Nelson, J., Lucas, M., Julius, J., McCrone, T. and Sims, D. (2020). *The Challenges Facing Schools and Pupils in September 2020*, National Foundation for Education Research, available at: https://www.nfer.ac.uk /media/4119/schools_responses_to_covid_19_the_challenges_facing_scho ols_and_pupils_in_september_2020.pdf, last accessed 10 September 2020.

Sharp, T. (2019). *Insecure Work*, TUC, 29 July, available at: https://www.tuc .org.uk/research-analysis/reports/insecure-work?page=1, last accessed 29 July 2020.

Sheaff, M. (2017). 'Constructing Accounts of Organisational Failure: Policy, Power and Concealment', *Critical Social Policy* 37(4): 520–39.

Shestakofsky, B. (2017). 'Working Algorithms: Software Automation and the Future of Work', *Work and Occupations* 44(4): 376–423.

Shirky, C. (2010). *Cognitive Surplus*, London: Allen Lane.

Sidders, J. (2020). 'The Retail Apocalypse is Getting Darker for Retail Landlords', *Bloomberg*, 2 July, available at: https://www.bloomberg.com/ne ws/articles/2020-07-02/the-retail-apocalypse-is-getting-even-darker-for-u-k -landlords, last accessed 2 July 2020.

Sinapi, C. and Gagne, Y. (2016). 'Financialization of Non-financial Companies: An Insight in the Automotive Sector', *LIMES plus – Journal of Social Sciences and Humanities* 13(1): 35–60.

Sirota, D. (2020). 'Trump Just Fulfilled His Billionaire Pal's Dream', *TMI*, available at: https://sirota.substack.com/p/news-trump-just-fulfilled-his-billionai re, last accessed 16 June 2020.

Slaughter, H. (2021). 'Earnings Outlook Q1 2021: Earnings in the Covid Crisis', The Resolution Foundation, 22 March, available at: https://www.resolution foundation.org/publications/earnings-outlook-q1-2021, last accessed 15 July 2021.

Smith, A. (2016). '"The Magnificent 7[am]?" – Life Articulation Beyond the 9[am] to 5[pm] "Norm"', *New Technology, Work and Employment* 31(3): 210–22.

Smith, J. (2021). 'The Greatest Debt History is Upon Us', *openDemocracy*, 19 March, available at: https://www.opendemocracy.net/en/oureconomy/grea test-debt-crisis-history-upon-us/?fbclid=IwAR18Ug_roGN3I9WuW7eMU DtbxhZtXaygdQ-VbEOANbFywCt2XZY77Uh1ir0, last accessed 13 July 2021.

Smith, M. (2020). 'Many More Middle Class Workers Able to Work From Home than Working Class Workers', YouGov, 13 May, available at: https:// yougov.co.uk/topics/economy/articles-reports/2020/05/13/most-middle-cla ss-workers-are-working-home-full-ti, last accessed 13 August 2020.

Smith, T. (1997). 'The Neoclassical and Marxian Theories of Technology: A Comparison and Critical Assessment', *Historical Materialism* 1(1): 113–33.

Smith, T. (2000). *Technology and Capital in an Age of Lean Production*, New York: SUNY Press.

Smith, T. (2012). 'Is Socialism Relevant in the "Networked Information Age"?: A Critical Assessment of *The Wealth of Networks*', in A. Anton and R. Schmitt (eds.), *Taking Socialism Seriously*, Plymouth: Lexington Books.

Smith, T. (2019). *Beyond Liberal Egalitarianism*, Chicago: Haymarket.

Smith, C. and McKinlay, A. (2009). 'Creative Industries and Labour Process Analysis', in A. McKinlay and C. Smith (eds.), *Creative Labour: Working in the Creative Industries*, London: Palgrave.

Smith, C. and Thompson, P. (1998). 'Re-evaluating the Labour Process Debate', *Economic and Industrial Democracy*' 19(4): 551–57.

Smithers, R. (2020). 'Sir James Dyson Named UK's Richest Person for First Time', *The Guardian*, 17 May, available at: https://www.theguardian.com/business/2020/may/16/sir-james-dyson-named-uks-richest-person-for-first-time, last accessed 2 June 2020.

Social Metrics Commission (SMC) (2020). *Measuring Poverty 2020*, available at: https://socialmetricscommission.org.uk/wp-content/uploads/2020/06/Measuring-Poverty-2020-Web.pdf, last accessed 31 July 2020.

Society of Motor Manufacturers and Traders (SMMT) (2020). *Risks and Opportunities: UK Automotive Trade in a Post-Covid World*, available at: https://www.smmt.co.uk/wp-content/uploads/sites/2/SMMT-Automotive-Trade-Report-2020.pdf, last accessed 23 June 2020.

Spencer, D. A. (2000). 'Braverman and the Contribution of Labour Process Analysis to the Critique of Capitalist Production: Twenty-Five Years On', *Work, Employment and Society* 14(2): 223–43.

Spencer, D. A. (2017). 'Work In and Beyond the Second Machine Age: The Politics of Production and Digital Technologies', *Work, Employment and Society* 31(1): 142–52.

Srnicek, N. (2017). *Platform Capitalism*, Cambridge: Polity.

Staab, P. and Nachtwey, O. (2016). 'Market and Labour Control in Digital Capitalism', *tripleC* 14(2): 457–74.

Stanford, J. (2018). Subsidising Billionaires: Simulating the Net Incomes of UberX Drivers in Australia, Canberra: Centre for Future Work at the Australia Institute, available at: https://d3n8a8pro7vhmx.cloudfront.net/theausinstitute/pages/2692/attachments/original/1519989285/Subsidizing_Billionaires_Final.pdf?1519989285, last accessed 23 June 2018.

Statistical Services and Consultancy Unit (2019). *Platform Work in the UK 2016–2019*, Hatfield: University of Hertfordshire.

StepChange (2020). *Coronavirus and Personal Debt: A Financial Recovery Strategy for Households*, June, available at: https://www.stepchange.org/Portals/0/assets/pdf/coronavirus-policy-briefing-stepchange.pdf, last accessed 12 August 2020.

StepChange (2021). *Stormy Weather*, January, available at: https://www.stepch ange.org/Portals/0/assets/pdf/Coronavirus-impact-dashboard-January-2021 -StepChange.pdf, last accessed 17 July 2021.

Stettner, A. and Novello, A. (2019). 'Faltering Factories May Presage a Faltering Economy', 8 July, *The Century Foundation*, available at: https://tcf.org/con tent/commentary/faltering-factories-may-presage-faltering-economy/?ses sion=1, last accessed 21 July 2019.

Stewart, P., Mrozowicki, A. and Danford, A. (2016). 'Lean as Ideology and Practice: A Comparative Study of the Impact of Lean Production on Working Life in Automotive Manufacturing in the United Kingdom and Poland', *Competition and Change* 20(3): 147–65.

Stiegler, B. (2010). *For a New Critique of Political Economy*, Cambridge: Polity.

Streeck, W. (2017). *How Will Capitalism End?* London: Verso.

Sturgeon, D. (2014). 'The Business of the NHS: The Rise and Rise of Consumer Culture and Commodification in the Provision of Healthcare Services', *Critical Social Policy* 34(3): 405–6.

Sum, N-L. and Jessop, B. (2015). 'Sense- and Meaning-making in the Critique of Political Economy', in B. Jessop, B. Young and C. Scherrer (eds.), *Financial Cultures and Crisis Dynamics*, London: Routledge.

Sunkara, B. (2017). 'Why Corbyn Won', 8 June, *Jacobin*, available at: https:// www.jacobinmag.com/2017/06/jeremy-corbyn-election-results-labour-there sa-may-left, last accessed 9 March 2020.

Sutherland, W., Jarrahi, M. H., Dunn, M. and Nelson, S. B. (2020). 'Work Precarity and Gig Literacies in Online Freelancing', *Work, Employment and Society* 34(3): 457–75.

Suwandi, I. (2019). 'Labor-Value Commodity Chains', *Monthly Review Press* 71(3): 1–25.

Suwandi, I. and Foster, J. B. (2016). 'Multinational Corporations and the Globalization of Monopoly Capital: From the 1960s to the Present', *Monthly Review Press* 68(3): 1–18.

Sweet, S. and Meiksins, P. (2008). *Changing Contours of Work*, Thousand Oaks, CA: Pine Forge Press.

Sweney, M. (2018). 'Amazon Halved Corporation Tax Bill despite UK Profits Tripling', *The Guardian*, 3 August, available at: https://www.theguardian .com/technology/2018/aug/02/amazon-halved-uk-corporation-tax-bill-to -45m-last-year?CMP=Share_iOSApp_Other, last accessed 8 September 2018.

Tapscott, D. (1996). *The Digital Economy*, New York: McGraw-Hill Education.

Tapscott, D. and Williams, A. D. (2007). *Wikinomics*, rev. edn., London: Atlantic Books.

Taskin, L. and van Bunnen, G. (2015). 'Knowledge Management through the

Development of Knowledge Repositories: Towards Work Degradation', *New Technology, Work and Employment* 30(2): 158–72.

Taylor, M., Marsh, G., Nicole, D. and Broadbent, P. (2017). *Good Work: The Taylor Review of Modern Working Practices*, available at: https://www.gov.uk/government/publications/good-workthe-taylor-review-of-modern-working-practices, last accessed 14 February 2018.

Thompson, P. (1990). 'Crawling from the Wreckage: The Labour Process and the Politics of Production', in D. Knights and H. Willmott (eds.), *Labour Process Theory*, London: Macmillan.

Thompson, P. (2016). 'Dissent at Work and the Resistance Debate: Departures, Directions, and Dead Ends', *Studies in Political Economy* 97(2): 106–23.

Thompson, P. and Smith, C. (2017). '*Capital* and the Labour Process', in I. Schmidt and C. Fanelli (eds.), *Reading 'Capital' Today*, London: Pluto.

Thompson, P., Parker, R. and Cox, S. (2016). 'Interrogating Creative Theory and Creative Work: Inside the Games Studio', *Sociology* 50(2): 316–32.

Tobias, M. and Rodriguez, R. (2020). 'Farmers are Forced to Let Crops Rot and Throw Away Milk while Food Bank Demand Soars', *Cal Matters*, 11 April, available at: https://calmatters.org/california-divide/2020/04/california-farmers-coronavirus-food-supply-food-bank, last accessed 20 May 2020.

Toffler, A. (1980). *The Third Wave*, London: Pan.

Tomaney, J. (1994). 'A New Paradigm of Work Organization and Technology?' in A. Amin (ed.), *Post-Fordism: A Reader*, Oxford: Blackwell.

Torfing, J., Ferlie, E., Jukić, T. and Ongaro, E. (2021). 'A Theoretical Framework for Studying the Co-creation of Innovative Solutions and Public Value', *Policy and Politics* early view: 1–20.

Trade Union Act (2016). Available at: http://www.legislation.gov.uk/ukpga/2016/15/contents/enacted, last accessed 4 May 2018.

Trades Union Congress (TUC) (2017). *The Gig is Up: Trade Unions Tackling Insecure Work*, available at: https://www.tuc.org.uk/sites/default/files/the-gig-is-up.pdf, last accessed 8 February 2018.

Trades Union Congress (TUC) (2018). *A Future that Works for Working People*, London: Trades Union Congress, available at: https://www.tuc.org.uk/sites/default/files/FutureofWorkReport1.pdf, last accessed 2 February 2019.

Trades Union Congress (TUC) (2020). *Job Security*, 4 July, available at: https://www.tuc.org.uk/research-analysis/reports/job-security, last 10 July 2020.

Trades Union Congress (TUC) (2021a). *COVID-19 and Insecure Work*, available at: https://www.tuc.org.uk/research-analysis/reports/covid-19-and-insecure-work, last accessed 15 July 2021.

Trades Union Congress (TUC) (2021b). *Transforming Public Procurement*, available at: https://www.tuc.org.uk/sites/default/files/2021-05/TUC%20response%20on%20Transforming%20Public%20Procurement%20FINAL.pdf, last accessed 16 July 2021.

Travkina, E. and Sacco, P. (2020). *Culture Shock: COVID-19 and the Cultural and Creative Sectors*, OECD, 7 September, available at: https://www.oecd.org/coronavirus/policy-responses/culture-shock-covid-19-and-the-cultural-and-creative-sectors-08da9e0e, last accessed 9 July 2021.

Tregenna, F. (2011). 'What Does the "Services Sector" Mean in Marxian Terms?' *Review of Political Economy* 23(2): 281–98.

Trugman, J. (2017). 'Why do Snap's IPO Shares Come with Zero Voting Rights?' *New York Post*, 5 March, available at: https://nypost.com/2017/03/05/why-do-snaps-ipo-stocks-come-with-zero-voting-rights, last accessed 12 September 2017.

Tussell (2019). *Amazon's Increasing Involvement with the Public Sector*, 11 June, available at: https://www.tussell.com/insights/amazons-increasing-involvement-with-the-uk-public-sector, last accessed 20 September 2019.

Tussell (2020). *UK Strategic Suppliers: 2020 Update*, February, Tussell.

Trussell Trust (2021). *State of Hunger*, May, available at: https://www.trusselltrust.org/wp-content/uploads/sites/2/2021/05/State-of-Hunger-2021-Report-Final.pdf, last accessed 13 July 2021.

UBS Global Wealth Management (UBS) (2020). 'Strategic Approach Pays Off for Family Offices amid Market Disruption', 16 July, available at: https://www.ubs.com/global/en/media/display-page-ndp/en-20200716-gfo-report.html?campID=CAAS-ActivityStream, last accessed 25 July 2020.

Umney, C. (2018). *Class Matters*, London: Pluto.

Unions NSW (2016). *Innovation or Exploitation: Busting the Airtasker Myth*, available at: https://d3n8a8pro7vhmx.cloudfront.net/unionsnsw/pages/3135/attachments/original/1474529110/Unions_NSW_Report_into_Airtasker.pdf?1474529110, last accessed 20 February 2017.

United Nations (2018). *United Nations E-Government Survey 2018*, New York.

United Nations Conference on Trade and Development (UNCTAD) (2013). *Global Value Chains and Development*, New York: UN Publications, available at: https://untctad.org/en/PublicationsLibrary/diae2013d1_en.pdf, last accessed 5 June 2018.

United Nations Conference on Trade and Development (UNCTAD) (2018). *Creative Economy Outlook: Trends in International Trade in Creative Industries 2002–2015*, available at: https://unctad.org/system/files/official-document/ditcted2018d3_en.pdf, accessed 31 July 2021.

United Nations Conference on Trade and Development (UNCTAD) (2019). *Trade and Development Report 2019*, New York: UN Publications, available at: https://unctad.org/en/pages/PublicationWebflyer.aspx?publicationid=2526, last accessed 1 October 2019.

United Nations Conference on Trade and Development (UNCTAD) (2020). *World Investment Report 2020*, available at: https://unctad.org/en/PublicationsLibrary/wir2020_overview_en.pdf, last accessed 19 June 2020.

United Nations Conference on Trade and Development (UNCTAD) (2021). *World Investment Report 2021*, New York: UN Publications, available at: https://unctad.org/system/files/official-document/wir2021_en.pdf, last accessed 26 October 2021.

United Nations Industrial Development Organization (UNIDO) (2020). *Responding to the Crisis: Building a Better Future*, April, available at: https://www.unido.org/sites/default/files/files/2020-05/UNIDO_COVID19 _External_Position_Paper.pdf, last accessed 19 June 2020.

United Private Hire Drivers (UPHD) (2020). 'UPHD Launches Emergency Legal Action to Force Government to Introduce Covid-19 Safety Standards for Uber and Other Private Hire Operators', 10 April, available at: https://www .uphd.org/news-posts/uphd-launches-emergency-legal-action-to-force-gover nment-to-introduce-covid-19-safety-standards-for-uber-and-other-private -hire-operators, last accessed 15 June 2020.

Unseen (2020). *Modern Slavery and Exploitation Helpline: Annual Assessment 2020*, available at: https://www.modernslaveryhelpline.org/uploads/202104 07114600907.pdf, last accessed 11 August 2021.

Urry, J. (2007). *Mobilities*, Cambridge: Polity.

Vandaele, K. (2018). 'Will Trade Unions Survive the Platform Economy? Emerging Patterns of Platform Workers' Collective Voice and Representation in Europe', *European Trade Union Institute*, Working Paper 2018.05, available at: https://www.etui.org/sites/default/files/Working%20Paper%2020 18.05%20Vandaele%20Trade%20unions%20Platform%20economy%20 Web.pdf, last accessed 25 June 2020.

Van der Pijl, K. (1998). *Transnational Classes and International Relations*, London: Routledge.

Van der Zwan, N. (2014) 'Making Sense of Financialization', *Socio-economic Review* 12(1):
99-129.

Van Doorn, N. (2017). 'Platform Labor: On the Gendered and Facialized Exploitation of Low-income Service Work in the "On-demand" Economy', *Information, Communication and Society* 20(6): 898–914.

Varghese, S. (2020). 'Gig Economy Workers Have a New Weapon in the Fight Against Uber', *Wired*, 17 February, available at: https://www.wired.co.uk/ar ticle/gig-economy-uber-unions, last accessed 25 June 2020.

Veen, A., Barratt, T. and Goods, C. (2020). 'Platform-Capital's "App-etite" for Control: A Labour Process Analysis of Food-Delivery Work in Australia', *Work, Employment and Society* 34(3): 388–406.

Vidal, M. (2013). 'Postfordism as a Dysfunctional Regime: A Comparative Analysis of the USA, the UK and Germany', *Work, Employment and Society* 27(3): 451–71.

Vidal, M. (2014). 'Incoherence and Dysfunctionality in the Institutional

Regulation of Capitalism', in M. Hauptmeier and M. Vidal (eds.), *Comparative Political Economy of Work*, London: Palgrave.

Vidal, M. (2019). 'Work and Exploitation in Capitalism: The Labour Process and the Valorization Process', in M. Vidal, T. Smith, T. Rotta and P. Prew (eds.), *The Oxford Handbook of Karl Marx*, Oxford: Oxford University Press.

Vidal, M. (2020). 'Contradictions of the Labour Process, Worker Empowerment and Capitalist Inefficiency', *Historical Materialism* 28(2): 170–204.

Vivant, E. (2013). 'Creatives in the City: Urban Contradictions of the Creative City', *City, Culture and Society* 4(2): 57–63.

Waddington, D. G. (2018). 'Online News Conference on 2017 Income, Poverty, and Health Insurance Coverage Estimates from the Current Population Survey', 12 September, United States Census Bureau, available at: https://www.census.gov/content/dam/Census/newsroom/press-kits/2018/iphi/news-conference-transcript.pdf, last accessed 5 November 2018.

Walby, S. (2015). *Crisis*, Cambridge: Polity.

Wallace, J., Ormston, H., Thurman, B., Diffley, M., McFarlane, M. and Zubairi, S. (2020). *Gross Domestic Wellbeing (GDWe): An Alternative Measure of Social Progress*, Carnegie UK Trust, available at: https://d1ssu070pg2v9i.cloudfront.net/pex/carnegie_uk_trust/2020/12/03165904/LOW-RES-4708-CUKT-GDWe-Social-Progress.pdf, last accessed 10 August 2021.

Wallace-Stephens, F. and Lockey, A. (2019). *Retail Therapy: Towards a Future of Good Work in Retail*, September, available at: https://www.thersa.org/discover/publications-and-articles/reports/retail-therapy-future-good-work, last accessed 10 July 2020.

Watkins, S. (2020). 'Britain's Decade of Crisis', *New Left Review* 121 (January/February): 5–19.

Watkins, S. (2021). 'Paradigm Shifts', *New Left Review* (March/April): 5–12.

Watt, N., Syal, R. and Malik, S. (2013). 'Universal Credit: Iain Duncan Smith Blames Civil Servants for IT Failings', *The Guardian*, 5 September, available at: https://www.theguardian.com/politics/2013/sep/05/universal-credit-iain-duncan-smith, last accessed 7 August 2017.

Webster, J. (2016). 'Microworkers of the Gig Economy: Separate and Precarious', *New Labor Forum* 25(3): 56–64.

Weil, D. (2014). *The Fissured Workplace*, Cambridge, MA: Harvard University Press.

Weise, E. (2018). 'After Losing Fight to Levy "Amazon Tax", Seattle is Back to Square One on Helping Homeless', *USA Today* 18 June, available at: https://eu.usatoday.com/story/tech/2018/06/17/after-amazon-tax-fails-seattle-has-no-clear-path-help-homeless/698575002, last accessed 8 September 2018.

Went, R., Monique Kremer, M. and André Knottnerus, A. (2015). *Mastering the Robot*, The Hague: The Netherlands Scientific Council for Government Policy.

Werner, M. (2016). 'Global Production Networks and Uneven Development: Exploring Geographies of Devaluation, Disinvestment, and Exclusion', *Geography Compass* 10(11): 457–69.

White House, The (2021). *The American Rescue Plan*, available at: https://www.whitehouse.gov/wp-content/uploads/2021/03/American-Rescue-Plan-Fact-Sheet.pdf, last accessed 14 July 2021.

Whitfield, D. (2006). *New Labour's Attack on Public Services*, London: Spokesman.

Whitfield, D. (2012). *In Place of Austerity*, London: Spokesman.

Whitfield, D. (2014). *Unmasking Austerity*, London: Spokesman.

Whitfield, D. (2020). *Public Alternative to the Privatisation of Life*, London: Spokesman.

Wilkie, R. (2011). *The Digital Condition*, New York: Fordham University Press.

Williamson, C. (2020a). 'Flash UK PMI Signals Marked Easing in Downturn during June', *HIS Markit*, 23 June, available at: https://ihsmarkit.com/research-analysis/flash-uk-pmi-signals-marked-easing-in-downturn-during-june20.html, last accessed 2 July 2020.

Williamson, C. (2020b). 'Flash PMI Surveys Hint at Global Economy Starting Recovery from Pandemic', *HIS Markit*, 23 June, available at: https://ihsmarkit.com/research-analysis/flash-pmi-surveys-hint-at-global-economy-starting-recovery-from-pandemic-June2020.html, last accessed 2 July 2020.

Will-Zocholl, M. (2017). 'Virtual Temptations: Reorganising Work under Conditions of Digitisation, Virtualisation and Informatisation', in K. Briken, S. Chillas, M. Krzywdzinski and A. Marks (eds.), *The New Digital Workplace*, London: Macmillan.

Wirsig, K. and Compton, J. (2017). 'Workers, Contradictions and Digital Commodity Chains: Organizing with Content Creators in Canada', in P. Meil and V. Kirov (eds.), *Policy Implications of Virtual Work*, London: Palgrave.

Wolf, M. (2018). 'Why So Little Has Changed since the Financial Crash', *Financial Times*, September 4, available at: https://www.ft.com/content/c85b9792-aad1-11e8-94bd-cba20d67390c, last accessed 7 August 2018.

Wolff, R. (2020). 'COVID-19 was a Trigger, but Capitalism Caused the Economic Crash', *Truthout*, 17 April, available at: https://truthout.org/articles/covid-19-was-a-trigger-but-capitalism-caused-the-economic-crash, last accessed 21 May 2020.

Wood, A. J. and Lehdonvirta, V. (2021). 'Antagonism beyond Employment: How the "Subordinated Agency" of Labour Platforms Generates Conflict in the Remote Gig Economy', *Socio-Economic Review*, available at https://pa

pers.ssrn.com/sol3/papers.cfm?abstract_id=3820645, last accessed 13 July 2021.

Wood, E. (1995). *Democracy against Capitalism*, Cambridge: Cambridge University Press.

Woodcock, J. (2019). *Marx at the Arcade*, Chicago: Haymarket.

Woodiwiss, A. (1990). *Social Theory after Postmodernism*, London: Pluto.

Womack, J., Jones, D. T. and Roos, D. (1990). *The Machine That Changed the World*, New York: Rawson Associates.

Worker Rights Consortium (2020). *Who Will Bail Out the Workers that Make Our Clothes?* March, available at: https://www.workersrights.org/wp-con tent/uploads/2020/03/Who-Will-Bail-Out-the-Workers-March-2020.pdf, last accessed 22 June 2020.

World Bank (2019). *The Changing Nature of Work*, Washington, DC: World Bank, available at: http://documents.worldbank.org/curated/en/816281518 818814423/2019-WDR-Report.pdf, last accessed 5 June 2019.

World Bank (2020a). 'Projected Poverty Impacts of COVID-19 (Coronavirus)', 8 June, available at: https://www.worldbank.org/en/topic/poverty/brief/pro jected-poverty-impacts-of-COVID-19, last accessed 31 July 2020.

World Bank (2020b). *Global Investment Competitiveness Report 2019/2020*, Washington, DC: World Bank, available at: https://openknowledge.worldba nk.org/handle/10986/33808, last accessed 3 June 2020.

World Bank (2021). 'The Global Economy: On Track for Strong but Uneven Growth as COVID-19 Still Weighs', 8 June, available at: https://www.world bank.org/en/news/feature/2021/06/08/the-global-economy-on-track-for-str ong-but-uneven-growth-as-covid-19-still-weighs, last accessed 12 July 2021.

World Ultra Wealth Report (2019). *Ultra Wealthy Analysis: World Ultra Wealth Report 2019*, available at: https://www.wealthx.com/report/world-ultra-we alth-report-2019/#downloadform, last accessed 10 June 2020.

Wright, E. O. (1978). *Classes, Crisis, and the State*, London: New Left Books.

Wright, E. O. (1997). *Classes*, London: Verso.

Zipperer, B. (2021). 'The Minimum Wage has Lost 21% of its Value since Congress Last Raised the Wage', *Economic Policy Institute*, 22 July, availa- ble at: https://www.epi.org/blog/the-minimum-wage-has-lost-21-of-its-value -since-congress-last-raised-the-wage, last accessed 30 July 2021.

Zwick, D., Bonsu, S. K. and Darmody, A. (2008). 'Putting Consumers to Work: "Co-Creation" and New Marketing Govern-mentality', *Journal of Consumer Culture* 8(2): 163–96.

INDEX